Chocolate and Corn Flour

Chocolate and Corn Flour

HISTORY, RACE, AND PLACE IN
THE MAKING OF "BLACK" MEXICO

Laura A. Lewis

Duke University Press

Durham and London | 2012

© 2012 Duke University Press

All rights reserved.

Printed in the United States of America on acid-free paper ♾

Designed by Heather Hensley

Typeset in Minion Pro by Tseng Information Systems, Inc.

Library of Congress Cataloging-in-Publication Data appear
on the last printed page of this book.

FOR LUKE, A FINE YOUNG MAN

Contents

Acknowledgments

I have had overwhelming institutional support for this project, beginning with the American Bar Foundation, which funded my initial trip to the Costa Chica in 1992 while I was a Dissertation Fellow in Chicago. In 1997–98 the Research Institute for the Study of Man and the Wenner-Gren Foundation for Anthropological Research (Gr. 6073) funded long-term fieldwork. I am particularly grateful to Wenner-Gren for providing grant money earmarked for the community of San Nicolás Tolentino. Those funds were used to make a road passable during the rainy season and to purchase sports equipment for young people, books for local school teachers, and reading glasses for the elderly. James Madison University generously contributed with a sabbatical for fieldwork in 1997 shortly after I was hired, a Faculty Summer Research Grant in 1999 for archival research in Mexico City and Chilpancingo, Guerrero, the Edna T. Schaefer Humanist Award in 2000 for research on visual culture, another Faculty Summer Research Grant in 2007 for work at the Schomburg Center for Research on Black Culture in New York City, and a sabbatical in spring 2010.

In 2002–3 the John Simon Guggenheim Memorial Foundation supported further research and initial writing with a Guggenheim

Fellowship. In 2002 the National Endowment for the Humanities also awarded me a summer stipend, and the University of Chicago / University of Illinois at Urbana-Champaign Center for Latin American Studies gave me a Visiting Scholar's Award, which enabled me to return to my alma mater for a month to peruse the wonderful resources of the "Reg." In the fall of 2004 I was fortunate to be awarded a Smithsonian Institution Senior Fellowship to conduct research in the National Anthropology Archives and the Human Studies Film Archives. A National Endowment for the Humanities Fellowship supported writing and revisions in 2007–8. Finally, the Rockefeller Foundation provided a wonderful opportunity to spend a month at the Bellagio Study and Conference Center in Italy in March 2008.

Although I first visited San Nicolás and a number of other Costa Chican villages in 1992, it was not until 1997 that I began long-term fieldwork there and, in 1998, with San Nicoladenses in Winston-Salem, North Carolina. Today I continue to maintain contact through visits, phone calls, and the Internet with people in San Nicolás and with the many San Nicoladenses—including my coparents, godchildren, and their own children—who live in Winston-Salem.

My fieldwork involved extensive participant observation in San Nicolás and in Winston-Salem. In San Nicolás it also included a household survey and interviews, and ongoing interactions with outsiders, including other anthropologists, cultural promoters, and local politicians. In addition, I attended regional, national, and international meetings and conferences that treated themes relevant to my research. I owe so many thanks to so many people for what has been a long journey full of encouragement, engagement, exchange of materials, heated conversations, invitations to present, and comments on drafts that I do not even know where to begin. Mary Farquharson and Eduardo Llerenas, producers of the Mexico City music label Corason, provided initial introductions to individuals on the Costa Chica, where they had recorded music. With his invaluable and superb Nahuatl skills Jonathan Amith patiently went through a lexicon from the Costa Chica for Nahuatl derivatives; he also helped me with Mixtec and, as an ethnographer of the Nahua Guerreran community Oapan, with indigenous customs. Claudio Lomnitz supported my Visiting Scholar Award at the University of Chicago Center for Latin American Studies. Jean Muteba Rahier invited me to present at a conference at Florida International

University, and he later commented on a chapter draft at the Latin American Studies Association meetings. Jose Antonio Flores Farfán invited me to present at CIESAS (the Centro de Investigaciones y Estudios Superiores en Antropología Social, or Social Anthropology Research Institute) in Mexico City in 1998, and Odile Hoffmann and María Teresa Rodríguez invited me to run a weeklong seminar, also at CIESAS in Mexico City, in 2005. They later sent me books that proved key to my own research. William Merrill, J. Daniel Rogers, Olivia Cadaval, and Jake Homiak provided office space and invaluable guidance through the maze of resources at the Smithsonian Institution, and Linda Arnold through a number of unfamiliar branches of the Mexican National Archives (the Archivo General de la Nación, or AGN). Daniel Althoff and Amy Paugh explained technical linguistic terms; and Adela Amaral, Jennifer Jones, and Alejandro Graciano shared their own student work on the Costa Chica.

Ira Bashkow, Liam Buckley, Hilquias Cavalcanti, Jennifer Coffman, Anani Dzidzienyo, Juan Flores, Shane Greene, Isar Godreau, Edmund Gordon, Charles Hale, Miriam Jiménez, Juliette Levy, Fletcher Linder, Kristen McCleary, John McDowell, Susan McKinnon, Jean Rahier, Matthew Restall, Rafael Sánchez, Katherine Snyder, Orin Starn, Ben Vinson III, Brad Weiss, Andrea Wiley, and others I am surely forgetting commented on drafts of chapters, made important interventions after presentations, and supported my endeavors in ways that helped me to move forward. Many university and conference audiences also provided invaluable feedback. I am also indebted to Craig Baugher for producing my maps on short notice, and to students I have taken to San Nicolás, especially to Magda Salazar, Emily Houdak, and Rose Salseda for support in the field, data collection, and coding, invaluable insights, cheerfulness, and impeccable behavior.

Judith Boruchoff accompanied me on my trip to the Costa Chica in 1992. She generously offered the use of her Jeep (and did most of the driving), adding her own keen ethnographic sensibilities as we visited Azoyú, Marquelia, Copalá, Huehuetán, Cuajinicuilapa, San Nicolás, Pinotepa Nacional, and Collantes. Judy saw me through the first of many gastrointestinal illnesses and spent an afternoon and evening with me in Huehuetán talking to people preparing for the performance La Conquista, a part of which we witnessed.

For their friendship and willingness to talk, I am grateful to successive mayors of San Nicolás, the former municipal president of Cuajinicuilapa, Andrés Manzano Añorve, his sister María de los Angeles Manzano Añorve, Father Florencio Robles Sánchez, Jesús Trinidad Zarate, Elena Zarate Conde, Enrique de Jesús Flores, Carlos Villalobos, and Father Glyn Jemott. Gratitude is due as well to the numerous scholars with whom I have had fruitful conversations throughout the years, especially Luz María Martínez Montiel, Malinali Meza Herrera, Gabriel Moedano Navarro, María Cristina Díaz Pérez, Jean Philibert Mobwa Mobwa, Carlos Ruíz Rodriguez, the late Miguel Angel Gutiérrez Avila, Taurino Hernández Moreno, Odile Hoffmann, María Teresa Rodríguez, Haydee Quiroz, J. Arturo Motta Sánchez, John McDowell, Patrick Carroll, Bobby Vaughn, and Ben Vinson III.

I also thank the anonymous reviewers at Duke University Press, whose comments were not only helpful but also made me laugh. Lorna Scott Fox, an editor and a long-time resident of Mexico, carefully reviewed my manuscript in London, and to her I owe enormous thanks. My editor at Duke University Press, Ken Wissoker, who also generously guided me through my first book, quickly steered this one too. All interpretations and any errors are, of course, my own, as are all translations, including of works published in Spanish.

For my first eight months of fieldwork Niklaus Stephan tirelessly looked after our son, Lukas, while I worked. Luke himself adapted after a fashion. He attended kindergarten in San Nicolás, returned with me for several summers, played for hours on end with Tavo, Eriberto, Javi, Damién, Ismael, Daniel, Jairo, Beti, Agla, Rosi, Loremi, Maybi, and Pelón, took his lumps and bumps, and still remembers a serious car crash when he was four and we were on the road from Pinotepa Nacional to CIESAS in Oaxaca City, where I was scheduled to give a presentation (we never made it). It was at this point, some two months into fieldwork, that I believe I crossed the "threshold of acceptance" among San Nicoladenses, for when I returned to San Nicolás with a whiplashed Luke while Niklaus looked after the car, Doña Lupe, Don Samuel, and Don Domingo paid us an unusual evening visit to make sure that we were alright. They were like parents to me, and they made me feel at home. Luke's life so far has paralleled my seemingly endless writing. He should know that his presence helped to foment my friendships with other adults and opened my eyes to children and to childhood, thus making this ethnography much richer.

Boys playing

I also thank Jessica Johnson and again Mary Farquharson and Eduardo Llerenas for putting us up (and putting up with us) in Mexico City when we needed to run errands there or were on our way to or from Virginia. My parents, Marjorie and Philip Lewis, also deserve thanks for having always stepped into the breach when Luke was young and I went off to Mexico without him.

Years ago the late William Roseberry commented to me that "villages matter," a seemingly small lesson but one that I never forgot. Because their village matters, this book is for the morenos and Indians of San Nicolás, who have always given me and my family a place in their home and have shown affection in ways too numerous to count. Don Domingo once told me after I gave him gifts of food that "God will pay you." I responded that God had already paid me by giving me permission to be there. A huge smile lit up his face.

San Nicolás is not a small place but just about everyone is related. Indeed, the community was started by six families, most of whose descendents remain connected to the village. "Almost everyone here is family; they marry each other," Sirina said. San Nicoladenses are identified with pseudonyms in the text, but I would like to mention several extended families, many of

Delia sitting with me on the artesa

whose members talked patiently with me, accompanied me to weddings, fiestas, and on errands, fed me delicious tamales, *pozole*, barbequed beef, fish, homemade cheese, and spicy chicken with rice, visit me in Virginia, open their homes to me in North Carolina, and still remain close friends and ritual kin: Baños, Bernal, Bruno, Castro, Cisneros, Domínguez, Garcia, González, Havana, Hernández, Javier, López, Magallón, Marcial, Marín, Medina, Mendoza, Molina, Morales, Moreno, Noyola, Oliva, Olmeda, Ortíz, Petatán, Peñalosa, Ramírez, Román, Soriano, Tacuba, Villarreal, and Zarate.

Many San Nicoladenses at first shook their heads when they saw me writing, or they asked if I was going to sell videotapes of them because they believe too many outsiders come and go without fulfilling the obligation to reciprocate. I can only hope that I have reciprocated by writing a book that makes them proud and does justice to their concerns, to their humor, and to their huge hearts. Proceeds from this book go to the community.

Portions of chapter 3 appeared in the article "Of Ships and Saints: History, Memory, and Place in the Making of *Moreno* Mexican Identity," *Cultural Anthropology* 16, no. 1 (2001), 62–82. Portions of chapter 8 appeared in the article "Home Is Where the Heart Is: North Carolina, Afro-Latino Migration, and Houses on Mexico's Costa Chica," *South Atlantic Quarterly* 105, no. 4 (2006), 801–29. All photographs in this book are by the author.

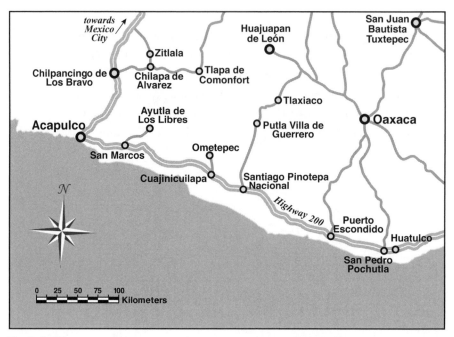

The Costa Chica. COURTESY OF CRAIG BAUGHER, CENTER FOR INSTRUCTIONAL TECHNOLOGY, JAMES MADISON UNIVERSITY

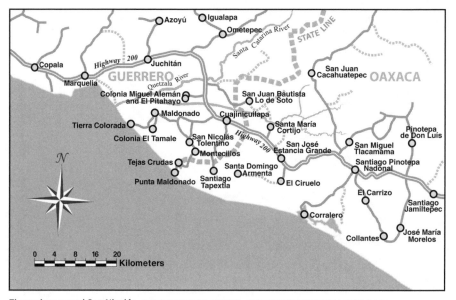

The region around San Nicolás. COURTESY OF CRAIG BAUGHER, CENTER FOR INSTRUCTIONAL TECHNOLOGY, JAMES MADISON UNIVERSITY

Introduction

In the summer of 1992 I perched on a low wall in the quiet and dusty central plaza of San Nicolás Tolentino, an agricultural village in a historically black region of Guerrero, Mexico. Pigs, chickens and dogs wandered the unpaved streets while cattle—I knew— grazed beyond village boundaries on land devoted to pasture, corn, sesame, mango, coconut, melon, and other produce for local consumption and regional markets. I was talking with Javier and Juan,[1] both in their twenties, who asked me about my work. So many outsiders had visited that they were convinced I was trying to make money taping dances and music and would leave with recordings and nothing behind. San Nicolás would then sink back into obscurity as the tapes took on a life of their own, beyond the control of those they represented. The men seemed bitter, though also eager to talk. But when Don Domingo joined us,[2] he was tired of talking. "Why do all the anthropologists come here?" he asked. "What do they want? They come for a few days, tape, and go away. They never pay." Javier explained: "We don't get paid for research- ing. So we just work in the fields."

San Nicolás sits on the coastal belt of the wedge-shaped Costa Chica—the "small coast," named for its narrow beaches—that runs from Acapulco, Guerrero, 400 kilometers southeast to the

Oaxacan port of Huatulco (first map). The Costa Chica's southern boundary is the Pacific Ocean and its northern one is the Sierra Madre del Sur mountain range. Fifteen of the Costa Chica's municipalities are in Guerrero and about fifty are in Oaxaca. Towns pertaining to these municipalities probably reach into the hundreds. Not all are on the coastal belt, but the belt alone contains about twenty larger African-descent communities and many smaller ones, the latter often unmapped (second map). San Nicolás ranks among the more prominent towns. Close to the Oaxacan border, it belongs to the municipality of Cuajinicuilpa (or Cuaji, as locals call it), whose seat, as in all municipalities, is a town of the same name.

That summer I spent several days in San Nicolás. I also visited a number of other coastal belt communities, but as a field site for ethnographic research San Nicolás attracted my attention in part because of residents' constant references to "all the anthropologists" and to others I call culture workers (politicians, artists, photographers, media types). Such people are known in San Nicolás as *la cultura* or "the culture." As Arlene Torres and Norman E. Whitten Jr. note in their own work on Latin Americans of African descent, pairing the Spanish article *la* (the) with the noun *culture* has the effect of elevating culture to a level of "refinement" and "civilization" that contrasts with "low" culture (1998:4). That San Nicoladenses collectively refer to culture workers in the singular and with the article *la* therefore speaks to the distance they perceive between themselves and those who study them. I became interested in San Nicoladenses' reactions to outsiders in part because San Nicoladenses self-identify as *morenos* (black Indians) and reject labels such as "black," "Afromexican," and "Afromestizo" imposed by culture workers, many of whom tape the music and dance to which Juan, Javier, and Don Domingo alluded.

I also wanted to work somewhere with an archived history. In Mexico City I met with Luz María Martínez Montiel, the director of the national project Our Third Root (Nuestra Tercera Raíz). The goal of the Third Root project was to salvage Mexico's "third" cultural and biological influence: the "footprint" or trace left by Africans in Mexico. Many of its associated researchers worked in villages on the coastal belt, including in San Nicolás. During our discussion, Martínez said that there was "no 'diaspora' of blacks in Latin America, no (unified) cultural identity." She emphasized archival work and the importance of establishing the histories of places to understand them. Because I had been told that San Nicolás was a town (*pueblo*), more prominent and with a larger population (about 3,500) than many other coastal belt locales, I was hopeful that it would yield the kind of archival material Martínez emphasized. To a great extent, it did. Such material has enabled me to begin this book with a history that enhances our understanding of contemporary identities.

In 1992 little was known about Mexico's present-day peoples of African descent, especially on the Pacific Coast. Although awareness changed rapidly as both Mexican and foreign researchers worked there and in Veracruz, the other region with a concentration of Mexicans descended from Africans, to date no one has produced the kind of comprehensive village-based yet "glocal" ethnography that I hope to have adequately laid out in the following pages.

In 1997 I returned to San Nicolás for a long period. My fieldwork there has now extended to more than a decade, with my most recent visit in March 2009. Since San Nicoladenses also migrate to Winston-Salem, North Carolina, a city not far from my Virginia residence, I also visit them there. Indeed, my presence among San Nicoladenses has been as constant as I have been able to make it. Don Domingo has read translations of two articles, I am a godparent (*madrina*) to numerous children, many now grown, and the comother (*comadre*) of many adult village residents.

Background

The ancestors of most San Nicoladenses were African and African-descent slaves and free persons, referred to as blacks (*negros*) and mulattoes (*mulatos*) in colonial texts. Because of demographics and social interactions between blacks and Indians, mulattoes in colonial Mexico were frequently of black and Indian descent (Motta 2006:121; also Lewis 2003:74–78). Mexico's history of slavery—in full force for about 150 years—has been amply documented, but here I highlight a few points, both general and specific. Until 1700, with the de facto end of the Mexican slave trade, Mexico hosted one of the largest black and mulatto populations in the Americas. Spaniards brought slaves directly from West and Central Africa during this period, but they also first brought some to Spain to Hispanicize and Christianize them before transport to the New World. Most slaves in colonial Mexico worked in mining and agriculture, and as urban domestics. Because manumission was achievable in several ways, the numbers of free blacks and mulattoes grew throughout the colonial period. While Indians (*indios* in colonial texts) made up the bulk of the colonial population even after the demographic collapse that accompanied the first century of colonial rule, a census of 1646 accounts for about 150,000 blacks and mulattoes in colonial Mexico (Bennett 2003:1), numbers that vied with those of Spaniards.

Although African slaves accompanied the conquistadors, in 1542 the Spanish Crown implemented the New Laws to protect only Indians from slavery and to limit the system known as *encomienda*, or the granting in perpetuity of Indian laborers and tribute to landed conquistadors. In part due to the limitations imposed by the New Laws, Spanish settlers augmented the Indian labor they did control with blacks. By the end of the seventeenth century, however, the Indian population had started to rebound, while the "mixed" population expanded. In addition, intensive plantation agriculture never developed in Mexico as it did elsewhere in Latin America. The Mexican slave trade had thus all but ended by 1700, even though slavery itself was not fully abolished until 1824 with independence from Spain.

Most slaves brought to the colony were men. They were sold at the eastern port of Veracruz and taken to other regions in New Spain, including to the Costa Chica, which was invaded by Spanish cattle ranchers in the late sixteenth century. These ranchers brought with them enslaved and free blacks and mulattoes to work as cowboys, laborers, and domestic servants. As elsewhere in Mexico, blacks and mulattoes on the Costa Chica entered into often contentious relationships with Indians. But contact also resulted in mixed black-Indian populations. In part because of this and in part because Mexico's slave trade—unlike that of Brazil or Cuba, for instance—informally ended rather early, African "survivals" in Mexico are difficult to identify. In San Nicolás, which outsiders widely identify as the "cradle of Afromexican culture," beliefs and practices—rituals, music, festivals, food, supernaturalism—are either largely Mexican or influenced by local Indian custom. San Nicoladenses know little of the Mexican slave trade because its history is not taught in schools and most middle-aged and older San Nicoladenses are not literate. There is no historical memory of slavery in the community and almost no knowledge of Africa. While before my 1992 visit I rather naively thought that I would find vestiges of "African" culture, I quickly realized that what John McDowell calls "the Africa thesis" (2000:9) was reserved for outsiders who tended to visit the coastal belt looking for cultural survivals.

Race

During my 1992 visit I became aware that local discourses about African culture existed alongside ones contrasting and entwining blackness and Indianness. For instance, I accompanied the forty-year-old musician Ernesto to see two artifacts encircled with barbed wire, situated on a plot of land some distance from the heart of town. The first was a round house (*redondo*) made of wattle-and-daub with a conical palm frond roof, which Ernesto said was "constructed by maroons; it's an ancestral custom." At first I thought it had been carefully preserved by local people as the adobe, cinder-block (*bloque*), and red brick (*tabique*) buildings that I saw all over replaced older dwellings. But when Ernesto added that the redondo was a copy, I realized my mistake. Don Domingo, then in his early seventies and also a musician, clarified that the late Third Root anthropologist Miguel Angel Gutiérrez Avila had asked local people to build the redondo around the time of the Mexico City earthquake in 1985. It was thus only six or seven years old. Next to the redondo Ernesto pointed out an *artesa*, an inverted trough made of a hollowed-out tree trunk, carved with a horse's head at one end and its tail at the other. The artesa is used as a platform for a traditional wedding dance that once accompanied the music known as *sones de artesa*. I discovered during this visit, however, that artesa music had all but vanished decades earlier and, like the redondo, had been revived by la cultura, which provided instruments and outfits. But the person who had taught the musicians to play had passed away. Young people wanted to learn neither the music nor the dance. Gutiérrez was going to pay people to learn, but after the earthquake everything stopped. "There was no more money," Don Domingo said.

As Ernesto showed me around San Nicolás that summer afternoon, he also remarked in rapid succession that the redondo and the artesa constituted "the African center of the village" and that he and his people were "very, very black." I realized that because Ernesto did not yet know me, he thought I was from la cultura and did what he thought I wanted him to do: he showed me local "culture." I came to see his claims as ambivalent and even contradictory. Although, for instance, he referred to an "African center," which was at some remove from the heart of town, he was clearly showing me—an outsider—what he thought I wanted to see, and describing it in a way that echoed the discourse of the culture workers with whom, as a musician, he had interacted. While he referred to his people as black, San

Nicoladenses reserve the term for ancestors, for people in other villages, and for people who are particularly dark-skinned. As one elderly woman said, "We are black Indians [*negros indios*]. [Blacks and Indians] marry each other and now the Indian race [is a part of us]." During my visit Ernesto also told me that "the Mexican" was an "Indian." Indianness figures prominently in local historical narratives, especially about land; in genealogies; in stories about the village's patron and patronymic saint, who "lives" among Indians; and in everyday life. Indeed, people morenos label "Indians," who are from the Mixtec uplands of the Costa Chica, have been San Nicoladenses since the mid-1960s.

In their iconic form, and mostly as Aztecs, Indians are also central to Mexican national mestizo ideology, as Ernesto indicated. Thus, not unlike mestizos of "mixed" European and indigenous ancestors, which is how most Mexicans identify, morenos embrace Indianness in part because "the Indian is Mexican." Moreno therefore racially signifies historical and ongoing mixture, which translates into a fluidity that enables morenos to both identify with and to distinguish themselves from Indians. It also separates Indians and morenos (and, by extension, blacks) from whites (*blancos*).

Peter Wade indicates that indigenousness (and sometimes whiteness) is as central to the self-identification of African-descent Latin Americans as is the "Afro part of the mix" (2006a:108). Thus every African-descent group must be engaged within its own cultural context, politics, and history. In this respect, black Indians (whether or not they call themselves morenos) are not anomalous in Latin America or in the United States. In Latin America they include the black Aymaras of the Andean Yungas (Urioste 1985), the Garífuna and their precursors the Black Carib (Bateman 1990; Gonzalez 1988; Prescod and Fraser 2008), the black Indians of Esmeraldas, Ecuador (Lane 2002), and the Miskito of Nicaragua (Pineda 2006). In the United States they include the Black Utes of Colorado (Brooks 2002), Oklahoma's Black Seminole, Afro-Cherokees, Afro-Navajos, and others (Katz 1997; Miles 2005; Miles and Holland 2006; Tayac 2009). Like the morenos of San Nicolás, each group gives meaning to its own black Indianness. Because of this, I take seriously the observation made by Edmund Gordon and Mark Anderson that ethnography is essential to understanding "black" identities in the Americas, which result from "creative" self-fashioning and the structural conditions around which self-fashioning occurs (1999:289; also Daniel 2006, Daniel and Haddow 2010a, 2010b; Wade 1997, 2006a).

While the morenos of San Nicolás see themselves as *of* Indians, they also belittle Indians as more rustic and less cultivated than they are. The contradiction between being of a people but also distinct from it recalls Marisol de la Cadena's description of "indigenous mestizos" in Peru, who identify as both but simultaneously denigrate Indians (2000). It is also a feature of Mexican mestizo ideology, which continues to fashion white Indian identities even as contemporary Indians are disparaged (Friedlander 1975). Contradictions like these are possible because race is socially constructed around local knowledge, history, and politics, and because it is deployed contextually toward different ends and with different meanings. In the United States race is construed in biological terms using scientific language, with careful percentages of ancestry that have shifted during the years but that even today make someone Native American or not, African American or not. In contrast, San Nicoladenses' race constructs rest on phenotype blended with history, space, place, language, clothing, and cultural practices. "Blacks" therefore do not exist locally in a reified material or biological sense. Instead, racial identities emerge from the dynamic merging of outsider interest with history and the consciousness and self-definition of individuals, who have particular understandings of their own experiences.

One of the most significant racial markers in many parts of Latin America, including in San Nicolás, is the contrast between rural and urban, with the former pertaining to the past, the foreign, the distant and the elemental and the latter to the present, the familiar, and the proximate. Because of this, the morenos of San Nicolás recognize various categories of Indians: The most foreign are the most "rural." They live up in the mountains or resided in the past. The most familiar live in San Nicolás itself, a space that is relatively urban. Morenos also temporally and spatially distance blackness through comments such as "our ancestors were black," "the village used to be really, really black," "those people in that more isolated town are black" (Lewis 2004; also Godreau 2002a). On the whole, then, "pure" blackness and "pure" Indianness do not exist in the village.

San Nicolás's morenos and, increasingly, its Indians, see themselves as more cultivated and cosmopolitan than that which is historically or geographically distant. They cultivate cosmopolitanism in part through upward mobility, made possible in recent decades by migration to the United States (*el norte*, the north, or *el otro lado*, the other side). Associating darkness with the past, San Nicoladenses also "race" the future as a time they will inhabit as modern Mexicans, removed from rurality and a more rustic way of life. In this context, if migration does not exactly whiten, it does lighten, by allowing San Nicoladenses to acquire the material goods, habits, and knowledge, both at home and abroad, that signify upward mobility (Lewis 2006, and chapter 8).

Multiculturalism and Social Activism

Culture workers consider San Nicolás the "cradle" of Afromexican, Afromestizo, or black culture, a place where "old" traditions have survived. But long ago the redondo Ernesto showed me crumbled following its removal to the outskirts of San Nicolás next to the shuttered culture house (*casa de cultura*), which was also built by la cultura in the 1980s to promote local but long-gone cultural forms, such as cotton weaving. No one attends to either of these houses, which are surrounded by overgrown brush. Public performances of artesa music no longer occur, as two of the musicians just passed away. During my years in San Nicolás it was occasionally played both inside and outside the community. But outside performances—solicited by la cultura—were embedded in showcases of Mexican or Latin American music; inside performances were generally at the behest of visitors. Both sorts were brief performances and did not, ironically, hold the significance that made culture workers value them: they were neither exotic African retentions nor did they illustrate contemporary community traditions. The redondo has also been displaced and decontextualized. Neither artifact holds much meaning for most San Nicoladenses anymore, except as vague links to the past and as not necessarily advantageous ones to la cultura. They are not part of "living" culture except insofar as they are made available for outside consumption.

San Nicoladenses do not struggle for ethnic recognition through such artifacts or in any other way. In great part this lack of struggle can be attributed to Mexico's postrevolutionary agrarian reform (1930–40), which granted communal land rights to most small farmers. Although not all Mexicans have fertile land, San Nicoladenses do, as their plots were carved out of the holdings of a U.S. rancher. And while land boundaries are still disputed, land rights are not.[3] Unlike in other parts of Latin America where people of African descent have had to argue that they are culturally "like Indians" to prove a special and officially recognized claim to land (Anderson 2007; Hooker 2005), San Nicoladenses have not. In Mexico there are no separate rights for them, and on the Costa Chica there is little group identity among moreno majority towns.

In 1997 the first Meeting of Black Villages was held. These meetings occur annually in a moreno coastal belt community, alternating between Guerrero and Oaxaca. They are meant to foment a regional black identity and to highlight cultural recognition to demand better infrastructure, agricultural support, and other necessities. In 1997 the umbrella organization Black Mexico was also founded. Both the meetings and Black Mexico are run by local intellectuals and outsiders. Most San Nicoladenses have politely refused to engage, including in the meeting held in San Nicolás itself in 2002. Largely this is because the appellations used by the meeting organizers and leaders—black, Afromexican, and Afromestizo—conflict with moreno identities, and the goals of activism do not correspond to San Nicoladenses' particular concerns with migration and holding together their families and community. Moreover, culture workers focus on no longer locally significant traditions. As San Nicoladenses show scant interest in the politics of multiculturalism, culture workers, in turn, often see San Nicoladenses as "uncooperative," if not downright hostile. Yet culture workers, including non-Mexicans, are still drawn to San Nicolás as they seek an African heritage in Mexico's multicultural mosaic: in early 2010 I met with a London-based television producer working with Henry Louis Gates Jr. on the PBS series *Black in Latin America*. During our long discussion about Mexico, I told her that her team would find little that to them would make San Nicolás "African." And if they did visit, they might notice San Nicoladenses leaving for the United States.

Migration and Homeplace

In 1997 I pulled into the central plaza of San Nicolás with my husband and our three-year-old son after a three thousand–mile car ride from Virginia. The only shade was under the concrete overhang of a small commercial strip where Doña Lupe, with whom I had stayed in 1992 and to whom I had written a letter in advance of our arrival, occupied a small corner space for a storefront and an interior room where she ate and slept. As we exited the car a man approached us with a wide grin. "Ah," he said, "Virginia," as he noticed our license plates. He introduced himself as Manuel, and told us that he had lived for several years in "Winston" (Winston-Salem). Manuel

San Nicolás's central plaza in 1997

pointed to a toddler perched on a long wooden table under the shade of the overhang. "That's my son Martín," he said. "He was born there." Manuel's house at the time was a cinder-block shell with no windows or doors. But it symbolizes his family's ongoing successes in el norte. As he once cheerily told me, San Nicoladenses are patient. Everything happens "bit by bit."

At the time I had no idea whether Doña Lupe had received my letter or whether she would remember me if she had. But she did receive the letter and she did remember me. We exchanged greetings and I stopped in to see the mayor, as we were looking for a place to live. He, in turn, identified Doña Lupe as someone who oversaw a number of empty houses for her sons and daughters, three of whom were in el norte. One of the houses, the mayor pointed out to us gringos, had an indoor bathroom.

Doña Lupe affirmed that she had an empty house that belonged, as she put it, to her daughter-in-law Amada, who was in Winston-Salem with Doña Lupe's son José. In 1997 Amada and José had already been gone for more than ten years, and all but one of their six children was born in el norte. The house had only recently been completed. They have yet to return.

As Doña Lupe brought out a large key ring, we all piled into our car and crossed the plaza. Soon we arrived at a single-story, boxy cinder-block dwelling with one front window facing the sandy road. I accompanied Doña Lupe through the green metal door and into the dim light while my son and his father sat in the shade across the way, magnets for curious children on their way home from the elementary school called Cuauhtémoc, after the last of the Aztec emperors, further up the road.

The house had two large rooms and a semi-open space with a low wall. The kitchen area held a cement cistern for storing water, and an unusual indoor faucet. In the back a wooden door opened onto an unfinished breezeway and a roughed-in bathroom, where the dead cat we found had spent its last days on the dirt floor. A tamarind tree offered welcome shade in the yard. Facing the road, a metal security curtain reached from floor to ceiling, taking up a whole wall. Doña Lupe had overseen the construction of the house, and it was her idea to ready it for a small business for her daughter-in-law, perhaps a pharmacy or a clothing store, with the metal curtain raised during the day to enable passersby to see what was inside. As an evangelical (an *evangélica*, *alelujah*, or *hermana* in local parlance), Doña Lupe refused to charge rent, which she did not feel would be right. In lieu of rent, we finished the breezeway and the bathroom, tiled the cement kitchen counter, painted, and installed windows on the west side of the house.

Although indoor kitchens and bathrooms are still uncommon, I did not know then that the house was typical of the new style taking hold as more and more people migrated. In 1992 occasional references were made to Santa Ana, California, where San Nicoladenses began migrating in the late 1970s. But by the late 1990s, at any given time a third of San Nicolás's residents were in Winston-Salem or in the nearby cities of Greensboro and Charlotte, and most households in San Nicolás now have several migrant members. The migration history of San Nicoladenses is relatively recent compared to that of other Mexicans and even to that of other Guerrerenses; only now are significant numbers of San Nicoladenses growing up in el norte, with the oldest in their twenties, using Facebook and having children.[4] Like other Mexican small farmers, San Nicoladenses have been affected by global trade that floods markets with inexpensive imports with which they cannot compete.[5] While they have fertile land, they do not receive sufficient agricultural support. Yet their most frequently stated motivation for migrating is not to feed their families. It is instead to "build my house" in San Nicolás.

Houses symbolize upward mobility and as such are both economic and cultural motivators. They are also potent symbols of homeplace. San Nicoladenses living in the United States send remittances to build these houses, and they remain oriented to their Mexican community in other ways: they travel between locales, send to and receive goods from Mexico, and are in constant communication with family members there, making the village space a prominent transnational symbol of the connections between migrants and nonmigrants.[6] Because migration is so central to how they and many other Mexicans and Latin Americans perceive their world and live their lives, the "community" of San Nicolás extends beyond geopolitical borders, which are technically closed to rural people, who cannot acquire any kind of visa because they do not have the skills, education, capital, or other property that would convince a consular official that they are needed in el norte or will return home after a visit. Yet because staying in San Nicolás means that it can take years to build a house like Amada's and José's, San Nicoladenses go to el norte anyway.

Nearly all San Nicoladenses are related, albeit distantly. Endogamy extends to migration: San Nicoladenses migrate with family, live with and visit family in el norte, find work in el norte through family, and while in el norte usually partner with others from San Nicolás or from nearby towns. Migration thus looms large in the identities of San Nicoladenses, whose migration patterns—or "journeys," as the philosopher Edward Casey might call them (1996:23)—follow routes that resemble pilgrimages. Indeed, their moreno patron saint, Saint Nicholas of Tolentino, journeys 300 kilometers every year from his Indian home to the village of San Nicolás for his festival.

Summary and Objectives

This book coheres around places and boundaries. My objectives are to show how race, with which I begin, draws one to an ongoing "past," while migration, with which I end, draws one to an urbanized, "modern," and elusive future. Race highlights the saint's connection to morenos, while migration highlights his sojourn far from home. Both race and migration thus bring focus to the village of San Nicolás: San Nicoladenses identify the moreno "race" with their homeplace, which is the nexus for much historical and symbolic mixing between blacks and Indians, and San Nicoladenses in the United States build houses in San Nicolás while embodying their Mexican community in gesture, word, taste, lifeway, and aspiration. Ultimately, race and migration are prisms through which homeplaces—cultural embodiments of history (time), space, and sentiment, what Casey calls the "dense historicities and geographies" that inform senses of place (1996:36–37)—are made meaningful by and to the people who inhabit them. From the perspectives of San Nicoladenses, what we might consider the instability and hybridity of migration and mixed racial identities actually make places that are as constant as the ground right before an earthquake.

I broaden the themes to include gender, especially as it relates to interiority and exteriority; the geography of race within San Nicolás; and houses as "empty" but deeply meaningful markers, as boundary making, as part of nature (mud-based, moveable, rural, like those of Indians and the past) or part of culture (concrete, fixed, urban, like those of the upwardly mobile). I also address anger, an "illness" that makes it difficult for people to maintain peaceful social relationships with others, which peace is resolved to restore the reciprocal bonds that make community. Such bonds, perhaps counterintuitively, are strengthened by migration, because as the community grows, remittances renew it, making it possible, faithful to the tradition, to continue to include everyone in life-changing events. Thus while displacement, uprootedness, and contestation are a part of people's lived experiences (Feld and Basso 1996), so is the maintenance of stability and place.

In chapter 1, "The Lay of the Land," I outline a regional history of the Costa Chica and San Nicolás based on archival and library materials, as well as oral histories. This chapter contributes to our collective knowledge of the Costa Chica, which is otherwise little documented. It also establishes a context for understanding the ethnographic material, especially the significance of land and moreno identities to San Nicoladenses. Chapters 2 and 3, "Identity in Discourse" and "Identity in Performance," draw on chapter 1 to establish the meaning of morenoness through analyses of local discourses about race and place. These stress "mixture" while expressing tensions and mutual accommodations between morenos and Indians. Chapter 4, "Africa in Mexico," traces the relationship in the 1940s and 1950s between the U.S. anthropologist Melville Herskovits and the Mexican researcher Gonzalo Aguirre Beltrán, who was the first to produce an ethnography of a "black" Costa Chican community and who used Herskovits's racial and cultural paradigms to do so. I also discuss Herskovits's legacy, filtered through Aguirre Beltrán. Chapter 5, "Culture Work," explores current social and political movements on the coast, particularly Black Mexico and the Meetings of Black Villages. These movements are designed to teach ethnic consciousness and solidarity, but they also replicate much of the discourse that differentiates "blacks" from other Mexicans, thus displacing San

Nicoladenses. Chapter 6, "Being from Here," explores cultural oppositions that make place. San Nicolás remains rather segregated by gender, and gender permeates almost every aspect of social, family, and ritual life. Gender is linked to notions of inside and outside, to home and the street, to the domestic and the public. Gender is also about marital discord, race, religion, work, and migration. Chapter 7, "A Family Divided?," addresses community tensions over "modernity" including drainage, literacy, and multiple political parties. It then moves to "cleansing" through festivals and weddings that draw people together. Similarly, personal conflicts, many of which are mentioned in chapter 6, also cause tensions. In trying to avoid or alleviate them, people remake place. Chapter 8, "Transnationalism, Place, and the Mundane," addresses San Nicolás as a magnet that draws people home. Many San Nicoladenses stay in el norte for long periods of time, but they always have a foot in San Nicolás. This chapter unpacks the most material sign of people's ongoing attachment to place—the cinder-block houses they build with remittances. Finally, people are always buried in San Nicolás, no matter where they die. The conclusion, "What's in a Name?," discusses ethnicity in el norte as San Nicoladenses come into contact with other groups. I suggest that they continue to fashion identities that connect their race (*raza*) and roots (*raíces*) to San Nicolás. As those identities are fluid, it makes sense to then summarize how globalization affects people who experience displacement but simultaneously give meaning to and confirm the ongoing existence of "their" village.

CHAPTER ONE

The Lay of the Land

San Nicoladenses use the terms *white*, *moreno*, and *Indian* in reference to the three broad "types" of Costa Chicans, which is why I use them too. As discussed in the following chapter, that terminology can become more complex. But for the purposes of imagining the geography of the coast it works because the locations of the communities associated with whites, morenos, and Indians largely coincide with socioethnic stratification. Thus at the macro level race can be spatially mapped onto place.

The Costa Chica's hot and humid savannah zone, or the "coastal belt" closest to the ocean, is historically home to morenos and continues to be one of Mexico's most important agricultural regions (Valdez 1998:19). The belt's temperatures range from 68 to 93° F (20 to 34° C), the soil is deep and fertile, the land quite flat, and production yields, especially of corn — the staple crop — relatively high (Bartra 1994:132). If the weather cooperates, "you can just plant any little sapling and it grows — here there's always fruit — maybe mangos, coconuts, then watermelon, cantaloupe," José mused as we discussed how few go hungry in San Nicolás. Indeed, the land is so fertile that white planters from Mexico City and foreigners from abroad (today including Japanese) buy or rent it for agribusiness.

From the colonial period on, Spaniards and whites were the

large landowners (*hacendados, latifundistas,* or *terratenientes*), and white professionals, traders, and businesspeople still dominate the Costa Chica's larger cities and towns, which embody "national [mestizo] culture" and control trade to and from moreno and Indian communities (Cervantes 1984:39–40, 44–45; Flanet 1977:212; Valdez 1998:44–49). These cities and towns cluster around or have easy access to federal Highway 200, which runs just north of the coastal belt. Part of the Panamerican Highway, it is one of the only upgraded thoroughfares on the coast. With the exception of stretches near Acapulco, it has one lane in either direction.

Indian communities are located north of Highway 200 in the cooler Sierra Madre del Sur foothills, and they are populated in the main by monolingual Amuzgo and Mixtec speakers,[1] the majority and linguistically related Indian groups on the Costa Chica today (*Así somos* 1994). Amuzgos live in and around the municipal seat of Ometepec (population 18,000), which is dominated by whites and reachable from Cuaji (population 10,000) via an upgraded branch of Highway 200, as well as in the neighboring municipalities of Xochistlahuaca and Igualapa. Mixtecs live in the Mixteca de la Costa, which includes the municipality of Pinotepa Nacional, Oaxaca, the coastal belt's largest city (population 35,000), and around Ayutla (de Los Libres) north of Cruz Grande.

Land in most Indian communities is less fertile than on the coastal belt. Typically, it is far from the villages to which it pertains, has been illegally usurped or leased to outsiders for minimal payments, lacks irrigation, or is located on deforested hillsides where erosion rates are high and soil quality poor (Bartra 1994:132; Flanet 1977; Valdez 1998:21, 36–37). Residents are forced to frequently rotate land as they are displaced into the mountains, further and further from their villages (Cervantes 1984:48; Flanet 1977:49). Much of it produces only one crop a year—mostly corn, hot peppers, or beans, which are staples of both Indian and moreno diets.

Moreno villages are socioeconomically sandwiched between white and Indian ones. Most are not as impoverished as the latter, but even though morenos speak Spanish as their native language, they do not have the material and political capital of whites. Inequalities also exist within and between moreno villages, due in large part to irrigation access. Thus, poorer San Nicoladenses, morenos from neighboring villages, and outside Indians work as peons in San Nicolás or for the region's whites. In San Nicolás, moreno peons are paid a bit more than Indians because the former live nearby, bring their own food, and return home each day. "Indian peons don't even bring tortillas," Rodrigo explained, "so they are paid and given food. They stay the whole week working in the bush, removing branches and the like." Because Indians stay for long periods, lodged with their employers, Rodrigo added that they sometimes keep "one or two small calves" in San Nicolás.

Highway 200 was completed through the Costa Chica in the mid-1960s. It was largely responsible for a leap in the region's economic and population growth.[2] Before the road was built and without access to a light plane, it took eight days to reach Acapulco from Cuaji on foot, or one night in a boat. "Only important people went to Acapulco," Don Gregorio recalled, "and even fewer went to Mexico City. News from Acapulco and Mexico City arrived on vinyl records. It would be played on a Victrola." Even today it takes three hours to navigate the 150 kilometers between Acapulco and Cuaji by car because Highway 200 is narrow, twists and turns, and passes through local towns with speed bumps. The trip is even longer on buses that make frequent stops.

Highway 200 constitutes Main Street in many coastal belt communities, such as San Marcos, Cruz Grande, and Marquelia close to Acapulco, Cuaji on the southeastern border with Oaxaca, and Pinotepa Nacional, Oaxaca, 50 kilometers southeast of Cuaji. The road is the only way for *costeños* (people from the Costa Chica) to reach Ometepec, which has two hospitals, Acapulco, the national highway to Chilpancingo, Guerrero's capital, or Mexico City, several hundred kilometers north of Chilpancingo. It is also the road to Pinotepa, with the closest banking centers, a supermarket, a large open-air market, opticians, and other amenities and necessities.

San Nicolás is about equidistant between Cuaji and the ocean. It is the largest town pertaining to Cuaji which, for San Nicoladenses, is the first stop for a variety of foodstuffs, medicines, some medical specialists, and services, including a recently installed bank branch whose ATM often runs out of money. Until the late 1990s most San Nicoladenses traveled there in open-air trucks lined with benches (*camionetas*), which ran on a fixed schedule beginning at 5:00 A.M. In the late 1990s several San Nicoladenses purchased taxis with migrant remittances. The fleet is now regularized and has replaced the camionetas. Taxis are the only way to get into and out of town without a private car, and they are expensive for many San Nicoladenses, who, depending on their needs, might have to reach Acapulco, Ometepec, Pinotepa Nacional, or points beyond.

The relationship between Cuaji and San Nicolás is similar to the one Karen Blu describes between the Lumbee, North Carolina, center of Pembroke and the nearby former cultural center of Prospect (1996:207–12). Like Pembroke, Cuaji is something of a miniature metropolis. Its more urban residents characterize San Nicolás as home to "country" folk who do not speak proper Spanish (variously said to be "wrong," "archaic," "uncultured," or "black") and who preserve the older ways, though many Cuaji residents remain ignorant about how San Nicoladenses live. For their part, San Nicoladenses insist that Highway 200 was supposed to come through their town, which would have made San Nicolás larger than Cuaji. Unlike Cuaji, San Nicolás still does not have a functioning, community-wide drainage system, a first-class pharmacy, consistently present healthcare providers, sufficient markets, or a finished plaza, which is a parody of the Porfirian ideal of a bandstand that should be surrounded by brightly painted walls, benches, and lush vegetation, all of which Cuaji has. Before each municipal or gubernatorial election minimal work is done, only to be quickly abandoned after a short time. Thus projects are completed bit by bit. Today the plaza's roads have been paved, as has the turn road from Cuaji at Montecillos. But the bandstand is still a shell, the plaza has no paint or vegetation, drain pipes burst, and electricity—only installed in the 1970s—constantly goes out, sometimes for days.

Mexican towns are subordinated to their municipal seats, which are subordinated to the state capital. Every six years, governors distribute checks to municipal presidents. The money is earmarked for communities in the municipality, but the presidents spend it as they wish, depending on which political party is in power in which community. Those communities whose mayors (elected yearly) are of the same party as the municipal president can expect their community to receive more funds.[3] Because Oaxaca has seven times as many municipalities as Guerrero, and a considerably denser population, money flows more freely there due to more direct interaction with the state government. Generally Oaxacan roads and infrastructure are superior. A recent study confirmed that "Afromestizo" communities in Guerrero have poorer access to medical services than those in Oaxaca or Veracruz,[4] and that moreno Guerrerenses lack the education to maximize agricultural production, as well as the economic infrastructure that would prevent young people from leaving (Rodríguez 2008). Because San Nicolás is always arguing with Cuaji over funds for infrastructure, in 2009

San Nicolás's central plaza in 2009

Cuaji's central plaza in 2009

it petitioned the state government to become its own municipal seat with jurisdiction over ten towns. As of this writing that petition has still not been approved.

Wet and Dry, High and Low

The Costa Chica is a tropical zone with a dry and a wet season. The dry season (*tiempo seco*) runs from November to June, and nights can be cool from November through February. As the air becomes more humid from mid-March on, daytime highs can reach more than 100° F on the belt. Just before the rains, the sky becomes overcast as clouds roll in and land is cleared for planting. In mid-June, if all goes well, the rainy season (*tiempo de lluvia*) begins, and the coast becomes astonishingly green and lush, providing rich pasture for its beautiful Zebu, Swiss, and Holland (Holstein) cattle (some of them cross-bred for the tropics), which often graze in majestic palm groves that punctuate the landscape.

Cattle have been integral to the region's political ecology since they arrived with Spaniards. They continue to be a source of sustenance and even wealth for many costeños, as well as for some state elites who graze their herds on the coastal belt, where new grass strains continuously permit more intensive cultivation (Sánchez 1987:268). Cattle are bred for both milk and meat. Some San Nicoladenses wake every morning at 5:00 A.M. to milk by hand, as there is no mechanized milking; others let their cows drip. Everyone drinks unpasteurized milk, and many women make cheese, rice pudding, and flan.

Cows bred for meat are fattened and slaughtered almost daily by local vendors such as Doña Lupe, who purchases a cow to be butchered in the interior patio of her family compound. The beef (*carne de res* or *carne*) is ready for sale by the early morning, when an announcement goes out over one of San Nicolás's loudspeakers. While good cuts are a luxury, every last scrap sells. Ranching is therefore lucrative, but with about one hundred head needed to make it viable, as cows only birth once a year, the cost for a herd runs into thousands of dollars, and milking or pasturing such a herd is impossible for most. Although a few wealthy families have more than one hundred cattle, most have between four and twenty.

San Nicolás lies in a savannah zone with elevations ranging from five to thirty meters. Its ejido consists of some eight thousand hectares.[5] Those

Locally owned cattle

with rights to community land (*ejidatarios*) include about eight hundred family heads, mostly men but also single women and widows.[6] Anticipating NAFTA (North American Free Trade Agreement) in the early 1990s, President Carlos Salinas de Gortari privatized ejidos by amending Article 27 of the 1917 Mexican Constitution. The ejidatarios of San Nicolás now own between 2 and 150 hectares, averaging 5 to 10. They produce corn for their own consumption, as well as sesame and fruit (mango, papaya, and watermelon) for markets where prices are always low, in part because imports undercut local products, which also enter the market all at once for seasonal reasons.

Field plots are divided between highlands (*los altos*), at twenty to thirty meters above sea level, and lowlands (*los bajos*), at five to ten meters above sea level. Those with hectares in the highlands, and land and irrigation in the lowlands, can produce three crops per year and water cattle year round, as cattle graze in the highlands during the rainy season and in the lowlands with irrigation in the dry season.[7] But people without lowlands or irrigation can only produce one crop a year, and then only if rain is sufficient. If it is not "there's hunger," Rosa said one year, "we don't have anything." By mid-June people start to fret if there is no rain or if it is inconsistent because cattle cannot graze nor can planting begin until the land is damp. Even then, if the rains stop, corn shoots wither and die in the sun. August can be a hungry month if a summer crop from the highlands is not yet ready, if a rainless summer has destroyed it, or if a spring crop from the lowlands is long gone. Cattle are sometimes sold off or die.

If summer rains are hearty, torrential afternoon downpours occur from June through September. But these can be *too* hearty, drowning cattle and crops in the lowlands. In October 1997, Hurricane Paulina hit the coast with a vengeance, causing mudslides that devastated Acapulco's hillside shanty-towns. Paulina wreaked havoc on coastal villages such as Collantes, where one person drowned, adobe houses were destroyed, and residents lived in the church on higher ground for five days. San Nicolás suffered crop and cattle losses. Trapped in their houses, Sirina and Rosa periodically called out "neighbor, neighbor, are you alright?" as the waters rose.

During the hurricane Sirina's cousin also tragically drowned when his truck was washed away by the rising creek known as the "Cold Waters" (*Aguas Frias*) that raged across a dip in the road to Cuaji. A bridge over Aguas Frias was finally finished in 2008, but only because taxi drivers had protested the situation. That paved but pitted road full of dangerous twists and cave-ins continues south to Punta Maldonado or El Faro (The Light-house), a small fishing village on the only significant bay between Acapulco and Puerto Escondido. El Faro supplies San Nicolás, Cuaji, and other communities with fish and seafood. During two days of the year—New Year's Day and the Saturday before Easter Sunday—it is packed with modestly dressed locals. Only occasionally does an intrepid foreigner find El Faro. Thus it sees few bikini-clad tourists, although tourism is Guerrero's principal industry and the state government periodically tries to promote its Costa Chica beaches.[8] San Nicoladenses once speculated that El Faro would become a resort. But Paulina devastated the village. While fishing survives, tourism has never taken hold.

An Ethos of Violence?

With few paved highways and little railway, Guerrero is still "at the margins of industrial growth," partly because of difficult terrain and partly because of ongoing interruptions to foreign investment, including during the Mexican Revolution of 1910–20 (Estrada 1994:12; Jacobs 1982:61). Although tourism and agroforestry are significant, they primarily benefit multinational corporations, politicians, and the federal government. Only in the colonial silver-mining town of Taxco, near Mexico City, do locals consistently benefit from tourism. The closest beaches to Mexico City are in Acapulco, but the latter city has become blighted by drug violence. In 2009, with battles raging between traffickers and the Mexican army, the U.S. State Department issued a travel alert after eighteen people died in a shootout that had tourists running for cover. Massacres continue to occur as the violence spreads down the coast. Last year it hit close to home when Sirina's brother was abducted from Cuaji in broad daylight, tortured, and murdered. A devastated Sirina told me over the phone that the police had not investigated, that unknown people were driving through San Nicolás at night, that residents were keeping their doors closed and locked, and that the lawlessness was just like that of "the revolution."

Agroforestry has wreaked ecological havoc in parts of the state and has caused violent conflicts between peasants and multinationals such as Boise Cascade, which extracted timber for export to the United States in the 1990s, including in 1995, when police in Aguas Blancas infamously murdered seventeen Guerreran farmers from the Costa Grande, north of Acapulco, who were on their way to join a protest, including against forest removal (Gutiérrez 2004; Wines and Smith 1998).[9] One year after the massacre, the EPR (Ejército Popular Revolucionario, or Popular Revolutionary Army) emerged on the Costa Grande. It continues to operate in southern Mexico.

By conventional economic measures Guerrero is one of Mexico's poorest states (Estrada 1994:8–12).[10] The Mexican national imagination also characterizes it as ungovernable, as a place where "violence" is "political culture" (Estrada 1994:63–64; Sánchez 1987:15). But instead of analyzing structural conditions, scholars too have regarded violence as something of a "social character" or "second nature" for Guerrerenses whose "inability to be governed" is considered inborn (Estrada 1994:63–64).

The state's reputation in part results from poverty and lack of infrastructure, exacerbated in recent decades by drug trafficking, electoral irregularities, increased military and police presence, and political instability. The EPR has little presence on the Costa Chica because, I was told, there is no place to hide. But in 1997 it did unfurl a banner in Cuaji with the slogan, "The fight is not against the people; it is against the government." "Zapata's fight has not ended," the municipal president, a member of the PRD (Partido de la Revolución Democrática, or Party of the Democratic Revolution), announced in San Nicolás during this period. "The struggle has to arrive here," Doña Leticia said. "It's the same as with the Carrancistas or the Zapatistas," she added with reference to the revolution. She told me that the EPR was sympathetic to the more progressive PRD, but that the PRD had to dissociate itself from the EPR because the centrist and entrenched PRI (Partido Revolucionario Institucional, or Institutional Revolutionary Party), which at the time had been in power for close to seventy years, was using the EPR as a pretext to repress the PRD. "The PRI is for the middle class and above," said Doña Leticia. "The PRD is for the poor people, the peasants."

Many San Nicoladenses are sympathetic to the EZLN (the Ejército Zapatista de Liberación Nacional, or Zapatista Army for National Liberation) in Chiapas,[11] as well as to the EPR. But Ernesto once told me—using language that revealed nationalism, pride, and autonomy—that he preferred the EPR to the EZLN: "Marcos fights for Mexico but . . . he engages in dialogue.[12] The EPR uses weapons . . . the government is beginning to understand that the EPR is strong. The EPR has lots of popular support. If the government says it's going to do something—like build a road—it has to because of the EPR. The EPR . . . doesn't try to 'communicate.' It's stronger. It pressures [the government] more than Marcos does. I like this better—more direct, rougher, without discipline. Marcos is disciplined and the EPR is not. It fights like a bull. I prefer the EPR."

In part because of its poverty and concomitant political upheaval, Guerrero is also one of Mexico's most heavily militarized states. An army barracks sits at the northwestern end of Highway 200, and the army runs checkpoints of buses, cars, and trucks, looking for caches of arms, drugs, turtle contraband, and undocumented immigrants from Central America. A small battalion was long stationed at El Faro, until the community complained that soldiers seduced young women without marrying them. Its official task was to protect from poachers the turtle eggs that are a delicacy on the coast. Its unofficial task was to intercept the drugs that—rumor has it—are still shipped by boats and small planes from Colombia. El Faro's military personnel used to occasionally drive through San Nicolás. Once I watched them jump down from their trucks with triggers cocked to scan the plaza. "They've never found drugs," a Pinotepa human rights worker told me, adding that they took seafood and fish from local fishermen without paying. Manuel said that since cultivators and dealers could get much more money in the United States, the drugs went there. The military, he said, was really looking for the EPR. But Ernesto also told me that in the fall of 1996 a small plane from Colombia did fly up the coast and drop drugs at El Faro, where people used fishing boats to recover them. "That's why the army is here," he said, as two trucks of soldiers rolled by.

San Nicoladenses maintain an ambivalent attitude toward the army and the police. Although neither does much to stem violence and the police—stationed in Cuaji—fail to investigate many crimes, both institutions provide jobs for men, and particularly at night local roads are unsafe. Commercial buses from Acapulco travel in packs down Highway 200 because bandits erect roadblocks and attack passengers, robbing men and raping women. Doña Lupe was once stuck all night on the highway when another bus was held up. All the women on the other bus were raped while the men were robbed. Sirina mentioned another bus holdup involving robbery and rape. I once passed an empty bus on the shoulder of Highway 200 with a single bullet hole through the driver's side window.

Kidnappings for ransom occasionally happen, though so far no one has been killed. But holdups do occur locally, sometimes in broad daylight. In 1997 police had a shootout with assailants on the road to El Faro. Around the same time, a man from Santiago Tepextla, a moreno village poorer than San Nicolás, held up a camioneta from San Nicolás on the same road. Doña Lupe, the camioneta driver's aunt, told me the assailant was dressed in rags. Her nephew begged the man to "come with me, put down your gun," and the assailant called him *jefe* ("boss" or "buddy"), but it was too late. The police shot the assailant dead. Rodrigo was sympathetic: "[Tepextla] is a community of morenos, but there isn't any irrigation, so they only harvest once a year. They come here to work as peons and are really happy when they find work. They don't eat anything more than tortillas with chile and salt—not even an egg. They suffer from hunger; they don't even have money for meat."

In general, Acapulco and poverty-stricken Indian areas of Guerrero experience more violence than the coastal belt. But while this might be so, and while Highway 200 is the main artery for tourists driving from Acapulco or points beyond to Oaxacan beach resorts, Cuaji—whose Museum of Afromestizo Cultures (Museo de las Culturas Afromestizas Vicente Guerrero) is close to the bus station—does not boast the amenities tourists generally seek. Thus most bypass it and the coast's smaller communities, which barely find their way into guidebooks.

Tourists also might not stop because many *costeños* (coastal residents) have darker skin than is the national norm, making the region appear alien to many Mexicans and to foreigners with particular visions of Mexico. This darkness might reinforce the myth of violence "as second nature" that adheres to Guerrero, to the Costa Chica, and to morenos within it. Even Mexican nationals typically refer to the coast's "blacks" as bellicose (*bravos*), as I was often told by taxi drivers in Mexico City who did not even know where the Costa Chica was. A Peruvian woman with whom I rode a bus to Acapulco in 2007 pointed out dark-skinned people as we arrived at the city's outskirts and asked me whether it was safe.

I often received startled looks even from coastal Indians and whites when I mentioned that I lived in San Nicolás. They would tell me that I needed to be careful because "blacks" are violent, impulsive, and uncivilized. "There are only black people" in Collantes, a Mixtec woman in Pinotepa Nacional told me as she made a face. San Nicoladenses, she added, "are bad; they're always killing each other." But she also seemed envious of the lush land and the seaside as she talked about the abundance of coconuts, plantains, citrus fruit, fish, and seafood on the coastal belt. A Mixtec woman from an illustrious family of Pinotepa mask-makers, whose uncle and husband had both been killed in land disputes, told me that morenos are lazy. "The men are jealous," she continued. "They're aggressive, they don't care about education, they don't want to work, they like music and eating." She then turned to her mother to explain that I lived "among black people. Can you believe it?" she said. "Aren't they bad?" she asked, turning back to me. "Do you feel comfortable there?" Elena, a white shopkeeper in Collantes, told me that "morenos refuse to study or work hard" because they like to "have a good time." For her, "indigenous people" were "more obedient and gentle." They "strive to better themselves, but morenos don't want to. The truth is they're lazy. Everyone has land, but morenos harvest the minimum to get by. They don't irrigate their land in the dry season because it takes more work, and they pay indigenous people to work the land for them." Morenos are "lazy," said a young cultural promoter from Pinotepa, as he contrasted them to "hardworking Indians." The ironies, of course, are striking, given morenos' generally higher socioeconomic status. But these depictions of blacks and Indians parallel nationalist sentiments that repudiate blackness and idealize Indianness. They resonate more profoundly in the comments of Elena's husband, who told me that "blacks" were "people in exile" and "without a country," as he linked "civilization" to indigenous and mestizo villages.

In linking the indigenous to the mestizo he was in no way indicating that the two were interchangeable. Instead he was suggesting that the two were equivalent *insofar as* they were different from "the black."

Land and Conflict

During the early colonial period the Costa Chica was known as the Southern Sea (Mar del Sur), with its Indians subject to royal tribute paid in gold. Whole villages were assigned to labor for Spanish *encomenderos* (encomienda owners), to whom Indians also paid tribute in kind. Most of the coast's early encomenderos were also conquistadors. After Don Tristán de Luna y Arellano, perhaps the most well known of them, "pacified" the eastern Mixtec upland zones, he was authorized to establish cattle ranches on the coast. When Arellano died his son inherited his land, which he sold to his brother-in-law, Don Mateo Anaus y Mauleón. Although the New Laws would eventually dispossess Mauleón of the family encomienda, this "insatiable hacendado" extended his dominion throughout the region (Aguirre Beltrán 1985:46). Indian villages disappeared because of European illnesses, overwork, ethnocide, reorganization into new towns, flight from Spaniards and their cattle, and judges' tendency to ignore colonial laws of protection. By 1600 the number of Indian tribute payers in Igualapa had fallen to 1,900. In 1625 it was 1,250. By this time Acapulco retained only 8 percent of its 1550 population, while Xicayán had lost 50 percent of its population (Aguirre Beltrán 1985:36; Gerhard 1993:150–51; Widmer 1990:158).[13]

As Indians died or voluntarily relocated inland, Spaniards also deliberately cleared Indian areas to make way for cattle and to consolidate land. From the late sixteenth to the early seventeenth century "the lower mouth of the Santa Catarina river passed from . . . indigenous agriculturalists to . . . Spanish farmers. . . . Pinotepa del Rey was successfully moved from . . . the border between Igualapa and Jicayán, to the site of the subsequent large [Spanish] ranch of Los Cortijos . . . [with its people] always fleeing from cattle" (Widmer 1990:174).[14] By 1656 one "Mariscal" (Marshall) owned Los Cortijos, which his descendents would inherit along with settlements to the south, until the end of the nineteenth century. By 1792 blacks and mulattoes constituted the majority of employees there (Motta 2006:125).

Few passable roadways to major markets existed during the colonial period. But cattle ranching remained lucrative as the port of Acapulco developed and demand for beef and cow by-products grew in Mexico City. The coastal belt held the finest grasslands, salt, and ports (Widmer 1990:127), and Indian villages were sparser there than in the uplands. But as Spanish encomenderos became ranchers, they invaded the humid lowlands of villages to which Indians descended for seeding. These holdings were often devastated by wandering cattle, such as those of Mauleón. Colonial law ostensibly protected Indian autonomy, including land rights, and Indians therefore petitioned colonial authorities to resolve disputes. In one late sixteenth-century case Indians from several coastal villages, including from Huehuetán, which mulattoes would populate by the mid-1700s, sought restitution from Spanish ranchers. These included Mauleón himself, who held cattle at a ranch site in Cuaji. The Indians accused the Spaniards of having unleashed "more than 100,000" cattle on their lowlands. They could not protect their corn plots (*milpas*), cotton, melon, beans, peppers, and "other vegetables with which we sustain ourselves," nor pay royal tribute because the cattle ate their crops. The ranchers claimed Indian communities were "located in high mountains that cattle can never reach." But Igualapa's local judicial officer (*alcalde mayor*) found for the plaintiffs and ordered the ranchers "not to allow the cattle to do it again in any manner whatsoever" (AGN Tierras 48, 6; Aguirre Beltrán 1985:45–46; Gerhard 1973:148–49, 151, 181). Mauleón and the others paid restitution, but they continued to graze cattle on Indian lands.

Indians were definitively excluded from the coastal belt by 1600, but cochineal and bananas (originally imported by Spaniards) helped resuscitate their communities from the mid-seventeenth century on, and the numbers of Crown tributaries grew (Gerhard 1993:150–51; Widmer 1990:76–177, 180). Indian villages continued to retain autonomy and some distance from cattle ranches, and Spaniards continued to employ blacks and mulattoes, many now free, to work their land as cowboys and even as ranch overseers (*mayordomos*) (Aguirre Beltrán 1985:59–60; Gerhard 1973:148–49, 151, 381; Moedano 1986:552).

As Arturo Motta observes, throughout the colonial period Indians were considered inappropriate cowboys and in fact needed permits to ride horses. They were relegated to goat herding, while blacks and mulattoes were considered superb horsemen (2006:121, 124–25). One colonial administrator noted that blacks in Pinotepa Nacional do "not like to walk. It is rare that a black does not have his good horses" (2006:125). Because of their expert horsemanship, blacks and mulattoes were also assigned to the so-called *pardo* militias established by the Crown in the late seventeenth century under the command of Spanish district officials and designed in part to subdue Indian uprisings (Lewis 2003:97–98; Motta 2006:125; Vinson 2001:51; Widmer 1990:189).[15] The division of labor that placed colonial blacks and mulattoes on horseback explains what Motta identifies as contemporary moreno cowboy culture (2006).

The coast was ideal for goats, and seasonal herding connected it to the Nahua uplands in Guerrero's Montaña region, 300 kilometers north of the Costa Chica. The history of San Nicolás in the eighteenth, nineteenth, and early twentieth centuries most certainly included Nahua goat-herding activities (Martínez and Obregón 1991:263–68; Widmer 1990:131–34). Today the few Nahuas remaining on the coast are still referred to as shepherds, although they no longer herd (Valdez 1998:59). San Nicoladenses do not have regular contact with these coastal Nahuas, who live north of Ometepec and are "descendants of the families of the stock-tenders" (Valdez 1998:94–95) ("There's another 'shepherd race' up there — they have a different language," Don Elidio said). But the "authentic" statue of San Nicolás's patron saint, San Nicolás Tolentino, resides in the church in the main plaza of the Nahua Montaña community of Zitlala ("place of the stars" in Nahuatl and once called San Nicolás Zitlala), a topic I return to in chapter 3.

Doña María Ambrosia de Vargas: Enigmatic Indian Noblewoman

Little reliable information exists about land distribution on the Costa Chica for most of the eighteenth century. Yet a land donation by the Indian noblewoman (*cacica*) Doña María Ambrosia de Vargas looms large in the historical memories of San Nicoladenses. Why she decided to donate land and how much was donated is unknown, and the intent and recipients of the transfer still remain contentious. The historical documents contradict San Nicoladenses' beliefs, but the idea of the transfer speaks to the mythological foundations of San Nicolás and to moreno indebtedness to Indians.

Doña María had rights to some fifty-five thousand hectares in and around Huehuetán. She seems to have been unmarried and without heirs. Thus *Doña* was likely an honorific recognizing her Indian nobility. She appears to have had passed away by 1755. On her behalf and according to her wishes, one Don Juan de Vargas donated the prime coastal lands she would have inherited to the mulattoes of Huehuetán.[16] Some researchers claim she sold another large parcel to Ometepec's Indians (e.g., Manzano

1991:22), and the morenos of San Nicolás insist that she *donated* land to them. As Taurino Hernández writes, according to San Nicoladenses "the almost mythical Doña María Ambrosia became ill, and when people from San Nicolás took it upon themselves to carry her in a hammock to be cured, she donated land to them in gratitude" (1996:22–23). In another version Huehuetán did not need all of its donated land and subsequently *rented* parcels to other communities, including to San Nicolás (Manzano 1991:22–23; Valdez 1998:64–65).

Don Domingo explained that "the cacica was the boss around here. San Nicolás was a small settlement, but when she left land to the people, everyone united to found the village. The people were her servants; the Petatán and Noyola families [two of San Nicolás's first families] were her servants. She didn't give anything to Cuaji. They weren't her servants." On another occasion he told me that "[San Nicolás] was a small settlement [*ranchería*]. A cacica named María Ambrosia de Vargas owned these lands at the time and had a cattle ranch. The people of San Nicolás were her cowboys. Then she left . . . she was an Indian. She donated her land to San Nicolás, to Maldonado, to Cuaji and to Huehuetán."

The Hernández family, which included five brothers, "founded the village," he later said. "They were cowboys—employees of María Ambrosia. It was after independence. She also brought black people as servants. [The Vargases] were Indians. She was a cacica—the boss [*dueña*] of part of Mexico. . . . On the creation of [San Nicolás] it was called Santo Petatán since the Petatán family was here. They were from another settlement the cacica owned. She had a lot of settlements. The Oliva, Noyola, Silva, and Cisneros families [names still common in San Nicolás] all worked for her. Some [other] Hernández folks were the 'Hernández Blanquena' family. But they weren't considered family. They were white. And this is when the town [pueblo] was founded,[17] when it was populated."

According to Don Domingo, Doña María's employees thus founded San Nicolás after independence around 1821. He also claims that she left land to a number of villages. Bits of this history are incorrect, including the chronology and that Doña María gave land to San Nicolás. Some published accounts are also incorrect. For instance, María Manzano claims that Don Francisco de Vargas was Doña María's father and that she sold land to Ometepec's Indians after independence (1991:22). But Doña María's father seems to have been Don Juan de Vargas rather than Don Francisco. The donation was also made before independence.

The Vargas family land can be traced back to the 1720s when Don Francisco, a cacique from Huehuetán, petitioned regarding possession of land that included Juchitán, about 32 kilometers northwest of San Nicolás and 16 kilometers from Huehuetán, and El Limón, still further north (AGN Tierras 472.2). Several decades later, Don Juan, stated to be Don Francisco's son, litigated to establish the boundaries of the family land to comply with Doña María's wish that her share be inherited by the "poor of the town of Huehuetán." As the frontispiece of the dossier states, "Cacicazgo [landholding] of the Vargas family. Evidence from witnesses made on behalf of the cacica of Huehuetán, Doña Ambrosia de Vargas . . . the record states the inheritors to be the community of the poor of the village of Huehuetán [Huhuetlán]" (AGN Tierras 3668.3). Although the records do not clarify the relationship between Don Juan and Doña María, clearly the two were kin. Given the chronology, Don Juan must have been either her father or her brother. Doña María died before he did, as Don Juan's testimony declares that the "poor people of Huehuetán" are to inherit Doña María's land *because of the choice made in their favor at her death*" (emphasis added). His litigation began in 1755 and ended in 1771. Forty-three years thus passed between Don Francisco's initial petition and the end of Don Juan's.

Mulattoes Become Natives

Numerous witnesses attested to the longevity of the Vargas cacique line, to the demarcation of its land (because the titles had been lost), and to the fact that no one had ever contested the family's ownership. Of great interest is that the witnesses—uniformly older men—are identified as mulattoes *and* as natives (*naturales*), a term normally reserved during the colonial period, as today, for Indians. The eighty-five-year-old free native mulatto Morales (whose first name is unreadable) thus testified that he knew Don Juan, his father Don Francisco, and even Don Juan's grandfather. Morales stated that the Vargas family was noble and that he could outline their land boundaries, which included Maldonado, a "spot" called Cacalote, and the banks of the Santa Catarina River, just north of San Nicolás. The seventy-year-old free mulatto Tomás Hernández was also described as a native of Huehuetán. Another witness, the eighty-four-year-old free mulatto and native of Huehuetán, Vicente Hernández, noted that everyone knew the land titles were lost but that he did not know where or how. The seventy-seven-year-old Salvador de Medina, another free mulatto native of Huehuetán, added that he thought one of the Vargas ancestors had lost the papers some seventy years earlier. Following testimony by these and other elderly mulatto men, an interpreter spoke to Nahua, Mixtec, and Amuzgo Indians in communities mentioned in the testimony. While several Indians contested the Vargas claims, they did not have the papers to prove the boundaries of their own land.

The places mentioned in the documentation are located just to the north-west of San Nicolás, that is, toward Huehuetán, although both Cacalote and Maldonado are today part of the ejido of San Nicolás. The testimony suggests that the Vargas land stretched as far north as El Limón and as far south as to the borders of where San Nicolás now stands.

Which territory was ultimately adjudicated as Vargas family land is un-clear. But some of it did go to Huehuetán's mulatto natives, as Doña María had wished, and some of it was given (rather than sold) to the "indige-nous people/town of Ometepec for free" (AGN Tierras 3668.3). Nowhere is San Nicolás mentioned, even though it existed by this time. It thus seems that Doña María did not donate to San Nicolás. For their part, San Nicola-denses deny renting land from Huehuetán, although primary sources con-firm that they did (Gobierno del Estado de Guerrero 1933:7). From their point of view, Doña María donated land to them, land then "stolen" in the late nineteenth century by a U.S. citizen, Charles A. "Carlos" Miller (Her-nández 1996:22).

Deep Colonial Roots

During Mexico's Independence Wars (1810–21) "Spaniards" became "whites." Liberal reformers suppressed entailed estates, but instead of going to the people, land went to private investors, who took advantage of the demise of land protection laws (Valdez 1998:54). Land also went to independence leaders, such as Generals Juan Alvarez and Antonio López de Santa María. According to Manzano, Santa María's rather than Doña María's holdings eventually passed to Carlos Miller (1991:21). Until the late eighteenth cen-tury one Mariscal de Castillo also continued to hold *estancias* (ranches or farms) in San Nicolás, Cuaji, and Maldonado (AGN Padrones 18). This Mariscal might well have been a descendent of Mauleón, as Motta implies

(2006:146), and it might be that his family lands went first to Santa María and then to Miller.

During independence, mestizos north of Acapulco, where there were few morenos—a term that, like *mulato* and *pardo*, meant black Indian and was in use at least by the mid-eighteenth century—quickly became followers of the independence leader José María Morelos, who had taken up the cause from Miguel Hidalgo after the latter's assassination in 1811. The majority of the Costa Chica's Indians also fought for independence. The independence history of the Costa Chica's morenos is less clear (Guardino 1996:53). But it appears that they often made political choices based on ties to white bosses. Indeed, a longer historical perspective that includes accommodation to a system tying moreno livelihoods to Spaniards helps make sense of regional and ethnic differences. Cuaji, Maldonado, and San Nicolás were all overshadowed by hacendados,[18] who employed moreno cowboys and left moreno peasants to their own devices as long as they produced cotton and other goods for sale. By independence, of greatest concern to such peasants were likely the same issues that concerned any other peasant: access to land, crops, and animals to maintain family and community. For morenos—as for some Indians—such access came through whites.

Early on Spaniards' black and mulatto employees included many hacienda overseers and cowboys, as well as the pardo militias. By 1761 several names still common today in San Nicolás, such as Cisneros and Marcial, appear in an order that freed from tribute such militiamen stationed in San Nicolás and in nearby estancias, including Maldonado and Cuaji (AGN Tributos 34.1).[19] But while pardo militiamen were exempt from royal tribute, other morenos were not. This situation likely precipitated tensions among morenos since most free morenos lived in poverty as independent farmers, sharecroppers on haciendas, or sometimes as both. With salaries and exemptions from tribute, militiamen would take advantage of their status. Thus in the late eighteenth century a group of "mulatto" soldiers, together with a "mulatto" corporal stationed in Cuaji, murdered another "mulatto" on the latter's estancia (AGN Criminal 457.2–3). Several years later a "mulatto" from Huehuetán denounced to a priest a "mulatto" captain from Juchitán for idolatry and witchcraft (AGN Inquisición 1223.13). At the risk of overspeculating, I would guess that such accusations resembled ones made by Indians who, during the early colonial period, tried to undermine the authority of political superiors by accusing them of witchcraft (Lewis 2003:134–35). If nothing else, such incidents speak to intra-moreno tensions.

Alliances between morenos and Spanish officials and bosses meant that many morenos fought *for* the Crown (Widmer 1990:189). As both volunteers and forced recruits, moreno Royalists were often led by moreno militiamen. As Gabriel Moedano writes, "When . . . Hidalgo's emissaries . . . managed to rouse to rebellion indigenous groups from Pinotepa and Jamiltepec, they found themselves enemies of blacks. It was the sadly famous [black] Juan José Candelas, captain of the provincial militias, who headed the coastal morenos [and] stifled the liberation movement initiated by the indigenous people in the zone . . . upon defeating [indigenous people] [blacks] succeeded in carrying [them] to the gallows" (Moedano 1986:553).

In 1821 Juan Alvarez took Acapulco from Royalists to dominate the northern part of the Costa Chica.[20] Alvarez was a follower of General Vicente Guerrero, who briefly became Mexico's second president, abolished slavery, and after whom the state of Guerrero was named. But the more conservative Florencio Villarreal (a name still found in San Nicolás, where one Villarreal told me that her grandfather was white) commanded the Costa Chica from 1830 to 1844, when he was replaced by Joaquín Rea. Alvarez then ousted Rea and controlled the whole of the Costa Chica until he died in 1867 (Jacobs 1982:6–7). Several decades later President Benito Juárez paid off Mexico's mounting debt in part by selling church lands to hacendados. Twenty-one percent of Mexico's national population became hacienda workers, and by the revolution of 1910, land in Guerrero was owned by a mere 1.5 percent of its population (Valdez 1998:56). Many morenos, including San Nicoladenses, remained tied to white hacendados, a situation that would continue until after the revolution.

The Revolution and the Casa Miller

Juárez's successor, Porfirio Díaz, governed Mexico for most of the following thirty-five years. Ushering in "modernization," he privatized land for industrial development, attracted foreign capital, and controlled "banditry" by setting up rural police forces to quell peasant revolts. Guerrero's rugged terrain made transportation infrastructure difficult (Estrada 1994:12). Much investment therefore bypassed the state. But the coast still produced cash crops, principally rice, coffee, tobacco, cotton, and copra turned into soap in Acapulco factories. Most production took place on haciendas. During the late 1880s, as U.S.-based corporations and national elites took over tens of thousands of newly privatized hectares,[21] Indian lands and small farms continued to be expropriated. By 1910, 834 haciendas (owned by foreigners and Mexicans alike) occupied 40 percent of Mexico's land (Jacobs 1982:62; Valdez 1998:56).

In the late nineteenth century Lewis Lamm and Carlos Miller, both U.S. citizens, owned the largest haciendas on the southeastern Costa Chica (Valdez 1998:65). Hacendados from the United States "preferred to buy land on the coast, where the sea provided relatively easy access to markets beyond the confines of the state" (Jacobs 1982:61). Lamm, Miller, and other white hacendados took land, often by force, from moreno and Indian peasants (62).[22] But they also employed moreno foremen, as well as Indian and moreno laborers (Valdez 1998:58; Vinson 2000:276).

Lamm was a railroad engineer and absentee landlord who married into a Mexican family and took over its landholdings around Xochistlahuaca. Miller was a mechanical engineer who originally came to Mexico in the 1860s at the behest of Juan Alvarez, who owned a small estate between Acapulco and Chilpancingo and had gone to the United States to purchase a turbine from the company for which Miller worked. One job led to another until Miller found himself in Cuaji to fix a broken cotton felling machine for the white Daniel Reguera, a local cotton processor. Miller settled in Ometepec and, like Lamm, married into a Mexican family, the Regueras, who were "landowners [and] a dominant political force in the Ometepec area since the Wars of Independence, when they had fought on the Royalist side" (Jacobs 1982:61). Miller and Daniel Reguera's daughter Laura had two sons, Guillermo and Germán. The former would become a judge for the State of Guerrero while remaining a member of his father's company, Carlos Miller and Sons. The latter would take over his father's business (Aguirre Beltrán 1985:41–51; Manzano 1991:33).[23]

Miller initially industrialized cotton seed oil, which he sold in Cuaji and throughout the Mixteca Alta and Baja regions of Oaxaca. In contrast to his father-in-law, who insisted that buying land "creates war" (Manzano 1991:34), Miller bought up land for cattle and cotton. As Germán put it, "when Don Carlos realized how great the land was and what the agroindustrial and cattle ranching possibilities were . . . he decided to extend [his opportunities]" (Manzano 1991:34).

Costa Chican haciendas were adjudicated to people with money for surveys and deeds. Miller claimed Huehuetecan land that, according to Germán, he bought outright from Vargas descendents around 1890. Germán also claimed that Huehuetán sold his father land pertaining to San Nicolás (Manzano 1991:35, 73). While Doña María had no descendents, Huehuetecans might indeed have sold to Miller land that they had once rented to San Nicoladenses even though San Nicoladenses deny to this day any such arrangement. What is clear is that by 1900 Miller owned some two hundred thousand hectares in the municipalities of Ometepec and Cuaji, "which he has devoted to the raising of live stock [sic] and cotton, and upon which . . . there are about eight thousand natives living, to whom he parcels out his land without rental and from whom he buys the cotton raised" (Jacobs 1982:61).[24] Some Huehuetecan lands were sold to other hacendados, including to one Miller allegedly later had assassinated for paying higher salaries to his workers than Miller did. But another account claims that Huehuetecans assassinated that hacendado for illegally cultivating their land, and that Miller vindicated the man's murder by sending his cowboys to "kill those who had killed [him]" (Manzano 1991:90).

Residents of Cuaji, San Nicolás, and Maldonado worked for Miller in his Cuaji soap factory or as cowboys and muleteers. But most were small farmers on Miller's estate, cultivating corn, tobacco, rice, and cotton, as well as coconut palms, bananas, and other fruits (Moedano 1986:557). In addition to providing for their own subsistence, they sold cotton, some corn, and sesame to Miller at low prices. He sent bales of cotton for processing to Puebla and fed his cattle with the profits. San Nicoladenses today confirm that Miller did not charge rent. But he was also the only local buyer and owned the store where workers purchased necessities—such as machetes—that they could not produce themselves (Manzano 1991:28–29, 31–32). Moreover, farmers sowed at their own risk and cost. A shortage of rain or a crop plague left them bereft and Miller free of any debt.

Nevertheless, many San Nicoladenses insist that Miller was their friend, always knew the land was theirs, and that it was his son Germán who caused problems. As Don Domingo put it,

Carlos Miller was a good man with respect to San Nicolás, but his son wasn't. Carlos gave the people tools; they called him Don Carlos. His son Germán was the bad one. . . . Carlos told [Germán] "the land isn't yours," but he tried to take it anyway. Carlos Miller arranged with the people of San Nicolás to close off some wilderness land to cultivate cotton. It was called La Culebra. There's still a village there. The people grew cotton and [Carlos Miller] bought it. He had a factory in Cuaji and another in Tacubaya. So the people worked this enclosed land. They were accustomed to working Don Carlos's enclosed land, but it wasn't his land. Germán heard about the enclosed land and knew it was for cotton. But as he grew up he'd fight because he thought the land belonged to his father. He wanted the land because he was rich. He had everything—other land, cattle—Carlos left him a lot of cattle. That's why he wanted a lot of land.

Don Gregorio said Miller was called "Don" out of respect. He was a "success with the people" and rented them land to pasture their cattle. Indeed, Don Gregorio associated the "golden years" with Miller. Like Don Domingo he claimed that "the fault lay with Germán," to whom he credited thirty years of agrarian problems in San Nicolás as the "rich" with government backing fought the poor over still disputed land boundaries.

Miller lent his small farmers money to produce cotton and sesame, thereby cementing their ties to him. Such loans "ensured the hacendado cheap and secure labor, and . . . created a relationship of protector-protected between the hacendado and the farmer" (Manzano 1991:31), a relationship echoed in Don Domingo's comments. Although by 1911 many Costa Chican towns, including Huehuetán, Azoyú, Ecatepec, Tlacochistlahuaca, Minas, and Pinotepa Nacional were demanding hacienda lands (Manzano 1991:75), by all accounts Miller's small farmers remained relatively peaceful, likely due to their semi-independence. While they were by no means well-off, land was plentiful, bountiful, and "free." Most parcels were around two hectares, since family labor could not handle more. Families planted their own crops, harvested for Miller, and had access to milk (Manzano 1991:45). They also owned pigs and chickens, hunted freely in the bush, including iguana with slingshots and deer with firearms, and fished in swamps and nearby rivers.

When Porfirio Díaz resigned in 1911, hacendados moved to protect their assets from the Zapatistas, revolutionaries named for the famed general of the Liberation Army of the South (Ejército Libertador del Sur), Emiliano Zapata. Hacendados engaged in fierce land battles with agrarian leaders (*agraristas*), many of whom were assassinated by Rafael Añorve, a supporter of Francisco Madero and a member of a powerful merchant and landowning family from Ometepec that was Royalist during the Independence Wars and remains prominent today.[25] Añorve was aided by Miller's in-laws, the Reguera family (Jacobs 1982:88). In early 1911 he controlled Ometepec, which he had taken with the support of its people and those of neighboring towns (Moedano 1986:558). By June of 1912 he controlled the whole Costa Chica (Jacobs 1982:88).

As Miller's loyal cowboys and peasants, many San Nicoladenses formed voluntary troops to fight *against* the Zapatistas (Ravelo 1990:259–60, 264). "Some people were on the side of the rich," Don Domingo confirmed. In another twist, many Indians did not rebel at all, even though their conditions were "less than ideal" (Valdez 1998:76). "While many of the indigenous people of Xochistlahuaca were in fact tied to . . . Lamm . . . as a resident labor force, they were able to experience a relatively high degree of autonomy made possible by [Lamm's] absenteeism and the lax form of . . . administration. The Amuzgo small farmers evidently did not recognize any significant advantages offered by the agraristas that would outweigh the perceived security that they already had as tillers and workers. . . . On the contrary, whenever [there were] rumors or evidence that Zapatistas were operating in the region, the villagers would all evacuate their homes to seek refuge in the hills" (Valdez 1998:76).

Among morenos the situation was complex: some aided Miller while others fled the fighting. Still others, including residents of Azoyú and Huehuetán, tried to retake Ometepec from Añorve with the help of the Zapatistas (Ravelo 1990:265). As Don Sebastián, a Huehuetán mayor, confirmed, Huehuetán was Zapatista and peasant, while Ometepec was full of "businessmen." Huehuetecans also had land clearly deeded to them by Doña María.

In March 1912 the Zapatistas managed to take Ometepec, only to be defeated by Añorve's troops and hacendado forces, including Miller's cowboys from San Nicolás (Ravelo 1990:264, 267–70). The Zapatistas decamped to Huehuetán, to where hacendados then advanced with the help of men again drawn from San Nicolás and other places "where hacendados were influential" (Ravelo 1990:265). In Huehuetán the wounded Zapatista leader Doroteo Pérez hid in the church. But "identified by the black Andrés Torres—a servant of the Casa Miller—[Pérez] was taken from his hiding place as Torres grabbed him by the hair, dragged him toward the atrium, hung him up by his legs and, without a second glance, cut off his head with a tremendous machete blow"

(López 1985:1.235, qtd. in Ravelo 1990:266). The bloodbath in Huehuetán left some seventy Zapatistas dead and houses burned to the ground.

With the help of Igualapa's Indians, however, the Zapatistas began to gain ground. As they did, Miller fled to Puebla, where he petitioned the Mexican government for men and weapons and lobbied the U.S. embassy for arms and protection (Ravelo 1990:264). By June 1912 the Zapatistas held the countryside, but most of the Costa Chica was controlled by the Regueras and another Añorve, Enrique,[26] as corporal Alfredo López convinced forty-seven morenos to join the anti-Zapatista forces as the "riflemen of the south" (Ravelo 1990:267–68; Jacobs 1982:88). As conflicts between Zapatistas and hacendados intensified, elite properties, including Miller's, came under attack, particularly by Huehuetán's morenos and Igualapa's Indians (Valdez 1998:72). By April 1914 forces of Venustiano Carranza—a Zapatista who would be elected president in 1917 and with whom Zapata would break ranks over the scope of reforms—had entered Omepetec. Several months later the Ometepec government was Carrancista.[27]

Before fleeing to Puebla, Miller moved his cattle away from the fighting, to Oaxaca and to his ranches closest to the sea (Manzano 1991:91). Germán tried to protect Cuaji family property partly with weapons from the U.S. embassy, with which he armed cowboys from Maldonado and San Nicolás. But the Zapatistas destroyed the Casa Miller, the family's store, and its soap factory (Ravelo 1990:263–64). "The Zapatistas burned it," Germán told Manzano. "Some 200 came armed and some 1,000 with lassos. They took the animals and sacked the house" (1991:53). But Germán also insisted that his cowboys were "very loyal. . . . Only one betrayed me . . . he joined [the Zapatistas] and took two horses" (Manzano 1991:92). One of Miller's cowboys confirmed the defense of the Casa Miller when it burned, yet he also claimed that residents of Cuaji and San Nicolás were Zapatistas (Manzano 1991:91). I return to this contradiction below.

After sacking the Casa Miller, the Zapatistas headed for San Nicolás and Montecillos, firing shots to hasten people's departure. Zapatistas allegedly looted San Nicoladenses' houses and killed to eat whatever cattle they found, while residents fled to Oaxacan towns. Soon Huehuetán, Cuaji, and San Nicolás burned to the ground. With the communities emptied, hacendados petitioned Madero not to rebuild them "because as long as they exist, so does public disquiet" (Manzano 1991:79).

Meanwhile, the battle for Ometepec and for the general region continued. Despite Carranza's redistribution of land to small farmers, the Zapatistas did not think that his reforms sufficiently diluted the concentration of wealth. The Zapatistas once again took Ometepec; forced out twice, they retook it twice. As battles raged, the Carrancista colonel Francisco López wrote that hacendados tried to "trick" peasants by telling them that *they* would redistribute property, including land, and that Zapata would not win (Manzano 1991:84–85).

By 1918 the Zapatista commander Ezequiel Olmedo controlled Cuaji and San Nicolás, though many residents had fled. Following Carranza's fall to Alvaro Obregón in 1919, Olmedo was assassinated while Obregón made concessions to foreign business interests to gain recognition from the United States. In San Marcos, agraristas organized peasants to take back land, as petitions such as the following one from the Guerrero Trading Company to the federal government attest: "An engineer, a propagandist of Trotsky and Lenin [*Trasky y Lenine*] . . . has been actively preaching to the agricultural and cattle tenants renting land from this Company. . . . These tenants for the most part do not ask for ejidos because the rent they pay the Company is comfortable enough [for them]. [The engineer] has preached and induced, with whatever invented pretext . . . to gain possession of the Company's land, only because it is owned by a foreign company" (AGN Dirección General de Gobernación 2.34.66, dossier 19).

Born Fleeing: A Divided Community

Doña Leticia told me that her father, Don Margarito, was "born fleeing." Don Margarito said that he was already "grown" (*grande*) when Carranza and Zapata came to blows. He was only a child of eight or nine, but he and Don Elidio recounted what happened:

> Many fled to the bush during the night. After a while, the government sent federal troops to pull everyone out. A boss commanded the people in the bush: "the commander of the peaceful people." We weren't armed and we stayed there, peacefully without any weapons. When it got dry a few people went to Ometepec and to other places. . . . People formed another village, La Bocana, which still exists. But the Carrancistas and Zapatistas were evil and ran everyone out of there. A colonel from Ometepec said he was going to prepare a party with music and everyone gathered. In the wee hours of the morning the government killed the

people in the bush. . . . They made a grave—they killed a lot of people, as if they were locusts. Everyone was dead. They are buried from here to there [Don Margarito made a sweeping motion across the patio]. Manuel Hernández, a colonel with the Carranza forces in Ometepec—he's the one who killed so many people. Zapata then killed him: cut off the soles of his feet and decapitated him. But the people were leaving anyway: "Let's go to the bush." They went to El Carrizal and made another village. [Soldiers] came to the bush, "leave, leave—go to work." The village here was all bush. There wasn't even one house [because] the Zapatistas and the Carranicistas burned [the village]. They only left the church and the saints. The village was abandoned. Deer and wildcats wandered around. . . . A lot of people died. . . . Everyone died. [Even] carnival was forgotten.[28] The government armed the people of San Nicolás, who returned. They made shelters, redondos. Finally the government took its soldiers away, but armed people came to steal what people had. These [armed] people were rich. The people fled again to the bush, where they stayed. The government returned. All the people fled—the whole night—making a path. They clashed with the government. When things calmed down the government said, "leave for your village." The village was empty for one or two years. Every night people from Santiago Tepextla would come to steal. One had to be vigilant. San Nicolás was armed night and day. Then the fighting calmed down. But many still fled. When the revolution ended, the people returned for good. A lot of people died in the revolution. Manuel Hernández killed a lot of people. Carranza killed a lot of people. The Zapatistas were in La Bocana. They went around with the peasants. They were friends.

Of interest is that Don Margarito and Don Elidio said the Zapatistas were both "evil" and "friends."

In her own ambivalent narrative, Doña Olivia referred to the Zapatistas as "bad":

There was a lot of hunger and they killed a lot of people. The village was abandoned. People would put their dogs and roosters down wells while they hid because if the dogs barked they would find people and kill them. They raped women, even married ones. This is how they lived in the bush. My father's mother would say, "Today the Zapatistas are coming." She would be making tortillas and my grandfather would put mud on her face so the Zapatistas wouldn't take her. The cowboys defended the people. The Zapatistas were against the government; they fought the government but also bothered the people. . . . People hid themselves. Government soldiers killed the Zapatistas. The [Zapatistas] were bad people. Fleeing, well, there wasn't anything to eat. Working while fleeing—those with cattle would kill them and grill beef. When the cowboys gathered here the village was full of bush because there weren't any people. After the war was over the village began again.

Doña Olivia thus mentions *cowboys* protecting people from the Zapatistas, while Don Margarito and Don Elidio contradict themselves but indicate that the Zapatistas were farmers' friends. The situation might best be understood as one in which San Nicoladenses themselves were divided: farming families were likely Zapatista sympathizers, while cowboys likely sided with "the rich." But just as pardo militias engaged in conflicts with local mulattoes, the revolution's local cowboys were on the payroll while farmers were not. On the Costa Chica, then, the situation during the revolution was much like that during independence: morenos with livelihoods tied to whites tended to be loyal to whites. Those with more tenuous ties, including Indians—who never served as militiamen or cowboys—were more likely to fight for land. Both scenarios have colonial roots, and they could even divide families.

Although the southeastern tip of the Costa Chica displayed some support for the Zapatistas, no deep agrarian insurrection ensued, and most San Nicoladenses did not take up arms. Instead, people fled until the situation calmed, and survivors returned to rebuild villages. Farmers then replanted traditional crops including cotton, which they continued to sell to Miller, who maintained his cotton-combing machine despite the destruction of the Casa Miller (Manzano 1991:95). The Millers also retained most of their cattle and other property until Agrarian Reform during the presidency of Lázaro Cárdenas (1934–40).

In the 1920s the government again sent engineers to measure Miller's land to then divide it. At least one engineer was assassinated in Cuaji. In 1931 a census-taker arrived in Cuaji. But hacendados challenged the census lists on which land redistribution would be based and therefore, as Don Domingo indicated, also the ownership of the lands around San Nicolás. Manzano claims that some peasants were confused by the legal complexities, even rejecting ejido land "because they trusted Don Germán" (Manzano 1991:102). But by many accounts, including those of San Nicoladenses, Germán was greatly despised, gaining the loyalty of his workers by engaging in extensive intimidation, above all by making them fear that taking "his" land was illegal. As one elderly farmer told Manzano: "Don Germán . . . tried desperately to avoid agrarian reform; he armed people and sent them to assassinate an engineer measuring the land. The people became afraid. Many neglected to receive their property titles. There are many ways of making the people fearful, and [Miller] took advantage of all within his reach, from subtle manipulation to making them believe that they acted against the law and were disgracing their boss . . . he had something like 30 armed cowboys. So the people were divided" (1991:103).

Despite Germán's intimidation, in February 1930 and again in June 1932 San Nicoladenses requested the restitution of some Miller lands, which they claimed to own anyway. Led by Nabor Ojeda, a local deputy and an advisor to the Costa Chica's agraristas, they organized land petitions while Germán claimed the "invasion" of his lands (Manzano 1991:109, 37).

Cárdenas's predecessors had tried to compromise with hacendados but Cárdenas aimed for their complete elimination. Peasants were invading lands anyway, and agricultural laborers were striking. During the Cárdenas years some 180,000 ejidos were created on 45 million acres of land for 750,000 landless peasants throughout Mexico. On 20 June 1933, San Nicolás was granted an ejido comprising 9,840 hectares, carved out of the 30,000 hectares still controlled by the Millers (Gobierno del Estado de Guerrero 1933:7–8). Each ejidatario in San Nicolás, Cuaji, and Maldonado received about 10 hectares. As in the rest of Mexico, Costa Chican ejidos were based on usufruct rights, with land rotated using slash-and-burn techniques. Most people cultivated only a few hectares at a time, since labor was family-based and a lack of heavy machinery limited productivity. Yet loose rules governing usage meant that larger families with resources were able to monopolize ejido land, while the majority simply survived. Despite being ejidatarios, then, many moreno small farmers—unable to subsist on their land—were forced to sell their labor to other landowners and to local businessmen (Manzano 1991:112).

During these years agraristas and private police forces formed by hacenda-dos (the White Guard or the Guardia Blanca) joined separate gangs (*gavillas* or *brosas*). Agraristas openly challenged local authorities and hacendados while the White Guard attacked agraristas. Manzano (1991:116) argues that gangs robbed and raped, but she only refers to agraristas.[29] Documenta-tion suggests that the White Guard actually fomented more violence, mur-dering agraristas and their wives while they were sleeping, robbing them and burning down their homes (AGN Dirección General de Gobernación 2.012.8[9] 20278).

In 1934, when municipal governments first formed, Enrique Flores Magón, a representative of the Mexican Peasant Federation (Confedera-ción Campesina Mexicana, or CCM) reported to his organization on behalf of Cuaji's ejidatarios that the state government had replaced Cuaji's elected town council with one headed by Filadelfo García. García brought with him a number of armed individuals "of atrocious origins." In Montecillos García's men murdered several men and a woman. A new schoolteacher also died when García ordered a group of "armed criminals" to go on a shooting spree and they surrounded a school. "Now," read the complaint, "no one will accept employment [as a schoolteacher]." García also owned a cattle ranch where he kept stolen animals watched over by an armed posse. When Porfirio Pastrana—who would become a famed agrarista for San Nicoladenses—attempted to recover his stolen cattle, García tried to have him and another man killed. In perhaps the most bizarre form of terror, authorities forced farmers to have their pictures taken without telling them why. One group was ordered photographed "in the company of the great landowner and reactionary Guillermo Miller, whom we hate because of his evil origins." The CCM asked the secretary of the interior to request that the governor of Guerrero "begin . . . a true step of peacefulness and of social and administrative reconstruction." The governor's secretary promised to investigate, but the tone of the response suggests that the complaints fell on deaf ears (AGN Dirección General de Gobernación 2.317.4.[9]-58).

Fearing for their lives, most people did not complain. But with support from Cuaji's municipal president, Pastrana lodged a request with the CCM for protection against assaults that included home invasion and the theft of his wife's jewelry (2.012.8[9]26474). According to Don Domingo, who was about twelve at the time, Pastrana had seen Germán's "people" assassinate the engineer sent to measure Miller property in the 1920s. Germán then forged documents that a "Señor Medina" had sold land to his father. As Don Domingo reiterated, Germán

> humiliated the people because they were poor and humble. [He] en-closed a river and the people were left dry. He wouldn't let people in. When Porfirio Pastrana saw this injustice, he took up arms against the Millers. Porfirio was an agrarista—he was a member of the opposition party. He fought the Millers. He killed their cowboys as well as a corporal from Cuaji. Yes, he killed him. After that, Germán sent federal agents to kill Porfirio because [Germán] was rich. He offered [the assassins] two jars full of money. Soldiers then killed Porfirio, and Presiciano García (from San Nicolás) killed two federal police because of Pastrana's death. I saw it. He shot them. One died on the spot and the other in Ometepec. But envy ran through the Pastrana family, so Germán's policy gelled. They were killing each other. They killed each other and Germán re-mained boss. The government of San Nicolás made Juan Rodríguez head of the rural defense forces. They killed him with forty shots. People from San Nicolás itself killed him. And this hasn't ended. It's in a song.[30]

Pastrana was assassinated in San Nicolás on 27 August 1937 "by federal forces accompanied by servants of the American landowner Germán Miller . . . whose crimes against the agraristas of this region have long been known" (AGN Dirección General de Gobernación 2.012.8[9]26474:40). According to Don Gregorio, federal troops also "took [Pastrana's] wife but didn't kill her. She came back and told the people." Pastrana, he told me, is known as "the Father of the Ejido" because he defended San Nicolás's land.[31] In response to Pastrana's assassination, federal forces stationed in San Nicolás were re-lieved of their duties (2.012.8[9]26474). Several regional deputies of the CCM also wrote to Cárdenas asking that Germán's brother Guillermo be fired from his position as a Guerrero state judge, "as much for his origins as for being the intellectual author of this assassination" (2.012.8[9]26474:44–45). This, apparently, did not happen: the following year several Costa Chica agraristas again informed Cárdenas that "the North American" Guillermo Miller "used his influence to stop the distribution of lands . . . [as] he has occupied various offices, including as a congressional deputy and now as a judge of the State Supreme Court" (2.012.8[9] 20278:21).

San Nicoladenses revere Pastrana, whose story connects more recent agrarian history to the chaos of the revolution by illustrating how agraristas fought not just hacendados such as Germán to force compliance with Agrarian Reform but also a military and judges—such as Guillermo Miller—who formed part of the white landed aristocracy. Some of that aristocracy drew private armies from the same moreno families as did the agraristas, most of whom were assassinated by those armies in cahoots with local and state officials (AGN Dirección General de Gobernación 2.012.8[9] 20278; Valdez 1998:84). As Don Domingo indicated, even members of Pastrana's family turned on each other.

This was not the end, for land transfers were halted during the presidency of Miguel Alemán (1946–52), who again defended hacendados. The conflict over Miller land subsequently went on for years. In 1953 Germán was shot and wounded (AGN Dirección General de Gobernación 2–380 [9] 59). And into the 1970s he claimed that the family had spent 2 million pesos on complaints and "never got a thing" (Manzano 1991:102). Although the Miller era seems like the past, Germán was still alive and complaining into the early 1990s. Moreover, the history remains very vivid for elderly San Nicoladenses. Indeed, Don Domingo's cousin was raped by a lieutenant stationed in San Nicolás in the 1950s (AGN Dirección General de Gobernación 2.380 [9] 42). Originally sent because two families were killing each other over a cattle inheritance, the lieutenant stayed on to become a henchman for Germán. At the time, Don Domingo served as the secretary of San Nicolás's governing council, many of whose members were murdered. He fled with his wife Doña Ana to Acapulco, where they stayed for twenty years. During that time they tried to adopt two children but, as Don Domingo said, the authorities would give such children only to the rich. The couple was later gifted (*regalado*) two children by relatives. The youngest child died and the older one, unwilling to study as her parents wished, ran off in her early teens.[32]

Contemporary Conflicts

Some Miller lands were sold rather than given to ejidatarios. These formed *colonias* (agricultural colonies managed like small properties) and included the nearby Miguel Alemán, founded by whites from other parts of Guerrero in the 1950s with the backing of the state government (Hoffmann

2007:372).[33] Its residents came into conflict with moreno small farmers, who wanted the lands for themselves (Manzano 1991:106, 107). But the colonists prevailed and today El Pitayaho, a moreno settlement founded by San Nicoladenses and part of its ejido, abuts Miguel Alemán. Although the two "communities" — with two churches, two schools, two town halls, and so on — are distinguished at the local level, at the state and national levels they are considered one urban center. Odile Hoffmann observes that the colonists' attitudes are "plagued with racist comments" about morenos, who do not understand why the colonists make them "less" and "backwards" (2007:381–82). Moreno comments about their neighbors, on the other hand, are not ethno-racial in nature. Instead they are based on class: colonists steal land, bear arms, and are backed by "the government." Yet everyday interaction between morenos and colonists is civil, and it appears to contradict their otherwise hostile discourse. I take up similar contradictions with respect to San Nicolás's contemporary moreno and Indian residents in the following chapters.

The El Tamale colony still has an unresolved land dispute with San Nicolás. The colonists took more than two thousand hectares of land from San Nicolás, but because they have been there a while, San Nicoladenses simply want boundaries settled. As Don Domingo explained when I was trying to figure out land ownership following a town hall meeting with representatives of Agrarian Reform:

> The government sold two lots to people from El Tamale . . . [El Tamale] took more land than it was given. A lot of people died over this. Now [government representatives] don't want to measure where they're told to. They want to defend the settlers' land. But we don't want to take the land away; we just want to know where the boundary is. . . . Another community, San José, also occupies land belonging to San Nicolás . . . 2,050 hectares. The deed says there are 8,000 hectares and the survey says 6,000.[34] Two thousand hectares are missing. People from Agrarian Reform came [in 1997], but with a fake plan. They were paid off so that they wouldn't focus on the matter. Now the Supreme Court is going to intervene so [those from San José] give the land to San Nicolás. People are going to tell Agrarian Reform not to come if they aren't going to follow the order. Before, there were usufruct rights; now everyone's land is enclosed so it can't be reclaimed. . . . It's important that the ejidos not

have problems. . . . The Agrarian Reform people, well, they come when people are fighting, but they don't want to fix anything. They just want their money.

Some days later he commented, "This problem of regularizing the land will never end. [The colonists] are white. They say that the people of San Nicolás don't want an agreement; that they don't understand because they're black, while people from San Nicolás say that *they* don't understand because they're white. But they're mixed; they have families together. There are white asses [*burros*] and dark [*prieto*] asses."

With the exception of the northern and northwestern parts of Guerrero, which are still dominated by haciendas, small farms today occupy 60 percent of the state's arable land. When the Miller monopoly came to an end, coastal belt farmers replaced cotton with sesame, which they already produced in small quantities. They sold seed to members of the local bourgeoisie, who sold it to the Acapulco-based oil company called 1–2–3, which is still one of the largest producers of cooking oil in Mexico. By the late 1950s and early 1960s, the ejidal bank Banrural had replaced this bourgeoisie, buying sesame at higher prices. From 1979 to 1999 farmers sold sesame and other crops directly to CONASUPO (Compañía Nacional de Subsistencias Populares, or the National Company of Popular Subsistence). The company supported prices and processed and traded crops with the aim of equal provisioning. It bought some corn on the international market but ignored direct input from local farmers, the smallest and poorest of whom did not have access to its guaranteed (low) prices (see Bartra 1994:133–43; and Yunez-Naude 2003 for detailed analyses). As globalization in the form of trade pacts such as NAFTA has undercut farmers' ability to compete even in local markets, San Nicolás and similar villages have been abandoned by the government. A lot of corn, and most tomatoes, apples, bananas, carrots, onions, and even sesame are now imported.

The Program for Direct Assistance in Agriculture (Programa de Apoyo Directo al Campo, or PROCAMPO), introduced in 1994 as a fifteen-year bridge program as the country transitioned to NAFTA, cyclically paid farmers according to their acreage and crops in an effort to compensate for NAFTA's negative effects on crop prices (Saudolet, de Janvry, and Davis 2001). Thus, for instance, in 1997 Don Domingo received a biannual subsidy of about 2,500 pesos (U.S. $250) for five hectares of land. But several

San Nicoladenses complained that they were not receiving subsidies, and the mayor of Collantes claimed that PROCAMPO had not given his town any at all. Thus PROCAMPO came to exemplify the "white" government's deception of small farmers. Moreover, as PROCAMPO comes to a close,[35] the government has been decreasing food subsidies just as final tariffs on corn importations are lifted, demands for cattle feed rise, and the cost of fertilizer doubles (Malkin 2008). Imported corn has therefore long been less expensive than that grown locally, thereby weakening small farmers' abilities to sell excess crops. Even though the demand for ethanol and the high cost of fertilizer raise the price of imported corn, small farmers still cannot compete (Hellman 2008:18).

By local standards San Nicolás is not desperately poor, but lack of assistance (fertilizer, price supports, access to markets, heavy equipment, and technical help) means that many ejidatarios cannot consistently make a living from the land. For instance, Ramiro complained that there is no money to plant or to buy cattle. Sebastián added that communities need more mechanized agriculture to get through bad times, such as a cyclone or a pestilence. When ejidos were privatized in the early 1990s, San Nicolás's land was allotted equally to heads of households. But in many ways a new and unequal distribution has emerged as some San Nicoladenses, along with outsiders, have bought up many hectares, often with migrant remittances, while others sell because of debts, medical emergencies, migration journeys, or an inability to care for the land.

Some people can produce marketable goods for regional and national consumption, but everyone is at the mercy of agricultural blight, inclement weather, and increasing capitalist penetration. Irrigation arrived only in the 1980s (Sánchez 1987:112). But even if one has it, access is uneven. During the rainy season it is not normally available unless the rains fail and wealthy cattle owners ask and pay for it so their cattle do not die. Farmers then piggyback on those who are better off. Yet in the parched summer of 2001 there was no water even for the wealthy, because rivers supplying irrigation canals remained dry. "If it doesn't rain soon," Rodrigo told me that July, "people will sell their cattle to middlemen in Cuaji," with a price per kilo too low to replace the slaughtered animal. "What will we eat?" Don Domingo asked after planting corn that summer. No rain meant the loss of his crop. "How are we going to live?" asked Doña Olivia. "The milpa is dry. . . . My father would say 'we're going to eat each other.' There aren't any clouds. And no money." Even when harvests are good prices fall just as produce is ready for market, as people plant when prices are high due to scarcity and seasonal rhythms, and everyone harvests at the same time. Out-migration continues. Some people go to Mexico City, Pacific coast resorts, or to Cabo San Lucas. But the vast majority goes undocumented to el norte, even with tighter border controls. On many small yard plots and in planters San Nicoladenses grow herbs, tomatoes, corn, and peppers in the middle of Winston-Salem, their daughter community.

Nonmigrants with remittances from the United States or employed relatives in urban areas can worry slightly less. But remittances can be sporadic, as they depend on the dispositions of people who have their own expenses and are not always reliable senders. In addition, those in el norte depend on the U.S. economy. When remittances do arrive, some go to purchase cattle, which, as Doña Lupe told me, "make you rich." "This is why they say *ganado* [cattle], because one 'gains' [*gana*]," Don Julio half-joked. Indeed, the wealthiest families of San Nicolás own many head of cattle. Beef is at the center of every ritual occasion and always in great demand because, even though it is a luxury, the ability to buy a bit of even a poor cut conveys status. Buyers say "'I want meat,'" Doña Lupe said. "They're very direct. They don't say 'I'd like' or even 'give me.' They say what [part] they want without even a 'thank you.'"

Like other animals, cattle of course breed, thereby augmenting a family's wealth. The federal program Alliance for the Countryside (Alianza para el Campo) currently sells cattle to farmers, lending them money for half the price. But the loans require collateral, which most people do not have. Even with remittances, cattle prices—and the possibility of a herd—are out of reach for many, since other necessities, including the desire to build a house, are more immediate. Land is still turned over to fodder production or grazing as cattle and dairy products remain an important part of the regional economy. But a large herd depends on ample land, since the size of holdings restricts the number of cows a person can accommodate without having to pay for access to pasture. Few San Nicoladenses have been able to amass more than six head; most cannot afford to buy feed or sufficient pasture that would enable them to rent land to wealthier cattle owners. Because land is still a precious and meaningful resource—for agriculture, for pasture, for houses—agrarian conflicts continue, though without the intensity they once had.

The Plagued Land

Agriculture on its current scale is only possible because in the 1970s the government deforested with heavy machinery. But deforestation destroyed wild animal habitats, thus making it harder to combine subsistence strategies. Although armadillos and iguanas are still hunted, they are much scarcer than they once were. Older people are especially disturbed by the disappearance of resources on which they used to depend. Doña Elvira started out speaking of material things, such as the *bules*, or hollow double calabash cups used to carry water that some men still take to the fields, and the plastic that is now everywhere. But she quickly moved to mourning the loss of biodiversity: "We used young squash shoots [*chicayote*] instead of bleach; we boiled the dirtiest clothes, but we didn't have a lot of clothes. We sewed and used grease soap. Before, everything was inexpensive. People hardly bought anything. Now there's money, but you have to buy things. Once there were iguanas, deer, rabbits, and parrots. Now there aren't any. Life is ending . . . there's more disease, there's no fish or deer—they died; rabbits, doves, parrots . . . people came and took the parrots and the long-tailed macaws. Now there aren't any. Before, people planted peppers; there wasn't any sesame. People came from outside to buy coconut, mango, limes. Now there's hardly even any watermelon. Now there are lots of mango orchards. Before, there were only orchards where Miguel Alemán is. People grew just what they needed for eating." I asked her if the changes frightened older people. She nodded and then sent me away so that she could do household chores.

"Some people say it was better before. The land was virgin," said Don Domingo. "There was a lot of food: berries, fish, iguanas, deer. Before, there weren't any pests. There were tomatoes, peppers, everything. People would barter. If you needed tomatoes you'd just ask your neighbor. There'd be tomatoes rotting all over the place there were so many—or you'd pass someone in the fields and they'd invite you to take a few watermelons." Doña Lupe said much the same: "We'd eat deer, beans, fish, doves, iguanas, wild pigs, badgers. Now everything is gone. The jungle, finished. The vegetation, finished. There were wildcats, parrots, parakeets, larks. A lot! Then they began to take down the trees—they cleared the bush and brought in agriculture. We had common cattle, ones you could get a cup of milk from. People were better nourished. There were native chickens, people planted peppers, tomatoes, and beans. They got salt from seawater and made their own soap. Clothes were cotton. They don't grow cotton or peppers anymore because there were too many pests. Now everything is bought and people want to buy everything."

Not the least of the changes wrought by agricultural "improvement" has been the heavy use of insecticides on both crops and cattle. As Don Domingo said, "You have to use insecticides, fumigate, to kill pests. Before, there weren't any pests. Neither were there insecticides. The pests came with the insecticides. Nature's strength. [The insecticides] took away nature's strength. Now the land is plagued." He told me of illnesses from insecticides that pollute well water and irrigation canals where some bathe and wash clothes. Having seen insecticide use firsthand, I suspect that poisonings are not uncommon. Once I drove through mango groves with Rosa to leave a gift of food for a couple who consented to be godparents for her youngest daughter's primary school graduation. They are from Mexico City and own orchards in San Nicolás, shipping the fruit to the capital, where it is sold at the Centro de Abastos Market, one of the largest wholesale markets in the world. The mango groves were beautiful, but their silence was deafening. Once I read Rodrigo a newspaper article about insecticides killing farmers. He said he used those insecticides and had mistakenly ingested them. I watched him delouse cows without protection, and mix the "liquid" with his bare arm, the way women mix large vats of food.[36]

Magical Money

Food, land, and markets invariably lead to the topic of mines or buried treasures because the land's abundance meant that ancestors did not need money, thus hiding whatever they had. "There was no money and no place to spend it," said Doña Lupe. As Rosa pointed out where mines might be, she said: "If a man had money he'd bury it and it would stay buried. On 24 June, the day of Saint John, they'd burn these mines at midnight. You'd go out to see the flames, mark the place, and return the next day to dig it out. The old people's fortunes are buried. San Nicolás is rich. My grandfather had a lot of cattle. He sold the cattle and buried the money. Instead of putting money someplace like a bank, they buried it in the earth. My grandfather didn't tell anyone where it was." Occasionally, I was told, a lucky person buys a house plot, starts digging, and finds a mine. But I never saw it happen. One family of outsiders arrived poor but became wealthy in San Nicolás. They had worked hard and resented the rumor that they had found a mine. Doña Olivia noted that people had come with metal detectors but never found anything.

That at least today no one seems to know where these mines are, and that people widely believe that ancestors hid money, suggests that money itself is fetishized in the sense that it has an almost magical significance. In secreting it away, ancestors "performed" value through rumor, through hiding value in the *earth* rather than using it for exchange (Graeber 2001:81). Thus, while the earth produces crops, turns twigs into fruit-bearing trees, and feeds animals; it also "grows" money. Obtaining a salary (*sueldo* or *salario*) in the global economy is subject to much discussion and consternation, and money is fetishized in various ritual and narrative contexts, as I discuss in chapter 3.

The recently deceased Doña Cata, who sang verses and danced the artesa until she was so old that she could barely move, would tell me how everything was simpler before. "If you want a house plot, now you have to buy it. Before you would just take wherever you wanted—everything is difficult now." This "fantastic" understanding of a past (Taussig 1983:6) that was in reality and by San Nicoladenses' own accounts violent and precarious, presents people growing their own food, making their own clothes, acquiring land freely, *and* getting "rich." Reminiscing about an idyllic rural past is not unusual among elderly Latin Americans (see Bourgois 2003:168 for a Puerto Rican example). Today, with money at a premium but with a generally more peaceful existence, people allude to the hidden mines allegedly left by the ancestors. As use-value has become exchange-value, some turn to money lending, charging exorbitant interest for loans, and women invest in gold jewelry as collateral.

While the line of reciprocity can be exceedingly delicate, traditional values do accommodate "modernity." Money can be gifted, for instance, and migration reinforces social ties because it makes possible in a growing community the maintenance of elaborate events that include everyone, such as fiestas and weddings. Population growth also leads to a proliferation of godparents for everything from kindergarten graduations to wedding dresses, thus increasing one's ritual kin. In short, people attempt to maintain a sense of community and their place within it even in the face of ongoing changes.

CHAPTER TWO

Identity in Discourse THE "RACE" HAS BEEN LOST

Many colonial ranchers on the Costa Chica were absentee land-lords. Those likely to live there, such as Mauleón, who also oversaw royal tribute, combined official and unofficial functions. Yet most Spaniards found the coastal climate "hot and ill" and suffered from gastrointestinal, respiratory, and other ailments they thought themselves more susceptible to than non-Spaniards (AGI Indiferente 107.1; Widmer 1990:143). Ranch responsibilities were thus often left to foremen. Sometimes these were Spaniards, but often they were blacks or mulattoes (Moedano 1986:552). Black slaves, as elsewhere in Mexico, also collected Indian tribute for encomenderos (Aguirre Beltrán 1985:53–54; Lewis 2003:68–72), and of course cowboys and many agricultural laborers were blacks and mulattoes. Spaniards and Indians grew to quickly attribute to them aggressiveness and "brutality," and they soon gained a reputation for raiding Indian communities (Lewis 2003:68–74; Widmer 1990:127). "Indians will be fishing and blacks and mulattoes arrive from the ranches and take their fish, nets, bows and arrows, and mistreat them. The cowboys scare the Indian women guarding the cornfields, taking their bananas and squashes and other things by force and against their will" (AGN Tierras 48.6). Thus what Rolf Widmer terms a "low-intensity war" pitting blacks and mulattoes against Indians began almost as soon as Spaniards brought the former to the coast (Aguirre Beltrán 1985:59, 65; Widmer 1990:131). Don Gregorio explained it this way: "Each Spaniard, each hacendado, had his people that belonged to him—Indians and blacks mixed together. Blacks did the hardest work because Indians were weaker. They couldn't take the work—the mining, panning for gold, cane cutting. They'd have to carry the cane on their backs. That's why they brought blacks, some of whom were given power over [other] blacks and Indians. Indians and blacks didn't get along. Blacks treated Indians very harshly. Blacks were more astute and clever; Indians were stupider and slower."

During this early period, maroons from the sugar plantations of Atlixco in Puebla state also fled to the coastal belt, forging relationships with people already there (Moedano 1986:552; Widmer 1990:138). Several scholars identify Cuaji as a maroon settlement (Palmer 1976:52; also Aguirre Beltrán 1985:59–63; Carroll 1977:493). But Arturo Motta makes a convincing case, based on Gonzalo Aguirre Beltrán's original sources, that Cuaji was a small agricultural settlement whose residents worked for Mauleón, and that no evidence exists for any true maroon settlements further north than Huatulco (Motta 2006:138–39).[1] Maroons on the coastal belt nevertheless seem to have developed—like slaves and freepersons—mutually dependent relationships with Spaniards, including officials with little oversight from superiors in Puebla, Oaxaca, and Mexico City (Carroll 1977:493; Widmer 1990:138). For instance, when Mauleón was forced to give up his encomienda, he apparently replaced Indian laborers with maroons, presumably including any who might have settled in Cuaji, whose residents already worked for him. In exchange for maroon labor, Mauleón offered protection. Settlements that likely included maroons, and black and mulatto descendents of Mauleón's cowboys and servants, eventually arose in San Nicolás, Maldonado, and Cuaji. Soon these places took on the characteristics of "true towns" (Aguirre Beltrán 1985:48; Manzano 1991:18–20; also Widmer 1990:139).

A Brief History of Black-Indian Mixture

Mulattoes and blacks of all statuses also worked with Indians, for instance producing for Spaniards cotton that Indian women transformed into thread and textiles (Widmer 1990:189). They learned from Indians to work the land and to manage local crops such as corn and peppers,[2] and they adopted "indigenous traditions like the evil eye and the *nagual*," the latter the most powerful figure in the Indian magical repertoire, which consisted of a person's destined animal double that, in the animal's guise, could harm another's animal double and hence that person (Aguirre Beltrán 1963:101; Widmer 1990:138, 140). Despite conflicts structurally embedded in the colonial political economy, by 1700, or perhaps even earlier, communities that were "afromestizo . . . culturally and biologically mestizo" began to replace Indian ones (Gerhard 1993:151; Quiroz 2004; Widmer 1990:131).

But while many blacks and mulattoes on the coastal belt lived like and with Indians, the hilly uplands remained almost entirely Indian (Aguirre Beltrán 1985:59–60; Gerhard 1973:148–49, 151, 381). Because of this, Ben Vinson III argues based on census data that *marriages* between Indians and "free-coloreds" were rare, due in great part to the cultural and geographical distance between their towns (2000:272, 281–82). While this might have been the case, it does not account for free unions or for marriages between male slaves and Indian women, which frequently occurred since under Spanish colonial law any offspring took on the legal status of their free Indian mothers. Indeed, such marriages were so common that colonial authorities complained about them. Many black Indian mulattoes likely grew up in their mothers' natal villages (Davidson 1979:86–87; Lewis 2003:77, 98–100). Some historical documents indicate that "mixed" individuals then "mixed" with each other. For instance, employees of mid-seventeenth-century Los Cortijos included a mestizo with a mulatto wife. Other employees included a free black woman, also described as a mulatta and *negrita*, who raised a free mulatta. One of her uncles was Indian; an aunt (caste unspecified) was married to a mulatto and, when he passed away, she partnered with a black slave (AGN Inquisición 439.14).

A non-Indian census of 1791 indicates that 235 Spaniards, 594 mestizos, and 5,206 blacks and mulattoes lived on the coast. Cuaji had about 270 families, San Nicolás about 126, and Maldonado about 91 (AGN Padrones 18; Gerhard 1993:151). All three were estancias under the tutelage of another Mariscal, this one "de Castilla," probably a generic reference to a Spaniard, as the translation is "the Spanish Marshall" (Aguirre Beltrán calls it an "inherited title" 1985:48). This Mariscal brought from Spain cattle and a hundred married slaves, likely augmenting the number of blacks on the coast by the end of the nineteenth century to at least 40,000 (Arce 1870:320, qtd. in Aguirre Beltrán 1985:58; see Motta 2006:125 on the Mariscal line). By 1800 or so San Nicolás had 1,134 residents or about 250 families (assuming each family had about 5 members), while Cuaji hosted about 1,700 residents and Maldonado about 600 (Aguirre Beltrán 1985:62; Moedano 1986:557).

As the records of 1791 are tribute records, and as slaves did not pay tribute, it is impossible to know from them how many slaves existed. The records distinguish "Spaniards, mestizos, and *castizos*" (non-tribute payers) from (free) "mulattoes" (tribute payers). The records also indicate that most residents of Cuaji, San Nicolás, and Maldonado were mulattoes, as were the "natives" of Huehuetán who resided on Doña María's land not long before. Given the coast's demographics—particularly the paucity of Spaniards, the black-Indian mixing that began early on, and patterns in other parts of New Spain—by the last decades of the eighteenth century mulatto often indicated a high degree of Indian admixture. The tribute records also refer to the mulattoes as "natives." Thus, as the documentation on Doña María's donation also indicates, Spanish authorities recognized mulattoes as natives in the same sense that Indians were natives. Coastal belt mulattoes were mostly black Indian; lived mostly like Indians, under the command—though often with different occupations than Indians—of Spaniards; and "mixture" had been a fact of life on the coast probably from the late sixteenth century on.

Raza and Raza

In 1997 Andrés Manzano Añorve, who self-identifies as moreno, was the PRD municipal president of Cuaji. His father was a doctor from Mexico City who knew Gonzalo Aguirre Beltrán, and his mother was a member of the prominent Añorve family of Ometepec. He once asked me if I felt bored in San Nicolás, and then told me that a moreno should be writing its history, not a "capitalist" gringa like me. I reacted with a shrug. Ten years later we were lunching at a Cuaji restaurant, the conversation much changed. Andrés told me that in 1998 he had been invited to Detroit by an African American school director who insulted him by asking how a "black" city like Cuaji could have elected a "white" municipal president like him. During lunch he talked at great length about his four brothers and sisters, some of whom "came out light and others dark." Father Glyn Jemmott, Ciruelo's activist priest who is well known in Cuaji, "thinks that to say that you are moreno buys into a mestizo ideology and denies blackness," Andrés said. But "I think moreno just reflects the mixture that people actually have." Moreover, he added, Father Glyn, a Trinidadian who self-identifies as black, comes "from an Anglo-Saxon country," just like the people in Detroit, and he "thinks like an Anglo-Saxon about race." Andrés was most indignant about his siblings. Indeed, he asked, how could one's own kin not be of the same "blood" simply because some were light-skinned, some dark-skinned, some had straight hair, and some curly hair? Where our conversation took place symbolizes contentiousness over how to define coastal identities, as well as a complex regional history: The restaurant's owner, Rita, is an ardent supporter of coastal social movements that emphasize an African heritage. But her father was an Añorve, like Andrés's mother. Indeed, Rita and Andrés are cousins.

In Detroit Andrés had been blindsided by the Anglo "one drop rule," or the social rule of hypodescent, that classifies as a "minority" any person—but especially one of African descent—with a minority parent. The rule only works for the purpose of social classification if "interracial" mixing is minimized, for it is buttressed by a visual sense that phenotype is synecdoche for blood. But because of the particular histories and contexts of widespread "mixture," throughout Mexico, as in the rest of Latin America, race is highly localized (Wade 1997). Thus Andrés and his siblings might appear by "Anglo" standards to be of different "races," when they are, in fact, of the same *raza*, a word that means both race and family.

On the coastal belt of Guerrero, the history of "mixture" was such that people of African descent self-identify as morenos, or as a race of mixed black Indians, a point that I myself have argued with Father Glyn (see also Amaral 2005). No simple Indian-black dichotomy exists in the genealogical and descriptive accounts of San Nicoladenses. Kinship and other ties between morenos and Indians are more pronounced than those between morenos and whites, largely because of questions of class and demographics: whites are "colonists," the government, hacendados such as Germán, the rich, and a numerical minority. Andrés, then, was not pleased that African Americans had identified him as white and therefore as a community outlier.

Although some of San Nicolás's morenos acknowledge white ancestry, and some morenos allied and continue to ally with whites, morenos are generally ambivalent about whiteness. In family descriptions moreno and Indian kin are much more prominent than white ones, although any combination of phenotype, including whiteness, can and does exist. Thus racial terms are both classificatory and descriptive.

As noted, throughout Mexico the word *raza* indicates both "race" and "family." Thus morenos entwine "blood" and kinship, which would also explain Andrés's indignation at the fact that his kin were supposedly not of his "blood." When Don Domingo explained to me that *raza* "means blood, family," he added that "[Indians and blacks] marry each other, so it's as if everyone is of the same raza. There are Indians who don't marry blacks," he continued, "but that's because of their language—they won't understand each other." When Don Margarito told me about his family he used both senses of raza interchangeably. "Our raza is moreno/Indian or Indian/moreno." His cousins' father, he said, was from San Marcos, near Cruz Grande, and from the "raza of [a man named] Viviano Carmona." Doña Berta used *raza* for "family." "Our raza" she said, "doesn't let children go to dances until they're fifteen—both boys and girls—our family. Me, my brother—everyone—me and my siblings—the whole family—that's the raza." As Manuel commented on the San Nicoladenses who come from el norte for fiestas, he added, "We say 'here comes la raza,' you know, the family." And when I showed Don Sebastián a photograph of a woman in Collantes holding a portrait of her own grandmother, he said, "That girl is of my raza; family." Raza thus encompasses family made up of "blood" relatives and those related by marriage. It further refers to the whole community, as Manuel's comment indicates, and even cuts across community boundaries, as Don Sebastián's remark makes clear.

In the Mix: We Are All Mexicans

I discussed race with many San Nicoladenses on different occasions and in different settings. Sometimes my presence obviously prompted such talk, but at other times it did not. Although I tired of the topic and suspect that they did too, race does indicate—especially given the region's history—people's attachment to place, how meanings shift with context and over time, what anthropologists (myself included) and other outsiders bring to the discussion, and how San Nicoladenses give meaning to the world. Race, in other words, is woven into the thickness of everyday life.

As I try to translate San Nicoladenses' concepts for those more familiar with a Northern European classificatory system, I am reminded that local people usually just say, "What does it matter, anyway? We're all Mexicans, whatever our color." Indeed, mixture (*mezcla*) is the predominant theme, as it is in Mexican national ideologies. As Marisol de la Cadena notes, mixture indexes "situated political statements that dominant and subordinate individuals make about the national place of subaltern identities" (2000:318).

Mexico is therefore not a "melting pot" or a racial democracy, as older Latin American theorists proposed (e.g., Freyre 1986; Vasconcelos 1924). Instead, mixture is itself a political concept, as I demonstrate in chapter 3. But so too are racial terms themselves, which shift within the multiple contexts in which San Nicoladenses live and in the comparisons they make between themselves and others. Race is therefore relative and almost impossible to pin down. But genealogies and the ways people describe their contemporaries offer clues to broad patterns, at least to the extent that what is otherwise a moving target freezes for the duration of a conversation. I begin with an older generation because it links to the past I have described. But the process continues with younger people, especially because of resident Indians, with whom morenos now routinely intermarry.

San Nicoladenses distinguish between "purity" (*limpieza*) and mixture, but no one has ever told me that they were "pure" anything. Instead, ancestors were the pure ones. Often the ancestral chronology is unclear, with purity located at an unspecified time in the past or even elsewhere in the present (Godreau 2002b:97; Lewis 2004). In 1992 Juan explained that blacks, whites, and Indians can all be pure, but that "here people are more mixed." He was not pure, he added, because he was of mixed blood (*sangre mezclada*). In Huehuetán, Alberto described San Nicolás as "mulatto" (the only time I heard the term *mulatto* used on the coast) and insisted that Collantes was where the "purest" blacks lived, a belief that San Nicoladenses often echo (Lewis 2004), though people in Collantes, such as Doña Aurelia, tell me that "almost everyone is mixed. Everyone is stirred together [*revuelto*]." Everyone is "mixed," the Huehuetecans agreed, and it was impossible to untangle their ancestries. "But we're all Mexican." In San Nicolás, Doña Lupe told me that her mother's mother was Indian, while her mother's father was white. Don Margarito, her father, said that one of his grandmothers was a "black Indian and that his own raza was also black Indian.... Now everyone is mixed. It's that way," he said, from Cruz Grande to San Nicolás. He also described the pure races of "the past" as "round-faced" Indians and "blacks," of the "thick-lipped race." Don Domingo's mother was an Indian from Cacahuatepec (north of Pinotepa Nacional), and he was born in Oaxaca. "They call me black, but my mother is Indian," he said. "I *am* Indian" (Soy indio), he insisted on another occasion. "The founders of [San Nicolás] were already crossed [*cruzados*]," he explained. "They were not legitimate, legitimate blacks. Indians were already here. Now one can't distinguish well because race was well-preserved before and now it's not—'the race' has been lost." Ernesto, the musician who brought me to the supposedly African center of the village, is married to Susana, an Indian from Tacubaya in the municipality of Tehuantepec, Oaxaca. Together they explained that "now the people from here are mixed with Indians." Rosa's mother Doña Mirna is from Jamiltepec, northeast of Pinotepa Nacional, and grew up speaking Mixtec. Like many colonial black Indian mulattoes, Rosa and one of her siblings lived for a time in their mother's natal town and spoke Mixtec when they were young.

Morenos talk amusingly and at length about bodies. Some comments are generally Mexican, such as *gordito*, "little fat one," a term of endearment. A thin person is *flaco* (skinny, but more in the sense of weak than *delgado*, which means slim and is less pejorative), and short people are *chaparrito*. More specific to morenos, thin-legged women are *guinchos* (cranes). A wide-hipped one is teased endlessly, as is a man with a protruding belly (*barrigón*) or excessive body hair (*peludo*). People comment on or mimic bowlegs and pigeon toes. But most bodily discussions involve hair and skin, the principal physical signifiers of race. Skin color terms range from very dark (*negro, prieto*, and even *morado*, meaning "purplish") to very light (*claro* or *blanco*). Hair ranges from straight (*lacio*) to wavy (*crespo*) to kinky (*cuculuste*) to very kinky (*chino*).

San Nicoladenses do use *black* (*negro* or *prieto*) to refer to ancestors, to insult particularly dark-skinned people, to describe residents of *other* places, and to indicate how outsiders speak of them. But, as Margarita confirmed, "*moreno* is used much more than *black*. *Black* is reserved for people who are really dark-skinned." Don Domingo focused on hair, but he also said that *moreno* is more common than *black*: "They don't say *black* unless you have very kinky hair; someone can [also] have moreno skin but be white because of his hair." Judit's grandfather was from Ometepec—"pure Indian people; little Indians come from there. But he spoke Spanish even though he wore Indian clothes. He had straight hair but [his skin] was moreno. He was short like the Indians." Her father's sister was tall, white, and blue-eyed. One of her grandmothers was white with kinky hair, while her grandmother's mother was moreno with very kinky hair. Judit has a white sister also with very kinky hair, and a moreno brother with wavy hair like her own. Doña Ana told me that her grandmother was white with straight "Indian" hair and that her father's hair was wavy. Her mother, she said, was moreno, while Doña Ana described herself as light-skinned and very kinky-haired. She added that her brother's grandchildren were white with straight hair.

Don Domingo, Efigenio, and I once composed a grant proposal to establish workshops for music and textile production in San Nicolás. At first they dictated as I typed: "We are of African descent." But Efigenio insisted on changing the wording to "we are of African, indigenous, and Spanish descent." (As I discuss in chapter 5, Efigenio later self-identified as Afro again after claiming a national cultural prize.) "Who knows what our origins are," Judit once said. Margarita concurred as we sat around and I asked her to describe for me people walking by. She called one woman *aindiada*, which, she explained, means "mixed"—lighter-skinned than a moreno and with long but wavy rather than straight hair. "Anyway," she concluded "even if you're white your siblings can be moreno," which Andrés Manzano and Judit had also pointed out. Margarita herself is light-skinned with long, wavy hair. One of her sisters is very light-skinned with very kinky hair, while another is darker skinned with long, straight hair. Margarita's daughter, Antonia, whose hair is thick, straight, and very long, might be mistaken for an Indian, though both Margarita and her husband Maximino identify as morenos.

The mixture that older San Nicoladenses describe still forms part of a younger generation's racial discourse. When my then twenty-one-year-old goddaughter Amalia described her first child to me on the phone from Winston-Salem, she immediately started with the child's skin (*blanquita*— whiter than Amalia's own), moved to her wavy hair, and then to her *grueso* (thick) lips, which Amalia likened to those of her own younger sister as she giggled. Amalia—the daughter of two morenos and the granddaughter of the Mixtec-speaking Doña Mirna—is married to Alfredo, one of San Nicolás's Indians.

Morenos always point out that even if "pure" blacks and Indians once existed, mixing occurred as soon as the two groups had contact. Even Don Vicente, an Indian who settled in 1939 at the age of twenty in San Nicolás, where he met the morena Doña Olivia with whom he had twelve children, also emphasized the purity of the past and the mixture of the present. Morenos are "not from here," he said. "They are from Cuba, from Africa, from over there."[3] Before," he told me with his fists clenched for added emphasis, "people were really, really black. You could only see their eyes. But now," he said several times during our conversation, "people are mixed." Don Margarito said that when he was a boy people were "black, black, black with kinky hair." But he did not know where these people came from. Indeed, he was under the impression that the government had thrown them out of Acapulco and sent them to San Nicolás "because there weren't any people in this corner [of the country]."

Ernesto once explained that "very black, black, black" maroons came from Africa on a ship, a widespread narrative I further discuss in chapter 3. They arrived through the Panama Canal and the port of Acapulco, escaped the ship, and founded coastal belt villages. These blacks had their own customs and spoke a "dialect," which Ernesto said was English. They never returned to their own land and immediately mixed with Indians. "There weren't any Spaniards," Ernesto explained, and "the two got along well—the Indians and the blacks." But he also said that when "blacks" first arrived to the coast, at some unspecified time in the past, Indians fled to the mountains as "blacks and Indians clashed."[4] Sensitive to history, Don Domingo contextualized this clash in colonialism. "Blacks weren't from here," he pointed out, "Indians looked at them with hate and not with trust, as blacks looked at whites, with fear rather than affection." "Blacks and Indians didn't get along," he continued. "They didn't understand each other because of the language, and they didn't know when they were teasing each other." Yet Don Domingo also pointed out that this all changed. Unlike whites, who "don't want their children to marry a black or a poor person, people in San Nicolás don't care—if the kids love each other it's alright. *So blacks and Indians are separate from whites.*" While "Indians used to be more insular," he continued, they soon "started intermingling with blacks." And "once the blood united there was more trust. Now it's even mixed in Indian villages—there are Afromestizo people there too. Among blacks there are Indian blacks and among Amuzgos [there are those] with Indian hair but the color of a black."

The Indian Barrio of San Nicolás

In the 1960s, when Highway 200 was completed down the coast, people from Tecoanapa, a town in the Mixtec region of Ayutla de los Libres in the northwestern uplands of the Costa Chica, began to settle in San Nicolás. Today they constitute about 5 percent of the population. They have lighter skin, higher cheekbones and nose bridges, longer noses, straighter hair, and a smaller stature than morenos. Morenos thus refer to them as "Indians," even though they do not speak Mixtec, at least publicly, and they do not wear indigenous dress.

Because they are from the Costa Chica (and therefore not "white" colonists), and because when they arrived San Nicolás was still battling Germán and colonists from other parts of Guerrero, San Nicoladenses gave them agricultural land and house plots. They settled at the northwestern edge of San Nicolás, which was then empty. Resident Indians average fewer hectares than morenos and have less access to the more productive lowlands.[5] With time they have begun to reach parity, but they still operate at levels closer to subsistence, and they struggle more than morenos to produce crop surpluses. They also began migrating to el norte later than morenos, because fewer had family members there to help. Many still have family in Tecoanapa, where land is scarce and unproductive, as well as in San Nicolás. Thus Mixtecs, who migrate in great numbers to the United States (Besserer 2004), also migrate within Mexico itself.

With some resentment Doña Ana once described these resident Indians as "outsiders" (*forasteros*) who had "grabbed" the highlands; Doña Adelaida wrinkled her nose when she mentioned the Indians at the edge of town; and Rosa said "they're outsiders, they're Indian. They speak with their accent, their language. They're not from here. They came as peons and brought their families, now they're mixing. But they're Indians." Yet Don Domingo defended them. They had not fought for land "or anything like that," he said. Germán was still after San Nicolás's land in the 1960s, and the Indians were settled to "get rid of Miller. The people here weren't interested in the land because at the time they had a lot of it." Thus the wave of Indian arrivals was politically expedient as it buffered San Nicolás from Germán. It was also the case, Doña Lupe added, that "there was a lot of unoccupied space, which was uncultivated and could be worked. They asked for land possession and the mayor gave it. Then they gave them land to build their houses. This was around 1962. They took some of the lowlands and registered as ejidatarios. They have the same rights [as other ejidatarios] and now they are of the village."

Today the Indians are "well-put" (*bien puesto*), although not all are well-documented. Resident Indians sit on the ejido governing committee—as Don Samuel pointed out, "their children are from here, so now they cannot be removed"—but the Indian Zenaida told me an anecdote that suggests some insecurity to Indian land claims: her Indian husband's family had documented rights to agricultural land in San Nicolás, but her father-in-law returned to San Nicolás from a trip to Tecoanapa to discover that the land had been taken over by a moreno. The family now has to rent. Resident Indians sometimes voice fear of ejection from San Nicolás altogether, because land is much scarcer than it was and population growth, coupled with privatization, puts market pressure on landholders.

A Mixture of Tongues

The Indians of San Nicolás come from a Mixtec region, but many words on the coastal belt have Nahuatl roots, which attest to the antiquity of the terms since few Nahuas live in the region now. In Nahuatl, Cuajinicuilapa means "place of the Cuajinicuipil trees" and Huehuetán means "near the upright drum." Many contemporary Nahuatl-derived terms, such as those for flora and fauna, are used throughout Mexico. Some deemed particular to morenos, such as *cuculuste*, *cuita* for excrement, and *chocoyote* for a family's youngest child (Aparicio, Díaz, and García n.d.), also derive from Nahuatl.[6] These words are not limited to the coast (e.g., *xocoyote*, or the youngest child in a family, has been found in Tlaxcala state since the colonial period; see Robichaux 1997:157, 161). Mixtec words are also found in places like Collantes, close to the Mixteca de la Costa of Oaxaca. One includes *pañu* (a Spanish-derived word meaning *rebozo*, or shawl), which I found in a story the mayor of Collantes showed me about a dance. Thus "mixing" is linguistic as well as geographical and "racial."

Although Indian surnames among San Nicolás's morenos and even among the town's Indians are rare, this red herring does not disprove mixture, as Bobby Vaughn contends (2004:83).[7] The names of indigenous people in the region are often a product of religious conversion during the colonial period. Thus, for instance, the name of the Mixtec highlands (Oaxaca) farmer who helped form the Center for Integral Campesino Development of the Mixteca (Centro de Desarrollo Integral Campesino de la Mixteca, or CEDICAM) is Jesús León Santos (Jesus, a Spanish City, and the Saints); one member of the community is María Magdalena Vicente (Malkin 2008). Morenos of course often have Spanish surnames of slave owners or, like Indians, had names bestowed on them on conversion. The names are neither African nor indigenous at all.[8]

Some Indian first names—such as Xitlali—are found among San Nicolás's morenos, and the surnames of Indians include López, Castro, Bruno, Tacuba and, ironically, Moreno, all of them common throughout Mexico. These surnames are not widespread among the moreno majority because most intermarriage has been between moreno men and Indian women. Indian men are often shorter than moreno women, who generally do not want to marry men smaller than they are. In addition, historically there were more black and mulatto men than women on the coast. Indians also tend to be less well-off than morenos. As Sirina pointed out, "Moreno women want their jewelry and to be dressed nicely. So they don't marry Indian men because [the Indians] are poor." "But," she added, "in San Nicolás everything is mixed. Indian men marry moreno women, [but] if the Indian is from outside it will be an Indian woman." Historically "mixing" has included especially these outside Indian women, who moved in, as residence patterns are patrilocal, and learned to speak Spanish. Indian women still marry in. "At first she won't speak Spanish and everyone will laugh at her," Sirina said, "but eventually she'll learn the language and traditions." Partnerships are therefore usually between moreno men and Indian women. Following Spanish and then Mexican tradition, offspring take the (moreno) paternal surname as the first of their two surnames.

Discord, Harmony, and the Geography of Kinship

Don Domingo's assertion that people from El Tamale and San Nicolás intermarry even as they express mutual hostility echoes Odile Hoffmann's observations (2007) about contradictions between discourse and practice in El Pitahayo and Colonia Miguel Alemán, where morenos and whites also bicker and marry. Don Domingo's and Hoffmann's conclusions can also be applied to San Nicolás itself, where squabbles between morenos and Indians are not uncommon, even as the two groups socially engage to make community.

In addition to insecurity over land, Indians sense that morenos question their *social* rights to residence, as they are criticized for failures of cultural etiquette—especially with respect to major ritual events such as weddings and funerals. While moreno customs are variations on general Mexican ones, San Nicoladenses own those customs and use them to make resident Indians outsiders. "They live here now," morenos say of Indians considered to have violated local norms. For instance, Rosa mentioned on our way to a wake for Zenaida's adult nephew that the Indians should have a two-night wake, as is the tradition for an adult, rather than one lasting only a single night. "People say to them, 'why don't you try to be more like us?'" Rosa said as we walked along. "But they keep on with their own customs." We agreed that they tried to conform, however, and when we reached the wake—only to discover that we had confused the date—the deceased man's sister explained somewhat sheepishly that the *rezanderas*, moreno prayer women who are supposed to instruct morenos and Indians on proper ritual practices, had told them how to conduct the wake. I once attended a pardon (*perdón*) in the Indian barrio. In this post-wedding custom, the bride's parents "pardon" the newlyweds for eloping or fleeing (*huir*) with ritual slaps. Normally the bride and groom both enter the house, but on this occasion only the bride entered. When I asked Sirina and Ernesto separately about it, they both told me that the Indians had not done it properly. Don Samuel said that initially the Indians did not perform the "customs very well." But, he added, the Indians "changed when they arrived." Sirina explained that "[the Indians] weren't born here, but now they've been here a while. When I was growing up there were already Indians here. They have other customs, but now they're taking up moreno ones."

The spatial organization of San Nicolás separates morenos from Indians, who continue to live on the outskirts of town because they are relative newcomers and because property is expensive in the center. Yet formal marriages between local Indians and morenos comply with more generally Mexican patrilocal residence (Robichaux 1997). Daughters thus typically move to their in-laws' houses. Moreover, inheritance is a partial system of ultimogeniture. The youngest son inherits his parents' house, but land and livestock are split among male siblings, while women generally inherit other goods (such as heirlooms) because it is expected that husbands will support them. Like patrilocality, ultimogeniture is more generally Mexican; indeed, it is probably pre-Columbian (Robichaux 1997:158–59, 162). Because race and class are gendered in ways that favor unions between Indian women and moreno men, and because the Indian women come either from outside or from San Nicolás's social and geographical margins, intermarriage results in "Indian" encroachment on "moreno" territory as Indian women move in with their in-laws. Because the youngest son stands to inherit his parents' house but domestic spaces are gendered as female, residence patterns mean that Indian wives sometimes come to de facto inherit the homes of their moreno in-laws, as Juliana recently did, and share moreno land and livestock.

Rosa once listed several Indian women moving in with their moreno in-laws. For her such women were "taking over" the center from the margins, as it were. In this respect, tensions between Indians and morenos concern territorial claims rather than race per se, but the tensions are expressed in racial terms. Thus, as Rosa voiced her annoyance, she commented that *her* oldest son, Ismael, "would never marry a *macuana*."[9] Her daughter Amalia did marry the Indian Alfredo, but from Rosa's perspective this meant that Amalia left the house, not that an Indian came in. Sirina appeared more accepting of marriages between morenos and Indians. Describing one wedding she said: "Indian men and women marry moreno men and women—the ones marrying today, she's Indian and he's moreno. . . . People go around all mixed up now. Now they have customs from here. They're 'Indian morenos.'" She used the term *champurrado* (chocolate and corn flour, or a chocolate *atole*, a traditional Mexican corn-based drink) to explain that if her oldest "chocolate" son Modesto married a "corn flour" Indian, their children would be natural-born (*criollo*) San Nicoladenses. She then added that it would in fact be better if Modesto looked for an Indian woman instead of for a moreno one with very kinky hair, because she herself preferred straight hair. "But it doesn't matter to me if he marries an Indian or a moreno," she added. "The only thing that matters is that he loves her."

Class tensions map onto the spatial organization of the village as well. This became clear when I accompanied the Indian Chela one day to visit Denalis, Chela's baby niece and the daughter of her Indian sister-in-law Gisela, who had married Pedro, a moreno. Gisela had followed Pedro to el norte and, as is the custom, had left Denalis with Pedro's family, where the couple had been living and where Gisela had given birth. Gisela's mother, Angela, was supposed to have Denalis on weekends. But Pedro's family, one of the most prominent in San Nicolás, would not allow Angela to see the baby, because they claimed she was spreading rumors of the baby's illness and therefore worrying Gisela. Indeed Denalis looked quite ill when Chela and I arrived. Two days later, perhaps because I had been there, Pedro's family gave the baby to Angela, who was so concerned that she took her to a doctor in Cuaji. With Denalis on the mend, Angela did not want to send her back to Pedro's family until she had been given the full week of medication the doctor prescribed. Chela and I thus returned to ask if Angela could keep the baby for the week. When we arrived, Pedro's great-grandmother ranted at Chela about "you people," referring to Indians. She said Indians were barren (at the time Chela could not conceive) and did not know how to raise children. It was too difficult to get up to the Indian barrio to retrieve the baby, she added, even though the family had a truck and we had walked. But for the great-grandmother not only did "backward Indians" live in an inaccessible part of San Nicolás, far from the center, where Pedro's family lived; Indians also did not know anything about the most natural practice, the raising of children. Since Angela had possession of the baby and Pedro's family members deemed it beneath them to retrieve her, Angela was happily able to nurse Denalis back to health.

Just as morenos disparage Indians, Indians disparage morenos, often by calling them "blacks" behind their backs. "There's a kind of bad racism toward Indians," Tomás told me. "But [the Indians] have their racism too." ("Nevertheless," he added, "indigenous and moreno people get along.") One day, as I was chatting with several Indian women, they started in. "We're Indians," they said, "because we don't have kinky hair." Blacks are the true "outsiders," they insisted as they emphasized their more authentic claims to Mexicanness. "They don't have permission to be here," said Angela. "We're the indigenous ones, not them." "The Virgin of Guadalupe was Indian," added Zenaida's daughter, invoking Mexico's (mestiza) patron saint. "They say, 'those Indians, we're going to get them out of here; we don't want them; get out, Indians!' Well, we'll see who wins. We Indians have a lot of children. We're going to fight for our land." Even after thirty years in San Nicolás, where both of her children were born, Angela complained about moreno food. "They put corn flour in chili sauce and in broth. We Indians eat white rice with our mole; morenos put stuff in the rice." She once told me that I was ill because I had eaten Sirina's homemade cheese. Resident Indians, however, also believe that they are discriminated against because they are not dark-skinned *enough* and thus not of interest to outsiders like culture workers. Thus their discourses about blackness and belonging express their own sense of displacement.

Reduplicated Indians

The Indians of San Nicolás speak Spanish and wear store-bought clothes. Morenos identify "really indigenous" Indians as "native" or as reduplicated "Indian Indians" (*indios naturales* or *indios indios*).[10] These include out-side Mixtecs as well as Amuzgos from the hills north of Ometepec. Don Domingo told me that historically "blacks crossed more with Amuzgos," who are geographically closer to the coastal belt, and that "native Indians of both the Mixtec and Amuzgo races" come to San Nicolás to work as peons. Amuzgo women sometimes join their husbands and are typically more "Indian" as they tend to wear traditional dress and speak only rudimentary or no Spanish (also De la Cadena 1991; Hendrickson 1991). They sell huipiles in Cuaji and San Nicolás, clothing they sometimes disparage, because even for them factory-made "Western" clothing—especially men's Westernized "pants of reason"—correlates positively with Spanish language acquisition and general Hispanization (Valdez 1998:29).

Throughout the coast Indian Indians are derisively referred to by whites and morenos as *guanacos*, also a common Mexican term.[11] Morenos sometimes refer to San Nicolás's own Indian residents as *macuanos*, as Rosa did and as Angela has told me. I once heard Sirina refer to Indians as "people without reason" (*gente sin razón*), an archaic colonial term that distinguished non-Christians from Christians, the subordinated classes from the dominant one, and non-Spanish speakers from Spaniards. By using this term Sirina was classifying herself with other "people of reason," that is, with the white majority, the "national" Mexican, while putting cultural distance between herself and Indians (also Aguirre Beltrán 1985 [1958]:70). Morenos also sometimes hurl the insult "you talk like an Indian."

An extended (generationally and laterally) family of Amuzgos from the hills north of Ometepec has lived in San Nicolás since 2001, and is routinely said to be filthy. The family settled in San Nicolás because a brother was working as a peon for Don Guillermo, who rented him a house that belonged to a son in North Carolina, and a connecting *tortillería*, which the Amuzgo family runs. The man brought his brother, both of their wives, all of their children, and the men's parents. Don Guillermo's wife, Doña Socorro, complained to me about the "mess" they made. "My son doesn't want the house all smashed up. Only one person is supposed to live there, and then they all came." Rosa called them "little farm dogs" because they "go to the bathroom wherever they feel like it and eat at whatever time." Everyone referred to them as "pigs." Amuzgo, morenos joked to me, sounds just like English to them. For their part, the Amuzgos referred to "blacks" as pigs and complained that although they cleaned up the garbage on the street, it always reappeared the next day.

Resident Indians also distance themselves from these Indian Indians because assimilation to the ways of morenos requires them to repress their own indigenousness. Zefraida thus told me that the Amuzgos could be swearing at you and you would not know, because they "speak their own language," while she spoke Spanish, just like everyone else. In fact, not until I had been coming and going for a year did Angela admit that her people were Mixtec, which she herself spoke.[12] Otherwise she and other resident Indians would duck the question, admit that "one or two" people speak "something," or comment that "we don't talk as 'one talks'" (as native Spanish-speakers do). Thus while more urban costeños disparage San Nicoladenses for what is considered their poor command of Spanish, moreno San Nicoladenses disparage resident Indians, whom they consider more rural than themselves, and resident Indians and morenos disparage Indian Indians, who are yet more rural.

Occasionally Indians from outside suffer attacks. One Mixtec came to San Nicolás to work as a bricklayer in the late 1990s, when construction was booming. After he fell down drunk one evening outside the house where he was staying with Don Domingo, a group of passing boys called him "indio." He responded with "you negros." The local police put him in the house so he would not be attacked. I asked Don Domingo whether such assaults were frequent; he affirmed that they were, though he added that boys would beat up any kind of drunk. In the summer of 2001 a young moreno man allegedly threw a firecracker onto the breezeway of the Amuzgos' home in the middle of the night. A child asleep in a hammock was burned. And my son's father told me that in a cantina one evening moreno men ganged up on an Indian Indian peon, swearing at him.

Whiteness in and out of Place

Paula told me that Angela's husband, Héctor, came from "Indian land near Ayutla—pure white people." Indeed, Indians can be white in a descriptive sense, but not in the classificatory sense that San Nicoladenses employ when using the term *white* to talk about the government, their history with hacendados, or the "rich." The hostility between morenos and Indians is mediated by integration through custom and newly formed families. Moreno hostility toward whites is not.

Late one night after a dance Sirina, Rosa, and I drunkenly picked our way through the bush; we all had to urgently urinate. As we decided to do it outside, we all laughed that my rear end would shine in the moonlight and be visible to everyone. Indeed, I am very light-skinned and San Nicoladenses identify me as white. But I am not a *güera*, or a nominally reduplicated white white person, because I do not have blonde hair, blue eyes, or freckles. My dark eyes and wavy black hair that frizzes in the humidity make me less strange to San Nicoladenses than other outsiders are. I am often mistaken for Mexican by people who do not know me. A teenager in Collantes was surprised to learn that I was not. "Oh," she said, "I thought everyone in el norte had blue eyes." Appearing Mexican was *not* to my advantage, however, because San Nicoladenses are hostile to white Mexicans. It was better to be a gringa.

All whites looked the same to Margarita because of their oval faces. And when I arrived in 1997 I was constantly asked not only if I was from la cultura but if I was evangelical, as white Chilean evangelicals were in San Nicolás at the time. Whenever I travel to San Nicolás after some months in the United States, I am told how fat and white I am, even though I have fit into the same clothes for years. And when people comment that I am fat, they invariably add white, as though the two always go together. People also endlessly point out the sunburns, pimples, mosquito bites, and heat rashes I suffer in San Nicolás. As Sirina jokes, I arrive all nice and white and clean, and then leave blemished and dirty because of the heat and dust. But when I leave I am always darker (*más morena*) and slimmer (*más delgadita*). Thus not just my body but also my "race" transforms during my stay, whether that stay lasts for one week or for two months.

Whiteness might confer social and political capital, but it also signifies a feeble physique. Rosa described "moreno skin [as] tougher. We can handle more—we eat peppers and tortillas. If you get a fever you turn whiter; if I get one I only turn ashen." Once her sister was visiting and everyone in the family had a fever, including one of her "white" sisters-in-law. Rosa's sister asked what was wrong with the sister-in-law. Everyone had a fever, but only the sister-in-law's was noticeable because she was so wan, Rosa told me with a guffaw. Then she mentioned a girl who fell and scratched herself because she was light and therefore weak and thin-skinned. "Morenos are strong, while güeros are weak," Don Zeferino's son teased a friend with whom he was playing soccer. Morenos themselves return from el norte whiter, fatter, and weaker than when they left. They are not working as much in the sun and are eating more (and often less healthy) food. Don Guillermo's and Doña Socorro's son complained of sunburn when he returned after five years in el norte, much paler and heavier than when he had left. A friend of Margarita's stopped me on the road one day to ask if Margarita had grown fat in el norte.

Don Domingo gave whiteness a political spin when he told me that no San Nicoladense would partner with a white person because "[whites] are more interested in money than in humanity." He qualified it by limiting it to Mexican whites, to Spaniards "seeking treasure," and in the context of a coastal history of whites dominating commerce, cattle, and politics. "There aren't any legitimate whites here now," he said. "White cattle ranchers were here, but they left. Today's whites are in Ometepec. The governor, he's white; the municipal president, he's white." He once told me in a drunken stupor that I was beautiful because I was white, but he later apologized and told me I was the only white person San Nicoladenses trusted.

Don Domingo's comments about rich whites open up a discourse about San Nicoladenses' real enmity, which is directed toward whites rather than Indians. He once narrated to me such hostility in a story that recounted without reference to time or place blacks' initial enslavement and the experiences of a mulatto (mixed white-black) boy with a wounded heart.

> I have a small story that the children used to tell, how the blacks first came to be slaves . . . the blacks . . . went to barter their merchandise . . . but the pirates entered and came out to rob them . . . they killed them. Later one pirate said, "We are not going to waste these people . . . let's grab one and take away his merchandise. Then we'll threaten to steal their water if they don't sign on as slaves. . . . There was a boat and an old man came with his granddaughter. She wanted to go about with her grandfather. He told her no because of the dangers . . . [but] she convinced him and the pirates seized her. . . . The old man and the young girl were the first to be enslaved and they sold them. . . . A white man fell in love with [the girl] and they had illicit love and a son. His parents denied he had had a union with a black girl; they sent him away. . . . They took the child and gave him care and education, but they never loved him very much as a grandson, and the boy was growing and saw how they treated the black slaves. He was born mulatto. . . . The grandfather was an old slave. . . . He told the boy to come and kissed him. The boy's lips became sweet because he was his grandfather, but the boy did not know it. The boy's father returned and saw him but could not embrace him because it wasn't permitted. He told the boy to come to his room. He said, I want to tell you something. He kissed him and the flavor came to his lips and his lips were sweet. He wanted to say that he was his father, but he was

never brave enough to do it. The boy's father saw them hit the blacks and did not have the courage to defend them, but the boy did, "I have it." The boy went off alone. He asked the old slave who his mama and papa were. The slave said he did not know.

This story is significant on multiple levels. First, a black girl and her grandfather are taken by pirates and sold into slavery. Don Domingo does not mention who the pirates were, but the assertion is reminiscent of his claim that bride theft, which I discuss in chapter 6, is a Spanish practice. "The custom of abduction is Spanish," he told me. "If Spaniards liked the Indian and black women, they would grab them. What could [the women] do?" Second, the mulatto senses the love of his slave grandfather, through a kiss bestowed by the old man, a kiss that leaves a sweet taste on the boy's lips. The sweet kisses indicated their kinship, Don Domingo said. Although the white father also bestows a sweet kiss that signifies an abiding and loving connection, his shame makes him reluctant to completely embrace his son, and thus his love cannot be fulfilled. Too cowardly to identify himself as the boy's father, the white man also cannot come to the aid of the slaves, who are in the end freed with the mulatto's help.

"Blacks believe that whites don't love them at heart," Don Domingo added. "There are still people that whites don't accept at heart." "Our ancestors' hearts were wounded by whites," he told me on another occasion. "Now there's little contact between blacks and whites. There's still some hurt." Morenos told me time and again that white people continued to hurt them. Not only was the white Germán evil (though Carlos was not), a former municipal president of Cuaji, who burned all of the archives pertaining to San Nicolás, was also white. Everyone mentions the white anthropologists who photograph morenos but do not say why they want the images. Morenos think whites want to make fun of them (Lewis 2004). All this puts morenos in something of a contradictory position because while whites do not accept blacks, blacks had to "adopt Spanish language and traditions to survive," Don Domingo said. "The Spanish influence is strongest," he added.

Whiteness has also become something of an extranational issue, given the difficulties of migration and encounters with *gabachos* (a slang and often derogatory term for whites) in el norte. Although San Nicoladenses do not have a long history with white U.S. Americans—indeed the only U.S.

American who looms large in their memory is Carlos Miller, whom many still esteem—they identify whites with *la línea*, or with the U.S.-Mexican border that most cross without documents. Referring to the United States, Doña Austroberta once told me that "whites from there don't really love blacks at heart." A drunken Luisa, celebrating a newly engaged couple, once recounted a border-crossing experience as she conflated gringos with whites and cried out to me, "We love you but you don't love us. We don't want your help, but we also don't want you to deceive us." She used "you" in the plural and so was not directing her comments to me in particular. But certainly as a white U.S. citizen I was partially contained within that plural. This was brought home when I hoped for food and sympathy the night I arrived dirty, sweaty, and tired after an eighteen-hour trip from Virginia. Instead, San Nicoladenses pointed out that at least I did not have to sneak across the border on foot.

Disrespect from local whites remains rampant. One Spanish priest who made weekly visits from Cuaji would gladly visit us, give candy to our son, and sprinkle holy water in the house to rid it of the dangerous light yellow scorpions known as little devils or *diablitos*. But he always made disparaging remarks about morenos to us, as if we were like him: a white dealing with recalcitrant blacks. During Corpus Christi he locked up the golden star representing Christ instead of leaving it in the church where, he said, someone would steal it. Only twelve men came to Mass he complained, and they only came because they were fiesta stewards (*mayordomos*). Only Indian men go to Mass, he added. The morenos think it a "feminine" thing.[13] He went on about a funeral where all the men were drunk and would not enter the room where he was saying Mass. He even disparaged the rezanderas, mimicking their voices and complaining that he could not understand them because they spoke too quickly. "The mestizos are the bosses," he declared. "The Indians are the workers, and the blacks are lazy—they don't do anything."

In 1999 a white PRD politician from Cuaji (fittingly named Blanca) came for a fiesta organized by la cultura. As soon as she saw me she invited me to sit with the dignitaries. I was clearly with Margarita, whom Blanca ignored. Sandra, a white woman from northern Mexico who married a local moreno stationed in the army, came to live with her mother-in-law when he went to el norte and spent the summer of 1997 trying to organize the women of San Nicolás through a state health and nutrition program. She was perplexed that only Indian women would go to the meetings and complained that moreno women fed their husbands first and gave children older than four what she insisted were scraps. "The Indians," she told me, "are more interested in progressing. Their neighborhood is cleaner. They sweep every day."

Moreno attitudes toward Indians thus need to be understood in the context of how blackness is depicted as defying social norms, especially by whites, who have power over morenos that Indians do not have. Whites' characterizations are not lost on San Nicolás's morenos, who are compelled to understand the difference imputed to them not as key to their acceptance, as culture workers would have it, but rather as a form of disparagement. In some ways morenos thus identify more strongly with whites than with Indians: after all, morenos speak Spanish and are *gente de razón*. Yet whites constantly remind morenos that the latter are not white. Furthermore, morenos view Indians' political, economic, and historical experiences as similar to their own, as both are subordinated to whites. Morenos point out, for instance, that neither they nor Indians can make a living through agriculture because white merchants first cheat both out of their crops and money and then are favored by the government in any arising disputes. The government in turn is said to "not want [morenos and Indians] to be educated," therefore failing to provide adequate schools. As morenos conflate whites with "the government," they also constitute class categories through racial idioms and refer to whites as "the rich."

Moreno ambivalence toward Indians is thus coupled with a consciousness of their comparable class position and relationship to the government and to whites. While Indian Indians are derided for their supposedly strange customs, Doña Lupe told me sympathetically that in their home region the Amuzgos grew coffee, chocolate, beans, and hibiscus (*jamaica*) but very little corn for their own subsistence because the altitude was too high.

Don Guillermo also felt sorry for them. "They're so poor; they don't have anything to eat." The Indians from San Nicolás, he said, were better off than those from outside. Anyway, he added, "the poor sleep better. Rich people are always thinking about how to make more money." Rodrigo commented one afternoon that, "we always say 'indios' [*inditos*, or "little Indians"]. I've seen on television how the Indians live. Now they've had enough. They are resisting, fighting back. We understand because we too have had it," he declared. "Little Indians," then, are coupled here with equally disadvantaged (and exasperated) morenos.

Just as resident Indians speak Spanish and dress as morenos do, in store-bought clothes, morenos themselves used to dress "like Indians." "Women wore huipiles," Doña Cata said, "not blouses, but ones like aprons around their chests and tied around their necks, like what Mixtec women wear." Eva told me that "the cotton clothes both men and women wore were white, white, white because there was no dye. It was the same clothing Indians wore. People would say my father 'dressed like an Indian.'" Doña Caratina, considerably older than Eva, described how women "just tied the fabric on their shoulders and wore wide skirts like the Aztecs, while men tied their trousers at the waist; everything was white."

Although morenos tease Indians for their Spanish and native languages, they sense that their own rural Mexican speech is also different. Sirina laughed one night as we walked home from a wake and passed two young women contracting phrases, such that "por dónde está mi mamá" (over by where my mother is; around my mother's house) came out "p'antá mi 'ama." Morenos drop the s from plurals, use apa for papá, qué instead of mánde (the convention for "what?" in more urban parts of Mexico), más mucho (much more) instead of mucho más, and vide and vido ("I saw" and "he, she, or you [formal] saw") instead of vi and vio. Thus Indians might speak "bad" Spanish, but so do morenos. And hostility toward Indians of course touches moreno families too. Once we were relaxing at Rosa's when a drunken moreno passed by and shouted "indita" at her mother Doña Mirna.

Despite ongoing verbal sparring between morenos and Indians, then, morenos in many ways clearly identify more strongly with Indians than with whites, and resident Indians are solidly integrated into the community, as are "outside" Indians who marry in, such as Susana. Thus discourse radiating hostility contradicts actual practice (see also Hoffmann 2007). Most telling to me is that no one is excluded from gossip networks. "People here are like tape recorders," Sirina once joked. Many times I heard the same tale told from an Indian at one end of the village as had been told to me by a moreno at the other end, in precisely matching words.

Feo

In part because of white disrespect, morenos view *black* as an impolite term reserved mostly for ancestors and to indicate the heightened consciousness of identities that culture workers attribute to local people. *Black* is also used to joke about or to insult others, and it is commonly applied to San Nicoladenses perceived to be dark-skinned or to people from other villages such as Collantes and Santiago Tepextla, both in Oaxaca (Lewis 2004). Thus Sirina and Rodrigo told me that those from Santiago Tepextla are very black. "You can't even make out people's features," said Rodrigo. They both put their hands up to their heads and made rubbing gestures: "Their hair: really kinky, really kinky." Using Sirina as an example, they noted that "she's not *as* dark as those from Tepextla, and her hair, while short, isn't *as* kinky as theirs." Sirina pointed out that a girl staying with Rosa was "*really* dark with *really* kinky hair, and from Tepextla." Beti's daughter is beautiful, she told me on another occasion, because the girl was light-skinned with straight hair, which Sirina indicated with a sweeping gesture from the top of her own head past her shoulders. Then she pointed out a girl from Collantes, whom she described as "black, black."

Morenos sometimes refer to themselves as "ugly" (*feo*), because dark skin is aesthetically unpleasing, an issue reinforced not just locally but also by national and even international media (Hernández Cuevas 2003; Lewis 2004). Grandmothers occasionally grumble about grandchildren, as did Doña Estefania when she deemed her newborn grandson "too dark." Parents might also complain if their children choose a dark-skinned partner. For instance, Petronila, whose family is from a town north of Juchitán, is lighter-skinned than her husband, Rubén. Her parents resisted the marriage because Rubén was too dark and poor, but Petronila ran away with Rubén, defying them. Petronila described her parents' attitude as "customs picked up [in San Nicolás]."

Sirina's mother-in-law also did not like Sirina. She called her "prieta" and "fea" even though she was dark-skinned herself, Sirina said. And then Sirina's own daughter Yanaris did not want a certain moreno godfather because he was too dark. Delia told me that Iris's children's father says that "all the younger ones are blacks, while the older ones are more beautiful than the other feas." The father, who is not married to Iris, once walked by our house and pointed out his youngest son. The child, around eight at the time, denied with a stony look that the man was his father. Iris said that he would call him *caldo* (broth), thus insulting him as "sallow." He and his next oldest brother, Iris said, have "too much affection in them — their father says they are too dark."

Doña Caritina took care of her ten-year-old great-granddaughter because the child's mother had gone to el norte. Her granddaughter's in-laws did not want the little girl because she is black and they are morenos. "Who wants to be black?" she asked rhetorically. "They are morenos, and they don't love her. The mother-in-law, she's very light-skinned. They're crazy in the head, people who reject their own family." Manuel commented that "a black man is not going to look for a black woman because people will say what a pity for their children when two blacks marry." Doña Berta told me how blacks "don't have a nose—their noses are flat and it's better to have a big nose, to be tall and white." "Do you like morenos?," her daughter Verónica asked me, and then she inquired if I was from Chihuahua because lighter-skinned Mexicans live there. Doña Berta also said that her son had married a very light-skinned woman from Mexico City, a güera. "One is happy when one's son marries a güera because people are going to say that she's beautiful," she added. Rosa told me about two daughters a man had with two different women. One, who lives in North Carolina, was "beautiful" because she was white. The other was "not beautiful." "She's black, black, with kinky hair. He won first place with the one in Carolina."

Morenos thus prefer lightness to darkness and long hair to kinky hair. But so does the dominant culture and so do Indians. Indeed, San Nicolás's Indians have their own internal color prejudice. Chela told me, for instance, how close she was to her father. "My grandmother says I'm my daddy's favorite. I came out whiter and my sisters came out darker." As Gisela prepared to marry Pedro, her Indian relatives and friends teased her: "If one marries a black the children are going to come out mixed. Do you want to change colors?" Pedro, in fact, is very light-skinned, but no one can predict a baby's features.

San Nicolás's morenos see themselves as less "countrified" and more modern, and therefore as less black than people from other coastal belt communities. Indeed, being "less black" has a class dimension that is often overlooked: dark skin is associated with rurality, manual labor, and poverty in Mexico, elsewhere in Latin America (Lewis 2004; Pineda 2006), and indeed around the world. Thus Petronila's parents coupled Rubén's skin color with his poverty. Dark skin means one spends time in the sun, which morenos often spontaneously mention to explain their skin color. According to Don Domingo, men do not want their wives to leave the house because they do not want them in the sun. To have a lighter-skinned wife or daughter means that a man has been able to care for her in such a way that she does not "need" to go out. Morenos thus combine a race and class prejudice that equates dark skin with backwardness. *Feo* therefore goes beyond skin color.

It means that one has not yet "made it" either by leaving field labor behind or by making enough money to protect one's family, especially its women.

The Middle Is the Best

The dictionary definitions of *moreno* and *crespo*, even if they can be found, do not entirely correspond to their local meanings. While *moreno* might mean "dark-skinned," it is a comparative term (see also Amaral 2005). Dark in relation to what, one might ask? *Moreno* is lighter than *prieto* (or black) and darker than white. *Lacio* does mean "straight," and *cuculuste*, which I noted derives from Nahuatl, does mean "kinky." Kinky hair aesthetically displeases morenos, but then so does completely straight hair. Indians have such straight hair, for instance, that it does not hold a curl well and, according to morenos, sticks up when it is short. *Crespo* does not mean "frizzy," as it would in some dictionaries, but rather wavy: less curly than *cuculuste* but not as straight as *lacio*.

Despite colorism among both morenos and Indians, in general the aesthetics of skin and hair do not favor whiteness or even straight hair as much as they do mixture (see also Candelario 2007:181–82; Godreau 2002b). When Manuel told me that he did not like "very black" women he added that he did not like "very white" ones either. A man I did not know once commented in passing about a blonde, blue-eyed student with me that the student might want to marry a moreno but that a moreno would not want to marry such a güera. Whites are sometimes referred to pejoratively as *bolillos* (soft, white rolls). "A moreno wants a morena from here," Manuel remarked as he linked physicality to place while also distinguishing morenos from blacks. Aesthetically, wavy is better than the extremes of straight and kinky; moreno and Indian are better than the extremes of really white or really black. Even dark-skinned Indians are "in the middle." "She's beautiful," Sirina says of her sister-in-law María, whose father is Indian. Her skin is tawny gold and her hair is long and wavy. Rosa once remarked that María's children all had their father's kinky hair. She then speculated that because María's son's fiancée had straight hair, perhaps their children would have wavy hair like María's and, indeed, like Rosa's own.

Part of the preference for this middle comes perhaps counterintuitively from a sense that people should marry "their own kind." Since the "blood" is already "crossed," this "improves the race" in the double sense of strengthening family ties and blood. Because morenos are already mixed, marrying Indians or other morenos makes sense. Paradoxically, mixture *and* endogamy together maintain moreno "purity." "To cross the blood is better," said Don Zeferino. "It's like a burro; it's stronger." To be moreno is to be normal and to maintain the rules and regulations of one's family. Indeed, San Nicolás is so endogamous that the names of the founding families Don Domingo listed remain among the most common surnames in town.

What It Means to Be Native

The Indians of San Nicolás try to fit into village life by performing rituals "properly"; they regularly develop ties of ritual coparenthood with morenos; and they participate in community events and politics. Indeed, as I have indicated, they also distance themselves from Indian Indians. Morenos and Indians intermarry, and they attend each other's weddings and wakes. Despite criticizing resident Indians, morenos contrast their own "selfishness" and indifference to public sanitation to the ways resident Indians sweep their roads every day, to their political unity, and even to their religious devotion ("they appreciate the saints more," Sirina told me). They are often said to be "clever." As Rosa explained, "the outsiders, the Indians, there are a lot of them. They have more land. They're cleverer than people from here. Where they come from there are hills, and so they came here and they made themselves clever. We don't take advantage of what we have. The Indians work harder."

In the late 1990s resident Indians banded together to bring electricity to their neighborhood, while morenos refused to work in a volunteer work brigade (*faena*) to help fix the drainage, repair the entrance to a school, or even to remove bush so that money I donated could be used to make a crucial road passable during the rainy season. Although all these things eventually got done, at the time Sirina commented that the "people here are not united. They are never in agreement. It's said that 'the people united will never be defeated,' but we're not united." Unlike morenos, who spent months before a local election arguing over who was a PRDista and who was a PRIista, and who benefited from belonging to one party or the other, Indians are not divided by political membership. "Some are PRI and some are PRD. But they don't let that affect them," Cosme said. "We, the proper members of this village, cannot work together." Both Sirina and Cosme maintain that morenos *are* San Nicoladenses. Nevertheless, Indian "outsiders" act more like a community.

Morenos refer to themselves as criollos and to Indians as naturales. Both words mean "native," but the term *creole* indicates that one is *born in* a place, while *native* indicates that one is *of* a place.[14] Thus, *natural* implies a more primordial character than *criollo*. The subtext to this distinction is that morenos recognize Indians as more rooted than they are. Morenos thus privilege Indian Indians with respect to territorial claims to the Mexican nation but themselves with respect to territorial claims to the village of San Nicolás. Privileging Indianness contrasts with the African primordialism expressed by Black Utes of Colorado, for whom the Indian "part" of their identity is cultural and shifting while the black "part" is elemental (Brooks 2002). The contrast likely relates to the different historical constructions of race in the United States and Mexico. Most pointedly, the importance of Indians to Mexican national identity cannot be overstated; nor can San Nicoladenses' sense of historical displacement, reinforced by both Indians and whites on the coast. In this sense, *criollo* grounds morenos in place—the village of San Nicolás—while *natural* recognizes that Indians "own" Mexico, which encompasses the village. "The authentic Mexican is Indian," Margarita once told me. "The flag, the money, an eagle, a nopal . . . if you are Indian, well, the flag is yours," said Manuel.

But morenos' common history of exploitation with Indians, their common habits, and even their common culture make both different from whites. Indeed, both have been *made different by whites*. The multiple affiliations with Indians that experience and consciousness have engendered for morenos thus ultimately link them through Indians to a nation in which whites have a rather tenuous place. "Moreno" thus challenges the category "mestizo" because, while both privilege Indianness, the former excludes whites. It thus undermines the dominant national discourse of *mestizaje*.

CHAPTER THREE

Identity in Performance

I now turn to three narratives that together express the exclusion of whiteness through the symbolic entanglement of Indianness and morenoness in the formation of place and identity. The significance of these narratives, which combine stories and performances and are oriented toward the past, rests on black-Indian "mixture." The first concerns a shipwreck and escaped maroons; the second the festival of San Nicolás's patron saint; and the third the ritual drama La América, which foregrounds Indian victory over Spaniards on Independence Day.

Magic, Money, and Maroonage

Throughout the coastal belt people talk about a foreign shipwreck slaves escaped sometime in the past. "Everyone here can tell you about it," said Judit. Stories about shipwrecks and escaped slaves abound in other African-descent regions of Latin America too, arising in particular with reference to black-Indian admixture. For instance, on the Caribbean coast of Nicaragua, *zambos* (black Indians) are thought linked to a coastal shipwreck that released slaves, who then intermarried with the coast's Miskito Indians in the 1600s (Pineda 2006:49–53). Scholars claim that blacks arrived on the island of St. Vincent after the wreck of another slave ship, intermarried there with Arawak Indians, and took on indigenous customs. Exiled to Honduras, Guatemala, and Belize by the British, who called them "Black Caribs," they became those today known as the Garífuna, whose language is a mixture of Arawak, Carib, English, and Spanish (Bateman 1990; Gonzalez 1988; Prescod and Fraser 2008:100–101). In Ecuador's Esmeraldas Pacific Coast province, a slave ship is said to have wrecked in the 1600s, its human cargo mixing with Indians on land (Lane 2002:ch. 1).

In San Nicolás the only shipwreck date ever mentioned was around 1873, when steamers were plying the Pacific waters from the United States. People nevertheless insist that this ship, routinely identified as the *Puertas de oro* (*Golden Doors*), sank off El Faro and carried "very, very black" slaves, who fled the sinking vessel and found freedom on the coast. Sometimes the story refers to a ship from the United States, with English-speaking Africans or ones who spoke "their own language," now forgotten; sometimes the ship's provenance is unknown. "The people from the ship came here; they were black slaves; I don't know when," Tivo told me in Collantes. Don Sebastián's more involved Collantes story included the "hypothesis (attributed to anthropologists) that blacks came from Sonora, passing through Florida and Baja California. The ship left the port of Acapulco and arrived at the port of Miniso, near Collantes. Blacks stayed on the coast because they were considering returning to Africa." He insisted that there were never slaves in Collantes.

Don Domingo and Don Gregorio additionally mentioned a ship called *La blanca* (*The White One*), which sank off the coast of Oaxaca in the 1940s. Don Gregorio did not know much about it, but Don Domingo told me it carried African American marines from Japan. While the marines did not stay, their children did. I did not look for records of that vessel, but people's lengthy genealogies never mention marines from the Second World War. I therefore doubt such marines stayed long on the coast, even if a ship did sink, or that they left children behind in Mexico. I found evidence of only one shipwreck in the nineteenth century, a U.S. merchant steamship that ran aground sixty miles south of Acapulco, far north of both San Nicolás and Collantes. It carried passengers, coal, and merchandise destined for Panama (DUSCA 1, July 18, 1823–December 19, 1853, file 143, roll 1).

According to Don Domingo, the slaves who escaped the *Golden Doors* remained on the coast. Others came through Acapulco, still others from the Caribbean, and some fled U.S. plantations,[1] "because Mexico was free," which it became in 1829. Don Domingo's grandmother was fifteen when the *Golden Doors* sank, which would place the event in the 1860s or 1870s. "This is why they put the lighthouse up, because there were lots of rocks," Don Domingo said. "[The ship] carried money," he added, "which washed up on the beach, and everyone went to rake it up." He did not know where the *Golden Doors* hailed from. "It wasn't Mexican because it carried blacks. Did it come from Africa? No. They were slaves. Slaves were from England? It was the first time it came down the coast and it didn't know the way. That's why it sank." According to Margarita, the *Golden Doors* carried African or Cuban slaves, who escaped and stayed on.

Doña Ernestina, probably the oldest person with whom I spoke, also identified the El Faro wreck as the *Golden Doors*. According to her the ship belonged to a rich widow and was full of paper money and weapons, but she did not know whether it carried slaves. This paper money, which she said her husband, nephew, and aunt went to collect, thus indicating that this ship, at least, sank not long ago, did not become damaged in the sea because it was made of special paper. Judit also told me of an El Faro ship with "a lot of gold and treasure," which people were unable to recover because the ship sat on the edge of a precipice. Don Gregorio confirmed the name of the ship and said—like Don Domingo—that it had run aground on the shoals of El Faro when his grandmother was young. "A lot of things ended up on the beach. People gathered them up, but the government took it away." The name of the ship, as well as mentions of gold, money, and other treasures that people either gathered and hid (the ancestors), could not collect but wanted to anyway, or that was "magical" recalls the fetishization of mines noted in chapter 1.

Although the ship stories vary in their details, they emphasize human mixture while reinforcing the coastal belt as a magnet for "foreign" blacks who became maroons. Thus the black Indian founders were already in the area, villages were already free, and escaped slaves mixed with the founders. The coastal belt might indeed have been attractive to maroons during the colonial period, even if no actual maroon settlement existed in Cuaji; and the shipwreck stories do coincide with other symbolic invocations of maroonage. These, in turn, can be linked to broader questions that morenos already semiconsciously project, in great part because they are asked: How did blacks get here? Why do people say that morenos are outsiders? In short, the arrival of people from elsewhere who mixed with people already present invokes questions of place and the cosmopolitanism that both James Clifford (1994) and Baron Pineda (2006) note mark the identities of African diaspora peoples elsewhere.[2] Don Domingo emphasized Mexico as free when he recounted the *Golden Doors*. Judit told me that people who escaped ships were never enslaved in Mexico. "They were slaves, but once they escaped they were guaranteed their liberty. My paternal grandfather was not a slave; and neither was his father."

The willfulness of maroons overlaps with notions of freedom to become perhaps the defining ideational complex characterizing San Nicolás's morenos' sense of themselves as "black." It figures in the story of the saint and figures as a constant in conversation. Freedom is also a central theme of the ritual drama La América, wherein it is attributed to Indians. Taken together, the stories of ships, saints, and independence identify San Nicoladenses as mixed, willful, and free, and as both native and creole, as Indians and morenos are linked spatially, culturally, and historically. The narratives ultimately turn on the broader ideologies of Mexican national identities—themselves infused with racial ambivalence and uncertainty—and on reconciliation.

Mestizaje with a Twist

Historically, Indianness has been the touchstone for important aspects of Mexican and other Latin American national identities, while blackness, with few exceptions, mostly remains invisible. Peter Wade argues that the difference between Indianness and blackness can be traced to Latin American colonial institutional and legal statuses, which carved out a special status for Indians while Hispanicizing blacks to make them useful to Spanish settlers by, as I note elsewhere, "putting difference to work" in the colonial political economy (Lewis 2003; Wade 1997:25–30). Indians were later exoticized through national ideologies and studies that disparaged or ignored blacks altogether (Wade 1997:35–36). Thus scholarly work itself needs to be historicized.

The Mexican national model has largely emphasized mestizaje, understood as the cultural and biological fusion of Spaniard and Indian and embodied in the form of the "hybrid" mestizo (Knight 1990:84–88; Phelan 1960; Stepan 1991:146–47; Vasconcelos 1924). The iconic mestizo represents the origins of "the Mexican," with whiteness as the imminent ideal. Within this framework, however, the Mexican patrimony is also anchored to a romanticized and ideologically powerful past that glorifies the Indian role in forging the national character, even while denigrating contemporary Indians (Friedlander 1975; Knight 1990; LaFaye 1976; Pagden 1987). Mestizaje thus stresses Indian assimilation to the Westernized Mexican while creating tension with an idealistic view of the Mexican character as primarily derived from Indian peoples. Such *indigenismo* (indigenism) became prominent after the revolution as emerging ideologies and anthropologies developed by elites simultaneously constructed Indianness and determined its value to a more progressive nation. During this period academic and government institutions were established to study Indian issues (Bonfil Batalla 1990:169–73; Dawson 1997; Wade 1997:32); the state promoted Indian education; Indian traditions were "woven into a new tapestry of folkloric nationalism" (Knight 1990:82); and the mestizo "protagonists" of Mexican history came to be tied more firmly to the "Indian race," the imagined foundation for revolutionary ideals (Knight 1990:76–77; Lomnitz 1993:277). Morenos highlight the centrality of Indians in this version of Mexican national ideology when they link Indians to the flag, to money, and to other national emblems.

Historically, intellectuals' indigenist and mestizo formations have consciously rejected blackness, in great part because of European racism against Latin Americans themselves. In the late eighteenth century the exiled Jesuit Francisco Javier Clavijero accompanied a defense of Mexico's Indians from such racism with the exclusion of the "vile Black slave and his descendants" from the nation (qtd. in LaFaye 1990:82). Blacks have "damaged blood and a disorderly physical constitution," Clavijero wrote (qtd. in Aguirre Beltrán 1976:26). "What could be more contrary to the idea we have of beauty and human bodily perfection than a pestilent man, whose skin is dark like ink, head and face covered with black wool in place of hair, eyes yellow or the color of blood, thick, blackish lips and flattened nose?" (qtd. in Aguirre Beltrán 1976:27; see also Aguirre Beltrán 1994:19). The same process that denigrated blacks while establishing the nation's racial identity later coincided in the writings of José Vasconcelos, the essayist of the revolutionary era who promoted the "constructive miscegenation" of mestizaje based on white-Indian mixing, while anticipating that the "Negro race" would vanish from the Mexican social body. "The inferior types of the species," he wrote, "will be absorbed by the superior type . . . little by little, by voluntary extinction, the ugliest races will make way for the most beautiful" (Banks 2006:219;

Hernández 2004; Stepan 1991:150; Vasconcelos 1924:30). Thus the idea of mestizaje does not just exclude blacks; it erases them from the face of the nation.

Mestizo and indigenist paradigms characterize Mexican scholarly and national traditions. Older scholarship incorporates mestizos into visions of a Mexico quite literally understood as a nation of "mixed-race" Spanish Indians sharing both ancestry and cultural ideas of what it means to be Mexican (e.g., Aguirre Beltrán 1970:14; Phelan 1960:767). Newer scholarship does deconstruct national ideologies in Mexico and elsewhere in Latin America by examining their rhetorics, practices, and symbols, but it also largely addresses the meanings people give to their own positions and identities as "Indians" in nation-states characterized as mestizo (Bonfil Batalla 1990; Dawson 1997; Friedlander 1975; Hill 1991; Knight 1990; LaFaye 1976; Mallon 1992; Muratorio 1993; Royce 1993; Smith 1990; Stutzman 1981; Urban and Sherzer 1991).

Because mestizaje is so prominent in Mexican nationalism, it also enters into the discourse of San Nicoladenses, where its flexibilities and tensions are echoed. Yet the narratives I present here embody a significant twist, for they consistently substitute the mestizo national icon with a moreno one, while retaining the *model* of mixing and the forging through such mixing of a *new* (moreno) *race*. Such a mestizaje "making sense" rests on a quintessentially Latin American racial logic. Indeed, it harks back to the colonial period, when caste categories spawned supposed mixtures and new categories through genealogies of descent.

Of the Saint

The village of San Nicolás Tolentino is named for an Italian saint. On a summer afternoon I encountered for the first time his "authentic" image, a dark-complected statue with a monk's tonsure. It reposes in the Catholic church of the Nahua Indian village of Zitlala, which means "place of the stars" in Nahuatl.[3] Zitlala is located in the heavily Nahua Montaña region of Guerrero, some 300 kilometers north of San Nicolás. The two zones were once connected by goat-herding routes, as discussed in chapter 1. By all accounts the saint is deeply venerated in Zitlala, where his flower- and star-bedecked statue occupies the most prominent position above the main altar of the church, which sits on the hilly town's high central plaza surrounded by panoramic views of fields. A large red heart with the words "San Nicolás

The gabacho saint

Tolentino, Zitlala, Gro." was nailed to the church wall to the left of the statue when I visited. Sánchez Andraka writes of Zitlala that "everyone loves San Nicolás, who is said to perform fabulous miracles. . . . The church is almost never empty" since Indians come from far and wide to worship the saint (1983:47). In 1982, when Zitlala's priest repainted the statue and made it whiter, Zitlala's Indians even protested that he had "no right" to modify the original skin tone and threatened him at gunpoint (Sánchez 1983:48). Morenos believe the saint was born and raised in San Nicolás, yet they fete him in Zitlala without any rancor toward his Indian guardians.

When I arrived one year in September for both the saint's festival and the performance of La América five days later, a new effigy (*bulto, figura*) for the church in San Nicolás had arrived. People had gone to the edge of town to greet it, and I went to the church to have a look. I thought it would be dark-skinned, like the one in Zitlala, but it was blond and white with unfinished eyes. A group of women decorating the church laughed that he looked like a gabacho and needed a bit more work. The saint was supposed to be moreno, said Judit. The new one was "not from here." "People lose their devotion because the statue is not moreno," Doña Leticia said. It had been made by saint makers in Cuaji, whose residents argue with San Nicoladenses about to whom the saint belongs. Even though the new white statue "does not belong," any statue of San Nicolás is said to be stronger than the other saint statues in San Nicolás's church. "The last time there were earthquakes here," Sirina said, "the statue [of San Nicolás] rotated toward the sea, but it didn't fall, while the other statues did."

The saint story raises interesting questions about how morenos understand history, race, and place, for Indians are prominent not only in the narrative of San Nicolás the saint but also in his namesake village's foundation and recent history, and even more broadly in moreno perspectives on the place of Indians and themselves within the Mexican nation. Similar to everyday discourse, historical narratives suggest ongoing tensions between blacks, Indians, *and* mixture. So do stories about the saint. For instance, after I visited San Nicolás's church that September, I went to Angela's for a meal. At the time she was embroiled in the dispute over her granddaughter and connected the moreno saint's presence in Zitlala to Indian munificence: "They call us Indians," she said, "but we're generous—we invite people into our homes and offer them food. Blacks never invite people into their homes." She then repeated what she had said a few years earlier, "We're going to chase them out—we're from here, from Mexico, and they're not." She mentioned someone who had lived close to them, a "black," who had said that "the Indians" should go back to their land.

Angela's bitter characterization of "blacks" contrasts with morenos' appreciation for the way Zitlala's Indians care for the saint. But the moreno-Indian relationship develops on different levels. Thus Angela expressed insecurity about her home in San Nicolás while morenos express their gratitude to Indians for giving one of their own a home elsewhere. Identity formations are therefore layered, while converging around concrete and interpenetrating historical events characterized by spatial and temporal movements that involve both morenos and Indians. These movements include the slave trade, colonialism, the search for arable land, independence from Spanish rule, the Mexican Revolution, and migrations—from Indian villages to moreno ones, from a moreno village to an Indian one, from countryside to city, and from Mexico to el norte. Thus, just as bickering and hostility contradict the fact of black Indianness, uprooting and contestation are at the center of the cultural processes through which identities and places are made.

On Freedom and Its Contradictions

Sometimes resident Indians use snippets of ship stories to assert their prior claims to the space they share with morenos. In so doing they are really expressing anxiety about their own security and status in San Nicolás. Resentment welled up one day as I sat with a group of Indian women making crepe paper flowers for the wake of Zenaida's nephew. "We're the indigenous ones," Angela burst out. As Esperanza joined the conversation she remarked that "blacks came in ships and aren't Mexicans, but Cubans or Chileans or something." "They're not from here," Angela emphasized. "They're from Cuba, from Africa, from somewhere around there. Before, they were really, really black. You could only see their eyes. They were brought as slaves with chains around their necks," she added. "Now they've been here more than a hundred years. The blacks here are the children of those who escaped." Resident Indians thus tell the ship story in a manner that circumvents their own tenuous connections to the village of San Nicolás, which has existed for centuries but where they have only recently settled. At the same time, they assert their prior claims to *national* space, while "blacks," who arrived "with chains around their necks" from faraway places, are foreigners in that space. By extension, "blacks" do not have prior claims to the village of San Nicolás and cannot kick the Indians out.

In contrast to resident Indians, who emphasize enslavement and the foreign provenance of the ship, morenos emphasize the freedom of the slaves who escaped the ship and the haven they found in Mexico. According to them, the wreck's emancipated human cargo settled and mixed with people who already "owned" this place. These owners were already mixed, but they "accepted [the others] as their raza," Don Domingo said. Indeed, the issue of Mexico's freedom often took on a life of its own whenever the ship story arose. Rosa explained that "a ship sank over there in [Tierra] Colorado, and they say the people were from Africa who married people from here. Who knows?" And she pounded her fists on her knees, "We are free! We are free!" When Manuel and I discussed the shipwreck he insisted that "there were never slaves here. Indeed, there were never slaves in Mexico at all." "Mexico is free," he said over and over, just as Rosa had. When I mentioned that some ancestors might have been slaves, Manuel refused to believe it. "Besides," he added, "Indians fought bravely for freedom, and they won the battle." He mentioned Cuauhtémoc as a brave Indian and, as Ernesto had years before, said that "the Mexican is an Indian." "The authentic Mexican is Indian," Margarita once told me, while Manuel pointed out that the Mexican flag has a nopal—an indigenous food—as well as the Aztec emblem of an eagle and a serpent. He also mentioned Indian images imprinted on paper money and coins, a suggestion that Mexico's "wealth," which morenos have never been able to quite "grasp," already belongs to "clever" Indians, the inheritors of the national patrimony.

When morenos do identify black ancestors as slaves, it is generally in the context of what they know from outsiders. To this end, they almost always preface their comments with the phrase "they say that" (*se dice que*; *dicen que*). It is, of course, likely that most moreno San Nicoladenses do not have recent slave ancestors at all, since most colonial blacks and mulattoes on the coast were, in fact, free, especially by the eighteenth century when none of the witnesses to Doña María's land were described as slaves and when residents of San Nicolás, Cuaji, and Maldonado were identified as mulattoes and (nonslave) tribute payers (see chapter 2). But the lack of information about slavery in Mexico results from the fact that older morenos, like other Mexicans, have not been taught its history and are frequently not literate. Judit's youngest daughter is a member of a generation learning that history. She felt "Afromestizo," she told me, because she learned the history of Africans in Mexico at school in Cuaji. She had also read magazines on the subject and seen exhibits, including the permanent one at the Museum of Afromestizo Cultures, a place older people do not visit. But most San Nicoladenses the age of Judit's daughter are already migrating, leaving the region before they have a chance to learn local history. This history is at any rate not an official Mexican one, for it does not appear in the Mexican textbooks that change with every administration, such that in 2010, the bicentennial of the beginning of Mexican independence, the conquest and colonialism had disappeared from the high school curriculum and peoples of African descent were ignored in the planned celebrations (Godoy 2009).

Moreno refusal to acknowledge slavery is also shaped by an understanding of Mexico as free, and thus incompatible with enslavement. But on closer examination, the ship story proves double-edged. For morenos it might have negative implications insofar as it accents the essential foreignness of blacks and enables Indians to use the notion of their arrival on ships to deny morenos membership in a community that, on the metalevel, includes Mexico itself. The ship that brought blacks originated abroad, making Indians the indigenous ones. This reading recalls a theme prominent in Mexican intellectual thought: that Indians are the key to the Mexican past and therefore to the Mexican character. It also emphasizes the absence of blackness from Mexican national identity. If morenos' ancestors were "foreigners" who came with "chains around their necks," as the Indians insist, it would undermine moreno claims to the physical space of the village, to their ejido, to being costeños, and indeed to being Mexican.

But the characterization of Mexico as free transforms the slaves into humans with roots in a community, roots made possible by a ship. Ships carrying African slaves can therefore also reinforce moreno claims to Mexico as a free people in a free place. Thus morenos tell the ship story in a way that emphasizes how blacks—originally outsiders—were emancipated as soon as they came on shore, crossing what Edward Casey calls the "permeable margin of transition" that makes places (1996:43; also Munn 1996:449–50). Here that margin would be the beach (the rocky shoals, sand, the coast), which the erstwhile slaves traversed to find not only a Mexico that, in the way morenos tell it, is always characterized as free but also the heart of their raza, located in San Nicolás itself. "All morenos are from here," Rosa told me. "It doesn't matter where they were born, their raza is here." In this sense, the homeplace comes to stand for the people (also Blu 1996:223), who are free because they are Mexicans.

Kinship and Escape

Morenos extend their ties to Mexico in general, and to their village in particular, by linking themselves genealogically to the saint. They argue that while Cuaji lays claim to the saint, he actually belongs to the village of San Nicolás, after whom he is named. The saint's statue in Cuaji, Don Efigenio told me, "is white. It's Saint Nicholas the Penitent." It is significant, however, that San Nicolás Tolentino's most authentic representation found a place among devoted Indians. Angela's comments aside, the saint stories represent an aspect of black Indianness that contrasts with the tension expressed through the different dimensions of the boat stories. Together these narratives frame the ambivalences of the black-Indian relationship and, consequently, the dynamics of belonging that rest on a conflation of blackness and Indianness in the figure of the moreno.

San Nicolás's morenos describe the saint as moreno and "sort of kinky-haired" (*medio cuculuste*). The saint's phenotype is thus tied metonymically to San Nicoladenses. "He's moreno like us," people say. "He's really big, he's moreno, he has kinky hair." They speak of his birth and upbringing in San Nicolás and refer to him as "Papa Nico," an endearing kinship term that uses the informal *papa* as well as a diminutive, Nico. By claiming that the moreno statue belongs to the village of San Nicolás and is the "papa" of morenos, morenos emphasize—through identification with the saint—that they belong to the village of San Nicolás too.[4]

Several stories recount the saint's journey from his natal village to Zitlala (Dehouve 1995; Gutiérrez 1987; Lewis 2001). In all of them, morenos stress Indian adoration of the saint (also Sánchez 1983:47–48). Zitlala is located on what was once the royal road and commercial route from Puebla to Acapulco. It was called San Nicolás Zitlala at least from the mid-seventeenth century through the late eighteenth century (AGN Bienes de Comunidad 6. 30; AGN Indios 102.1; 30.393; 30.472; AGN Tierras 32. 21). It appears to have received San Nicolás Tolentino as its patron saint from the Augustinian order in the early seventeenth century (Dehouve 1994, 1995; Gutiérrez 1987; Sánchez 1983:45–48), and indeed the church was probably built around 1624. The saint was likely brought to the coast by Indians and/or Augustinians from the Montaña region sometime during the late eighteenth century, and San Nicolás Tolentino was feted in Cuaji by 1782, if not earlier (AGN Criminal 457.2–3). Given the close relationship between Cuaji and San Nicolás, it is likely that either the saint was feted in San Nicolás by this time as well or that San Nicoladenses attended his festival in Cuaji.

According to Danielle Dehouve, a mid-eighteenth-century version of the story of San Nicolás recounts how mulattoes from the Los Cortijos hacienda solicited a statue of San Nicolás from an Augustinian friar living in Puebla, who was said to be an excellent sculptor. As they were carting the finished statue back to the coast, the mulattoes stopped for the night in Zitlala. The following day they found themselves unable to continue their journey because the crate containing the saint had become so heavy that no human force could lift it. When a Mass failed to make the statue portable, the mulattoes decided to donate the statue to Zitlala, while promising to visit it yearly. A priest was then able to lift the crate with one hand (Dehouve 1995:119–21).

A modern variant of this story, told to Dehouve by a middle-aged resident of Zitlala, recounts how a white priest took the statue from the village of San Nicolás for repairs. Although he had planned to return it, the statue willfully planted itself in Zitlala (1995:134). Because Indians represent Mexico, and whites are traitors, the story of the moreno saint choosing to leave his "children" behind to reside in an Indian village resonates with moreno ties to Indians through common descent, and it cements claims to national identity and belonging made through "race" (see also Stutzman 1981:76).

Likewise, versions of the story told in San Nicolás sever the link between Spaniards and the saint, rather than between morenos (or mulattoes) and the saint, as the saint decides to stay in Zitlala in defiance of a Spanish priest. But the morenos of San Nicolás say the priest *stole* the original statue because the village of San Nicolás was just a small hamlet and "unworthy" of such a miraculous saint.[5] Everyone sent me to the elderly and bed-ridden Don Adalberto for the full story.

Don Adalberto said that "a priest came from elsewhere and took the saint to be fixed. There they were, walking along, and the saint didn't want to continue. He made himself heavy near a small village. One of the people with the priest tried to grab the saint, but the saint didn't want to move. The people from the small village took him and made his temple there." Don Adalberto had once gone on a pilgrimage to Zitlala himself, and the pilgrims brought a portrait of the saint with them. "My mother-in-law was very small when she saw all this," said his wife, Doña Consuelo, taking over for her infirm husband.

> It was a Spanish priest. He said that San Nicolás [the village] didn't deserve such a miraculous saint. "I'm going to take him," the priest said. But not even they [Spaniards] could carry him from there [Zitlala]. He stayed there. There he wanted to stay. A lot of people love him there. The church is full of older people. The saint is kinky-haired and moreno. They say that he was born here and was a child here. And the child—just playing all the time . . . playing at bullfighting. That's what he did. And his mother would say "come and eat now." But he played and danced all

day. He didn't eat because he was playing all the time. They're not going to bring him here. Those from Cuaji said that San Nicolás Tolentino was from Cuaji. [People from Cuaji] went to Zitlala, but they wouldn't give them the saint because he's from here. People from here went to the saint maker with a stamp to make San Nicolás from here. Someone from Cuaji asked the saint for a huge cornfield and a wife, but the saint didn't do it. The man got angry and they threw him out. People began to cry. . . . No one says anything about the saint living among the Indians. They've taken the bull dance [the *toro de petate*] there. The Indians make a lot of food and are really welcoming. Many from San Nicolás don't want the saint to be there, but people love the saint like they do their girlfriends: First they're all over him and then they don't pay him any attention. People here don't know the whole story of the saint—they talk about him in bits.

The priest "from elsewhere" was probably from Chilapa, the colonial site of the Augustinian bishopric and about two hours' walk (14 km) from Zitlala. According to San Nicolás's morenos, as the priest passed by Zitlala the saint "planted himself" (*se pegó*) there; he "made himself heavy" (*se puso pesado*), "he wanted to stay there" (*allí quiso quedar*), they built his church and the priest could no longer lift him. Don Samuel echoed Don Adalberto and Doña Consuelo when he pointed out that although Cuaji claimed the saint long ago and had even gone as far as to try to bring the statue from Zitlala to Cuaji, those from Zitlala would not allow the town to take it, asking instead for a "seal" and three signatures from San Nicoladenses. As these were never procured, the saint remained in Zitlala. "The one here is a copy," he said, "and so is the one in Cuaji." Doña Ernestina explained that "they say that [people from Cuaji] went to see the saint in his land [Zitlala]. The saint says that they're not my people. They're not from my village; I know those from my village. They say the saint is ours; that he doesn't speak with other people. He made himself heavy because he didn't want to go, and the people from Cuaji couldn't lift him."

As if to plant the saint in her own home, Rosa's sister Beti built a shrine to him in the main room of her two-room cinder-block house. At the center of the shrine is a large photograph of the Zitlala statue, even though no one is supposed to photograph it. But Sirina told me that Beti's husband was a photographer and that they "really revere" the image. During his saint's day,

The photograph of the authentic statue

the photograph moves from house to house. Thus, in 2002, the photo was at Doña Leticia's, and dancers paid it homage the whole night. Rosa told me that the year before she had taken it to the church on the saint's day. When she went to retrieve it a week later, "he didn't want to leave; it kept raining and raining." She finally tricked him by getting an umbrella so that he would not realize it was raining. Thus the saint's willfulness is part of his authentic essence, manifest even in the photographic replica.

Sirina added that the saint grew up in San Nicolás and wanted to play all the time, especially with toy bulls, and that his mother could not get him to eat. But she added that one reason he did not return was because a storm destroyed his wattle-and-daub redondo, something San Nicoladenses themselves have also experienced. Thus variations on the saint's characteristics and personal history are prisms through which morenos understand their own.

San Nicolás's morenos told me over and over that "the [Indians of Zitlala] really love [the saint]." A kinship idiom thus links morenos directly to place through the saint, their "papa" and their village's namesake, as ethnic identities are constructed through a network of religious worship and spatial organization that connects a black village to an Indian one, where residents care for Papa Nico in such a loving way and welcome morenos when they arrive to celebrate him. Zitlala's devotion and hospitality suggest that blackness is meaningful to Indians just as Indianness is meaningful to morenos. By way of comparison, Colombia's Indian shamans recognize blacks as they go through stages of an initiation process that conjoin, at one point, blackness and freedom from slavery (Whitten and Corr 1999:219). And Mexico's indigenous Chontales incorporate blackness into their dances, as *negritos* (little black ones) are given symbolic permission to retaliate against cruel "Turks," thus acknowledging "Afro-Mexicans as influential compatriots in national struggles" (González 2009:139). These performances show the historical and cultural—and ongoing—amalgamation of blackness and Indianness, which makes it impossible to imagine the black without the Indian, and vice versa. As Norman Whitten and Rachel Corr note, "all culture is interethnic . . . and all ethnicity is intercultural" (1999:216; also Wade 1997).

San Nicolás's morenos refer to Zitlala as a special, almost magical place. The saint has the power to heal and to bestow fertility on land, animals, and people. As Doña Consuelo said, "The saint performs miracles—if I want someone, if I do something wrong, if I have to get well, that I don't die. People ask for a lot of cattle and goats from him." A barren woman is supposed to touch his *pajarito*, the dove that arises from the plate he holds, and also a Mexican slang term for penis. The saint's connections to food, rain, children, growth, barrenness, and starvation cohere around the issue of fertility. Indeed, when I visited Zitlala, its residents were returning to the church with the saint, whom they had just taken out to their fields to pray for rain. Sirina pointed out when I returned that it had indeed rained because of the saint's intervention. She wanted to know whether in Zitlala they could carry the saint. When I replied that they could, we agreed that this was no doubt because the saint wanted to be carried. Although I did not think

Doña Lupe would be impressed by my trip because she is an evangelical, even she broke out in smiles when I told her that I had seen the saint.

Often during the early days of the saint's days-long festival in September, which takes place both in San Nicolás and in Zitlala, those who can will go to Zitlala to perform the *toro de petate*, while Zitlala's Nahuas dance in the streets in flowered skirts and ply visitors with beef and drinks. San Nicolás's dancers and pilgrims visit Zitlala on September 8, returning on September 9 to be in San Nicolás on September 10, the day the saint "returns home." "Their dance is really beautiful," Ernesto and Susana remarked of Zitlala's Indians. Sirina had never been, but she knew that "when people from here are in Zitlala they see a letter saying he's happy that people from his land are there." Zitlala's Indians greet San Nicoladenses warmly, as they together fete the saint who will soon be visiting San Nicolás, "his" village, where the toro de petate is also performed in his name and on his day. San Nicoladenses maintain that when Papa Nico is feted in San Nicolás, the dark-skinned statue leaves Zitlala on his own to return home. During this period the doors to Zitlala's church will not open. "The Indians say they don't know why," Sirina told me. "They say, 'the boss is angry.'"

The toro de petate is a performance that commemorates the saint's life as a ranch child who played with toy bulls. It thus mythologically reinvents village history. The saint's connection to cattle and thus to wealth rooted in colonization, as well as his residence in Zitlala, also recall the association of Indians with wealth in its literal incarnation as bills and coins — more pointedly made in La América — and the Indian association with the patria.

The toro de petate centers on a bull (the toro) made largely from mats woven of natural fibers (*petates*). During the several days of the festival, the bull — given mobility by a young man hiding under the petate — is accompanied by people playing ranch hands, overseers, and the "bosses," the Spaniards "Don Pancho" and his wife "La Minga" (for Mariana Dominga), also referred to as *mojigangas* (masked ones, hypocrites). When I saw the performance Don Pancho wore a silver mask, while La Minga wore a white one with a prominent beauty mark; she (actually a "he") had a large bosom, wide hips, and held a white boy doll.

Cowboys wearing head coverings called *coletas* to represent tails (*colas*) danced in two straight lines while a cloth image of the saint was brought into the church by the festival steward and candles were lit outside. The toro

Minga with her white infant in San Nicolás

de petate followed them and was then put aside, to be hidden in the bush the following day. While the saint was blessed inside the church, outside reigned what would seem like complete chaos to anyone who did not know the sequence of events. An enormous crowd gathered around Pancho and Minga. Pancho wore baggy clothes and a sombrero, and he carried a lasso to tease young women. Sirina told me the women represented calves, but I also suspect their relationship with Pancho recalled the former practice of young men on horseback abducting young women, a Spanish custom taken up by morenos, as Don Domingo had told me. Indeed, as noted, his own cousin was kidnapped and raped by a white lieutenant.

With his lasso, Pancho chased young women and girls, forcing them to dance with him. He made a beeline for me, since I stood out — the only white and the only foreigner there. While I did not learn until later who was playing him, as he was masked, he did know me. Sirina screamed, "She's afraid," as I tried to hide behind her. But given that Sirina is much shorter than I am it was a losing proposition, so I danced, while everyone laughed approvingly. As Pancho frolicked with young women, Minga went about thrusting her baby at them, which further suggested that the crowd was symbolically one of servants, as it was common during the colonial era not only for servants to look after white children but also to be their wet nurses (Katzew 2004:57). As the dancing came to a close, the night ended with a burst of fireworks and the explosion of a wooden castle made by Indian Indian specialists, an explosive, flaming wooden bull, and a procession through town.

Following this "hard" (*fuerte*) or central day of the fiesta, Pancho and Minga went door to door with the cowboys asking for coins to offset expenses. The whole village thus participates to make the festival a success, as it does for other festivals. Later in the afternoon the toro de petate reappeared with "Don Pancho" written in large letters on its rear end. The cowboys from the previous day were now mounted, whipping the toro with *gorros*, or three-pronged whips, which the statue inside the church also held in its hand instead of the usual white dove. Pancho and Minga played the crowd, Minga with a gorro and Pancho with a lasso. At one point Pancho, whom by then I knew was Hilario, asked to talk to me. "You've respected us," he said. As I thanked him and Minga came our way, we assured her that "we didn't do anything," jokingly defusing any jealousy. With the young men running the toro de petate about finally exhausted, the festivities ended with parts of the toro parceled out to onlookers and participants.

Pancho and Minga represent past ranch life. As Don Margarito told Doña Leticia, the dance is about cowboys. But Doña Leticia herself added her insightful symbolic analysis when she told me that "each person has good and bad. The saint became a saint because he removed himself from wickedness by not even eating. But," she added, "in the popular festivals it is recognized that we are all made of flesh and bone [*carne y hueso*]." Thus the saint's sacred dove is replaced by a profane whip. But then the saint too was once flesh and bone, and one of his favorite activities was to play cowboy. Indeed, because La América follows two days later, the cowboy theme extends beyond the saint's festival, as both come to an end with a rodeo. The first rider is *monochato* (a monkey-masked scarecrow), who is always thrown. "He's black," Sirina told me, and then joked that "he must be from Cuba." (Nothing is really off-limits in San Nicolás.)

The prominent themes of cowboys, rodeos, bulls, and ranching in the festivals of San Nicolás, including for Santiago (Saint James) in July, when even young women ride horseback from village to village, supports Arturo Motta's claim that the "culture" of the region is cowboy culture (2006). But while Motta discounts maroonage as significant to the region's history, an argument I believe to be empirically accurate, maroonage—the act of running away and finding freedom—is nevertheless clearly a vital part of San Nicoladenses' self-identification (see also Leland and Berger 1998). Indeed, maroonage is a powerful metaphor—a trope—that roots San Nicoladenses to their "place."

Of Ships and Saints: Blacks, Indians, and Whites

Ships and saints make complex memory statements about community and belonging on different levels. In weaving themes together I tease out further connections to a broader racial politics. Although the moreno-Indian relationship is in many ways ambivalent, such ambivalence finds some resolution not only through the day-to-day behavior described in the previous chapter but also through the juxtaposition of the two stories: ships become narrative vehicles for Indians to alienate blacks from place, and they enter into morenos' own uncertainties about their claims to that place. But the stories also tie morenos to the central symbol of place, their patron saint, because he can be understood to represent a transition from freedom (identified with his place of origin, the village of San Nicolás) to enslavement (represented by the Spaniard who carries him away) to a recapturing of freedom in Indian Zitlala, where he is well cared for and where San Nicoladenses are well received when they visit, performing a dance about ranching that commemorates a history so distinct from that of the Nahua Indian Montaña. That dance honors the saint's life before he was taken away and settled among Indians, a time when whites dominated a region that was populated, if not by slaves, then by cowboys and servants who did whites' bidding, often under duress.

A compelling symbolic connection between an escaped slave and the saint is most obvious in the moreno version of the saint story, when the saint is said to have *defied* the will of the Spanish priest who took him from San Nicolás. Against the priest's wishes, the saint himself made the decision to stay in Zitlala. In the ship stories we also find blacks escaping from whites, in this case slave owners. These slaves-turned-maroons also made their own decisions about where to settle, and some ostensibly chose to mingle with morenos already on the coast. The saint's willfulness (often expressed as weightiness, an inability to be displaced) is one of his defining features. Thus the will of the saint achieves a thematic coherence with the will of the enslaved.

What Orlando Patterson terms the "social death" of the slave is of course marked in part by the negation of the slave's human will—a will recovered in the present case when some ancestors of these morenos, who today celebrate the saint in an Indian village, made their escape from the wrecked slave ship. Social death also signifies a state of kinlessness. When the escaped slaves found San Nicoladenses, they mixed with them and thus became kin. And while the saint lives apart from his real kin—his children or the morenos of San Nicolás—his Indian "kin" still venerate him and treat him with the respect accorded a papa while also welcoming the saint's children, thus establishing a kinship with morenos through the saint.

The saint—who is after all the "boss"—not only decided to stay in Zitlala long ago. He also decides to temporarily leave Zitlala on his feast day, close the doors to the church there, and make his way to the village of San Nicolás. He thus reinforces his willfulness as he travels to receive homage from his real kin, among whom he grew up and who are reenacting his story in his honor. Perhaps most startling of all, on the saint's return from his festival in San Nicolás, when Zitlala's Indians open the doors to the church—"they keep an eye on [the church] to see if he has come," Don Samuel told me—they find the saint's feet covered with sand from the coast, that "margin of transition" between sea and land that the shipwrecked slaves also had to breach to reach freedom in Mexico. Thus the saint resembles a maroon—a slave who breaks free from whites and owns his destiny.

The Independence Day celebrations in San Nicolás glorify Indians as the quintessential Mexicans and the ones who "broke the chains of slavery" in their victorious battles over Spaniards. If Indians are ritually represented as responsible for making Mexico free, as owning Mexico, and even as being Mexico, then by extension they are responsible for making the village of San Nicolás, the place within Mexican territory where maroons found a haven and the place where the moreno saint was born and to which he returns. It is telling in this respect that in addition to venerating La América, who is Indian, morenos claim that the Indian cacica Doña Maria donated land to them. Although this is untrue, it is nevertheless *meaningful* as it indexes another level on which San Nicolás's morenos feel indebted to Indians. Moreover, their territory, which passed from hand to hand from the eighteenth century through the early twentieth, was finally wrested from the white

Miller family—whose son Germán fought until the bitter end—with the help of Indians from the Ayutla region, who are today an integral part of the community and also morenos' kin.

Thus, like escaped slaves and the saint, today's morenos owe debts to the Indian "owners" of Mexico who gave them land and later populated some of it to fend off encroachment by Germán. Zitlala might therefore be understood in a more expansive sense as representing Mexico itself, while the coastal belt is the resting place of escaped, kinless, and willful slaves. Zitlala serves as an iconic reminder of the "Indian who owns Mexico," the wider territory in which the free village of San Nicolás exists and where the saint torn away from his own kin by a Spanish priest chose to settle. The saint story thus entwined with the ship story indexes the importance of Indians to morenos. For Indians are said to have made Mexico "free" and to have given San Nicoladenses their land. Conversely, moreno identification with a place that is said to have offered their ancestors that freedom cannot be understood without reference to the dark-skinned runaway saint who is today deeply venerated in the Indian village of Zitlala, a community that does not bear his name or, perhaps, his raza.

If Indians represent Mexico and morenos are linked genealogically to San Nicolás, then Indian veneration of the saint can be read as an embrace that Mexico (represented by Indians) itself offers to blackness. In the course of this embrace, blackness transforms into a hybrid racial form represented by Indian and moreno claims to San Nicolás the saint, whose beneficence is shared.

The Veneration of the Nation

When morenos mention local customs to interested outsiders, invariably the first is the two-day ritual performance for Independence Day (September 15) called La América or Los Apaches. Thus, when I called San Nicolás in August 2002 to tell people that I was coming in September, everyone mentioned La América, even though I also planned to be there for San Nicolás the saint as well.

In Huehuetán, Los Apaches takes place on October 12, Columbus Day in the United States and Día de la Raza in Mexico. This "Day of the Race" actually commemorates the history and contradictions of conquest, which generated not just domination and discrimination but also mixture. While I have not seen Los Apaches in Huehuetán, in San Nicolás La América/

Los Apaches is perhaps the nail in the proverbial coffin as it cements ties between morenos and Indians through the defeat of whites and the consequent birth of the nation.

"Apaches" refers to the Indians made prominent in the performance. "It's a symbol," said Don Guillermo. "It's a fierce Indian. They fought the Spaniards with arrows and did not compromise." Along with blacks, such "wild" Indians, including northern Mexican groups that incorporated Apachean peoples, were excluded from the "Indian as Mexican" construct of the postrevolutionary period (Dawson 1997:20). It is thus telling that in La América the Indians are Apaches and not the sedentary Indians conquered by Spaniards with the help of blacks.[6] And during the unfolding of the performance there are no blacks at all as these brave Indian warriors defeat Spanish conquerors. Instead, San Nicoladenses dress up as Spaniards (*gachupines*, a derogatory colonial term for Spaniards), as a young Indian woman, La América, and as male Apaches. Ultimately the ritual speaks to the centrality of Indianness in the Mexican nation. Together with the ship and saint stories, the symbolic, historical, and political threads help clarify the tapestry of black Indianness, as well as the importance of place-identity processes.

Typically, Mexican conquest plays reenact battles between Spanish conquistadors and Indians. Such plays developed out of the sixteenth-century theatrical performances that missionaries introduced to evangelize Indians as they "taught" them through role-playing how to be Christians by conquering Moors (Trexler 1984). Conquest plays featuring righteous Indian (and sometimes mestizo) protagonists are common throughout Latin America. Indeed, in Pinotepa Nacional, whose population dropped dramatically after the conquest (Tibón 1981:16), Mixtecs enact conquest themes during Carnival through the performance Los Tejorones (the Badly Dressed Men), during which Mixtecs dress in white and black wooden masks made by well-known Mixtec mask-makers. The white-faced men are "Spaniards" (there is also a female "Minga") and the black-faced men are cowboys and henchmen who carry arms.

Such ritual performances are the "yearly renegotiation of the historical basis of modern society" and communicate visions of fundamental aspects of national cultures (Rowe and Schelling 1991:56–57). Rituals are also "large worlds writ small" (Van Young 1994:349), and each incarnation requires a thick description (Van Young 1994:349–51). In other words, context is everything. Nevertheless, in interpreting ritual acts one gains insight into

Minga and a
black cowboy in
Pinotepa Nacional

the systems of meaning and value that constitute a worldview, even if that view or ritual is "open-ended, frayed, indeterminate" (Van Young 1994:349), as every human action is. Indeed, when someone fainted during La América in 2002 it came as little surprise to San Nicoladenses. Although unscripted, it had happened before, and it was part of the consequences of community bonding and worship through ritual acts. Accidents do not happen during every ritual event, and for each enactment people make their own costumes and individual decisions. But there are also templates, rules, and sometimes even texts to follow.

Conquest plays are found throughout Guerrero. Huehuetecans perform La Conquista (The Conquest) for San Juan Bautista's saint's day on June 24, part of which I saw in 1992. They dress as Moctezuma and as Spaniards, following a book of instructions and scripts, handwritten by a schoolteacher decades ago and passed down through the years. While contemporary conquest plays such as this one typically reenact the *defeat* of Indians by Spaniards, they also speak to a variety of historical ideas and therefore need to be positioned within specific worldviews. In this vein, Max Harris, following James Scott, notes that the conquest plays he studied, which were staged by Indians, often had "hidden transcripts" as Moctezuma triumphed or was resurrected, thus subverting the defeat of Aztecs at the hands of Spaniards (1997:106–34).

In San Nicolás, La América follows the template of a conquest play, but it is really about reconquest (independence) as Indians take territory *back* from Spaniards, thereby freeing the Mexican nation from its captors. On the surface the play seems straightforward: Indians defeat Spaniards and Mexico becomes an independent nation. But it also contains a hidden transcript as morenos align with the Indian victors and thus work themselves into a nation that has historically excluded them. It is *whites* who are now written out of the nation as black Indians take its center. Rather than highlighting the tensions between marginalized peoples and a conflated nation-state (Cohen 1994:150), La América assimilates blackness to Indianness as it effects a split between the nation, feminized and black Indian, and the state, which is masculinized and white. Thus the state and the nation are raced, gendered, and split apart.

La América begins every year on the morning of September 15. Here I describe the version I saw in 2002, which I compared with a videotape of a performance several years earlier. Most of the ritual process was the same, with minor differences in elaborate costumes over which women labor for days. It might appear difficult to have been in all the places I mention, but San Nicolás is not that big and I spent a lot of time racing madly about, sometimes in a local taxi, to get the fullest possible sense of community involvement.

San Nicoladenses began to gather at about 9:00 A.M. in the central plaza around the town hall, which was draped in patriotic bunting: the green, red, and white of the Mexican flag. Up front women and children sat at a long table, while men stood around the sides and at the back. Two floats—so high that they brushed against electric cables—soon arrived on the backs of pickup trucks. One was for La América; the other for La Reina, the Spanish queen derisively referred to as *la gachupina*. Unlike the ritual's Indians, the queen and her male *gachupín* protectors faded into the background as the ritual progressed.

The Apache warrior

Like the town hall, La América's float was decorated in the colors of the Mexican flag, while La Reina's was decorated in the red and white of royalty. When the floats arrived in the plaza, the two young women who played La América and La Reina were home putting the finishing touches on their outfits with the help of female friends and relatives. Young men were gathering in the central plaza, dressed as Indian warriors wearing small feathered headdresses and red tunics sewn at intervals with coins that clinked when they danced. The coins again associate Indians with wealth; they also reference the gold and silver Spanish conquistadors chased from the silver mines of Zacatecas in the north to the river gold in the south. These young men were some of Los Apaches, La América's protectors. Her float was painted on one side with a bare-torsoed Apache warrior, crouching on one knee with his face raised toward the sky, a bandana around his forehead, decked out in gold bracelets and an earring as he shot an arrow toward freedom.

La América on her float

Los Apaches first accompanied La Reina on her float from her house to the center of town. Once they arrived, they switched to La América's float to pick her up. With her float decorated in the same patriotic colors as her elaborate gown, she was accompanied to the town hall by several Apaches dressed in loincloths and by small boys playing "little Indians" (*inditos*).

When both young women arrived, a civic program arranged by local schoolteachers (mostly outsiders) ensued with schoolchildren reciting poetry, singing mariachi songs dressed in ranchero outfits, and performing the Mexican hat dance. These cultural forms are not local, but they symbolically incorporate morenos into Mexico because they are emblematic of Mexican national tradition. A more pointed and local moment that folded San Nicolás more securely into the nation came when several older women recited the verse "I love San Nicolás, my country" (*amo a* San Nicolás, *mi país*). With these words, Mexico and the village of San Nicolás became one.

La América then descended from her float in front of the town hall while the mayor recalled how "Mexicans" and *criollos*, here a reference to Mexican-born natives, including morenos, defeated Spaniards during the independence wars, with Indians leading the way. As the mayor finished speaking, whooping Apaches in red tunics danced with La América to cheers from the surrounding crowd as La Reina descended from her own float to be crowned. But no one paid attention to La Reina as she entered town hall. When the two young women returned to their floats, the Apaches accompanied them on a route that took both through town and back home.

The following morning, uniformed students, including older people — almost all women attending the "open school" (*escuela abierta*) adult literacy program — accompanied La Reina and La América, again on their floats and again around town. With a squadron of drummers preceding her, La Reina threw candy to the crowd, while La América brought up the rear, accompanied by Apaches on foot as the crowd of onlookers built. When the two reached the town hall, La América descended from her float, and she and the Apaches again danced. La América now wore an elaborate feathered headdress with her green, white, and red outfit, which was adorned with a sequined eagle and serpent, Aztec symbols and the central emblem of the Mexican flag. She thus simultaneously became more Indianized (the feathered headdress) and more nationalized (the colors and emblem of the Mexican flag). The Apaches' headdress feathers had been replaced with little Mexican flags, thus also symbolically uniting the Mexican nation with Indians.

With bows and blunted arrows, the Apaches prepared to fight the Spaniards, male gachupines amassed in the plaza with shortened hand-launched firecrackers (*cohetes*) representing firearms. Unlike the Indians, the gachupines wore no special clothing. Moreover, La Reina continued to be all but ignored as she waited in the town hall while the real action took place outside. These two features of the performance recall Harris's observation that the hidden transcripts in Latin American conquest plays coincide with the ritual centrality of Indians, indexed by their elaborate clothing and the crowd's focus on them, both of which contrast with the crowd's lack of interest in the Spanish conquerors (Harris 1997).

Throughout the long and hot second day of the festival, Apaches and gachupines engaged in a village-wide mock battle as the gachupines tossed their cohetes in the Apaches' direction while the Apaches, accompanied by and protecting La América, took shots with their arrows at the gachupines. Occasionally someone was injured by a cohete while, as noted, one Apache fainted. But even though there were fewer Apaches than gachupines, the Apaches won, as they always do. They broke into a foot-stomping dance and again headed toward the town hall surrounding La América in a protective circle.

When she entered, community members—already squeezed in and braving the sweltering heat and dust swirling from the unpaved roads—broke into cheers of "Viva Mexico." La América took a seat on a red, white, and green platform, where she and her cohorts were surrounded by Mexican flags large and small. Next to her waited a crowned La Reina, who now held a scepter. La América lifted a large Mexican flag, which she waved back and forth while the crowd sang the national anthem. She then gave a speech praising the heroes of independence—whose pictures graced the wall behind her—as well as the people of San Nicolás, thus once again identifying the village and its people with the birth of the nation.

The town hall ceiling was now draped with green, white, and red crepe paper chains. The denouement came when La América took her bow and pulled these "chains of slavery" down as the crown was removed from the Spanish queen's head and the Apaches literally "whooped" it up. When I asked Don Domingo why Indians "break the chains of slavery," he responded rather matter-of-factly that "Indians fought and blacks did not."

Race, Gender, and the Nation

La América is symbolically rich on multiple levels. First, removing the chains of slavery indicates that Mexico is free, a theme replicated in the ship narratives in which escaped slaves find their way to a free Mexico, and in the saint narrative in which the saint decides where he will live. Second, such removal confirms that Mexico "belongs" to Indians, who break the chains of slavery after they triumph over Spaniards to free their nation, a theme again repeated in the stories of the saint, who frees himself from a Spaniard and plants himself in an Indian community, and in the ship stories, as slaves escape bondage to join morenos already mixed with Indians on land allegedly bequeathed by an Indian. Third, and on a deeper level, the performance of La América solidly joins morenos to the Indians with whom they identify as the victors and, in many ways, as cleverer than they are themselves. Finally, the performance cements the village of San Nicolás and its residents to Mexico, as San Nicolás's morenos speak to their Indian "roots" and, through Indians, to their own national belonging.

San Nicoladenses typically describe the Mexican government as white and as an institution that withholds help from moreno and Indian farmers. In Spanish, *government* is a masculine noun (*el gobierno*), and political institutions in Mexico are dominated by white men. One could thus argue that during the ritual not just whiteness but whiteness embodied by the masculinized Mexican state is "banished" (Cohen 1994:150). In contrast, the nation, as indicated by the feminine noun (*la nación*) and the personage of La América, is female. Her ritual dress is the most elaborate, all eyes are on her, she is protected by the Apache victors of the street battle, she takes possession of the Mexican flag, and she symbolizes, by breaking the paper chains that symbolize slavery, the birth of a nation rescued from a Spanish government. In this interpretation the nation is female, Indian, and loved, while the state is male, white, and despised.

This vanquishing of whiteness speaks to the amalgamation of black Indianness, which also threads its way through people's genealogies, the stories of the Indian cacica Doña Maria, and the peregrinations of the saint and his followers. It additionally points to the historical memories of San Nicolás's morenos, whose ancestors first battled Spanish colonization, then white landowners backed by the government, a current generation facing a government that does not fulfill its promises, and further migrations to el norte, the land of gabachos.

While La América is sartorially Indian, her physicality embodies moreno notions of hybridity, which speak to local conceptions and enactments of mixture. Mestizaje is replicated, but with a twist. For the mixing that validates local experiences and cements local claims includes morenos and Indians but excludes whites, who are the slavers, the estate owners, the priest who dared to steal the moreno saint from its home, and the gachupines defeated at independence. This mixing is not about the mestizo, then. It is about the moreno, who both echoes and challenges traditional mestizaje.

Being moreno or black Indian involves a particular aesthetic as well as a particular understanding of politics, history, and genealogy. La América has to be a young woman with long wavy hair, not straight hair like an Indian's or the kinky hair of someone considered "too" black. Yanaris would never be La América, Sirina told me, because her hair was too kinky and one has to be able to put one's hair in corkscrew curls or waves (*olas*), which even straight-haired Indians cannot do without a perm because their hair will not hold a curl. La Reina has to be light-skinned. Even if no young woman wants to play her, one will if asked, as everyone is obligated to take part in rituals that bind the community together. When I saw the performance, La Reina was the daughter of the light-skinned Tomás and his wife Isabel, who is also light-skinned and originally from Ometepec. That La Reina is ignored while La América is given all the attention suggests again that the preferred aesthetic is moreno. The white statue of San Nicolás that sits in the local church offers a perfect example: "He's not from here." Instead, Papa Nico is.

As Sirina described Papa Nico, she said that he was "moreno, kinky-haired, and large like the Virgin of Guadalupe; she's moreno also, moreno like us." The Virgin of Guadalupe is an Indian-Spanish virgin said to have first appeared soon after the conquest to the converted Indian Juan Diego. San Nicolás the saint is the patron of San Nicoladenses, but the Virgin of Guadalupe is the patron saint of Mexico. She is also one of the most densely symbolic of the syncretic figures that exemplify a mestizo Mexican identity. Like the moreno one, that identity holds important the primordial ties of Indians to a national space (indeed Zefraida's daughter claimed that the virgin was an Indian), but one that whites have had to work at making, while fearing, like blacks, that somehow that space is not rightfully theirs.

That the most prominent Indian in La América is also female duplicates a national ideology that feminizes the nation through the Virgin of Guadalupe, while drawing attention to the importance of gender in ritual contexts (Van Young 1994:349). It also speaks to local genealogies and patterns of intermarriage, as Indian women are more likely to marry moreno men than the other way around, and they therefore might "take over the center of the village" as well as the household. On one level, then, the village belongs to morenos (men), who are embodied by San Nicolás the saint. But on another level the village belongs to Indians (women) whom, after all, La América and the Virgin of Guadalupe embody, and who are the original owners of the Mexican nation in which San Nicolás is situated. La América might also exemplify Doña Maria. Thus interpersonal relations, replicated historically, also map onto the themes of black Indianness and national belonging. Moreover, the ocean from whence enslaved blacks are said to have come, and where the saint journeys on his way to and from Zitlata, is referred to as a "she" even though *el mar* (the ocean) is a masculine noun. "She's called Ana María," Sirina told me. Doña Soccoro repeated this on a completely different occasion. "The sea is a woman; her name is María." Thus the feminized sea is also a fount of freedom.

That blacks as such are not obviously present in a ritual that commemorates freedom in a historically black region of Mexico, indeed the emancipation of blacks after independence is not mentioned at all, raises a number of questions. Their absence recalls Edmund T. Gordon's and Mark Anderson's observation that "black" identity formations in Latin America are not made through "free play" (1999:287). Taking up their point that ethnography is central to understanding such identity formations (Gordon and Anderson 1999:289; see also Yelvington 2006a), we might understand La América not so much as a denial of blackness as a story of resistance to Spanish governance and to whiteness more generally. Such resistance necessarily foregrounds morenoness and maroonage as it unites blacks and Indians against a common enemy, in much the same way as Papa Nico's journey does. Not surprisingly in this regard, Whitten and Corr (1999) note that in Ecuador for white elites the category "moreno" (also black Indian) is the most dangerous of all because it disallows the possibility that whiteness will have any place in "civilizing" blacks or Indians.

Indians symbolically represent the Mexican nation in La América, and morenos are linked genealogically to Papa Nico. Indian veneration of the saint can therefore be interpreted as an embrace that Mexico, represented by Indians, offers to blackness. In the course of this embrace blackness transforms into a hybrid racial form represented by Indian *and* moreno claims to the saint, whose beneficence is shared. For San Nicolás is a moreno, and morenos explain the term with respect to their own "mixed" Indian and black "blood," while Zitlala's Indians venerate a moreno saint. Today in San Nicolás there is no term for someone of black and white ancestry. And there have been no white residents of San Nicolás, except for schoolteachers, anthropologists, and occasional evangelicals and military personnel, since the mid-1950s, when several white traders (*comerciantes*) from Ometepec were murdered. As Don Domingo once told me with a wry smile, "very few whites have come and gone [from here] without problems."

Because there are no African survivals or even blacks in La América, morenos dressed up as Indians stand for Mexicans in a country that, as morenos repeatedly insist, has always been free, but one they know also rejects blackness. Indeed, for San Nicoladenses, even runaway slaves cease to be black once they reach land, where they mix with people already mixed. Unlike Indianness and whiteness, blackness has no symbolic or capital value in Mexico. The ritual therefore continues to efface blackness from the nation. This effacement repeats in coastal discourses centered on blacks' alleged violence and laziness, and, from the perspective of San Nicoladenses, also in culture workers' stress on blacks' differences from other Mexicans because of their Africanness, related in both direct and indirect ways to a heritage culture workers essentialize in "blood," an issue addressed in the following chapters.

Significant, then, is that through a symbolic-cum-biological abridgment with their Indian kin and therefore with the nation, morenos engage a hegemony that has made them different because of their "race." But in the final analysis it seems that this move makes these black Indians more Mexican than anything else, because it replicates national mestizo ideology that also holds Indianness as the key to Mexico's allure. In forging a common history and set of identity issues with Indians, whom the national tradition already romanticizes, morenos thus anchor themselves to the nation as particular kinds of (black Indian) Mexicans (Lewis 2000, 2001).

As they amalgamate blackness and Indianness, however, they at once replicate mestizo ideology and give it a subversive twist: for they exclude from their version of Mexicanness the whites they see as thwarting the upward mobility of nonwhites. Yet while whites have the power to thwart that mobility, they also embody it on television, in films, through urbanization, through material acquisition, and through the wealth represented by el norte. Thus, whites enter San Nicoladenses' consciousness as simultaneous barriers to and bearers of advancement and modernity (also Bashkow 2006).

CHAPTER FOUR

Africa in Mexico   AN INTELLECTUAL HISTORY

This chapter explores "the Africa thesis," as John McDowell (2000:9) terms the ascription of Africanity to coastal belt morenos. I begin by reconstructing an intellectual genealogy that began with Franz Boas's student Melville Herskovits, the first academic to establish African and African American studies at a major university in the United States. As my reconstruction shows, scholars of peoples of African descent in the New World were engaged in transnational dialogue long before the term *transnational* came to describe circular migration. Yet culture workers today almost universally neglect the genealogy of the intellectual paradigms they often unconsciously deploy. As a result, models derived from the earliest dialogues are still current in scholarly evaluations of San Nicoladenses. These models focus on race, impose a Eurocentric model of such, and overlap biological and cultural constructs, so that "black" becomes Afromexican or Afromestizo, while a particular ethos is attributed to peoples of African descent.

Melville Herskovits and the Concept of Survivals

In an essay published in 2006, Kevin Yelvington establishes Herskovits as a "key actor" in initiating cultural and historical knowledge about New World Americans of African descent as

Herskovits's "theoretical positioning came to occupy a central place in . . . anthropological investigations" (2006b:38; see also Price and Price 2003:77–29; Vinson 2006:11). In recent years Herskovits's work with students, his influences on and influences by Latin and African American researchers such as Fernando Ortíz, Jean Price Mars, Arturo Ramos, Arthur Schomburg, Alain Locke, W. E. B. Du Bois, and Lorenzo Dow Turner, and the milieu of the Harlem Renaissance of the 1920s and 1930s—which created an intellectual and cultural climate for the theoretical inscription of black and Afro-centric identities—have become better known (Jackson 1986; Mintz 1990; Price and Price 2003:77; Yelvington 2006b).

As Herskovits's teacher, Boas, of course, deeply influenced his pupil's intellectual development (Jackson 1986; Mintz 1990:x–xi; Yelvington 2006b). Although Boas did not escape the intellectual shackles of his day that reified race, he did separate race from cultural achievement, understanding cultures as unique and equal. This understanding leaves Boas's work characterized by a tension between universalist-assimilationist strategies and the expression of cultural difference. The same tension resurfaces in Herskovits's work (Jackson 1986) because he, like his teacher, linked cultural uniqueness to history and historical transmission.

Early in Herskovits's career he affirmed the "assimilation" of African Americans into "white" culture and insisted on "complete acculturation" (Yelvington 2006b:45), thereby taking a stance perceived as antiracist. Soon he entered into dialogue with the African American intellectual vanguard of the Harlem Renaissance, "a product of the 'talented tenth,' . . . disproportionately made up of the multiracial elite" (Daniel 2006:112). In the political climate of the day this vanguard could not acknowledge its own multiracial background and therefore confronted something of a paradox: On the one hand, it formed part of a select group, mostly from the urban northeastern United States, that operated within a "European American sociocultural tradition" (Daniel 2006:114). On the other hand, it wished to reconnect with a more distant blackness in the rural South (Baker 1998:161–62) and in northern inner cities to develop a "distinctive cultural tradition with roots in the African past and in Afro-American folklore" (Jackson 1986:101; see also Yelvington 2006b:45–49). In the context of Jim Crow laws and the increasingly constricting rule of hypodescent, which prevailed over an earlier and more "liberal" definition of race that allowed for degrees of admixture, African American intellectuals "became" black (Daniel 2006:115–16). Influenced particularly by the Afro–Puerto Rican Schomburg and the African American Locke, Herskovits modified his initial position, developing in its place a typology of intensities of so-called Africanisms. This typology allowed him to resolve tensions in his work by arguing simultaneously for assimilation (African Americans) and for the retention of African survivals (the Saramaka Maroons) (see also Price and Price 2003; Yelvington 2006b:66–67).

The most intense Africanisms were African cultural forms transmitted intact across time and space. These included attitudes toward the dead; plural marriage; flexible religious worldviews; and types of music and dance (Herskovits 1990:63–64, 70–72, 75–76). In accentuating the distinctiveness of peoples of African descent, Herskovits, like Boas, attempted to avoid arguments about racial inferiority or superiority by focusing on culturally and historically constituted "behavior patterns" (Jackson 1986:107). Yet in emphasizing ties between New World peoples of African descent and African cultures, Herskovits also risked interpretations of New World peoples as "African," and as therefore inassimilable to the societies of which they were a part.

Herskovits's argument was antiracist insofar as he tried to recuperate cultural heritage for deterritorialized Africans (Mintz 1990:xii–xiii). Denying such a heritage, he argued, infantilized "Negroes," suggested that only the "poorer stock" of Africans (those without "culture") had been brought to the New World, and that "African culture" was "savage" anyway (Herskovits 1990:1–2). But Herskovits's argument also allowed an interpretation in terms of biological inheritance, which fed rather than combated racism (Mintz 1990:xiii). Indeed, even as the social and hard sciences deemed and deem race a social construct rather than a biological fact, what Audrey Smedley calls the "folk belief" of race (2007:19) continues to have a central place in Western knowledge systems.

Herskovits and Gonzalo Aguirre Beltrán

As Herskovits devoted the remainder of his life to identifying a scale for Africanisms in black New World culture (Jackson 1986; Mintz 1990; Price and Price 2003; Yelvington 2006b:48), he became increasingly interested in possible connections between Africans and peoples of African descent in the Americas. Some argue that he created those connections, often spinning them out of thin air or from his own preconceptions. For instance, in Suriname, for which he received his first field funding and where he first tested his hypotheses, he found among the Saramaka Maroons what he considered "a large number of West African words and place names . . . and West African music, folklore, religion, and art" (Jackson 1986:108). As Richard and Sally Price argue, "throughout his stays . . . he was 'seeing Africa,' inducing it and insisting upon it repeatedly . . . instructing the Saramaka of Suriname (so-called Bush Negroes) about the origins of their practices from his first weeks there" (Price and Price 2003:19–20). Herskovits and his wife, Frances, showed and explained to the Saramaka African images from books they had brought along. "They attribute[d] to [Saramaka] canoemen the exclamation '*mfundu*,' which [the Herskovitses] explain means 'deep.' In fact, the Saramaccan word for 'deep,' today as in the eighteenth-century, is *fundu*, from the Portuguese *fundo*, and the 'African' phoneme 'mf' does not exist in Saramaccan" (Price and Price 2003:21–22).

The Prices identify other "convoluted African etymologies" and point out that "Herskovits arrived in Suriname with the firm belief that Bush Negroes would view Africa and things African as the deepest and most authentic aspect of their own culture, representing their most dangerous and powerful domain and the most difficult for the ethnographer to penetrate," an idea that carried over into the 1960s with Thomas J. Price, one of Herskovits's final PhD students (2003:24–32). Throughout the late 1960s and 1970s, the Prices point out, "from Alex Haley's *Roots* and Robert Farris Thompson's *Flash of the Spirit* to the African-names-for-your-new-baby and 100-traditi onal-African-hairstyles booklets at supermarket checkout racks, from Harvard to the streets of Watts, Black was Beautiful and roots were in. There is no doubt that the staying power, within the academy and out, of Herskovits' diasporic vision, and its revitalization over the past several decades, has as much to do with ongoing identity politics as with its originality or truth . . . that [Herskovits] never quite got the Saramaka ethnography right seems in the end not to have mattered much, to him or to anyone else" (2003:87).

Herskovits never carried out fieldwork in Mexico, but the compelling idea that African culture migrated to and stayed in Mexico nevertheless descends directly from him. My main objective in now tracing the connections between Herskovits and Gonzalo Aguirre Beltrán, who conducted the first ethnographic work on the Costa Chica, is not to determine the accuracy of Aguirre Beltrán's conclusions as much as it is to highlight the intellectual influences and traditions formative to his thought—which substantially inspire contemporary studies of morenos (Hoffman 2006a:117)—and to show how Aguirre Beltrán leaned toward both African survivals and a racial model of hypodescent, both due in large part to his interactions with Herskovits.

Herskovits's influence on Aguirre Beltrán is little known. To my knowledge, except for mentions by Odile Hoffman (2006a:111) and Gabriel Moedano (1980:19), no one has explored their relationship, which is central to the direction of Aguirre Beltrán's work, to that of subsequent scholars, and even to some morenos' understandings of their own history. Aguirre Beltrán's principal contribution was the monograph *Cuijla: Esbozo etnográfico de un pueblo negro* (*Cuijla: An Ethnographic Sketch of a Black Village*, 1985), written after he spent six weeks in Cuaji. *Cuijla*, an antiquated term for Cuaji,[1] focuses on that place but also on San Nicolás and other municipal towns. As the first and still the only full-length monograph about Mexicans of African descent from the Guerrero coast, the book and the models Aguirre Beltrán outlines in this and other writings unsurprisingly influenced subsequent culture workers and interpretations of local identities. Because it shaped the way culture workers approach San Nicolás, and therefore identity formations within the town, *Cuijla* remains relevant to any ethnography of contemporary San Nicolás and constitutes the starting point for understanding the trajectory of thought that produced various iterations of culture work and social movements on the Costa Chica. It is also critical to identifying why San Nicoladenses understand being African in the ways that they have expressed to me. Their knowledge is not based on direct readings of *Cuijla*, but rather on widespread and superficial local knowledge of the book's themes. Among those with whom I spoke, only Don Gregorio had read the book. And as he told me twice with much insistence, "Aguirre took information there in Cuaji from the rich—the rich people of Cuaji. And they give it in their way. Not in the sense of the people. One day," he told me, "morenos will write their own history."

Most scholars describe Aguirre Beltrán (1908–96), raised in the Gulf state of Veracruz, as an ethnographer. Yet his formal training was in surgery, which he practiced before taking up a position as a biologist in the Demography Division of the Ministry of the Interior (Secretaría de Gobernación). There he met Manuel Gamio, the pioneer of Mexican anthropology and an indigenist, who influenced Aguirre Beltrán's future research directions by encouraging him to take up ethnography, and more particularly the study of Mexicans of African descent (Hoffman 2006a:111).

Aguirre Beltrán's participation in the transnational academic dialogue in the Americas that Yelvington and others outline is not widely known. He was, however, at least as immersed in that dialogue as other Latin American scholars. Indeed, perhaps even more so because, on receiving $1,890 from the Rockefeller Foundation in 1944, Aguirre Beltrán came to the United States to study with Herskovits in the field of "Negro Studies" at Northwestern University, several years before Herskovits established African studies there (NUA-HP). During his year-long stay, Aguirre Beltrán worked on his first book, the influential historical study of Mexico's African-descent population, *La población negra de México: Estudio etnohistórico* (*The Black Population of Mexico: An Ethnohistorical Study*), published in 1946. This thorough study of Mexico's blacks and mulattoes during the colonial era demonstrates Aguirre Beltrán's demographic skills.

Throughout Aguirre Beltrán's sojourn in the United States—and throughout the 1940s, long after his return to Mexico—Aguirre Beltrán and Herskovits corresponded. Herskovits wrote in English, which Aguirre Beltrán could read but not speak well, while Aguirre Beltrán wrote in Spanish, which Herskovits could read but not speak well. Many of their letters are personal, concerned with family, health, and similar matters. But most of them focus on publications, conferences, and other aspects of each scholar's work. The letters also make evident the hierarchical nature of their relationship: Herskovits was the teacher while Aguirre Beltrán was the student. Aguirre Beltrán addressed Herskovits as "Esteemed Dr. Herskovits," while Herskovits rejoined with "Beltrán."

The correspondence began toward the end of Aguirre Beltrán's fellowship, during which, in conjunction with his grant activities, he visited universities and scholars throughout the United States with Herskovits's introductions. Aguirre Beltrán's goal, Herskovits wrote to Ira D'A. Reid of Atlanta University, was to gauge the state of the "field of Negro studies and to get to know something of the bibliographic and research problems in that field" in the United States (NUA-HP 1945).

Herskovits also corresponded on Aguirre Beltrán's behalf with Alfonso Caso, the noted Mexican archaeologist and the director of the National Institute of Anthropology and History (INAH), urging Caso to offer Aguirre Beltrán a teaching post in the "African field," in "African ethnology," in the "field of New World Negro Studies," or in ethnohistory (NUA-HP 1945). Caso replied that it would not be possible at that particular moment to offer any position. Thus, when Aguirre Beltrán returned to Mexico, he returned as a demographer.

On that return Aguirre Beltrán and Herskovits began to move forward with the new journal *Afroamerica* for the International Institute of Afroamerican Studies. With articles published in English, Spanish, Portuguese, and French, the journal's editorial board included Herskovits, Ortíz, Price Mars, Ramos, and other Latin American and U.S. scholars. Ortíz and Aguirre Beltrán were part of the institute's executive committee (as director and vice director, respectively), while Herskovits served as a consultant. The journal was published in Mexico, but funding and editorial problems meant that only two volumes came out (*Afroamerica* 1945–46). Herskovits contributed the first article to the first volume, "Problem, Method, and Theory in Afroamerican Studies" (*Afroamerica* 1945), while Aguirre Beltrán contributed the second article to the first volume, "Comercio de esclavos en México por 1542" ("The Mexican Slave Trade by 1542," *Afroamerica* 1945), as well as the final article of the second volume, "Problema, método y teoría en los estudios afroamericanos, según Melville J. Herskovits" ("Problem, Method, and Theory in Afroamerican Studies, According to Melville J. Herskovits," *Afroamerica* 1946).

When the journal failed, a distraught Herskovits brought it up repeatedly in his correspondence with Aguirre Beltrán, at one point scolding him for not publishing in a timely manner and inquiring as to why the Mexican division of the Institute of Afroamerican Studies "has shown so few signs of life" (NUA-HP 1948). One particularly admonishing letter might reflect a tendency toward what Price and Price identify as Herskovits's "intense irritation" in other situations (2003:71), as well as his concerns for his own career. He and other members of the institute were "distressed," he wrote, "that after the auspicious beginning your group made, so little has happened. . . . Certainly, there were half a dozen occasions in the last year when I was tempted to suggest that articles be sent to Afroamerica, articles for which, in all fairness, I had to indicate other sources of publication. I found it sad that the significant paper by Juan Liscano of Caracas, which he wrote me had been sent to Afroamerica, had to be published in Venezuela, where it will be lost, because something happened when he sent it to Afroamerica. I think you will agree with me that this is not a desirable state of affairs and that those of us who are interested in the field must cooperate to do everything we can to remedy it." He was "rather in despair about the whole matter" (NUA-HP April 1948).

Toward the end of the 1940s the Mexican government named Aguirre Beltrán director of Indigenous Affairs. Yet Aguirre Beltrán remained equally interested in the indigenous and Afroamericanist fields, as his work attests. In March 1948, during the presidency of Miguel Alemán, whose father of the same name was a revolutionary general but whose administration was marked by rampant corruption, rapid industrialization, and the neglect of agrarian reform, Aguirre Beltrán attempted to explain to Herskovits the political problems induced by Alemán's conservative government. These problems, which directly affected rural communities, led Aguirre Beltrán to renounce his post. Herskovits seemed to have little understanding of Mexico's political and economic difficulties, writing to Aguirre Beltrán that he had heard "rumors" about the political situation in Mexico and had thought of writing earlier, but that he was sure that when matters resolved he would hear from Aguirre Beltrán.

Now unemployed, Aguirre Beltrán attempted to obtain funds to carry out ethnographic work among Mexico's "mulatto population," but he could not find money to meet his basic needs. He was, in fact, contemplating a return to medicine when he was invited back to the Demography Division of the Ministry of the Interior. Soon thereafter, in December 1948, Aguirre Beltrán arranged a trip to the Costa Chica. He wrote to Herskovits that he was preparing "to begin an ethnographic study of the black population that so many times I have had to postpone. My trip will be an exploration. . . . I will stay for two weeks in Cuajinicuilapa" and later go back. "The work I will do is due to a little bit of help that the Anthropology Institute and the Vikings Fund offered, and my stay in the region will depend on the cost of living there and the permission I receive from the Ministry of the Interior." He also expressed hope that *Afroamerica* would again be published (NUA-HP December 1948).

Herskovits replied with best wishes for "an excellent field trip. We will look forward to hearing of the results, particularly since this is, as far as I know, the first field ethnographic work among the Negroes in Mexico that has ever been attempted." At the same time, Herskovits sent comments on Aguirre Beltrán's book *Medicine and Magic* (*Medicina y magia*), a study focused on the colonial period, which would first be produced in 1955 in folio form by an unknown publisher and then published by the National Indigenous Institute in 1963 (Aguirre Beltrán 1963; NUA-HP December 1948).

African Elements in Cuaji

When Aguirre Beltrán returned from the Costa Chica in January 1949, he wrote Herskovits about "the first results of my fieldwork in the village of Cuajinicuilapa . . . a village with a high percentage of blacks and only four families of mestizos who, in accordance with North American patterns, would surely also be classified as blacks" (NUA-HP January 1949). Early on Aguirre Beltrán was thus at least aware of a U.S. racial system that would classify as "black" four families he identified as "mestizo" (his language is ambiguous).

He told Herskovits that he had gathered a lot of material on economic life, social organization, and religion, and then he immediately set up a typology of cultural patterns. Aguirre Beltrán noted that "the majority [of these patterns] . . . are indigenous, although one could uncover some clearly black [patterns] and others that one would not be able to say if they were black or indigenous." He then asked Herskovits to review his interpretations of his data.

Especially in the published edition of *Cuijla* Aguirre Beltrán elaborated on the themes about which he wrote to Herskovits, but with an emphasis on Africanity. Indeed, even the title of the book does not reflect Aguirre Beltrán's initial interpretation of cultural patterns as majority indigenous. Among *cuijleños* (people from Cuaji) the "African" elements Aguirre Beltrán found included "motor habits, such as straddling a child on the hip or carrying weight on the head" and "the type of house called a redondo, which indigenous groups such as Amuzgos, Mixtecs, and Triques, among others, borrowed [from blacks] . . . in agricultural work, in social organization—particularly in the system of kinship—in the distinct crises of the life cycle, in religion, and even in language, it is also possible to recognize unequivocally *African forms*" (1985:12–13; emphasis added). Although Aguirre Beltrán linked a violent ethos and aggression to maroon resistance to colonial rule (1985:12, 130; 1994:26–27), he also obliquely made such violence another "black" or "African" trait since he established Cuaji as a maroon settlement and its inhabitants as blacks. This alleged ethos of violence can be traced to the colonial period. It is an ascription of which scholars and contemporary morenos on the Costa Chica are acutely aware, and to which some respond (e.g., see Lara 2007:94–97). For Arturo Motta (2006) such an ethos is rooted, first, in Aguirre Beltrán's erroneous claim that Cuaji was a maroon settlement, second, in the need for contemporary urban intellectuals to "find" a political identity unrelated to genetics (in which case "maroon" becomes a euphemism for "black" [Motta 2006:116]), and, third, in some local people's efforts to boost their self-images by symbolically invoking a fierce ancestral past. Although I have complicated the idea of maroonage in the previous chapter, this is not to completely negate Motta's conclusions, but rather to evaluate the theme of maroonage as an asseveration of willfulness and freedom that drew people to Mexico, more than as one of a "fierceness" that makes them "un-Mexican."

In Aguirre Beltrán's letter to Herskovits recounting his fieldwork in Cuaji, he focused on a number of cultural traits, without identifying particular patterns. He claimed to have found "surprising" the issue of bride theft (*casamiento por robo*). But one might read his reaction in itself as surprising since Aguirre Beltrán did not know or did not want to acknowledge that bride theft was common throughout Mexico, as well as in other parts of the world.[2] Indeed, Edward Tylor had first described it in his article "On a Method of Investigating the Development of Institutions, Applied to Laws of Marriage and Descent" (Tylor 1889). Aguirre Beltrán identifies Cuaji's particular form of bride theft as "institutionalized," and he breaks it into seven parts: (1) theft or flight; (2) the return of the bride; (3) the *sacar del parecer*, or gaining consent from the bride's parents; (4) civil marriage; (5) church marriage; (6) the giving of gifts (*el presente*); and (7) the pardon of the bride and groom for fleeing.

Rather than finding something distinctive in the process, his goal appears to have been to link bride theft to an aggressive ethos: "The whole cultural complex [of marriage]," he wrote, shows an "aggressive" tendency related to other "aggressive" local cultural patterns. He then went on to "assume marriage by 'theft' had African origins." "'High society' marriage is by request [*pedida*]," he noted, thereby "conforming to the urban [and by implication "whiter" and more "civilized"] pattern"; on the other hand, "among the 'black population' [*negradita*], marriage is by 'theft,' a local pattern indubitably of African origin, although there are a number of additional elements of indigenous or Western origins" (NUA-HP January 1949).

Although Aguirre Beltrán thus acknowledged bride theft as a syncretic practice, he ultimately dismissed indigenous and Western elements as "marginal" and as not always present, thereby focusing on the supposedly African core of the process. "It is possible," he claimed, "that in the original African pattern the theft and return of the bride were the fundamental traits of the complex and that these are enough for the society to accept this form of marriage as valid. Another fundamental trait, nevertheless, appears as much in the actual African pattern as in the local pattern in Cuaji, which is the payment of compensation to the family of the bride by the family of the groom. This compensation that, among some Bantu tribes is called 'lobola,' is known in Cuaji as the 'gift' [el presente] and . . . is nothing but symbolic compensation for the loss suffered by the family of the bride. Following this payment, both the groom's and the bride's families not only return to their former friendship but it even increases" (NUA-HP January 1949). The consent of the bride's parents in essence "breaks" a hostile marriage pattern in which "aggression has been the primordial characteristic." Here, then, Aguirre Beltrán links aggression and bride wealth to Africanity and to the core of a cultural form, marriage by theft, a theme with which he follows through in the published version of *Cuijla* and in the article "Casamiento del monte" ("Marriage in the Bush") in 1951, most of which recaps a chapter of *Cuijla*.

Although Aguirre Beltrán never indicated which aspect of the marriage complex he deemed "indigenous," he noted that the importance of a "stolen" woman's virginity was "not an original African pattern." Rather, it derived from colonial Christian ideals, "which have persisted in the region with an *unusual vigor* . . . helped by another complex, machismo, which together give regional culture the ethos of violence and aggression that characterize it" (1985:161; emphasis added). It is unclear whether Aguirre Beltrán ascribed machismo to Spanish culture, but he implied that certain elements of that culture amplified a preexisting ethos of violence on the Costa Chica, since such elements had an "unusual vigor" on the coast (1985:161). Thus, in his estimation, costeños adopted and then reinforced aggression, whose origins were elsewhere.

Further inconsistencies appear in Aguirre Beltrán's argument with respect to marriage. First, he attributed the most aggressive attributes of the marriage complex (especially bride theft) to Africa, without any evidence that this might be so; second, in contrast to his letter to Herskovits, in *Cuijla* he claimed that indigenous influences were marginal. Yet even so he failed to pinpoint those influences, while identifying the importance of a bride's virginity—still significant today—as central to a successful marriage by theft, and as Western or Spanish. He also identified what one would construe as Spanish machismo as central to the aggressive character of costeño culture, even though elsewhere in his correspondence and in *Cuijla* he links aggression to Africanity, first through bride theft and second through claims that the persecution of maroons during the colonial period "created an aggressive hostility" still found in the region (1985:60). Given that indigenous people were also persecuted—both by Spaniards and by blacks and mulattoes under Spanish control—one has to wonder why Aguirre Beltrán did not identify a supposed ethos of aggression just as arbitrarily as an indigenous trait.

Aguirre Beltrán's writings about religious beliefs likewise demonstrate the lengths to which he went to tease Africanisms out of local practices. People from Cuaji, he wrote to Herskovits,

> consider the human person to be integrated by four principal elements: 1.—the body; 2.—the soul; 3.—the shadow [*la sombra*] and 4.—the *tono* (as defined below). The soul has its Western connotation. The shadow is something distinct from the soul. It is lost because of "frights" [*sustos*] during sleep, out of fear of death, etc., and should be recovered if the individual [who lost it] is not dead. There are many procedures in place for recovering the shadow, and I discussed them at length with the wise man, that is, with the village healer. This concept appears African for its similarity to the *susuma* (presumably the Gold Coast Ga word for "soul," which also means spirit or shadow). The fourth concept, the tono, is indigenous, more specifically "Zapotec." At birth a child is exposed to a cross in the road where a ferocious animal takes it under its protection, signaling this by licking and stroking [the child]. From this moment on the individual is tied to the "tono animal," which is commonly a wildcat, a bull, a lizard, etc., in such a way that if the animal dies the individual dies, if it is sick the individual is sick. Also, I collected a number of versions of this concept that also appear among the ancient Zapotecs. The problem I have and that I mentioned to you is the similarity that exists between this concept of the "tono" and that of the "bush soul" of Nigeria. Where can I document this last issue?" (NUA-HP January 1949)

Just as with the marriage complex, wherein Aguirre Beltrán linked particular elements to Africa, here he related the shadow to the Ga *susuma* without evidence of a correspondence, especially since the *sombra* is prevalent among indigenous Latin Americans (Signorini 1982). Aguirre Beltrán does the same in *Cuijla*, where he states that "[its] introduction and diffusion in Mexico is owed to the black African" (1985:177). But several pages later he insists that "indigenous peoples . . . share the black concept of the shadow, as among the Amuzgos" (1985:180). In point of fact, concepts similar to "frights" are common throughout the world, and especially prevalent among Latin Americans (indigenous and not) from the Southern Cone to the United States (Rubel 1964). Connections to indigenous complexes, especially to those associated with Nahuas, have been amply documented, including through the use of codices and including during Aguirre Beltrán's lifetime (Signorini 1982).

On the Costa Chica the condition known as *espanto* (fear), essentially the loss of the shadow in a living person, is commonly cured by Indian healers, even today and even among San Nicolás's morenos. The custom of "rousing the shadow" (*levantar la sombra*) after a scare involves ensuring that it returns to its owner. This, too, has indigenous antecedents (Weitlaner 1961). Today in San Nicolás no one sleeps in a dead person's house for eight days because the person's shadow might not be at rest. During the day people pray in the house to placate the shadow. At night they sleep, play music, and cook outside. After eight days they carry a cross to the graveyard and place it on the deceased person's tomb to reunite the shadow with its person. The music played for an adult during these eight days is Mixtec, Manuel explained to me.

In his letter to Herskovits, Aguirre Beltrán first linked the idea of the *tono* to Zapotecs, but then queried whether it might be related to the so-called bush soul of Nigeria. While he did not discuss *nagualismo*, this concept, also indigenous, is similar to *tonalismo*, as he notes in *Cuijla* (1985:187–88), where he also states that Amuzgos use the two terms interchangeably. Nagualismo derives from the ancient Mexica belief in the *nagual*, or one's animal double (see chapter 2), while tonalismo derives from *tonalli*, or the Mexica word for "destiny." Like shadow loss, variations on destiny are pan-Mesoamerican (Foster 1944; Holland 1961; Kaplan 1956; Parsons 1936; Saler 1964). In his correspondence with Herskovits, however, Aguirre Beltrán tried to link both shadow loss and destiny to ancestor worship and respect for elders, both of which he saw as African.

Aguirre Beltrán's attempts to root various practices in the Americas,

Europe, or Africa are full of inconsistencies, lacunae, and leaps of logic. They reveal more about Herskovits's influences than about local culture. One might think that because Aguirre Beltrán was a scholar of indigenous cultures as well as of ones of African descent he would not have been so quick to make spurious connections. Indeed in his later ethnohistorical work *Medicina y magia*, which was already written before *Cuaji* was published, he devotes almost a chapter to nagualismo, destiny, and the shadow, stating that "the [Guinean and Bantu] concept of the shadow loss is so intimately related to the loss of the tonalli that *the transition of the indigenous concept to the black* must have been psychologically very easy. There is no other way of explaining the presence of the concept among the mixed population" (1963:109–10; emphasis added). Here he thus acknowledged that the concept of shadow loss was so widespread that to derive its Mexican variant from Africa proved problematic. He also noted that "the black" adopted it from indigenous people. He probably would have done the same in *Cuijla*, and in his correspondence with Herkovits, had he not been so eager to find Africanisms in Mexico to please his mentor. Indeed, the forcefulness of Herskovits's fame and personality, as well as Aguirre Beltrán's respect for him as a teacher, seems to have led the younger man to relate the core elements of bride theft, bride wealth, and both shadow loss and destiny to Africa.

Any doubts are laid to rest by Herskovits's response, in which he again pushed Aguirre Beltrán by asking whether he had found any "forms of socially sanctioned mating that do not have either church or civil ceremonies," because this would "tie in pretty closely with the pattern elsewhere among New World negroes," although it would mean cutting out the last four of the seven marriage steps Aguirre Beltrán outlined. Reinforcing the "Africanness" of the shadow, Herskovits also wrote that "the ideas of the soul [using what would be a Western concept] are certainly very African though, of course, as you say, the 'tono' has many American Indian elements." He also provided Aguirre Beltrán with some references to the "Bush soul" (NUA-HP February 1949).

In response to Herskovits's query about socially sanctioned mating, Aguirre Beltrán wrote that "in Cuijla there also exist, as there do among other Afroamerican groups, patterns of unions not sanctioned by law or religion, but by the group. A man can have a 'woman' and one or more lovers." In March he hoped to return to Cuijla to "refine his data" with respect to this issue (NUA-HP February 1949).[3]

Clearly the Herskovitsian paradigm encouraged Aguirre Beltrán to identify cultural traits as Africanisms and culture itself as consisting of these traits, which might be "African," "indigenous," or "Western," and possibly operating in amalgamated fashion but conceived as pure retentions from the past. Aguirre Beltrán seemed to ignore the prevalence of some of the beliefs and practices he described, which led him at least to write, if not actually to prove even to himself, that some elements were "specific" to "blacks." He did not appear to realize that bride wealth was a widespread practice in Mexico, in Latin America, and in other parts of the world, as was the sombra in whatever language. He also failed to acknowledge that the custom of a man having a female lover in addition to a legal wife was and is a well-documented Mexican and Latin American practice (Nutini 1967, 1965; Smith 1995). As Don Domingo probably rightly once insisted to me, "the custom of openly having another woman is Spanish." Aguirre Beltrán also presented unions as if they were frozen in time, when in fact during a marriage cycle a man might be monogamous, then take a lover (with whom he might have children), separate from his wife, leave the lover, return to his wife and "legitimate" heirs, and so on. In San Nicolás today this is certainly the case, as I discuss in chapter 6.

In 1954, long after Aguirre Beltrán's fellowship had ended, Herskovits met up with him in Brazil for a folklore conference and for the Thirty-First International Conference of Americanists, mentioning in a letter to Frances both a talk and a film of Aguirre Beltrán's that he had attended (SCRBC-MFHP, Personal Papers, box 67, 1954).[4] He also referred to Aguirre Beltrán as an "old friend" (box 67, 1954). In 1958, in a letter to Frances written from Mexico City, Herskovits referred to himself as "Beltrán's patron" (box 1, 1954), thus reaffirming the hierarchical nature of their relationship. In 1963 Aguirre Beltrán sent a condolence letter from Mexico to Frances when he learned of Herskovits's death (box 54, 1963). Aguirre Beltrán also dedicated the first edition of Cuijla to Herskovits.[5]

A Voice Forgotten

Aguirre Beltrán notes in the prologue to the second edition of La población negra de México that "although publication of this work in 1946 was well received, it did not stimulate among Mexican researchers the desire to follow this interesting line of investigation; therefore, we continue, as in the past, to not account for the black's contribution to the composition of the population, to the economy, and to national culture" (1972:11). In reality, however, shortly after the publication of *Cuijla* another Mexican researcher visited the coast. This was Gutierre Tibón, an Italian immigrant, "anthropologist, philosopher and historian" (Quintana n.d.), a dean of the Colegio de México and a professor at the National Autonomous University of Mexico. Although Tibón produced an interpretation of coastal customs and identities to counter Aguirre Beltrán's by the early 1960s, subsequent researchers always cite *Cuijla*, while Tibón's quite different work remains barely known and is never addressed, even though he was a prolific writer, an avid traveler, and garnered much respect in the Mexican academy. When I brought up his name during a seminar I led at CIESAS in Mexico City in 2005, one of the participants dismissed Tibón with the comment that he was "a Jew."

In the early 1960s Tibón visited Collantes, which prompted him to reflect on a number of Aguirre Beltrán's claims, especially those regarding redondos. In *Cuijla* Aguirre Beltrán had classified redondos as black, African, and even Bantu. "Everything appears to indicate," he wrote, "that such a style of house is a cultural retention of African origins, more specifically, Bantu" (1985:93). Such houses were already being replaced by adobe structures when Aguirre Beltrán spent his brief period in Cuaji, but he did note that Amuzgos, Mixtecs, and Triques also lived in round houses. "In our estimation," he wrote, "this is a cultural loan that Indians took from blacks; but it is also necessary to take into account that the construction of round floors was not unknown in the pre-Columbian era, and that the granaries of many ethnic groups often have a cylindrical form and a conical roof" (1985:93). Yet he also insisted that the construction of redondos as living quarters "follow to the letter African architectural patterns," even though the building materials were local (1985:93). Whether or not they were a cultural loan Indians borrowed from blacks, and whether or not the architectural style was African, redondos quickly became the flash point for those who would debunk any connection to Africa, as well as for those who would underscore such a connection. Indeed, they have become a prominent symbol of the "black" Costa Chica.

When Tibón spotted redondos from the window of the small plane that brought him to the coast, he asked himself somewhat rhetorically, "African cottages on the American Pacific coast?" (1981:39). Noting that round structures were characteristic of the pre-Columbian Cauca Valley of southeastern Colombia, a gold-mining region to which African slaves were imported after 1560 (Wade 2002:4), as well as to indigenous areas of Mexico (such as Teponaxtla near Putla de Guerrero far north of the Oaxacan coast, a region in which blacks and mulattoes never arrived), Tibón questioned the logic of Aguirre Beltrán's argument. "And the round houses of the Mixtecs? Are they pre-Columbian or a cultural loan from the Africans? Some African experts, like Aguirre Beltrán," he continued, "see in the round huts proof of the influence of the black redondo in Mixtec habitations, which adopted the new form, originally from the African continent" (1981:49). In Collantes, however, he pointed out earlier in the text, "there is no *macumba* or voodoo . . . I would have liked—why not confess it—to have come across a zombie on the Mixtec Coast. But if some ancient tradition survives in Collantes it is not African but rather Indoamerican" (1981:41). "To speak of a Mexican Congo," he somewhat harshly concluded, "is a cheap literary device" (1981:49).

Tibón referred to Collantes's population of African descent as moreno in the vernacular, or as an *Afromixtecan* mixture that had taken place throughout centuries of interaction between African-descent people and Mixtecs (1981:48). Asking himself whether the people he saw were "the Congolese in Mexico" (1981:39), Tibón carefully noted phenotypical variation, especially combinations of noses, hair, lips, and skin color, such as in this description of a groom: "Skin as dark as ebony, but with straight hair, a thin and well-drawn nose, delicate lips" (1981:44). "They tell me that there is incompatibility between the blacks and the aborigines of the coast, the Mixtecs," he wrote. But then such was also the case between "blacks and Anglo-Saxons in North America, which does not impede the existence there of more than 10,000,000 mulattoes. The mixture of blood has been equally verified here, in the course of four centuries" (1981:40). The people of Collantes, he went on to write, descended from the "mixtures" of the colonial period.

Tibón approached local culture rather in the manner of a modern ethnographer. Instead of generalizing, typologizing, essentializing, and interviewing supposed specialists, he wrote about himself and his direct observations, which makes his account almost literary. While local people told him that consensual abduction was the norm, he attended a marriage arranged not through abduction but through request. With a clear sense of humor he described in detail the meeting of the couple's two "clans," during which a "comedy of modesty" played out as the bride was insulted by her family while the groom's family members, who did not know the names of the bride or her mother, replied that they did not care that the young woman could not sew, grind corn, or thread a needle. Tibón noted that the custom of disparaging in song the qualities of the bride by her family was also common in the Sierra Mazateca, a mountainous indigenous region in northeastern Oaxaca. Moreover he noted that the burial customs of morenos were almost identical to those of Mixtecs. "I have seen," he wrote, "a dead boy child, dressed like an angel . . . in the graveyard of Jamiltepec [a nearby Mixtec town], and another little angel, dressed equally, with wings and crown, in Collantes" (1981:49).

Drawing on his vast knowledge of Indian Mexico, Tibón claimed that the "Dance of the Devils" (*"Danza de los diablos"*), performed by masked residents of Collantes on the Day of the Dead, was "a loan from the Indians to the blacks of the coast" and resembled a dance in "one of the most isolated indigenous zones in Mexico, the Sierra Mazateca" where, "on the second of November the dancers, who wear odd masks, visit the people, house by house, while they do their ritual dances" (1981:49). Anita González invokes the "Dance of the Devils" as an "exotic and violent archetype of the Afro-Mexican" (2009:136), but it is doubtful that is archetypically Afro-mexican. Morenos, especially from Collantes, do perform the dance, indeed with such forcefulness that Motta (2006) connects it to the "cowboy culture" that permeated and still permeates the coast. But scholars other than Tibón have linked similar dances to many indigenous groups in the Americas, including to Nahuas (*American Indian Quarterly* 1974; Blau 1966; Fortún 1961; Grossberger-Morales 1995). One of Motta's elderly collaborators, who was ninety-two when Motta interviewed him in 2001, placed the "parent source" of the dance in indigenous villages (2006:129–30). Certainly the Day of the Dead, an ancient indigenous custom dedicated to a goddess of the Mexica underworld and now a Mexican national tradition, cannot in any way be construed as an African "survival." Moreover, devils and other evil spirits have, of course, become iconic figures of colonial repression throughout Latin America both among peoples of African descent and among indigenous ones (e.g., Feinberg 2003; Nash 1993; Taussig 1983).

One Drop and Cultural Survivals

From the 1940s until his death in 1996, Aguirre Beltrán produced two key monographs on Mexico's African-descent population (1985, 1972), as well as several essays and essay collections (1951, 1970, 1994). From his perspective, post-independence national statistics, which omitted the caste-based cen-

sus data of the colonial period, reflected a biological disappearance of Mexican blacks and mulattoes, who had, in his words, "blurred into" the process of mestizaje or "race-mixing" that came to characterize the new nation
(1970:12). He also believed, however, that Costa Chican blacks had never
blended into what he identified as "the national society that could offer them
an identity (as Mexican) and a status (citizen)" (1970:22). In *Cuijla* he notes
that while blacks were told by some whites that they were "foreigners" and
from Africa, blacks considered themselves Mexican and, "in their songs
and ballads [*corridos*], they like to affirm their nationality with true pride"
(1985:30). Thus while in some respects Aguirre Beltrán seemed to want to
follow the "integrationist" mestizaje model advocated by José Vasconcelos
(Aguirre Beltrán 1972:277–80; Hernández Cuevas 2004:8), his contention
that black Costa Chican communities had *not* blurred into the process of
mestizaje ultimately exposes an intellectual model that promoted "recovering" the culture of those communities and, by extension, a Mexican heritage
as yet unrecognized. As Marco Polo Hernández writes in homage to Aguirre
Beltrán, "28 years after Aguirre Beltrán's revision, these black enclaves continue to flourish" (2004:8; see also Martínez Montiel 1991:2).

Aguirre Beltrán separated the issue of race from nationalism. In other
words, he failed to see how racial ideologies meshed with national ones,
which is surprising given that Mexican national ideology has been, at least
since the revolutionary period, explicitly based on the idea of the mestizo "cosmic" race. He himself recognized that even in the 1940s blacks
were strongly patriotic with deep-seated Mexican national identities. Yet
instead of acknowledging the intersection and coconstruction of national
and racial ideologies, he based his arguments on the racial thinking of the
day, including on models of hypodescent prevalent in the United States and
Europe. Aguirre Beltrán thus concluded that while Cuaji's local population
was clearly mixed, "it is also apparent that through hybridization the black
factor [is] predominant and that, because of this, the mestizo cuijleño is,
in fact, predominantly black, that is, an Afro-mestizo" (1985:65). Thus even
"mixed" residents of Cuaji were black, the one-drop rule making them so.

The same emphasis on hypodescent emerges in Aguirre Beltrán's letters to Herskovits. As I noted earlier, Aguirre Beltrán concluded that the
"four families of 'mestizos'" would "surely" be classified as "black" in accordance with "North American patterns." We can only guess at what he meant
by patterns, but given contemporary race paradigms—even Boas thought

races existed, although he did not believe they were connected to achievement—we might conclude that "patterns" did not refer to social constructs but rather to biological processes on which popular and many intellectual ideas about race were founded.

From Aguirre Beltrán's point of view it did not matter that blacks thought of themselves as Mexican. In keeping with his emphases on purity, Africanity, and black enclaves, they were to him "unassimilated" and "unnationalized," no matter their self-perceptions and history. Indeed, they retained cohesion and a group identity that set them apart from majority Mexicans, as well as from certain indigenous groups that similarly maintained a distinctiveness (1970:14, 22; 1985:30). Blacks' "isolation" from majority Mexican society, where the mestizo dominated surviving indigenous groups, coupled with their alleged lack of assimilation made it less problematic to study Mexicans of African descent as "living fossils" of the African diaspora.

Aguirre Beltrán's intellectual framework thus entwined the unsubstantiated issue of survivals with the reification of race by insisting on the material fact of mixing and, as a corollary, that some people—such as Mexicans of African descent on the Costa Chica—did not mix (see also Torres and Whitten 1998:24–25). As Aguirre Beltrán carved out Costa Chican blacks as objects of study by severing them from the social (national) body, he therefore also generated their cultural-cum-biological difference through what Arlene Torres and Norman E. Whitten Jr. call the "objectification of 'outsidership'" (1998:24). For as I have demonstrated, in Aguirre Beltrán's view local life displayed an assortment of unmistakably African "cultural elements transmitted by the first blacks to immigrate to Mexico" (Aguirre Beltrán 1985:12).

Although Herskovits's conceptualization of Africanisms constituted an antiracist argument meant to establish the endurance of African cultural traits in the face of the dual onslaughts of slavery and colonialism, many scholars today find the concept of survivals, applied to peoples of African descent or to any other peoples, intellectually indefensible. Although historical connections are a plausible feature of diaspora, Jean Muteba Rahier argues succinctly that the concept of survivals is ultimately "spaceless" because it ignores meaning while favoring formal likeness by "denying any real importance to the socioeconomic histories, political processes, and geographies of the Americas" (1999:xvii). Peter Wade points out that tracing origins and therefore identifying survivals is almost impossible because of similarities in practices and the entanglement of such practices over time, which allows for conflicting interpretations (1997:78).

With respect more specifically to Mexico, Colin Palmer (1976) notes in his influential history of the earliest slave trade that possibly only maroon communities retained aspects of ancestral cultures. Yet even in such communities colonial accommodation prevailed, as I discuss in chapter 2 (see also Carroll 1977; Davidson 1979; Widmer 1990). In addition, Palmer writes that "the vast majority of slaves did not escape but remained with their masters. They embraced aspects of Spanish life both voluntarily and involuntarily" (1976:52–53). He also notes that the "intermixture" of African, Indian, and Spanish cultural elements appeared quickly in Mexico. According to Palmer, although one can discern something of a "slave culture" in religious and folk beliefs, it is not possible to "identify precisely those features of the slaves' folk culture that were African or Indian or Spanish in origin . . . since none of the component parts apparently survived in pure form" (1976:145–46).

For Aguirre Beltrán, just as for many of his contemporaries, the boundaries of race and culture thus blurred such that the biological survival of a people pointed to the survival of cultural elements. Culture was therefore almost literally carried in the blood. In the end his work does precisely what Herskovits wanted to avoid: it links race and culture, turning what are presented as cultural arguments into biological ones.

Aguirre Beltrán's Legacy

In the early 1980s the art historian Robert Farriss Thompson once again addressed Aguirre Beltrán's identification of round houses as African in *Flash of the Spirit: African and Afro-American Art and Philosophy* (1984). Unlike Tibón but like Aguirre Beltrán, Thompson sought to defend a connection between Africa and Mexico through material culture. In one chapter he discusses both Saramakan maroon textiles and Mexican redondos (which he calls "rondavels"). Sally Price (2006) masterfully critiques Thompson's treatment of the textiles. As she writes, Thompson's methods were haphazard and his citations altogether missing. Not only are his traceable sources full of "silent misrepresentations" (2006:96, 98) but his analysis of textiles is weak, for he tends to "assert" connections between textile traditions such that "what begins as an art historian's marveling at visual similarities of color and composition becomes, in recycling, historical fact" (2006:95).

Following Aguirre Beltrán's African emphasis, Thompson's treatment of redondos reveals the logical fallacy based on the sorts of specious claims highlighted by Tibón and Price. Thompson begins by acknowledging that "blacks intermarried with the surviving Native Americans, as reflected in the physical type prevailing on the Costa Chica" (1984:199). Yet he then immediately cites a well-known text of 1591 regarding the Huatulco maroons, "whose African manner of cultivation and architecture," in Thompson's own words, "were noted as early as 1591" (1984:199). This text describes "black runaway slaves" living "*with their houses*, maize cultivation, cotton-growing, and other things, as if they were in Guinea" (Thompson 1984:199; emphasis in original). The original has been cited both by me (2003:31) and by Rolf Widmer (1990:135). But in the first case it is an example of the perceptions of colonial authorities that blacks were living "loosely" (*suelto*) and would revert to a "savage" state if they were not under the supervision of Spaniards, thus "as if they were in Guinea." In the second case it is cited as historical evidence of the Huatulco maroon community discussed in chapter 2, debunked by Motta as a maroon source for the settlement Aguirre Beltrán argued existed in Cuaji.

Although the colonial text does not mention anything about the style of the houses it references, Thompson seizes on the phrase "their houses" to establish the existence of "African survivals" while ignoring the text's references to maize and cotton, indigenous cultigens adopted by blacks and mulattoes. While Thompson qualifies his contention that redondos constituted "African architecture," he nevertheless describes such houses as African-influenced: "The priority of arrival of Wolof and Mande in Mexico and *most likely* the re-creation of their houses there by 1591 is a momentous event in the history of African-influenced architecture in the New World" (1984:200; emphasis added). Thompson then focuses on redondos "still being built by Afro-Mexicans and their Native American neighbors" (1984:200) and compares them to what he considered their African counterparts and origins. He also points to their spatial arrangement "in circular plans, [which] evinces further ties to western Africa . . . the reconstellation of round houses in circular compounds was also the prevailing plan on the Costa Chica for which, evidently, there was no clear Iberian or Native American precedent" (1984:203–4).

Thompson's sparse citations regarding redondos refer to Aguirre Beltrán's work, unpublished papers (e.g., the sources "Eddy," on which he "relies heavily" [1984:294n12]; and "Yecies"), and personal communications with unnamed sources (e.g., 1984:294n16). Some of these unpublished sources are likely the same Yale undergraduates that Thompson relied on for his textile studies (Price 2006:96).

Thompson uses the phrase *most likely* with respect to the African origins of redondos, while noting that Native Americans also build such houses. Of four basic Mande round-house construction techniques, he observes that only the last two, technically the simplest, were practiced in Mexico. These techniques included the plastering of woven wicker walls with wet clay (wattle and daub) and the construction of a ring of posts to support conical thatched roofs. Detailing the differences between Mande and Mexican house types, Thompson suddenly argues that Afromexicans were influenced by Soninke, rather than by Mande, building techniques (1984:201–3). He also links to western Africa in general the spatial organization of Mexican redondos, stating that such organization had no clear "Iberian or Native American precedent," yet he provides no citations to support his claim. In a similar vein, Bobby Vaughn notes that "most of the homes in the [Costa Chica] region were round mud huts, whose roots have been traced back to what is now Ghana and the Ivory Coast," also without supporting his argument.[6]

Accessible to both Thompson and Vaughn (as well as to Aguirre Beltrán) would have been Frederick Starr's *In Indian Mexico* (1908), which includes a clear photograph of a set of redondos with wattle-and-daub walls and thatched conical roofs from the Mixteca Alta, or the Mixtec Highlands, an indigenous region that stretches from Oaxaca to the northeastern part of Guerrero state, and one without morenos. Other Mixteca Alta houses included rectangular-shaped adobe brick ones with thatched roofs (Starr 1908:123). Although Starr's book gives no textual description of the redondos, the set in the photo not only look like those built on the coast; they are shown to be organized as a cluster, with houses spatially set out in an oval pattern (1908:139; chapter 8).

A Mexican newspaper shows a photograph of similar wattle-and-daub houses—one rectangular and one round, both with thatched roofs, in an article about the Spanish version of *Zapotec Civilization* (Marcus and Flannery 2001). The photograph depicts contemporary Zapotec houses, includ-

Mixtec redondos from Starr 1908:139

ing a round one, from the Valley of Oaxaca, an enormous distance from the Costa Chica (*La Jornada* 2001).

Perhaps most intriguing is an archival document of 1583 with a map of the Mar del Sur (AGN Tierras 48.6, 162). The map, from documentation about Indians from villages around Ometepec protesting Mauleón's cattle trampling their fields, names various locales, among them "Huehuetlán" and a small estancia called Coyotepec de Ganado. The location of this Coyotepec, just north of the ocean and to the east of a river that is probably the Santa Catarina, suggests that it was close to where San Nicolás stands today. Of more than passing interest is that each estancia and pueblo is marked with a round thatched structure and that each structure is topped with a cross. While it is not possible to say whether these are churches or houses, since the documentation does not specify and both structures would have had crosses at their apex, as Aguirre Beltrán noted in the 1940s and as San Nicoladenses have told me, they are nevertheless round structures and the only structures represented on the map. This suggests that Indian villages, as well as the small estancias that likely belonged to Mauleón and were populated by black and mulatto cowhands, contained round structures in the late sixteenth century. Given that blacks and mulattoes would have only recently arrived to the coast, the presence of these structures in a complaint brought by Indians regarding protection of their land and on a map drawn by a court official makes the strong case that such structures are indigenous to the region.

It is worth repeating that simply because something *looks like* something else, in this case West African round houses and moreno redondos on the Costa Chica, this does not mean that the two things are related. Indeed, other redondos within Mexico itself—those of the people of the Mixteca Alta, those of the people of the Valley of Oaxaca, those of Ometepec's Indians in the late sixteenth century—also look like the redondos of morenos on the Costa Chica. Given that Zapotecs and Mixtecs inhabited Mexico long before Africans arrived, it seems a stretch to claim that Indians suddenly adopted the ways of peoples of African descent, whom they saw as their oppressors and whose presence did not even extend to the Valley of Oaxaca or to the Mixteca Alta. If blacks and mulattoes adopted maize and cotton cultivation from their Indian neighbors, why not houses made of locally available materials? Why does Thompson ignore the comments of colonial officials about maize and cotton cultivation, while projecting a particular *kind* of house onto the words "their houses"?

Mexican Roots

Rahier argues that "for Herskovits, the cultures of the African diaspora in the Americas were nothing but, in the final analysis, some sort of emigrated African cultures. The obsession of his work for the study and/or discovery of 'africanisms,' 'African retentions' and 'cultural reinterpretations' that allowed Africans to survive in the Americas are well known" (1999:xvi). In his view, there is nothing "American" about Herskovits's African Americans. Indeed, logically for Herskovits, Africanists rather than Americanists should study the diaspora (1999:xvi). It was indeed an Africanist, Luz María Martínez, a Yoruba specialist, who directed the Mexican recovery project Our Third Root from its inception in the late 1980s to its recent demise. The project began soon after the publication of Thompson's work. Under the auspices of the Mexican government's Office of Popular Culture in conjunction with the National Institute for Anthropology and History (INAH) and the history department of the National Autonomous University of Mexico (UNAM), it developed a number of cultural and historical projects (Meza 1993). The recuperation movement focused on Mexicans of African descent, including on the Costa Chica, referred in its name to something not Spanish or Indian, and thus to something not traditionally part of Mexican mestizaje. Its collective character ("Our") is situated in a "past" ("Root") that stretches deep into Mexican soil and is African ("Third"), as opposed to

Indian or Spanish. Martínez long ago characterized the Third Root's goal as the acknowledgment that "the American peoples have an African cultural heritage that is part of national societies and therefore a part of national identity and culture" (1991:2).

As Third Root researchers searched for this cultural heritage, they invented and valorized local traditions as pieces of a past linked to Africa (Lewis 2000; 2004; see also Torres and Whitten 1998), thus equating moreno culture with African survivals and rehabilitating those survivals, such as redondos and sones de artesa (see also Rahier 1999:xv–xxi; Wade 1997:77–78). Such survivals are depicted as isolated and leftover "bits" of a tangible past to which the value of the present adheres, but without reference to local understandings of the past or to the social dynamics of the present (Torres and Whitten 1998:4). Researchers' approaches to morenos typically emphasize the past, fixity, and contributions based on things long-vanished from people's day-to-day lives. To illustrate this I return to the imagery of the artesa and the redondo in the construction of an ethnocultural space in San Nicolás, a space that Ernesto, as I noted in the introduction, referred to as "the African center" of the village because he thought I worked for la cultura. Some San Nicoladenses have indeed learned about Africa and, just as culture workers do, now link Africanness unproblematically to cultural survivals, which then are identified with moreno contributions to national (pluri)culture.

Although Aguirre Beltrán specified southwestern Bantu influences on the Costa Chica, even that constitutes a vast linguistic and cultural category. Culture workers who follow the survivals paradigm broaden it further, mostly positing Africanisms without specificity or any deep knowledge of the continent's history or cultures, thus implying a singular African tradition (Patterson and Kelly 2000:16). By simplifying Aguirre Beltrán's model they also ignore the intricacies of coastal belt history and culture. In turn, and in keeping with the Third Root theme, they make spurious distinctions between African descent and other Mexicans.

Liisa Malkki notes that "roots" is an arborescent, territorializing metaphor related to others such as kinship, homeland, and nation, all of which "suggest that each nation is a grand genealogical tree, rooted in the soil that nourishes it. By implication, it is impossible to be part of more than one tree" (1992:28). Such a tree evokes both "territorial continuity of essence and territorial rootedness" (1992:28). Yet in the case under consideration here, national identity, kinship, and even homeland are forged out of *three* distinct roots. Moreover, as Hilda Lloréns and Rosa E. Carrasquillo note in the Puerto Rican case, although the "national genealogical tree is popularly believed to be composed of three hierarchically ordered and distinct roots that coexist democratically in the making of one organism/nation" (2008:109), blackness in Puerto Rico is still marginalized from the "national body" (2008:110). The ways in which rootedness is organized—as hierarchical, separated, and so on—can thus come to invoke boundaries and segmentation rather than merging and integration. While the Mexican Third Root was meant to validate African culture—to equalize it with respect to the indigenous and Spanish cultures that sustain the idealized Mexican national imaginary, to imagine Mexico as a tree with multiple roots—the use of the "Afro" appellation in *Afromexico* or *Afromestizo* also indicates morenos' displacement or uprootedness (also Malkki 1992:25): not only is their root "third," last, something of an afterthought and distinct from Mexico's other roots; it is also located on another continent.

Rootedness, as Malkki also notes, "involves intimate linkages between people and place" (1992:24), especially insofar as place is often explicitly conceptualized in botanical terms (soil, roots, trees, land) (1992:27–28). Yet the soil in which coastal belt peoples are rooted is not in Africa but in North America. They died for their American territory, soil, trees, animals, land, and roots. Thus the concept of arborescence, at least on a regional scale and from the point of view of San Nicoladenses, is misplaced because it in fact displaces them. The Spanish words *raza* and *raíz* (root) have a common etymology, and for San Nicoladenses, their "roots," genealogies, and "tree" are not in "Africa." They are in San Nicolás.

At the inception of Our Third Root, the Mexican anthropologist Guillermo Bonfil Batalla headed the Office of Popular Culture. His work focused on the non-Western orientation of Mexico's "forgotten" indigenous peoples (1990). Martínez wrote with reference both to Aguirre Beltrán's work on blacks and to Bonfil's work on Indians, "since Aguirre Beltrán opened the path, there has been no black without an Indian nor an Indian without a black, both reside in the Deep Mexico of Bonfil Batalla" (1991:2; see also Meza 1993:9). Although her words could be interpreted as a call to investigate black Indians, the Third Root project specifically targeted Mexicans of African descent, who were construed as constituting a substratum (a root) distinct from that of Indians or Spaniards, thus replicating a model of survivals. Because Mexican national ideology defines the mestizo as an amalgam of Spaniard and Indian, blacks therefore remained separate, even though they, too, participated in the cultural and historical processes from which mestizaje allegedly emerged. Investigating the "Afromexican" caught on so quickly that Martínez told me in 1992, "There are some ten theses being written about Afromestizos." In her opinion, however, "Afromestizo culture does not exist. Anthropologists have an artificial feeling . . . there is no black diaspora in Latin America. There is no cultural identity," she said. Fourteen years later Hoffmann noted that nevertheless "there are almost 1000 titles, and masters and doctoral theses in anthropology multiply" (2006a:114).

In keeping with the root metaphor and the idea of exploring a substratum of Mexican culture, the Third Root project was meant to recognize the African heritage of the American peoples (Martínez Montiel 1991:2), or "vestige[s] of African inheritance" (Manzano 1991:37), and to give "blacks" a voice by exposing the "footprints" of the "African contribution" to Mexican "multiculturalism" (Valencia 1993:14). A footprint suggests something concealed to everyone but the most talented tracker, and Third Root researchers fanned out to find these footprints. Politically, they linked the Third Root project to the then looming Columbian quincentenary (Meza 1993:9), to the history of African American civil rights struggles, to the Brown Power movement, and to African decolonization (Valencia 1993:14; for a critique of this discourse as applied to Brazil, see Daniel 2006).

These points reinforce the transnational and even international exchange of ideas and social protest movements out of what are historically very particular configurations of race and power. They thus make equivalent the experiences of peoples of African descent everywhere in the Americas. As a result, the U.S. civil rights struggle, which overturned de facto and de jure segregation in a country that saw the world in black and white, was transposed onto a country in which racism and discrimination exist against dark-skinned people, as well as against those who are poor, those who are rural, and those who do not speak Spanish; but also onto a country with a history that conceptualized race in a manner both similar to *and* significantly different from the United States. In Mexico, in fact, segregation, intimidation, and even deportation most notoriously and officially targeted the Chinese in the first decades of the twentieth century.

The regional branch of the Third Root project in Guerrero attempted a kind of salvage ethnography meant to "revitalize and revalorize aspects of [local people's] own culture, particularly things on the verge of extinction" (Meza 1993:10). Although Enrique Valencia Valencia noted in the prologue to a collection of coastal belt stories dedicated to Bonfil's memory that the "third root" in Mexico "was quickly absorbed by the process of mestizaje" (1993:13), he also, in a nod to Aguirre Beltrán, observed that "many and diverse traits of Afromestizo culture have survived, principally in the Gulf region—above all in Veracruz—and on the Pacific Coast—above all in Guerrero" (1993:13). Third Root researchers sought to recover Mexico's forgotten African peoples. With *Cuijla* as a guide, the Guerreran project focused on three coastal belt communities: San Nicolás, Maldonado, and Huehuetán. On the Costa Chica, and to a lesser extent in Veracruz, Third Root researchers variously found, echoing Aguirre Beltrán's own thematics, isolation and violence coupled with distinctive "Afromexican" cultural traits, many seen as endangered (see especially Aparicio, Díaz, and García n.d.; Díaz, Aparicio, and García 1993; Díaz and Catalán 1991; Gutiérrez 1988, 1993). Even in the early stages San Nicoladenses were "skeptical and indifferent," one of the researchers noted (Meza 1993:9). As I shall show, such reactions have had implications for subsequent projects, particularly for the Meetings of Black Villages, which began in 1997 and which I discuss in chapter 5.

Reviving Aggression, Blood, and the Marginal

Along with African cultural traits "found" by Third Root researchers such as redondos, sones de artesa, the Dance of the Devils, and women carrying babies on their hips and water on their heads, contemporary scholars revived and linked to morenos the notion of aggression—first propounded by Aguirre Beltrán with reference to a former (and ongoing) runaway slave mentality of resistance to colonial rule (Aguirre Beltrán 1985:130; 1994:26–27).[7] For instance, María de los Angeles Manzano noted that blacks "repressed" their misery during hundreds of years of slavery. They subsequently channeled that misery against each other through violence. "They kill each other," she wrote (1991:116). While Miguel Angel Gutiérrez pointed out that San Nicolás and other "Afromestizo" communities had no higher rates of violence than Indian ones (1997a:106–7)—indeed, land disputes result in violence throughout rural Mexico—he paradoxically also faulted Veronique Flanet (1977) for an insufficient focus on violence,[8] which he considered a "pillar of group identity" reaffirmed by "Afromestizos themselves"

(1988:19). He referred to the "extreme violence" of local Afromestizo communities (1997a:98) and followed Aguirre Beltrán and Manzano in attributing this "ethos" to a maroon mentality that "profoundly marked the character of Afromestizo society" (1988:20). Like Aguirre Beltrán, Gutiérrez also used bride theft as an example of local violence (1997a:101–2; 1997b). Moreover, and again like Aguirre Beltrán, he considered bride theft an "African retention" (1997a:101).

People of African descent elsewhere in Latin America have to create a cultural distinctiveness to be heard. This generally follows an indigenist model resting on primordial ties to land, since indigeneity and land are almost coterminous throughout Latin America and land struggles are found everywhere. That agrarian reform gave community land to Mexican small farmers regardless of ancestry means that land is not the touchstone around which organization can successfully take place. Land disputes still exist in Mexico, as do hacendados, and agricultural support is lacking. But San Nicolás and other coastal belt communities generally have good and sufficient land.

Latin American multicultural movements are often promoted by the state, with which ethnic organizations have to negotiate. These movements match state objectives as they contain within their paradigms a "fragmentation that coincides with a neoliberal vision of the atomization of social, political, and economic life" (Hoffmann and Rodríguez 2007:23). State elites, including indigenous ones, deny racism. But their denial in fact reveals racism, or at least racialization, because it rests on the false acknowledgment that races exist (Anderson 2007; Daniel 2006; Dávila 1997; de la Cadena 2000; de la Torre 2005; Hale 2006; Hooker 2005; Lloréns and Carrasquillo 2008; Rahier 1999, 2008; Wade 2006b). An example of this can be found in Mexico, where "Afro" Mexicans have a place alongside Indian and Spanish ones, their "root" lauded as a cornerstone of a modern, multicultural Mexico, a nation open to all. Despite Valencia's admission of no identifiable "pure" African cultural traits (1993:14), in their multicultural quest, a quest supported by the state, Third Root researchers directly and indirectly index an "African presence" to a cultural heritage essentialized in "blood," "genes," and phenotype. As José del Val asserts in the introduction to Maya Goded's *Tierra negra* (1994), "the black component of the formation of modern Mexicans was immense . . . a torrent of black blood runs through our veins" (n.p.). Thus "change agents," to borrow a term from Jean

Jackson,[9] emphasize differences between morenos and other Mexicans as they conflate culture and biology.

Researchers who videotape and photograph dances, rituals, and "a few" aspects of daily life (Meza 1993:10) have therefore referred to "African culture in America" (Martínez Montiel 1991:2); Mexico's "African roots" and "the African essence and presence across the Mexican Republic" (Chávez 1997:11); a culture of "African origins" (Valencia 1993:13); "Afromestizo for the physical characteristics of the inhabitants" (Martínez Maranto 1991:7); and the "genetic memory of the culture" (Martínez Montiel 1997:9). The introductory comments to an exhibit mounted in 1998, *Soy el negro de la costa* (*I Am the Black of the Coast*) spoke of "underscoring the presence and significance of the African biological and cultural heritage in our country, and its survival today" (Díaz 1998). Elsewhere María Cristina Díaz refers to "today's contemporary African population located on the Costa Chica of Guerrero" (1993:20); while others claim the "phenotypical distinctiveness" of Mexican blacks on the Costa Chica to be "unquestionably African in origin" and that "the endurance and persistence of communities of African peoples in Mexico are . . . characterized by a distinctive culture and by African 'biological remembrances'" (Hamilton and Téllez 1992:6). Quite recently Marco Polo Hernández wrote jarringly and repeatedly of "black genes," "black African genes," and "black African blood" (2004:xviiin3, xviiin5) even as he argued that "José Vasconcelos was unable to conceive that all human groups including those present in Mexico actually are, each and every one, the product of millions of years of evolution of Homo sapiens sapiens" (2004:12).

Researchers have typically elided the complexity and diversity of Africa, the slave trade, and the historical and cultural specificities of local experience. They have also made only the vaguest attempts to trace practices from Africa to Mexico. Thus, under a photograph of a woman carrying a basket of bread on her head, Vaughn writes that "while there are indigenous people throughout Mexico who carry burdens on their heads, there is little doubt that in the Costa Chica, the custom is of African origin."[10] Linguistic peculiarities are said to be "African" (but also common to the Costa Chica and to Guerrero in general); corridos are said to reflect the "oral tradition of Africa" (Martínez Montiel 1997:10; see also Moedano 1997:4), as supposedly does the custom of narrating stories in the evening hours (Gutiérrez 1993:24–25); in other instances story themes themselves are characterized variously as "popular tradition," "popular peasant culture" and "African" (Díaz 1993; Valencia 1993). Interchangeable usages of the terms *African*, *Afromexican*, *Afromestizo*, and *black* add to the confusion, for no attention is paid to what these terms signify, either for the scholars using them or for the local people they ostensibly reference. While some costeños, especially in more urban areas, use these descriptors too (McDowell 2000), McDowell notes that "Afromestizo . . . is an esoteric label with little currency in the African-descendant population. Residents of the coast who are comfortable with this term are typically those who have left the region for study in Mexico City or elsewhere and returned with a nativist political agenda" (2008:6).

Díaz, one of the original Third Root researchers, writes that "the contemporary Afromestizo population on the Costa Chica of Guerrero is a cultural and biological amalgamation of European, African, and indigenous elements—in greater or lesser proportion" (1993:19). While the idea of "proportions" is reminiscent of Aguirre Beltrán's need to typologize, the statement at least pays lip service to the idea that morenos are not "pure Africans." Yet nowhere do researchers explore at length the significance of this "amalgamation." The most in-depth treatment of the relationship between blacks and Indians (conceived of as separate groups) can be found in Flanet (1977), a French anthropologist and not a Third Root researcher at all. Gutiérrez (1987; 1988:23–24) and Díaz (1995:22–23) acknowledge the issue without systematically exploring it. I suspect that it has been neglected because it complicates the idea of black singularity and therefore undermines neoliberal multiculturalism and the ability of culture workers to obtain funding and achieve upward mobility for themselves.

Although the Third Root project began in the 1980s, the language and even structure of culture work have scarcely evolved. In 2007 the First Afromexican Forum took place in José María Morelos, a Oaxacan town on the Costa Chica. Organizers included the Colectivo Cultural Africa (Africa Cultural Collective); México Negro (Black Mexico); and the Museo Regional de las Culturas Afromestizas (Regional Museum of Afromestizo Cultures). I did not attend, but the unidentified author of a newspaper article about the forum used the terms *blacks*, *Afromestizos*, and *Afromexicans* interchangeably. Since ordinary community members generally refer to themselves as morenos (see also Amaral 2005), it is unlikely that many were there. Indeed, the article notes that participants consisted of "more than 100 *rep-*

resentatives of organizations from Veracruz, Guerrero, and Oaxaca" (*La Jornada Guerrero* 2007; emphasis added). Given my experiences with the Meetings of Black Villages that I discuss in the following chapter (see also Motta 2006), I suspect that the organizers were local or even outside intellectuals, who "in their discourses incorporate words such as Afromexican and ethnic group" (Lara 2007:101). Ordinary community members would have been scarcely involved because they do not understand the objectives of such attempts to organize or are not sufficiently consulted. This disconnect prompted the 2001 newspaper headline "Researchers Show That Meetings of Black Villages Have Lost Their Original Roots: Differences Have Arisen among Costa Chican Afromestizos" (*La Jornada El Sur* 2001). And as McDowell recently commented to me, had community members been asked about the name and the content of the Museum of Afromestizo Cultures, more might feel a sense of ownership and visit the museum.

The forum's objectives were political, as the organizers insisted that "the three levels of government [municipal, state, and federal] . . . attend to our demands with respect to education, health, nutrition, living standards, natural resources, the environment, the economy, culture, and rights" (*La Jornada Guerrero* 2007). They also called for national government recognition of "the African presence" in Mexico, while claiming that Poza Verde, the early name of the village of José María Morelos, derived from Cape Verde off the West African coast. A positive outcome of the forum was the *Centro de Documentación Afromestiza* (*The Afromestizo Documentation Center*), an archive of materials held in José María Morelos, Oaxaca.

My critique of the forum does not in any way deny the needs of people on the coastal belt. Certainly small farmers need government and medical attention, just as the history of Mexicans of African descent needs to be recognized, which it is evidently not, even as Mexico celebrates its two hundredth anniversary of independence from Spain. Yet even today, sixty years after *Cuijla*, organizers and researchers (1) use language that does not reflect the ways in which local people see themselves; (2) blithely equate the terms *Afromexican, Afromestizo, African*, and *black*; (3) make demands similar to those of peasants and rural peoples everywhere yet couch them in terms of blacks' ethnic and cultural uniqueness; (4) emphasize African roots and ethnicity as the basis for political and social claims—thus neglecting the centrality of morenoness to local identity formations, conflating black and moreno identities, alienating many of their constituents (see also Amaral

2005), and excluding Indian and mestizo small farmers. The last point is perhaps of particular concern, because it thwarts the political and economic alliances that small farmers might otherwise make. Instead of promoting economic class and occupational solidarity, then, or other regional criteria for collective action, culture workers undermine it.

Although Africanness is intended to be inclusive, insofar as it is construed as a "third" Mexican root, given racialized national and local discourses about the aesthetic, cultural, and character inferiorities of black people, scholarly claims about moreno difference actually contribute to morenos' perceptions of their marginality (also Torres and Whitten 1998:24–25). In other words, from the perspective of San Nicolandenses, the so-called Africa thesis replicates the differences engendered by racism: blacks are not from Mexico, and neither are Africans. Moreover, the rule of hypodescent remains operative, as it was in Aguirre Beltrán's work, wherever blackness is found. Thus Wade writes that the use of terms such as *Afro-Latin* "[obey] a U.S. logic of putting everyone who has some African descent . . . in the same ethnic-racial category" (2006a:107–8). Hoffmann makes a similar point in her review of *Afroméxico* when she writes that "[Bobby Vaughn] adopts, without explanation, the concept of the U.S. 'color line' (a black is someone with a drop of black blood)" while ignoring the "intense interactions between blacks and indigenous people. These interactions are precisely what make impossible the use of these two terms (black and indigenous) in many contexts. . . . Claiming that there exists no mestizaje between both groups is simply absurd" (2006b:177).

Due to the emphasis on blackness as the sole criterion for determining identity and therefore the construction of diasporic connections between morenos on the Costa Chica and peoples of African descent elsewhere, local understandings of research objectives sometimes conflate antiblack racism with the interests of culture workers. Thus, while a few white Mexican researchers, such as Díaz and Gutiérrez, stayed in San Nicolás or visited for long periods, San Nicoladenses say they bickered with each other, while others often take film footage and photographs and then leave "without paying anyone." Wariness about whites who pass through San Nicolás ostensibly to learn about local customs prompted Doña Cecilia to once declare to me with some bitterness that "whites come to take pictures to make fun of us." Because morenos are the objects of both derision and cultural promotion, "making fun" comes to include "making money," because whites often sell the pictures and film footage they take of morenos (Lewis 2004).

Ultimately, the third root model not only extends Aguirre Beltrán's cultural paradigm of the late 1940s; it sets the stage for ignoring a Mexican mestizaje that has always included people of African descent. Researchers continuously emphasize the possibilities of recovering the African "footprint," a tendency that might help explain what Malinali Meza characterized as San Nicoladenses' "skepticism and indifference" when faced with inquiries that disregard their self-definition as morenos and claims to Indianness, as well as Indian claims to belonging in San Nicolás. In the final analysis, the irony is that what outsiders tend to do with blackness—exoticize it, displace it, distance it, focus on it, and turn it into an object of consumption for the curious—has the unintended effect of indeed making blacks like Indians. For even if shared roots should suggest a common kinship and assumed social affinity, in setting blackness apart, culture workers construct a new national identity still located in a romanticized and primitivized history situated in a pre-European past of which only showy vestiges remain (Stutzman 1981:64–65; Wade 1997:ch. 3). This history excludes contemporary morenos much as contemporary Indians have always been excluded, even as their "past" is extolled and preserved for elite consumption (Friedlander 1975). In the end, not only are blacks and Indians thus both exploited; both are also folklorized. We might thus want to understand the "Africanization" of morenos as a further sign of their "Indianization."

CHAPTER FIVE

Culture Work   SO MUCH MONEY

Scholars of other African diaspora populations have worked within the particularities of American histories and experiences, offering stellar examples of the nexus of ethnicity, race, and nation and, more broadly, of what Kevin Yelvington (2006a) calls transnational "dialogue." This is exemplified by J. Lorand Matory (2006), who draws Africans deeply into the picture. Indeed, research on people of African descent in other Latin American contexts displays a remarkable diversity of experience (e.g., Candelario 2007; Daniel and Haddow 2010a, 2010b; Godreau 2002a, 2002b; Goldstein 2003; Gordon and Anderson 1999; Miles and Holland 2006; Pineda 2006; Price 2006; Rahier 1999, 2008; Sheriff 2001; Wade 1995, 2006a; Yelvington 2006a).

Recent Mexicanist and Mexican scholars have also produced meticulous work (e.g., Hoffmann 2006a, 2007; Lara 2007; McDowell 2000; Motta 2006), yet culture workers seem not to engage this scholarship. Indeed, when Andrés Manzano complained in 2007 that he was identified as "white" by the Detroit teachers and accused Father Glyn of using "Anglo-Saxon" racial logic, it appeared that there was new discord among the concerns and thought processes even of Costa Chican intellectuals like Manzano and Father Glyn, such that Manzano—once Cuaji's munici-

pal president—became more like a local community member as he encountered models that conflicted with his personal identity and family history.

Cultural promotion and organizing does not always involve whites. But
it does involve "white" discourses about race. Culture workers thus emphasize morenos' African descent or their blackness, operating with "a terrible
(and terrifying) international *lingua franca*" of U.S. origin, such as the one-
drop rule (Bourdieu and Wacquant 1999:43; Daniel 2003; Hoffmann 2006b;
Wade 2006a). This muffles San Nicoladenses' voices and, in the process,
complicates the moreno-Indian relationship as well as Indian identities.

Because several of the first Third Root researchers (Malinali Meza,
Miguel Angel Gutiérrez, María Cristina Díaz) conducted their work in San
Nicolás, San Nicoladenses were subject to much of the earliest contemporary talk about African roots. In this chapter the intellectual genealogy previously outlined becomes something of a metaethnography, one of interactions among culture workers, including social movement leaders, regular
community members, and me.

Culture workers intend to draw "Afromexicans" into Mexico, but for San
Nicoladenses being Afromexican makes them *different* while inventing and
valorizing the past in ways mostly meaningful to outsiders (Lewis 2000;
Torres and Whitten 1998). Outsiders thus ignore parallels between research
and national interests that might explain the relatively sudden emergence
of "blacks" on the national landscape. As noted, intellectuals such as Clavijero and Vasconcelos never romanticized blacks the way they did Indians.
Instead, they deliberately excluded blackness from their ideal image of a
mestizo nation. Recent attempts to reevaluate morenos as "blacks," "Afro-
mexicans," or "Afromestizos" sometimes follow a template that adheres to
official state multiculturalism, which pays lip service to celebrating rural
people for their customs but does nothing to ameliorate their living conditions. Like Indians, then, Afromexicans become a kind of exotica drawing
outside interest.

Ironically, erasures of the past thus reemerge in a different form: one
that is not, of course, avowedly racist but one that nevertheless effectuates
a newly configured separation of blackness from Mexicanness because it
imputes an identity that local morenos do not claim, thus once again distancing them from the mainstream. "Why should we be 'Afromexicans' if

whites don't call themselves 'Spaniards'?" an exasperated Don Domingo once remarked to me. "[Whites] say they're Mexicans and that we're not from here." "Well," he continued, "they're not from here either." When Ernesto showed me the "African" center of San Nicolás, he emphasized that it was "of the people." But "the people don't support culture workers; what they do doesn't interest them. They don't want it," Don Domingo said. For Rosa, people were not interested "because they just want to get on with their lives."

Because rights to land, and the construal of a special relationship to it, are not the basis for recognition, culture workers emphasize distinctions allegedly founded, as they have been since Aguirre Beltrán's day, on culture and "blood," which often seep into each other. Because of this, thick descriptions of the Costa Chica's peoples of African descent have been sidelined in favor of essentialisms aimed at reinventing blackness as part of a political and antiracist process of minority recognition. As a top-down approach, this ignores the views of community members about who they are and what they see as the major impediments to improving their lives. Some leaders also use social movements as vehicles for their own upward mobility in a context in which culture work is a way of gaining both social and financial capital. As Manzano discovered, such a position can come back to bite.

Peter Wade notes the limited impact that black Colombian ethnic mobilization has had on isolated, nonliterate, poor rural peoples (1995:343). George Reid Andrews makes the point more recently and more generally that not only does such activism only engage social mobility for a few; it also does not speak to its "constituencies": "Throughout Afro-Latin America . . . black activists tended to be either of middle-class background . . . or upwardly mobile individuals who had acquired high school and, in some cases, university educations. Their target constituencies were overwhelmingly poor and working-class. The prejudice and discrimination that middle-class activists felt . . . were much less salient in the lives of lower-class blacks and browns, for whom immediate issues of survival . . . were far more pressing" (2004:189, see also Daniel 2003). This situation seems to hold in the present case, where more urban intellectuals from Cuaji, Chilpancingo, Mexico City, and even the United States attempt to communicate to small farmers what they think those farmers' concerns should be: promoting group cohesion among blacks and fighting antiblack racism.

Folklorization: Turning Blacks into Indians

One way in which such cohesion is promoted is by identifying certain traditions as emblems of identity, in keeping with what is termed "folklorization" with reference to relations between *Indians* and the state in Latin America (Friedlander 1975; Godreau 2002b; Lewis 2000; Rowe and Schelling 1991:58–59; Urban and Sherzer 1991:10–11). Such folklorization adds another dimension to the "Indianization" of "blacks" (Lewis 2000). Supposed traditions such as redondos, music, and even phenotype are touted as part of Mexico's rich and varied heritage—as part of a "menagerie, one of several semi-independent traditions that together make up the whole" (Urban and Scherzer 1991:11; see also Rowe and Schelling 1991:58–59). They create "Afromexico," which is grafted onto the new, multicultural nation, "one in its wholeness and diverse in its plurality" (Martínez Montiel 1991:2). Folklorization typically transforms such traditions through spatial and temporal decontextualization: the redondo and artesa Ernesto showed me were initially set up in a field rather than in town; outsiders arrange performances of artesa music, which usually take place outside of San Nicolás; portable pictures and replicas of redondos replace the real thing; and images of people, such as *La Cuculusta* (*The Kinky-Haired Girl* [pictured]) that Cuaji culture workers produced for the First Traditional Fair in San Nicolás in 1998, which outsiders also organized, insult community members' sensibilities ("She hardly looks like anyone here," Margarita said; while Sirina claimed she appeared to have "corn dough in her teeth").

Redondos were still common in the 1940s when Aguirre Beltrán conducted his fieldwork. Today they surface principally in contexts controlled by outsiders and linked to morenos' difference. Not only was the crumbling replica originally commissioned in the 1980s by anthropologists (Gutiérrez 1993:18) but redondos also featured on the painted backdrop for the First Traditional Fair, which also depicted a short-haired woman with large breasts in a miniskirt parading past palm trees with a bucket of water on her head. They further surfaced on badges made for participants in the first Meeting of Black Communities, discussed below, and on the original design for Cuaji's Museum of Afromestizo Cultures, which included concrete replicas of redondos outside the main museum building. They are also on the cover of a published collection of Afromestizo narratives (Díaz, Aparicio, and García 1993).

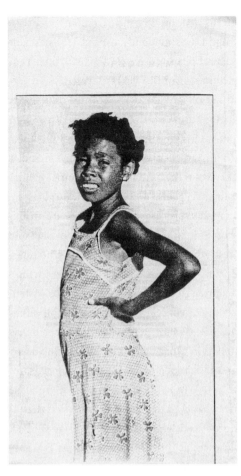

La Cuculusta

Even more than redondos, however, artesa music, which is portable, culturally denser, and usually performed at events featuring San Nicoladenses, signifies difference, while its relationship to regional and even international traditions is neglected. Parts of it might well be African influenced; but ultimately it is syncretic and has transformed over time. Like every cultural practice, it must be contextualized. Indeed, it tells a remarkable tale of the Costa Chica (see Ruíz 2001, 2004), including for San Nicoladenses.

The *artesa* (trough) is a dancing platform (*tarima*) carved from *parota* wood and turned upside down. The term *son* literally means "sound." Thus sones de artesa could be translated as "trough sounds." *Son* dates to sixteenth-century Spain, with its original meaning located somewhere between "noise" and "music" (Stanford 1972:67). Early Cuban son was "based on simple

European-derived harmonic patterns" (Moore 1997:90). Its mounting popularity among the Cuban working classes evidently caused "considerable anxiety among those devoted to European music" (Moore 1997:95). Thus son might be regarded as a form of music for the "less cultivated."

Artesa music is a regional variant of son consisting of "musical, literary and choreographic" components (Stanford 1972:67). It is played throughout the Costa Chica by whites, morenos, and Indians alike, but it is most strongly associated with morenos. In San Nicolás the instruments include a violin, a normal and pan-regional part of the ensemble (Ruíz 2001:63; Stanford 1972:67), a low, rectangular drum (cajón),[1] and a cylindrical ridged instrument called a guacharaca, scraped to produce sound. Violins are prominent in other forms of musical expression in San Nicolás, but the cajón and guacharaca are reserved for artesa music. Miguel Angel Gutiérrez refers to the guacharaca as "Afroamerican" (1993:20). Carlos Ruíz also inclines toward African origins because although it resembles indigenous instruments, he has never encountered any direct reference to an autochthonous Mesoamerican one (2001:61). Yet this type of percussive scraper is found throughout Latin America, as well as in other parts of the world, including in Africa. It has a host of names and is made from different materials, including gourds and wood (Petre 2003). In San Nicolás it is made from the local guarumbo tree (Aparicio, Díaz, and García n.d.). Ernesto said that its name comes from the rasping produced when the tree's bark is rubbed. Its origins, then, are clearly unknown, as the ethnomusicologist Eduardo Llerenas told me.

The artesa, sometimes called a "canoe" (Ruíz 2001:39, 47), likely originated in Oceania and arrived through the port of Acapulco, where it was adopted by coastal fishermen (Ruíz 2001:46). It is inverted and acts as its own instrument as people dance fast-paced chilenas on it. Moisés Ochoa identifies chilenas as the "most Latin American of Mexican dances" (1987:15). Like corridos, they are not particular to San Nicolás, to the Costa Chica, or to morenos, although they are more popular on the Costa Chica than elsewhere in Guerrero and Oaxaca (Guerrero n.d.; McDowell 2008:5). Chilenas originated in seventeenth-century Spain, blended with the Chilean cueca, and arrived in Mexico with Chilean sailors through Acapulco in the early nineteenth century (Ochoa 1987).[2] Ruíz (2004) likens them to Spanish flamenco and to the jarocha music of Veracruz. Mexican coastal fishermen traditionally danced chilenas barefoot on the artesa (Ochoa 1987:135).

An artesa performance

The inverted trough and barefoot dancing are both features of artesa music as performed by San Nicoladenses, although they do not refer to the trough as a canoe. Their trough is unadorned wood carved with a horse's head at one end and the tail at the other, representing ranch history (Ruíz 2004, 2001:42). The dancers' formal costumes, like those of white and Indian dancers, include cotton shirts and trousers for men and embroidered or beaded blouses and full skirts for women. Men and women both carry handkerchiefs in their upraised right hands. Chilenas are courtship dances (Stanford 1998), and because of this artesa music is interspersed with humorous verses laced with sexual themes, improvised by a man and a woman.

In the past artesa music was played for hours at a time at weddings as couples danced chilenas atop the trough. But the late 1990s saw probably the last generation of artesa musicians in San Nicolás, who had been taught to play fifteen years earlier, when Gutiérrez revived the music to inaugurate the local casa de cultura that never functioned. The music's popularity had waned in the 1940s and 1950s with the advent of orchestra or big band music. Colombian *cumbia*, which is popular all over Mexico, electric instruments, rap, and techno imported from North Carolina then replaced orchestra music, including at weddings. In the 1990s and into the early 2000s the musicians played mostly as parts of showcases outside San Nicolás, or within the community at visitors' requests. In both cases performances would last only a few minutes. The musicians generally enjoyed playing for audiences, and San Nicolás, the site of the music's recuperation, was also considered its last bastion. In the early 1990s the filmmaker Rafael Rebollar requested a new artesa to record the music (Ruíz 2001:51). In 1992 the musicians received state funds for instruments. In 1995 they received funds for costumes "because they wanted us to look good when we travel to performances," said Don Samuel.[3] The musicians represented Afromexico to the outside, and they developed roles as local intellectuals exposed to the Africa thesis through interactions with researchers and travel to cultural events, sometimes far from the coast. Thus when they claimed that something was African, as Ernesto did, it was because they had been told that it was (Ruiz Rodríguez 2001:61).

If the music no longer holds local importance it is partly because morenos do not value the past in ways that outsiders do. For one, young people are no longer interested in learning artesa music, in part because so many migrate and because, as elsewhere in the world, new technologies and forms of popular culture attract their attention. Don Domingo grouped blacks with Indians as he expressed confusion over and exasperation with cultural promotion, which obfuscates people's real needs. "Whites are really worried about blacks and Indians losing their customs, but I haven't figured out why," he told me. "Why do they spend so much money on this?" He noted that white business owners from Ometepec who lived in San Nicolás in the 1950s originally liked "the customs of the blacks here in the village. But then they prohibited them because there was too much noise. They were rich; they had influence. The rich gave the orders. All they had to say was 'this noise of these stupid people is useless.' The rich have everything in order—whites prefer order. They want things the way they want them. We were accustomed to doing things our way, so it was better not to do them if we couldn't do them the way we wanted to. Before, there wasn't any schedule and the whites protested. They wanted to go to bed."

The class relationship between morenos and whites has clearly not changed, and neither has white control of local music. First they liked it, then they did not, and then they did again. That whites like it again, however, has not benefited San Nicoladenses. Despite attention to the music, performances often became fraught and efforts to maintain it difficult. The musicians would complain that performing and traveling, while enjoyable, meant that they had to set aside other obligations, such as agricultural work; they were never paid, even when money was promised; and they sometimes had to negotiate coverage of their transportation and food costs. In 2001 they applied for funds from Cuaji's municipal president to replace a battered artesa. When the request was ignored, Don Domingo remarked to me—not for the first time—that while whites amuse themselves with artesa music, it no longer held local importance. In fact, he added, the musicians themselves were losing interest. What money might exist for cultural activities, he said, is "hidden" in Mexico. He then joked that because morenos were not from Mexico anyway, perhaps they should ask another country for funds. In October 2002 that in fact happened: the Eastbay Center for the Performing Arts sponsored a trip to California for the musicians, who participated with other groups in a review of Mexican son. For the first time they were paid for their efforts, and yet this was one of their last significant performances. In 2008 Doña Cata, the oldest member of the group and one of the vocalists, died, as did Don Oscar, another musician. Manuelito, whom Doña Cata had taught to dance and who was a key performer when he was twelve, had gone to el norte.

From the late 1980s through the late 1990s the musicians also clashed with culture workers, who squabbled among themselves and whose genealogies San Nicoladenses rattle off as fluently as their own—first there was so-and-so, then so-and-so, and so on. As an example, in 1996 the musicians were invited to participate in an event at the Smithsonian Institution, which I did not know until I went to the Latin American Studies Association meetings in Guadalajara in 1997, where a Smithsonian official asked me why San Nicoladenses had not shown up the previous year. I did not have an answer. When I returned to San Nicolás and asked, Don Samuel told me that everything had been ready for the trip: the musicians had their visas, passports, and tickets. But Miguel Angel Gutiérrez, who had sent his student Malinali Meza to San Nicolás to organize the musicians, fell out with Meza, apparently because she wanted to accompany the artesa musicians to the Smithsonian event, while Gutiérrez thought it was his place to go. He believed the musicians were taking sides and that Don Domingo, in particular, had betrayed him. Don Domingo responded, "Look, you sent her [Meza] to us, and I just did whatever I was supposed to; I never asked for money; I thought we were friends." In the end no one went. Gutiérrez especially left an impression. People talked about how he drank, went after local women, and embarrassed María Cristina Díaz in public by criticizing her fieldwork. Once I went by Margarita's house to retrieve a plant only to find an elderly woman randomly discussing how "Miguel Angel" had written down all the artesa verses and taken them away.

As traditions long vanished from people's day-to-day lives became folklorized, San Nicoladenses thus grew more cynical about those who professed to act on their behalf. In part this was because cultural promotion did not speak to the community's social and economic concerns. Furthermore, many community members—including the musicians—saw themselves giving away cultural capital. And finally, cultural promotion had traditionally focused on just a few local residents, who other people thought benefited unfairly from outside help. Indeed, other villages financially support those who represent them outside their communities, but San Nicoladenses do not.

Nonmusicians often voiced conflicted feelings. Thus Rosa told me about a white woman who spent two months filming reenactments of traditional dances. She went around with "only one or two people," including Ernesto. She "taped and taped, but never paid anyone a thing," said Rosa, who herself did not much like artesa music and made a face while thumping out the rhythm on a nearby chair. She would not have wanted it at her wedding, she insisted, even though her beloved grandfather was an artesa musician. He "played and played" for outsiders but was never paid or "given anything." He also worked for the "gringo" owner of the mango orchard near Miguel Alemán. When he died, the "gringo didn't even buy him a coffin." Thus Rosa conflated the filmmaker with the orchard owner. Both were outsiders, both were white, and both exploited San Nicoladenses. Rosa also spoke to the "objectification of outsidership" when she linked artesa music to Africa. She remarked that while she had heard it said that "we" are from "Africa or Cuba or something, this hardly interests the people around here." "Anyway," she added emphatically, "we're Mexicans. We don't want to be from Africa," thus excluding from San Nicoladenses' calculations of who they are a place that is meaningless to them as well as to the larger national imaginary.

México Negro, the Meetings of Black Villages, and the Conflation of Culture and Race

A number of Costa Chican organizations address issues within what they call an Afromexican, Afromestizo, or black framework. In some ways Third Root researchers created the context for these organizations simply by bringing attention to coastal belt villages and by giving those who wanted to promote a certain kind of activism a connection to the state. The organization most directly concerned with San Nicolás, generally as part of a constellation of moreno coastal belt communities, has been México Negro, founded in 1997 after the first Meeting of Black Villages. These meetings take place yearly for a number of days, alternating between communities in Oaxaca and in Guerrero. The organizers ignore the term *moreno* while grouping all people of African descent into the same category. Often they use the terms *black, Afromestizo,* and *Afromexican* interchangeably. As Amaral (2005) points out with respect to her fieldwork in Corralero, Oaxaca, the labels "México Negro," and, I would add, "the Meetings of Black Villages," conflict with local labels. Amaral concludes that a "lack of ethnic political organization" is due in great part to contrasting views of race, since Corraleros also self-identify as moreno. I would add that the prefix *Afro* also situates local people in Africa, a continent with which they are largely unfamiliar and with which they do not identify, while mimicking the language of hypodescent and creating a new Mexican "type."

I arrived not long after the Third Root researchers left. My introduction to México Negro occurred at its inception in 1997, when I attended the First Meeting of Black Villages in Ciruelo, Oaxaca, where Father Glyn, the meeting organizer, lives. I subsequently attended the meeting in Cuaji in 1999, during which the state governor inaugurated Cuaji's Museum of Afromestizo Cultures, and the meeting in San Nicolás in 2002. In part I attended meetings and engaged in conversations with organizers and cultural promoters as an anthropological interloper, as I rooted myself in San Nicolás and among San Nicoladenses as best as I could during events that promoted culture or aired social issues, trying to obtain both a bottom-up and a top-down perspective. I lived with San Nicoladenses, but I went to local meetings that San Nicoladenses did not attend. I did not capture everything, of course, but I did pay close attention to San Nicoladenses as we discussed events, and I listened to culture workers complain about local residents. I also occasionally ventured to make suggestions for better communication. I therefore was not *like* a San Nicoladense insofar as I participated and observed, whereas San Nicoladenses generally ignored the proceedings, even when they were held in San Nicolás; but nor was I *like* an activist or organizer, as I never had an official role and always returned to San Nicolás in the evenings.

One of the first things I noticed at the 1997 meeting was the badge depicting a redondo, an early indication to me that this house form had been folklorized through the circulation of images and duplicates. Díaz, who had completed her bachelor's thesis in San Nicolás under the auspices of Our Third Root, served as the meeting secretary. Other outside attendees included foreigners such as the U.S. photographer Ron Wilson, who would later, with his wife, Joyce, and their friend the late Norma Abi Reed, become quite special to me. Participants also included local schoolchildren and teachers such as Sergio Peñalosa from Cuaji. Alejandra Cárdenas, a historian from Chilpancingo, was there, as were three students studying anthropology in Ometepec's college prep school, Catholic lay workers and nuns, and a man introduced as an "African" who I later learned was a Nigerian studying in Mexico City. Father Glyn was present as was Father Florencio Robles, a Mexican priest who lived in Cuaji while serving many local parishes, including San Nicolás.

The political objectives of the meeting were to encourage people to talk about their local communities as *black* communities, with the understanding that they would begin to make connections among communities and, eventually, over the course of the meeting's three days, with other black communities in Mexico and in the Americas more generally. Only by understanding their past, the organizers stressed, could blacks understand how to move forward to demand their rights. I was sympathetic to the organizational objectives, but they failed to cohere because the organizers never took seriously the idea that a "moreno" might be something different from a "black," or that subsistence and migration were, from the perspectives of small farmers, more urgent than the revitalization of traditions, or that Indian customs figure in moreno ones.

As Arturo Motta argues, having also attended several of these meetings, the "past" is reinvented or constructed ad hoc by intellectuals (2006:166). During the first meeting, for example, understanding the past meant appreciating Africa. To this end, the organizers taped a series of posters depicting the "Great Kings of Africa" on a blackboard in an outdoor plaza under a shelter. The Nigerian student discussed African civilizations, mentioning that the Egyptian pyramids built by blacks were much bigger than Mexico's pyramids built by Indians. When Díaz began discussing Mexico's "African heritage," however, he grabbed the microphone to announce that it was "difficult to say if something was African," that "only God knows." Later he told the attendees, "You're not African. You're black Mexicans, living here with all the mixture. Blacks, blacks as I am, there aren't any anymore. But something of the culture, yes, there is and it is necessary to recover what is positive for our identity, in order to be ourselves. This is central to identities battered by racism." Father Florencio, a mestizo, interjected: "We're not African. We're Mexican. All of us together." Yet not everyone was ready to let Africa rest. Peñalosa correctly noted that the Costa Chica and blacks are barely mentioned in school textbooks. He then went on to say, indirectly referencing Aguirre Beltrán, "Redondos come from over there [Africa] and we find round houses everywhere. How did they get to the Mixteca? The influence of blacks."

Almost immediately, then, a continuum of identities, from mixed to black to African, emerged. But the organizers quickly pushed attendees to focus on their differences from other Mexicans. As the conversation got under way, they also immediately distinguished Indians from blacks based on custom. One organizer pointed out that "in indigenous villages there are no brotherhoods [*hermandades*] as there are in black villages." Although such brotherhoods are a Spanish Catholic institution and have been closely related to other kinds of confraternities (*mayordomos* and *cofradías*) since the colonial era (Gruzinski 1990), the point was clearly to head off discussion of similarities between Indian and African-descent Mexicans, as was the comment about who built larger pyramids. To paraphrase Odile Hoffmann, the objective was to promote the "absurd" notion that there was no intermixture.

The organizers then grouped participants loosely by village. Since no one from San Nicolás was present, I randomly joined a group. A series of questions were posed: What are the origins and history of your community? What festivals do you celebrate and how are they organized? How is a black identity lived in your community? How do blacks live with others (Indians and mestizos) among them? Responses to the first question focused on community founders. For instance, someone pointed out that Ciruelo was founded by families from Pinotepa Nacional, who were then joined by residents of nearby coastal belt Oaxacan communities such as La Estancia and Santo Domingo. Later on, however, one participant referred to Pinotepa Nacional as "not completely a black village; there are brothers from there, but properly speaking Pinotepa is not a black community. It's an indigenous one." Thus one might guess that Ciruelo was founded by Indians. It was not clear.

Festivals, foods, traditional medicine, agriculture, and customs lost to time, such as the ability of a farmer to start a fire with a bit of wood and a machete, were popular topics. But virtually no description focused on anything specifically "black," except that some people insisted that "black" is the joy people get from dancing and from dancing when they want to, whether anyone else is dancing or not. Morenos indeed like to dance in San Nicolás. But so do Indians. No one ever dances alone, unless they are drunk. As examples of specific black customs, people also mentioned traditional medicine, saints' days, the Day of the Dead, and foods, none of which are particular to morenos. Yet so insistent were the organizers on fomenting a black Mexican identity that when a woman brought up migration, which even then deeply affected the region, someone cut her off with "right, let's leave that for now because this boat is going to sink."

Indeed, on several occasions the organizers interrupted responses to steer discussion back to blackness. This happened especially around ethnic group identity, and more specifically around the relationship between morenos and Indians. One man pointed out that "our villages have blacks and Indians." Another volunteered that he was "mixed Indian and black" and went on to refer to morenos, a term that participants used interchangeably with black but that the organizers rejected. On several occasions people asked to "speak frankly," thus implying that they could not. They wished to continue discussing mixed ancestries, but this was discouraged.

Yet local people persisted in returning to ethnicity and to mixture. For instance, one woman stated that "here in Ciruelo we do not discriminate against indigenous people. There are marriages between indigenous people and blacks, and we get along—not very well, but we try to ease this." A man mentioned that his mother was Indian and his father was black. "Two races," he said, "Indian and black." Within my group, one man noted that he felt that now "the race is mixed. I have chino hair but there are also mestizos." Someone identified Cuaji as a place both "black and mixed," with a "minority of the indigenous race." A man spoke about unification through religion or social activities. "Black or Indian, everyone goes—Indians, blacks, mestizos . . . they can coexist—we're all equal. The color of one's skin doesn't matter." One of the organizers again interrupted with "very good" as he asked for applause. Peñalosa insisted that even though anthropologists said activists and organizers were wrong, he was black and he wanted his students to learn the customs, as well as how different ethnic groups live.

Efforts to foment group identity were rife not just with ethnic confusion but also with differences concerning class, gender, age, and the rural-urban divide. Thus a student from Cuaji mentioned that dancing minuets at a child's wake, and again eight days later when flowers are brought to the grave to reconcile the soul with the body (*levantar la cruz*; see also chapter 7), were no longer practiced. Yet I had just witnessed the whole process in San Nicolás, when a three-year-old had tragically died from a scorpion sting. By the time the student made her comment, Ernesto had arrived and joined my group. He was the only participant from San Nicolás until the following afternoon, when the artesa musicians were scheduled to perform. We indicated that minuet music was indeed still played, and when the student asked why, Ernesto explained rather matter-of-factly, "Because they're children; they're heaven's angels." The student went on to ask what minuets were, and Ernesto simply said that they were a type of music.[4]

This exchange caught my attention because it exposed distinctions between people from more rural and more urban locales, and between younger and older people. It also indicated what did and did not become folklorized: that a young woman from Cuaji did not know that minuets were still played at children's funerals in a town near her own does not so much signify her ignorance as it highlights such folklorization. Certain practices—in particular ones that could be construed as African—become fodder for public consumption, while others, such as minuets, are ignored because their Europeanness makes them not exotic enough. This gives weight and value to things that might or might not hold meaning to the people with whom they are associated. Outsiders knew about artesa music but they did not know about death rites nor, it would later become clear, about rural subsistence. Thus, San Nicoladenses' daily lives are ignored as the meaningfulness of their lives is imposed from above. As a result, the model the organizers wanted, and the model mostly delivered, conflated space (the coastal belt), culture (different), and identity (blackness or Afromexicanness), a conflation that benefited the outsiders.

Akhil Gupta and James Ferguson warn anthropologists about the prob- lematic ways in which "distinctiveness" is "predicated on a seemingly un- problematic division of space, on the fact that [societies, nations, and cul- tures] occupy 'naturally' discontinuous spaces" (1997:33; see also Appadurai 1996), but it is certainly the case that the "old model" correlating a people with a place, an identity, and even a language is prevalent not only among some academics (Julien 2007) but also among some of "the natives" who forge their identities around "imagined communities." This seems to be the case with representatives of local organizations on the coastal belt. A native essentialism might present a dilemma for anthropologists, as it is frequently used in Latin America by ethnic groups to claim their rights, as Martin Diskin noted long ago (1991). But in the present case the rep- resentatives spoke in much more essentialist terms than local community members, perhaps because there was more at stake for the former. Indeed, without being present there is no way to know for whom "representatives" speak. San Nicoladenses, for example, certainly feel connected to a "natural" space—their village. But they refer to mixing, complex histories, migration, and the flux of their identities when they return to that space, which thus might be imagined as concrete but also as unbounded. In the meantime, those who would speak *for* them essentialize them by distinguishing them from fellow Mexicans and by linking them to Africa.

During the first meeting, Father Glyn handed out cards showing a slave ship and its captive passengers crammed together. "How do they look?" he asked the crowd. "Happy? They are half-naked. Maybe your grandma or grandpa is there.[5] Where do we all come from? Africa. Do you recognize your grandfather? Sixty-six percent of those who left did not arrive." Par- ticipants arranged themselves by town and walked around in lines, pretend- ing to be on slave ships. While ships are certainly relevant to San Nicola- denses, as I have shown, outsiders use them to signify place in ways that San Nicoladenses do not. Artisans from Ciruelo make vessels fashioned from coco husks to sell to tourists, complementing a handicraft repertoire tradi- tionally Indian. These vessels include fishing boats, the source of livelihood for seaside communities (which Ciruelo is not). But they also include the kind of schooners that brought African slaves to Mexico. In fact, for Father Glyn the inverted trough of artesa music signifies death: it is a slave ship, whose overturning represents blacks' victory over their enslavement. "For me," he said, "it's a boat turned upside down, and we dance on top of this boat. In some way we're doing a dance about something very sad; the artesa is also a casket. . . . It's for weddings, but it's also for death." Yet to Ernesto the trough signified blacks' domination of horses and a joke on whites, also symbolically dominated. "It shows that the black is dancing on top of the white," he said at the meeting to hearty applause. For San Nicoladenses, then, these platforms certainly have to do with a history of domination. But that domination is not linked to Africa, slavery, or to death per se. Instead, the trough is a rather concrete metaphor for the historical situations of blacks and mulattoes brought to the coast to work for Spanish ranchers (also Ruíz 2001:48–50). In the end, then, even the history most meaningful to activists is not the one meaningful to regular community members. This does not mean that Father Glyn cannot interpret the artesa. It simply means that culture workers are more likely to steamroll over local meanings—which should be the starting point for any cultural analysis, and in fact are more complex than the ones imposed by culture workers—and replace them with their own.

That same afternoon Father Glyn gave Ernesto two hundred pesos for a camioneta and asked me to round up the artesa musicians for a performance the following day because I had a car. When Ernesto and I returned to San Nicolás that evening in the dark, we drove from house to house— including to the bush where Don Domingo was living in the lowlands— asking the musicians to "get ready" for the performance. They had been invited months earlier, but no one had ever told them the date. Don Samuel complained that this was what always happened. "They never tell us until the last minute. I'm not going," he insisted. But the others convinced him to, and as Ernesto and I drove around, he told me that the "priest from Cuaji" (Florencio) had invited them to Cuaji a few months ago but had not sent a truck to pick them up. They had gathered in San Nicolás's plaza in their jaro-cha outfits with their instruments and the rather heavy artesa. There they waited for a truck that never arrived.

The next day—the closing day of the meeting—the oldest of the artesa dancers, Doña Cata, rode in my car while the musicians went in the camioneta along with several young dancers. Ernesto told me that Doña Cata "always wanted a little something" since the musicians were never paid, and so I gave her some money. The musicians and dancers were at the meeting the whole day, playing for Ciruelo's dancers, since the latter did not have their own musicians, and then again on their own. Unfortunately, as we wandered around before the performances, we spotted a book display that included Maya Goded's *Tierra negra* (1994). As we flipped open the book we came to a photograph of Rita, one of the young dancers' severely mentally and physically handicapped aunt with whose family Goded had stayed and whom Goded had enticed to pose nude from the waist up. Horrified and embarrassed, we agreed not to say anything to her mother for fear of upsetting her (see Lewis 2004).

The musicians were fed twice, as were all the attendees, but not, of course, paid. The audience was more interactive than it would have been during, say, the Folkloric Ballet in Mexico City, and the performance was joyful and long, but the dancers and musicians still had a disembodied quality. They were performing not to "root" themselves to a place or to cement a marriage, but as entertainment for an audience of onlookers. And no one knew what we had just seen.

The Meeting before the Meeting: Mutual Distrust

The third meeting, held in Cuaji in 1999, was much more public and commercial. I have discussed it elsewhere (Lewis 2000, 2004) but highlight the main issue here, which is again the disjuncture between "the people" and their "representatives." On a Monday evening before the five-day meeting was to begin, Peñalosa, now president of the Organizing Committee of Black Villages, arrived with two women from Cuaji for a pre-meeting in San Nicolás to discuss making the village a "seat" (*sede*) of the Meeting of Black Villages. "He wants to have this [preliminary] meeting," the mayor Hugo told me, "because he doesn't think the people of San Nicolás are organized enough to go."

I had just arrived after an eight-month absence, but within a day I learned that Don Jesús's son, my neighbor across the road, had died, allegedly of AIDS, in the United States. The body arrived at 4:30 A.M. a day or two later, when I went to visit his wife, bringing the traditional candles and pesos and sitting with the body for a while. I learned that thirty people had just left for el norte, the way San Nicolás had voted in a recent election, that Sirina's and Rodrigo's son had moved from California to North Carolina, that María's son Jaime's girlfriend still did not want to get married, and that Isidra had a baby girl as yet unnamed, though she wanted "something from the Bible." Delia brought me a watermelon; Rosa told me that two men, one from Montecillos and the other from San Nicolás, had shot each other in North Carolina over a woman. She also complained about Don Jesús's daughter, who made calls on Rosa's telephone without paying for them. Sirina and Rodrigo mentioned a wedding in el norte, to which I had been invited by Margarita, but which I could not attend because I was going to be in San Nicolás. We giggled over the irony, as we did about the fact that because I could read newspapers and had access to the Internet, I knew more about what was going on than San Nicoladenses themselves did. Everyone mentioned how long I had been gone.

People immediately told me the important things in their lives, and no one mentioned the Cuaji meeting. In fact, although I had called several times to arrange for my arrival, including from Mexico City the day before, I had learned neither the location nor the dates of the meeting from San Nicoladenses. These observations foreshadow my position as I tried to follow the meeting preparations and participate in the meeting itself while endeavoring to see it from the perspectives of San Nicoladenses, who basically ignored it until it came to them.

I immediately became a potential resource for the meeting organizers. For instance, as I was walking with friends to San Nicolás's church, a woman from Cuaji spotted me and invited me to the pre-meeting. The next day another woman from Cuaji asked me if I was with the meeting people. Doña Lupe remarked that I was the one singled out, although I had only just arrived. She did not say that I was not from San Nicolás. Although she told me that "everyone" was going to attend the pre-meeting, when the time came the only people present were Peñalosa and two women from Cuaji, me, the mayor Hugo, two school teachers who taught in San Nicolás but who were not from there, and an Indian woman from Igualapa who lives in San Nicolás.

Peñalosa opened the discussion by mentioning in quick succession people coming to Cuaji from abroad. He then explained the purposes of the meeting, which would run from 11 A.M. until 8:00 P.M. over several days. The first aim resembled one from the meeting in 1997: to encourage people from various communities to talk about their history, founders, and problems. The second was to have such communities reflect, and the third was to display culture through traditions. "San Nicolás is changing," Peñalosa said. "It's the capital of Afromestizo cultural traditions." He announced that because there were "more traditions" in San Nicolás than in Cuaji, San Nicolás's role would be to entertain meeting attendees who would travel from Cuaji the final afternoon of the event. The only reason the meeting itself was not held in San Nicolás was because "San Nicolás isn't welcoming." He then asked that San Nicoladenses contribute by preparing a meal for the Cuaji visitors.

Hugo humbled himself: "Frankly," he said, "my people don't understand what you're doing. They're blind. The young people don't want to study. They prefer to go to el norte. They don't have anything new in their heads. The people don't see." The Indian woman pointed out that "people from here didn't come to the meeting." One of the Cuaji organizers interjected that although "there's a lot of resistance" from San Nicoladenses, it was important to involve everyone. At one point Hugo addressed Peñalosa as a moreno. The latter corrected Hugo and described himself as black. He also rejected Hugo's contention that preparing a meal would be a problem. "Money is a problem for everyone," he said, "[but] we have a commitment to these outsiders and we don't have any money to show them around." The "we" did not include San Nicoladenses, who were nevertheless drawn into culture work.

A teacher who taught in San Nicolás told the Cuaji organizers that they had not started early enough as it was "difficult to get people around here to do anything." The other teacher noted that "people didn't attend [this meeting] and now it's time. The only thing I can do is to tell the kids that they should go to the inauguration [in Cuaji]." Peñalosa emphasized that cows had been butchered to feed attendees during the first and second meetings, indicating that there was no reason why San Nicoladenses could not do the same (although the meeting of course was to be held in Cuaji). But he quickly gave up on the food, noting that the "cultural program" was the most important part. Hugo mentioned Los Cimarrones (The Maroons) a ballad group led by Ernesto's brother Efigenio. He then added, catering to the widespread belief that San Nicolás is dangerous and San Nicoladenses uncooperative, "My people are more ready to learn the bad than the good—it embarrasses me—a meeting in San Nicolás."

A discussion ensued as to exactly what the program should be. Peñalosa wanted everyone to participate, including young people. One of the teachers added that it was a question of getting them to try. With a different model of culture in my head, and in an effort to familiarize the visitors with San Nicolás, I suggested that they tour the village to meet people and to gain an understanding of daily life. One of the Cuaji organizers quickly shot me down. "That's not our goal," she said, "our goal is 'the culture.'" "Afromestizo culture," Peñalosa added. "People will be coming from other parts of the Costa Chica and they'll want to see the culture, the customs; here they dance the artesa." He then mentioned that he thought San Nicolás would be ready to host a meeting in a few years. "The seeds are planted." He listed a number of dances that he thought San Nicoladenses could showcase for the cultural program. One teacher responded that "we'll have to see what we can do and let you know." The other proposed gathering children to dance chilenas. I asked where the Cuaji meeting was to be held and received contradictory answers from the organizers.

When they departed it became clear that the exchange had been something of a public transcript, as both sides tried to politely cooperate. One of the local teachers thought I was a Cuaji organizer, indicating that the organizers are often white. But when she discovered that I was not, the tone immediately changed. Hugo pointed out the organizers' arrogance, including the expectation that things would be done at a moment's notice without payment, even for the food San Nicoladenses were asked to prepare. He did not again want to let down the artesa musicians, since Manzano had promised to take them to Detroit in 1998 but had taken Cuaji schoolchildren instead. Hugo joked that "the culture here is one of *cholos* [gang members]." Everyone rolled their eyes about the reception of my idea for a tour of San Nicolás. "They didn't understand what you meant," they laughed. "So you really get this," Hugo said, turning to me, "this" being the constant pressure from culture workers to make San Nicoladenses live up to their reputation as bearers of Afromexican culture and the unrelenting suspicions that they were hostile and uncooperative, as Meza had written long ago. A teacher noted in this regard that Ciruelo was very organized because Father Glyn made everyone jump to attention all the time. If he says, "do this," they do it. If he says, "do that," they do it.

The next morning Hugo, who is also an electrician, came by to fix a short at my house. I told him that I had been thinking about the pre-meeting and how the Cuaji people thought that San Nicoladenses were not accommodating. Hugo laughed. "That's what they always think." He was going to try to pull something together, even though the organizers did not know how many attendees there would be or how they would reach San Nicolás. We also discussed the fact that even if San Nicoladenses wanted to go to Cuaji they did not have the resources, as at the time it cost about $1 for a one-way trip and a small farmer's monthly income, without remittances, was only about $30. Hugo also mentioned that the musicians were invited to play but were never paid and rarely fed. He raised his hand to his mouth in an eating motion as he told me that the money for the meeting was coming from Manzano who, as it turned out, was hosting the people from Detroit who had invited him to Michigan the previous year. Sirina later told me that some people would be interested in the meeting "thing" but that most people would just "pooh pooh" it. Doña Lupe said that she would be interested but that she was not going to go, that no one would spare the time.

During a quick visit that morning Angela asked me about "Africa," recounting how some time ago a group of people had come to the church. They were from Africa, she said, "foreign blacks," and they gave handouts, but only to people whose skin was dark enough, overlooking her for being Indian. With hostility she expressed her alienation: "The meeting would interest people here if they knew what it was about, but they don't. They're thick." Later I saw a large sign posted in the town hall: "The Coordinating Committee of Black Villages, the Civil Association of Black Mexico, together with the Municipality of Cuajinicuilapa, Guerrero, Convene the Black Villages of the Costa Chica of Guerrero and Oaxaca and National and International Organizations for the 3rd Meeting of Black Villages of Oaxaca and Guerrero. Place: Cuajinicuilapa, Guerrero. Dates: 10, 11, 12, 13 and 14 of March 1999. We Await You So That Together We May Reinforce Our Culture."

It was illustrated with a light-skinned couple dancing chilenas barefoot on an artesa, palm trees, and someone who looked like a tourist, wearing sunglasses (which no locals wear) and taking pictures. I asked a policeman in San Nicolás, wearing a uniform issued in Cuaji with an emblem showing a redondo and Cuaji's church, what he thought of the meeting. He did not know what it was.

It seemed as if no one really cared to explain the meeting to San Nicoladenses, that no one cared about the people whose village was, as Peñalosa enthused, "the capital of Afromestizo culture." Those from Cuaji took on the "burden" of organizing San Nicoladenses, but assumed, for instance, that everyone could read the announcement when most adults are not literate. They also assumed that San Nicoladenses self-identified as black and that the announcement therefore spoke to them. No one thought about the time and money small farmers would have had to spend to travel to Cuaji, and no one noticed that San Nicolás's Indians sensed discrimination because of the color of *their* skin.

In Cuaji

The next day, as I was leaving for Cuaji, Hugo told me that Peñalosa had twice called looking for him, but that Hugo had been running around trying to organize for Saturday because the program had already been printed and San Nicoladenses therefore felt pressured to perform. Felipa's headdress for La América had been dismantled and used for other purposes, and her grandmother, Doña Lupe, did not want to pay for another one (Felipa's parents were in el norte); Petronila had taken her newborn to the hospital for severe diarrhea, and Don Jesús and his wife mourned their dead son. Sirina was working at her mother's bakery for the following two days, but said she would try to make it and laughed when I told her I was going to Cuaji. "Oh, to your *mujeres morenas* [moreno women] thing," she said. "And what is it again?" The passengers I rode back to San Nicolás with late one afternoon from Cuaji also laughed at the title: "The meeting of blacks?" they exclaimed, emphasizing "blacks."

When I arrived in Cuaji, I ran into Delia in front of the town hall, where the meeting—as it turned out—was to be held and where some two hundred chairs had been set up. I asked her whether she was going in, but she replied that she did not want to, not even for a minute. She "had things to do." Most people present at this point were costumed schoolchildren, musicians, and African Americans mostly from Detroit. Soon Father Glyn arrived, followed by Manzano. We all walked across the street so that Manzano could speak in front of the Museum of Afromestizo Cultures, with its concrete redondos outside. When we returned to the town hall, the functionaries sat at tables facing the audience. Applause ensued in succession for people who had come from other countries, from Cuaji, Acapulco, and from Oaxacan and Guerreran villages. When San Nicolás was called only one person stood up: Rosa's uncle, who worked in Cuaji.

As young women dressed in Indian costume passed out fruit drinks, Peñalosa announced that México Negro was registered with the state, whose governor would be inaugurating the museum. Like the federal government's funding of the Third Root project through the Office of Popular Culture, which, like the museum, is under the auspices of the Mexican National Office for Culture and Art (CONACULTA), the official co-optation

of México Negro underscores the role of the state in forging multiculturalism and cultural preservation initiatives that trade the national effacement of blacks for a celebration of their objectified culture.[6] During the first
meeting two years earlier, one of the organizers had whispered to me that
the state had sent spies, possibly because it feared that the meetings, and
then México Negro, would foment discontent. By 1999 the state had tamed
a potential ethnic movement by co-opting it with "official multiculturalism." This might have given the organizers token funds and a visit from the
governor, but it also strengthened state control (Wade 1997:105–7). Indeed,
whites ended up controlling the museum itself, which was almost moved
to Ometepec. Moreover, for local academics and intellectuals, who have a
stake in the formalization of their roles, the state's recognition—whether
national or local—provides a positive change in status.

I returned to the meeting after a meal to no audience and only a few
people speaking. One discussed the revival of lost traditions such as the
artesa; another how people used to grow their own food but now bought
everything. Yet in San Nicolás people do grow a lot of their own food. They
even still hunt. "Before," the man continued, "people worked with machetes."
But in San Nicolás, where there is little heavy machinery, people still work
with machetes. Indeed, some still tend to their fields or cattle on horseback.

Díaz mentioned to me how few people had come from local communities and that the meeting, at five days, was too long. She shook her head,
saying that it "seemed to be for foreigners." One such foreigner, the photographer and filmmaker Bob Richards, approached me to ask if I would
show him and his wife Marty around San Nicolás. I said that I would meet
them there the following morning, but requested that they only photograph
with people's consent, as I did not want to be associated with outsiders who
might offend local sensibilities. Bob and Marty made it to San Nicolás, but
so late that they had time only to view the church before we headed back to
Cuaji. On the way I mentioned that San Nicoladenses seemed disinterested
in the meeting. Marty responded: "Well, you try to do something for people
and they don't realize it." They told me about an African fashion show I had
missed in Cuaji the night before, because I had returned to San Nicolás with
the last of the taxis as evening fell. I had no idea what this show was like,
but Motta notes in something of a rant against the "messianic" foreigners
and Mexicans who run the meetings that "in three of the Meetings of Black
Villages I saw them haranguing people so that they would dress in *bubus*

(West African dress), dance in an African style and play drums . . . in order to show them what they had lost of Africa" (2006:121).

When we arrived at Cuaji's town hall, I ran into Don Gregorio, Margarita's father, who lives in Cuaji. He immediately told me that he wanted to go to "Carolina," bemoaned the fact that he had no place to stay in San Nicolás since his daughter had left, and chatted about passports and visas, without understanding that his chances of getting a visa were practically nil.[7] He asked me when Margarita was coming back, but as of September 2011, Margarita still had not returned. Indeed, while she sews curtains for a living, her husband Maximino, who for a long time could not find work, just found a new job.

As the organizers divided people into groups to discuss history (especially agrarian), the loss of traditions, music, and dance, I overheard snippets of conversation such as this answer to what religion blacks had brought with them to Mexico: "Tonos and naguales." Elsewhere someone explained that the corridos of the Costa Chica were played in minor keys while those elsewhere in Mexico were played in major keys, making those of the Costa Chica sound melancholy.[8]

The following day Sheila Walker, a professor at the University of Texas, Austin, opened the proceedings with a talk about segregation in Texas. She referred to "us" to include her audience and noted that while the United States exploited Mexico, "we are black like you," and so not a part of that exploitation. She had perhaps attended an earlier meeting in Estancia Grande (Oaxaca), as Motta notes the "absurdity" uttered by a "functionary" of the African and African American Studies Center at the University of Texas at Austin, "an African-descent woman herself" who "said to attendees . . . that they should give their last names since she, from her position in the United States, could trace their African origins" (2006:121). But at least Walker spoke Spanish. While Father Glyn encouraged other U.S. attendees to share their knowledge, this proved impossible for a man affiliated with the Museum of African American Cultures in Detroit, who stressed the value of a "good, strong education" as the most powerful weapon for young people. It was a pity, really, because many points the visitors wanted to make were important for young people, teachers, and officials to hear. Along with others I translated when I could, but as there were more groups than bilingual speakers, much went uncommunicated.

I sat in on the groups for a while and then wandered outside to look at the exhibitions. Marisela Zamora, an amateur photographer and painter from Cuernavaca, had set up her work in one of the museum's concrete redondos. With what could only be described as a shocking lack of sensitivity she was offering photos of black people in one of the sites modeled after dwellings indexical of the region's "primitive," "African" past, dwellings that are themselves reproduced and circulated by outsiders. The photos consisted in the main of children, including one of Rosa's niece, titled "Girl with Enchiladas." They were priced at two hundred pesos, or twenty taxi rides between San Nicolás and Cuaji. One child wanted a photograph of his sister and burst into tears on hearing that he would have to pay for it. Díaz was upset when I asked her why the organizers had permitted such a display. There was no way to control these things, she lamented. Rosa's reaction was intense when I told her about the photograph of her niece. No one had paid to take the picture, she said, and no one had given the child a copy. Besides, the "photo belongs in the family." She was reminded of the filmmaker who had twice come to San Nicolás. She "never paid anyone," Rosa fumed. "And she made money from [her film]. It came out on television. That's why people don't like to have their pictures taken." Her comadre Liliana, she added, would not let her picture be taken by outsiders at all (Lewis 2004).

The meeting was not without its honest moments. The following day I sat with a group of mostly local women, many of whom directed anger at men who abandoned their families, beat their wives, or brought other women into the home, issues I discuss in the following chapter. The pain was palpable, especially when one revealed that her mother had not wanted to marry her father because he was "too black," but her father had kidnapped her anyway, keeping her for eight days in the bush where he repeatedly raped her with the consent of his family, who helped hold her captive.

As this discussion concluded, a local man declared that "the black race" had suffered. "They were slaves, see?" He claimed that Cuaji and San Nicolás were founded by fugitive slaves who built huts (*jacales*) and were accustomed to killing, thus associating violence with maroonage. This was an example of what Motta asserts: that *maroon* has become a euphemism for *black*, and that some local people try to defend—through claims to descent from maroons—the violence that has been imputed to them by outsiders anyway (2006; chapter 3).

I returned to San Nicolás that afternoon to await the Cuaji visitors. While Peñalosa worried that San Nicoladenses would not be prepared—just that day he had mumbled that "San Nicoladenses don't want to cooperate"—San Nicoladenses worried that the Cuaji visitors would not show up, that they had readied themselves to play the artesa and perform bits of festival dances for nothing. Yet several minibuses did, in fact, make their way over the bumpy roads from Cuaji. As they arrived in the central plaza, where no food had been prepared, and the visitors poured out of minibuses, cars, and taxis, almost all holding cameras and video recorders, four men came down the road toward the church, carrying the casket holding Don Jesús's son. The church, of course, is also in the central plaza, and its courtyard cross is always the first stop during the long procession to the cemetery outside of town.[9] The visitors raised their cameras and video recorders in unison as they raced from one side of the plaza to the other, while Díaz and I tried to shield the funeral procession from the clicks and whirs.

On the sidelines, Delia, always the wit, asked me with a guffaw if the people who arrived from Cuaji were *mollos*, a derogatory term for African Americans,[10] while Rosa told me how she hated the beat of the Dance of the Devils, which Collantes dancers had come to perform. But as darkness fell the artesa musicians played and danced for five minutes, people performed the toro de petate without the toro, and the whole thing was over by 8:00 P.M. "They should have had it in the morning," Don Gregorio told me the next day, "so that they could have done a whole program." He read me a poem he had written about the meeting and asked why San Nicoladenses had not come. I told him they did not feel invited, and he retorted that they wanted to be paid. But of course once again they were not paid for performing "authentic Afromexican culture." Instead, they sold beer and food to the visitors, who were happy to oblige because they got their photographs. Peñalosa was relieved that San Nicoladenses had done their bit.

In San Nicolás: Tension under Wraps

In 2002 the sixth meeting was held in San Nicolás, for three days rather than five. It began with Israel Reyes, another Cuaji organizer, introducing México Negro in the town's ejidal hall. He assured a sparse audience that "we're demonstrating to the country that we're black on the coast. They say that in Oaxaca they're Indians, not blacks, and that there are few blacks in Guerrero." He then announced the program and asked for cheers for Guerrero, Cuaji, and San Nicolás. When he insisted that "it's necessary to accept that we're blacks" and asked, "Where are my black people?" he elicited few cheers. So he more emphatically warned that "we" have to accept it and then we will cheer. "We have to learn." This time there were few foreigners: a television news team of whites from Mexico City, a few out-of-town Mexican visitors, and Ron Wilson, his wife, Joyce, and Norma Abi Reed. Father Glyn appeared later. No San Nicoladenses greeted the visitors, who again consisted of schoolchildren from Cuaji, intellectuals who stayed overnight in Cuaji, and a smattering of individuals from nearby villages.

Before the cultural program that evening, Cuaji schoolchildren milled around San Nicolás's central plaza, approaching everyone who looked foreign for interviews. As they took pictures of foreigners, the foreigners took pictures of them. At one point a white Mexican woman ran over to snap a moreno eating watermelon. "That's what mollos eat in the United States," the man eating the watermelon cracked. When the children tried to photograph me with Joyce and Norma I shied away. Both Norma, who passed away several years ago and was a self-identified Afro–Costa Rican who spoke fluent Spanish, and Joyce, who does not speak Spanish, were puzzled by my reaction. But I had become so averse to photography in such contexts that I could not be in front of a stranger's camera (Lewis 2004). I later explained my position as I accompanied Joyce, Norma, and Ron around town.

The evening program included a parade of children and a "cultural" event in San Nicolás's newly built dance hall. Hundreds of San Nicoladenses now turned up, as they do when the circus comes to town, when a couple marries, or when evangelicals come through with films they show on outdoor screens. Like everyone else, they want to be entertained.[11] I went with Sirina, her children, her sister-in-law María, and María's children.

Reyes began the program asking for applause for "all the black people." People applauded. He then asked for applause for "*my* black people," and few applauded. When he asked for applause for the people of San Nicolás, everyone again applauded. Because the vast majority of the audience consisted of San Nicoladenses, the level of applause for each call-out suggests that most did not consider themselves black, even as Reyes repeated "black community" and "black people" over and over. "The black race has a place at the national and international level," he proclaimed into a microphone. "We want to emphasize that we're a race living alongside everyone else, also with a cultural tradition, which we carry in our blood so as not to lose it. We haven't lost our roots." When he repeated, "Where are my black people?" again, few clapped. I was not the only one who noticed. The TV news reporters did too, as they mentioned to me the following day. They also commented that hardly anyone had come from "the outside."

When Reyes introduced the program, he named only Efigenio, Ernesto's brother, also an artesa musician and the lead guitarist for Los Cimarrones. No one clapped. Unbeknownst to most outsiders, the previous month Efigenio had collected a national prize after someone from the National Office of Popular Cultures had faxed an award letter to the artesa musicians, which Efigenio received, signed, and returned. The person who had faxed the letter assumed that Efigenio spoke for the musicians for whom the award was intended. But few San Nicoladenses had known about it until they saw Efigenio on TV with Vicente Fox, then president of Mexico, or heard about it on the radio. Thus, as the meeting got under way, a cultural row was brewing. Indeed, Popular Cultures had asked the rest of the artesa musicians not to make waves.

Efigenio allegedly had kept the money, telling people it was only 50,000 pesos, which he would donate. But it turned out to be 400,000 pesos (some $40,000 at the time), the amount he had given me over the phone when I was in the United States. He apparently received one check for 50,000 pesos, which was supposed to be split among the five artesa musicians, and another for 350,000, which was supposed to go toward new instruments and the casa de cultura, where the musicians hoped to give young people lessons. When newspapers printed the full amount Efigenio claimed they were lying. And when Don Domingo insisted on full disclosure, Efigenio resisted for fear of being kidnapped. He gave 5,000 pesos to each musician.[12]

As people from Popular Cultures tried to keep the tension under wraps for fear that the artesa group would fall apart before the meeting, the extent of the ill feelings became clear. Rosa, for instance, refused to go to the evening cultural program because Efigenio had not informed everyone of the award. The parents of the young women set to dance that evening for 300 pesos apiece (paid by Efigenio) wanted 1,000 pesos. Don Domingo sighed. "I didn't want a scandal," he said. "I want to go to your country so I don't hear anything. The ambition for power, for money, it's too much." The musicians had picked out a special parota tree for a new artesa, he told me, but they could not afford to pay someone to hollow it out and carve it. The next day Doña Lupe told me "400,000 pesos is a huge sum of money"—why, not even the wealthiest people in town had that much. She said Efigenio's wife bought gold jewelry with the money, which she would then sell for a profit.

Doña Lupe continued, "Efigenio claimed that he had taught Don Domingo to play artesa music. But that's not true! My father played that music. [The money] is for the people, for the community, not for him." Delia went on about all the money Efigenio kept, while her aunt, Doña Cata, did not have any for food and could barely walk. Efigenio started identifying as Afro-mexican when a year earlier, as I had been typing a grant proposal for the musicians, he had insisted that they self-identify as "African, indigenous, and Spanish."

The situation clearly demonstrated the disconnection between state institutions and local mores and expectations. Popular Cultures assumed Efigenio spoke for the whole group when he signed the letter; Efigenio, suddenly finding himself with a windfall, was frozen out of the community; and Popular Cultures was more worried about what would happen during the meeting than about setting things right, which it never did.

The emcee only introduced Efigenio. Like Reyes, he asked where "his black people" were. The first time no one cheered, so to elicit a whoop he joked that he knew they were there because he could see their teeth. When I whooped, Sirina and María laughed so hard they almost fell out of their seats. The emcee followed with a joke about La India María, a Mexican staple about a country bumpkin who comes to the big city and urinates on the street. Schoolchildren danced, Los Cimarrones played, and part of a wedding ritual was reenacted, which the emcee described as a past custom, even though it is still current in San Nicolás. A desultory artesa performance without Efigenio ended the event.

The following day I attended the meeting in the ejido hall. Sirina, who accompanied me, was the only San Nicoladense there, as a clinic doctor present to check people's blood pressure noticed. Everyone else was from Cuaji, from Mexico City, from the United States, or from other villages. San Nicoladenses were amassed outside, waiting for taxis so they could run errands. Sirina felt uncomfortable, but she joined one of the discussions as I went to fetch water for the two of us. There were almost no men at all. Finally two elderly men from San Nicolás arrived, but they sat outside until I motioned them in. Somebody muttered that all the blacks were outside the meeting hall, while Israel noted that "indigenous people" had been organizing themselves for five hundred years, as if organizing were some sort of competition. "We have to know we're Africans," he said, "before we can carve a space for ourselves in this multicultural nation." Suddenly a

Traditional cotton coverlet

light-skinned woman stood up and said that her father was black but that she was obviously not. "Now we're evolving. The mestizo people," she continued, "want to know our roots." I was not sure that I had heard her correctly until someone angrily shouted that she was equating whiteness with progress. An elderly moreno farmer from another community stood up and pleaded with the organizers to explain what it was that they wanted. "We don't understand the point," he said, because the organizers did not speak in the people's own "language," meaning that their concepts were incomprehensible.

The following morning I waited in the plaza for Norma to arrive from Cuaji, as Angela had asked me to invite "la molla" for a mid-morning meal. As Angela later told Norma herself, she was unsure whether Norma would come because Angela is Indian and Norma was black. As I waited for Norma I saw myself in photos displayed of past meetings. Handicrafts were for sale, including painted shells of the endangered turtles that biologists were protecting with army backup on the coast. But San Nicoladenses do not produce handicrafts. Those once made were principally cotton coverlets sewn by women, such as the one shown in the photograph here.

I waited a while for Norma, but as the hour had passed and I was un-sure of whether she would, in fact, show up, I left for Angela's house, know-ing that Angela would be nervous and would have cooked up a storm. A few hours later I discovered that Norma had arrived after I had given up and eventually found her way to Angela's. As the three of us stood around talking, Angela remarked that she could not go to see the doctor in atten-dance at the meeting because she was Indian. The other Indians had warned her that she could only go if she was of the "black race." I told her that it was alright, that surely the doctor would take anyone's blood pressure, and explained to Norma the exclusion felt by people like Angela, who live in San Nicolás too. Angela went to the plaza and reported back that the doc-tor indeed refused to check her blood pressure because she did not have "black blood." But, she added in a bemused way, the doctor did check that of her daughter-in-law Chela, also an Indian, because the young woman's last name is Moreno.

Later that afternoon I attended a series of meetings with the organiz-ers. At each pass they insisted that the issue was about blacks, dismissing a local woman's comment that the focus should be regional rather than racial identity. They refused to see that one cannot study racial disparities in Latin America without accounting for their historical entanglements with socioeconomic class (Wade 1997:22–24). This is not a question of ignor-ing racism. For it is true, as Father Glyn pointed out, that Cuaji's political leaders, businesspeople, and professionals are all white. It is simply another way of saying that all race is local and that even in San Nicolás wealth dis-parities are tied to history and ethnic origin, both among people called mo-reno and between them and those called Indian.

The organizers discussed México Negro's community role. All these people come from outside, said Reyes, and treat it as a party, while those who stay and do the work keep coming back to the same thing: "Black Mexico hasn't reached its goals." While I made it clear that my commit-ment was to San Nicolás rather than to México Negro, I tried to help, first pointing out that if the organization's goal was to combat racism, La India María jokes were inappropriate, especially as people were preoccupied with the reissuance of the comic book character Memín Pinguín. As Marco Polo Hernández notes (2003), this dark-skinned "pickaninny," whose exagger-ated physical characteristics suggest "a chimpanzee," is meant to instill a desire for whitening in the national imagination. That Mexico's Memín Pinguín postage stamps sold out almost immediately in 2005 attests to the character's popularity. México Negro, I suggested, should have several goals: combating racism wherever it happens and representing local people more broadly. One of the organizers indeed admitted that one of the organization's errors was its inability to communicate its goals to small farmers.

Notably distinct from the first meetings was the absence of mentions of Africa. The organizers had also dropped *Afromexican* and *Afromestizo*. Instead, they focused entirely on being black and therefore having "black culture" in Mexico. Yet this raised questions as to the criteria used. Whereas previously traditions were linked to Africa, the question had since become one of naming things particular to blacks. But there is really nothing particularly distinctive about moreno "culture" in the ways that the organizers reified and saw it. Because of this perhaps unconscious acknowledgment, the focus came to be more about skin color and "blood," but with an attempt similar to those of previous meetings to distinguish blacks from Indians. Father Glyn thus noted that while there were censuses of Amuzgos, Mixtecs, Chatinos, and other indigenous groups, there were none of people he referred to affectionately as *zanates* (black birds). Officially, however, Indians are classified principally by language. Zanates are not only Spanish speakers but also dress as majority Mexicans do and share national and local customs with both mestizos and Indians. Indeed, separating zanates from Indians has the effect of doing what Hoffmann notes, pitting blacks against Indians to maintain the position of white urban elites (2006a:126). I wondered how México Negro would conduct a census. Would they ask people if they were black? What would that mean in the Costa Chican context where people of African descent identify as moreno, a label organizers reject? Who would they ask? Would they go to villages locally identified as Indian where morenos also live? How would a moreno with an Indian mother respond? How would one with a white grandfather? Or a moreno man married to a white Mexican woman whose children are "mixed"? Or a moreno woman married to an Indian man? These last questions are especially compelling since racial labels shift over time, through space, and in relation to other people.

Ultimately, Motta calls attention to the fact that culture workers use the indigenous to create the black. That is, in the process of positing distinct but not local classifications, they also construct them. Both Indian and black, moreover, are colonial categories that still serve to generate dissimilarities and therefore barriers between people of color. Thus the idea endures that

CHAPTER SIX

Being from Here

Culture workers find positive value in San Nicolás principally around the abstract qualities of Africanity or blackness. But for San Nicoladenses such qualities are either negative or not engaged at all. The meanings they ascribe to being moreno and to being from San Nicolás rest on modes of being and acting that are tied to their village, and they distinguish principally between "inside" and the home, and "outside" and the streets. These poles map particularly onto gender roles, which become increasingly fixed as people age. During the life cycle the freedom San Nicoladenses ascribe to maroons, to Mexico, and more generally to themselves becomes strongly linked to men, such that women become almost entirely "enclosed" (*encerrada*), while men are "of the streets" (*de la calle*). Together these associations constitute the placement of the body and the embodiment of place by establishing the acceptable boundaries around which individuals operate to maintain the social and spatial norms of community life.

In general, a criollo is born in the village or to moreno San Nicoladenses. For this reason, even first-generation resident Indians are still sometimes referred to as outsiders and their parents' handling of rituals questioned. But not belonging can also be ascribed to moreno San Nicoladenses who do not, for instance, engage in reciprocity, or to women who wear shorts, smoke, and drink outside of dances and other ritual contexts, unlike a typical woman from San Nicolás (Lewis 2004). During my longest stretch of fieldwork I was out and about while my son's father stayed home, shopped, cleaned, and cared for him. Because we were married, parents, and not Mexican, evaluations of our behavior were more flexible and curious than judgmental. But my son's father sometimes joined groups of men for rounds of beer, and he never cooked. In turn, I cooked, shared food—the primary gift in the reciprocal exchanges among friends and family—and socialized mostly with women. "People don't have problems with you," Sirina once remarked when I began to go to San Nicolás alone,[1] "because you're very respectful, don't flirt with anyone, and don't give any man an excuse to come after you." After my years of coming and going, learning proper comportment, and developing godparenthood (*compadrazgo*) ties with numerous families, people said that I was "from here now," urging me to buy land and to build a house. Thus belonging is a flexible concept that applies to most morenos and can also apply to outsiders if San Nicoladenses deem them deserving.

Papa Nico, Kids, and Freedom

San Nicoladenses often refer to freedom in their everyday discourses about how Mexico is and, by extension, about how they are. This characterizes their approach, for instance, to Mexican independence, when the village is conflated with a Mexico that Indians freed, to maroonage, and to Papa Nico's willfulness. It also characterizes the rearing of male children especially. Thus the words on a *reliquia* hanging on a young boy's neck read "everyone is free to do what they want."[2]

Papa Nico in particular symbolizes childhood and freedom. He is said to have been stubborn as a youngster—his mother would hit him when he refused to come eat—and he liked to play, especially with small bulls, in keeping with the cowboy culture of the region. The saint holds a soup plate in one hand, with a dove soaring out of it. The released dove signifies the saint's "discipline," I was told, which I interpret as a kind of sacrifice, as the saint was vegetarian and San Nicoladenses deem animal protein an essential, if luxury, part of their diet. The dove also signifies a love for freedom, as San Nicoladenses believe that especially young animals want to be free but also keep birds, in particular, as pets. Papa Nico's childhood story is thus an allegory about San Nicoladenses themselves, including about the relationship between mothers and boy children, who are allowed to roam when they are young and who, as teens, are not "ordered about" (*mandado*).

As in English, children under the age of seven or so are kids or *chivitos* (baby goats).[3] "They don't yet have complexes," Jaime once noted of a toddler who defecated in public, meaning that they are not self-conscious about their persons. They are like young animals and compared favorably to children raised in el norte, who are described as enclosed. Thus when the twelve-year-old Yanaris announced that she wanted to go with us to el norte, Sirina dissuaded her by pointing out that she would "be shut in all the time. You can't run all over the place like you do here."

Encerrado has the same roots as a sheep or cattle pen, *encerradoro*. To be enclosed is therefore to be like a caged animal, and indeed Doña Austroberta compared children to animals. "Here children go around playing in the open air," she said. "[In el norte] they are completely locked up indoors. They're like animals—look, I have a kid goat locked up and in the open air it leaps, jumps, skips. Out of happiness. They want freedom—a little animal, a bird. Over there children lack freedom. They've got toys and everything to entertain them, but they don't have liberty. They should do what they want. The [kids] they bring from el norte, they're soft [*blanditos*], sick. And once they've been here a while they're ruddy and strong, massaged by the sun. They grow [over there], but they don't have their little friends." In San Nicolás, then, young children are free and healthy like young animals, while those in el norte are weak and caged.

"Children run around loose here," Sirina said one day about her four boys, at that time all under the age of ten. While children who arrive in San Nicolás from el norte for a visit typically wear shoes and remain under their parents' watchful eyes, those raised in San Nicolás rush about barefoot with abandon, run around in packs, spin and wrestle on the sandy roads, and slowly make their way home at night, falling asleep together in the same room or bed when they wear out. They form gender-segregated groups, typically with cousins and siblings, who then provide protection, including from other groups of children. My son had to fend for himself. Like other boys, he learned to throw rocks with precision, once pegging Lourdes's ten-year-old son on the head and once going after the much older Yanaris in anger with a broom. Sirina, Rodrigo, and I still laugh remembering how Rodrigo called out "careful Yanaris" as my furious four-year-old chased her.

Playing in the breezeway

As it was for Papa Nico, playing is a constant. We initially let children through the front door to play inside our house, although adults advised us not to. One stole a significant amount of money, and was caught and punished. Regretfully we began to confine them to the back entry and the rear breezeway. This taught me, at least, that while breezeways are for catching breezes, they also enable one to invite people into one's home without actually having them in one's home. They are thus physical spaces for spontaneous public activities—children's play, conversations with passing neighbors, and visits from friends and relatives—that are public and private, or outdoors and indoors. As children do, breezeways link the inside and outside.

Like the young boy who stole, children have to learn the limits of freedom. Papa Nico's story indicates that too much might result in a whipping. As women are more responsible for children, such discipline falls to them. Indeed, I never observed a father's aggression with a small child (see also Guttmann 1996:77). Physical punishment has to be understood within the context of adult expectations, for being "free" does not mean that a child can do anything he or she wants, despite the boy's reliquia message. Thus Doña Socorro told me that her two- and four-year-old grandchildren, sent from el norte where their parents worked,[4] were "chivitos" and "mischievous" without their parents there to guide them. As she took out a belt and threatened them, I asked if she hit them. She said yes, but that their grandfather, Don

Guillermo, did not; he just scared them with stories. She then said "see?" after she threatened but did not hit them and they became quiet and lay on the ground. "Well," Doña Socorro continued, emphasizing a value San Nicoladenses hold dear but one to which children born in el norte are unaccustomed, "those born in el norte are more mischievous because when they get here they're suddenly free and go a bit wild." To properly "grow" children, one has to "cultivate" them and hope for a "good crop," Estafania told me. Thus, like the bush, children are "wild" if they are not properly tended. The festival for Papa Nico, the saint of fertility who aids barren women as well as barren land, takes place in September toward the end of the rainy season, in hopes for a good winter crop.

From Uncultivated to Cultivated: How Children Grow

Newborns and toddlers stay mostly with their mothers, but men often have young children in tow, a reminder of Matthew Guttmann's assessment that Mexican men's closeness to their offspring is largely a product of class, as wealthier men in Mexico City find carrying babies "unmanly" (1996:52). I once asked Manuel whether people thought it strange that my son's father took care of him. He responded, "No, not at all. When my wife is busy I take care of the children," just as a working-class man might do in Mexico City.

By the age of four or five children are given more freedom, receiving little supervision except in school.[5] Yet San Nicolás holds its dangers. People remember two siblings who fell down an uncovered well and drowned, and a young girl run over by a truck while playing in the street. Children are thus taught to be safe and reprimanded for misbehavior, especially for serious infractions that put themselves and others at risk. "Te voy a pegar" (I'm going to smack you), a mother or grandmother might threaten, just as Papa Nico's mother threatened him. Sometimes they follow through. Thus Doña Mirna whipped a young grandchild with a switch for climbing into the backyard cistern where a child can drown. Cisterns are also the only source of water when the flow stops, which it frequently does. Adults are constantly cleaning them to prevent mosquitoes from breeding and to conserve water for dishes, clothes, and bucket baths. "I punish my kids," Sirina told me after she beat two of her sons for climbing onto the back of a truck racing down the road, "but I don't do it to calm my own nerves," implying that other people did.

In fact, brutality is rare, and it indicates that a parent is either absent or "not from here." Rosa once brought by a five-year-old with parents in el norte whose body was scarred from his grandmother's whippings. "They put people in jail for this in el norte, don't they?" she asked. And when I mentioned scars from cigarette burns on the arms and legs of a young boy who often came over to play, and saw his mother whip her young daughter hard on the legs with a stick, people expressed their disapproval, emphasizing that the mother was *not from* San Nicolás, which indeed she was not.

Older children begin to learn that their contributions to the household count. While still young themselves, boys and girls look after younger siblings (see also Díaz 1995:41), run errands, and sweep. Once girls reach the age of seven or so they help around the house, learn to cook, make quick trips to grinding machines for corn dough, clean, and bathe younger siblings. Boys take on more arduous outdoor chores, such as gathering kindling for their mothers' kitchens, tidying yards, climbing fruit trees, and eventually helping their fathers in the fields.

Part of a young person's training includes punishment for failing to properly carry out an important chore. Thus when Yanaris ruined a sauce because she left the top off the pot and something fell into it, she was punished. She not only needed to cook for her natal family; she also needed to learn how to later be a good wife and mother. Boys tend to be punished not so much physically as mentally by their fathers ignoring them, as happened to Modesto while he was in the fields helping with the cows. One stepped on his foot and left him in tears, but his father ignored him while his mother ceded his masculinization to his father.

As boys mature, they are given more freedom than girls. Indeed, while the label "mischievous" might apply to overly wild children (who are likened to cats that steal food off the table), the ways in which core values map onto gender mean that the term is also applied to preteen girls, who are too old to be flitting about but too young to be thinking about marriage: when the twelve-year-old Linda climbed up on our roof without our permission and brought down mangoes from a neighbor's tree, everyone exclaimed how mischievous Linda was.[6]

Because unmarried teenage boys (*solteros*) are not given orders, the elderly often complain that they need supervision because migration sends many parents to el norte. With parents gone, "there's no one to keep an eye on them," Margarita and Eugenia both told me; "grandparents can't control them." "They used to work," a woman relaxing at Doña Lupe's remarked. "Now they just wander around looking for trouble." "It's that marijuana," another woman said, with reference to a relatively recent phenomenon tied to migration. Indeed, young men swagger like *cholos* as gang affiliations start even among boys, who pick up such connections from older siblings and the media, or during their own trips to el norte. One can find in San Nicolás gang colors, signs, and even graffiti in English. A musician from Pinotepa Nacional, who had played at a wedding dance in San Nicolás, once remarked that the cholo thing is "really strange" and particular to San Nicolás. He had to shout "calm down" as teenage boys got out of hand, while older guests and girls who had come with their parents started to leave. I suspect that this "strangeness" has to do with the fact that San Nicoladenses are highly endogamous and tend to migrate together. Migration to an urban area means that gangs might develop, as there are enough San Nicoladenses to form one.

Because everyone hails from the same community, however, gang violence is not a serious problem in San Nicolás itself. Nor have I encountered talk of such violence in el norte. Only at dances do fights occasionally break out over interpersonal conflicts. Thus the cholo behavior is mostly bluff. Indeed, once teens are reunited with their families and the "warmth of their parents," as Doña Lupe observed, they take on the familial roles expected of them, whether home is recreated in San Nicolás or in el norte. Teens work, contribute to the household, avoid trouble, and obey mandates that enable the family to remain a unit.

Such unity means that parents' threats and acts are balanced with the fact that their offspring are also their security for old age. The elderly Doña Eusebia lives alone because her husband long ago left her; she does not get along with her only child who lives in San Nicolás; another was killed in el norte; another became disabled there; and another does not speak to her. She is pitied because children and grandchildren should care for their elderly parents and grandparents. When Don Gregorio sold without his daughter Margarita's permission land she had inherited from a relative, and then squandered the money, Doña Lupe made the consequences clear as she shook her head and rhetorically asked, "Where is he going to go when he gets really old?" implying that his children would not look after him.

The Body Public

The liberty children enjoy means that outsiders think they are not well cared for, but to San Nicoladenses "really dirty" (*choco*) is a derogatory description of a child with negligent parents. In general, that which is inside, personal, or private, merits protection; that which is outside, or public, does not. This distinction holds especially true for the family, the primary social unit. This unit extends to its property, which is almost always surrounded by an enclosure. Anything within that space, including the family itself, is as well maintained as a given family can manage. Thus adult San Nicoladenses normally bathe twice a day; and younger children are bathed before bedtime by a mother or an older sister. Indeed, because of their freedom young children are always dirty by nightfall, as was my own son. (Everyone knew his bath time because he displayed his displeasure at cold-bucket baths with piercing screams.)

People save their "good" clothes for special occasions, including trips to Cuaji. Women constantly wash their hands as they cook, and both men and women sweep the interiors of their homes, even if the floors are dirt, as well as their exterior yards. One of the tasks children learn early on is how to flick water from a plastic container just so to keep the dust down and to sweep more efficiently. Most women walk around with a towel or a rebozo (an indigenous shawl) to cover their heads, as men do with sombreros. Partly this offers protection from the sun, exposure to which is associated with dark skin and thus with socioeconomic class and a husband's improper care. But head coverings are also handy to wipe soiled chairs before one sits down and to wipe dirt and sweat off the hands or face.

While private spaces and bodies are well cared for, however, public ones are not. A really dirty child with negligent parents is one who is unsupervised and therefore too "public." (Thus a foreign white evangelical neighbor of Rosa's once asked her why her toddler daughter was so dirty, implying that Rosa was a bad parent. Rosa simply laughed and said that it was so hot the child liked to bury herself in the ground.) Such public values apply to village space as well. When Kimberly Grimes returned after several years to Putla in the Mixteca Alta, 135 kilometers north of Pinotepa Nacional, she was "shocked and dismayed by how much trash had accumulated in and around town" (1998:51). She ties the problem to increased modernization, including consumption and drainage that contaminates the ground with sewage. This is also true in San Nicolás, where more trash indicates a higher standard of living and where what drainage does exist also causes problems outdoors. But it is additionally the case that, in contrast to what is inside and private, what is outside and public is not maintained because San Nicoladenses paradoxically see themselves as "from here" but not as a collectivity.

Only when people return from el norte are there occasional grumbles about garbage, which on a practical level, someone could probably make money collecting, since San Nicolás has no trash service. But doing so is considered lowly, for it would mean, essentially, that one was like a pig or a dog: unconcerned with dirt and an outside forager. People therefore burn *their* garbage, including plastic, in *their* yards, but do not touch street litter unless it is front of their store, in which case it is an extension of an interior space and part of the home. The outside could therefore be seen as an undomesticated space that, like bush, does not belong to anyone.

The private is valued in other ways as well. For instance, because freedom is in many respects individualistic, people are often reluctant to cooperate for public projects. While other migrant communities collect donations to improve infrastructure in their Mexican hometowns (Boruchoff 1999; Goldring 2002; Viramontes 2008), San Nicoladenses do not. Nor do they routinely form agricultural cooperatives to improve economies of scale. I discovered that a kind of individuality can conflict with the collective when I donated several thousand dollars to repair the road impassable during the rainy season. While the road was public and therefore benefited everyone, no one wanted to sign up for the voluntary labor (*faena*) needed to clear the bush so that gravel could be poured. Then complaints came in that the road would give advantage to the camionetas that at the time were the only form of public transportation and to the one man who owned them. Although the road was built and proved a life saver during the rainy season years before the bridge was constructed over Aguas Frias, the process of getting it done explains why many moreno San Nicoladenses refer to their own egocentricity, a theme I return to in chapter 7.

Interiority

Until the age of five or so boys can run around nude, while even infant girls must wear panties. Boys' genitals are thus as free and exterior as boys themselves are. When I asked Rosa about the difference she explained that if her toddler daughter's "parts" were seen by a man she would feel as if her own were on view. A young girl is thus a gendered extension of her mother, whose genitals are hidden (interiorized) and private.

Boys older than ten or so are also free to roam. Young men are expected to lose their virginity with prostitutes (*guinzas*) at about the age of fifteen. They are then no longer "boys" (*niños*), Manuel told me, but solteros: "They go looking for love and look for a prostitute. But it's always hidden until a parent suddenly realizes it, because the boy doesn't say anything to his parents." Girls, by contrast, are mostly kept at home to help their mothers with chores, including for the males of the household. A girl's vagina remains intact (closed) until she "flees" or elopes (*huir*) with a young man, who is said to "steal" her (*se la robó*). At that point she ideally loses her virginity and is no longer a *señorita* (a virgin), an occasion that marks her womanhood and her engagement. Indeed, a young woman's purity is sacrosanct, and young men are warned about the "dirty" women in el norte, who might carry HIV or other sexually transmitted diseases.

Mothers of course have opinions about the best ways to raise their daughters, including the amount of freedom they should have and the amount of sexuality to which they are exposed. Rosa thus kept a tight leash on Amalia, while Sirina allowed Yanaris to attend dances with her. While Sirina thought Amalia would probably flee at fourteen to escape her mother's house, Rosa thought Yanaris would flee early because Sirina allowed her too much liberty. As it turned out, both fled at what is the normal age for a señorita: around seventeen.

Because most señoritas are watched carefully by their parents, young couples do not stroll around San Nicolás's central plaza in the evenings as they do in other Mexican towns. They instead meet at school or at dances—where señoritas are accompanied by parents and girlfriends. Once a señorita has a boyfriend (*novio*) and is therefore a *novia*,[7] she might spend time with him during the day or in a public place, but she will not be alone with him for long unless it is to flee. If she does, and all goes well, she becomes a woman and, after the marriage that ideally follows, a wife.

Once the novios have fled, they return to the novio's parents' house, where the novia's virginity is ascertained by the novio's baptismal godmother,[8] who checks the novia's underwear for blood, sheets for blood (if the couple had intercourse on a bed), or her forehead to see if she is warm. If the godmother determines that the novia is *not* a virgin her novio will usually not trust her to stay with him because she might "have eyes for" another man. Since people believe that a man's penis shapes a woman's vagina, a nonvirgin's interiority as well as her faithfulness will have been compromised. Girls are so concerned that a local clinic doctor told me they will not use tampons for fear of breaking the hymen and misshaping the vagina.

If the novio still wants to marry someone who is no longer a señorita, he needs his parents' consent because they pay for the wedding. If they do not consent but the couple insists, the parents will say, "If a woman wasn't afraid to do it with someone before, she's not going to be afraid to do it with someone else after," said Judit. "The novio's parents pay a lot for the wedding. The young people can't afford one, and they're not going to want to marry without a party. But if the son really loves the novia his parents will pay. They're obligated to." The novio's parents might, however, still make the novia feel unwelcome by, for instance, threatening to serve tortillas with holes in the middle at the wedding dinner, thereby indicating that the bride was already "open." One woman told me that if her son's novia did not turn out to still be a "girl" (niña) she would put something with a hole in it on her front door so that everyone would know.

If the parents object and the novio agrees with them, the novia is no longer a novia and her family is disgraced. Unless she finds a man to marry—which is unlikely—she will become a querida, a married man's lover. Conversely, if the novia is a virgin but the novio does not want to marry her, his family pays hers a fine. Thus there is some flexibility within the system, which is basically a negotiation over the worthiness of the novia and her family and the honor of the novio and his. In that sense it rather classically follows the Mexican ideals of machismo and marianismo, insofar as the young man and his family are expected to uphold their commitments while the young woman and her family must accept the outcome with a certain amount of abnegation. Because of this, young women, especially those whose parents look after them, are careful about the company they keep and will only willingly flee if they are quite sure about the outcome. If that outcome is positive the novio's family announces it community-wide in the middle of the night with the firecrackers that are always shot off in specific sequences to broadcast important events, such as deaths and impending marriages. Thus a girl's loss of virginity is quite public, in keeping with its value, while a boy's is not.

Because the novia stays at her novio's parents' house to begin her training as a daughter-in-law (nuera) months before the couple is married—a practice not unusual in Mexico, where "free unions" and patrilocal residence are both common—her family might not know that the firecrackers are for their daughter (although they might suspect it since she will not be home) until the novio's family tells the mayor, who then tells her family. The novia's family is not always happy. For instance, when Gisela fled with

Pedro, Angela lamented that Gisela was her only daughter, that her husband was a drunk who beat her, that her son, Oscar, was in the fields, that Gisela would not be back to see her mother until the wedding, and that they had no money for the perdón, the ritual pardoning of the couple and the only part of a wedding for which the bride's family pays. "Life is tiring," Angela said. "My husband is drunk all the time; Gisela is gone."

From Novia to Nuera

Today most young women flee once they finish secondary school.[9] Once one does and is accepted by her in-laws, her novio and his family, rather than her parents, control her. If she has not finished school, her in-laws and her novio/husband decide whether she will continue. Thus one reason for Angela's distress was her fear that Gisela would not be allowed to finish school, which turned out to be true. Amalia's story is also telling in this regard. Rosa asked me to be a godmother for her graduation from primary school. I agreed on the condition that Rosa allow Amalia to continue studying, as was Amalia's wish. Rosa insisted that she needed Amalia at home, since she was the oldest girl in a family with three younger children, two of them boys. We discussed it, as Rosa brought up the example of Pati, Don Jesús's daughter, who had gone to secondary school—at no small expense for uniforms, donations for classroom materials, and the like—and had then taken off for el norte. This reflected, of course, a double standard, as many young men attend secondary school and then go to el norte. But for some, secondary school is considered a waste of time, especially for girls. I prevailed, and one of my gifts to Amalia was her uniform for secondary school. I left money with Rosa for school donations, and each time I went to San Nicolás over the next few years I would check on Amalia's schooling, once reenrolling her when Rosa ran out of money for donations. But in 2001 Amalia fled with Alberto several months before her graduation. Alberto decided that she did not need to complete school because she would "learn everything she needed to know" from him, and so she never finished.

Civil marriage can occur at any time, and if the novio's family cannot afford a wedding, the couple might only have a civil marriage. Similarly, if the novia is too young, the couple will also have a civil marriage, sometimes followed by a Catholic one several years later.[10] Sirina's cousin's novia was fourteen. During the civil ceremony Sirina remarked that although she was young she was "well developed," which is one way San Nicoladenses determine a young woman's readiness for marriage. Juana's new nuera was also fourteen. Because of the girl's youth, Juana postponed her plans to go to el norte to show her how to run the house, especially because Juana was leaving youngsters behind. The morning after the nuera fled with Juana's son, she was at her in-laws' serving food and beer to visitors celebrating the impending marriage.

Novios are usually older because they have more freedom, can have intercourse with no repercussions, and want to be able to support a family either by working in the fields with their fathers or by going to el norte, making money there, and returning to find a novia. Thus Filadelfo worked for several years in el norte before returning to San Nicolás to "look for his wife" (*buscar a su mujer*). The couple's wedding took place in San Nicolás; his mother, Margarita, who lives in el norte, asked me to attend as a godmother, as she could not be there, so I did. Filadelfo then returned to el norte with his wife, Dorotea, ready to make a home and a family. With two youngsters of their own, they still live with Margarita and her husband Maximino.

Church marriages and weddings generally take place several months after a couple flees, after Easter but before it rains.[11] Weddings cannot conflict as every family wants the entire community at the evening dance, where barbecued beef, tortillas, and green salsa are always served to those who have been formally invited (*invitados*, or those who receive written invitations). Women prepare vats of food with their neighbors and comadres, as they do for fiestas and visiting dignitaries, while men prepare the event's infrastructure.

Weddings take place in the morning. Though the bride's parents attend, only afterward is she meant to visit her family home for the couple's perdón and a breakfast of chocolate and sweet bread, served to neighbors, ritual kin, and formal guests. During the perdón the couple kneels at the feet of the bride's parents, as her father ritually slaps them, a symbolic punishment for fleeing and stealing. Although perdóns are more common in San Nicolás than in other Costa Chican towns, and certainly more common than in the more urban Cuaji (Diaz 1995:14), in San Nicolás one will not take place if the bride's family cannot afford it, as was the case when Chela and Oscar married, or if the bride's parents are not there, as was the case when Aquiles married.

Following the perdón the couple visits the groom's baptismal godparents, where a party and a meal ensue. They then go back with the godparents to

Food preparation for a wedding

the novio's parents' home. Here the bride, accompanied by her own baptismal godparents and parents, who bear small gifts for the groom's family, is literally returned to her in-laws. This is sometimes accompanied by a ritual known as an *entregamento* or *entregamiento*, the handing-over of the bride, a formal ceremony I only saw during Aquiles's wedding, which was also "old-fashioned" in other ways: artesa music was briefly played because Aquiles, an Indian, had a moreno father to whom he was gifted, and his father was an artesa musician.[12] During the entregamiento, two officials handed over and received the bride with religious and congratulatory verses (see Diaz 1995:15–18). She then accompanied her in-laws to an open palm-frond shelter (*ramada*), which extended and symbolized the interior space of their home.

In what David Robichaux would describe as a "Mesoamerican household formation system" (1997:150), young couples reside patrilocally for a time, but eventually they have to buy house plots and build their own homes to make way for the next son's wife to become the new nuera of the household. This pattern continues until the youngest son's wife takes over the running of the household permanently from her mother-in-law (*suegra*) as the latter ages. Ideally, then, a family always has a nuera, who lives with her in-laws sometimes for several years until she and her husband are ready to set up their own household and make way for a new couple in the husband's parents' house. But while houses technically belong to men, everyone refers to them as a woman's because the domestic is female and because women bear much responsibility for funding the building of homes, as I discuss in chapter 8 (see also Pauli 2008).

As long as a nuera lives with her in-laws they control her, burying her if she dies before they do and overseeing the births of her children. "They have complete control over the couple," a clinic doctor told me, in great part because they pay the bills, including for the births of grandchildren while the couple still resides in their house. Occasionally the bride's family will not have sons, or the bride's family will be wealthier than the groom's, in which case a nuera might lack the proper training for her suegra's household. For instance, Judit knew of a young woman who did not even know how to make tortillas. In such cases, the bride's parents pay for the wedding and the couple lives with them. They then control the couple. "Whichever in-laws marry them," Don Domingo said, "have the right to control them. The father-in-law will order the novio about, and if he gets drunk and lacks respect the father-in-law has the right to punish him. And if the wife doesn't follow [her parents'] orders they will punish her too—they'll whip her."

A couple does not necessarily set up a separate residence even after a child is born. This depends on whether a younger son has married, whether a couple can afford it, or whether a nuera has been left behind, with or without children, by a husband who has gone to el norte.[13] Tensions easily ensue, especially between the nuera and the suegra whose house she lives in and runs but does not and will not possess, unless she is the wife of the youngest son. Oscar is Angela and Héctor's only son. When Oscar and Chela, two of my (Indian) godchildren, married they lived with Angela and Héctor. Chela suffered the indignity of being unable to conceive, the latter central to the sometimes quite lengthy rite of passage that makes a girl a woman and proves that her husband's penis fits properly. As Chela's situation was quite public, everyone speculated that she refused intercourse with Oscar, and Angela, my comadre, threatened to throw her out if she and Oscar did not have a child within a year. "The suegra is angry because [Chela] doesn't have children," Paula, Chela's mother and also my comadre, told me. "And because [Chela] is not her daughter she pressures her."

Infertility is considered a woman's problem because a woman is not deemed complete until she has children. Thus, as a matter of proper coupledom, infertility *is* her problem, even though people know that a man can be infertile too. A barren woman is called a *machomula*, the name of a dance meaning "male/female mule." A mule, of course, is a hybrid and sterile animal. Thus a childless woman is *like* a man in that she has not borne children and sterile in the sense that she will not carry on her husband's lineage or have a "purpose" in running a household. She is neither a man nor a woman. Men do not necessarily leave because of infertility. Instead, the couple might take in a gifted child. But apart from the mentally or physically handicapped, who never marry,[14] I only knew of one childless couple.

Chela would often complain that Angela would not let her out of the house (see Pauli 2008 on the use of the word *encerrada* by Mexican daughters-in-law; see also Hellman 2008:47–48). "Nueras used to be treated like princesses," Don Domingo told me. Doña Lupe agreed that they would go out all the time with their suegras. "Before," she said, "when a girl became a nuera she wouldn't work right away. But now she does." Indeed, the nuera now occupies the lowest position in her husband's family. Whenever I visited Doña Olivia, who had a dozen children, one of her nueras would always cook and serve food. Doña Delfina's nuera Elena, whose husband was in el norte and who never left her in-laws' yard, washed everyone's clothes. After Chela and Oscar's wedding, Gisela insisted that she would never marry or be a nuera because she had seen what Chela did around the house. In addition to having to ask her in-laws for permission to go out, especially after Oscar left for el norte where he stayed for years without Chela because he did not want her to work and therefore to be "on the streets," Chela washed the dishes and clothes, including Gisela's, cleaned the house, made tortillas, and otherwise cooked, all the while engaging in ongoing conflicts, especially with Angela. But a nuera-suegra relationship can evolve over time: Chela and Angela developed an affectionate relationship as they came to depend on each other through the years, especially after Gisela fled and both Héctor and Oscar were in el norte.

No one could tell me why nueras had gone from being "princesses" to shut-ins whose days are filled with domestic drudgery. I suspect that if such a change occurred it did so at least a generation ago. It might be that the more frequent absence of husbands, who are often young and in el norte, precipitates a tenser relationship between nueras and suegras, as the husband cannot or will not mediate. In addition, if the husband is not there to keep watch over his wife the "burden" of making sure she stays within the confines of his family falls to his parents. Yet even if a husband is there, because he too initially depends on his family, he often does not interfere in conflicts.

Judit, who is quite a bit older than Chela, told me about her experience as both a nuera and as a potential suegra. She led her narrative commenting that

the in-laws pay her expenses but the nuera cooks for everyone. She cleans, she washes the clothes. Sometimes the nuera lives with her suegra for a long time. The husband gives all the money to his father because they work together in the fields. Sometimes the couple can sleep apart, but some houses don't have rooms—all the beds are in the same room—the couple, single youth, parents. Almost always the father tells the young man that his wife doesn't want to be there anymore. So they do a little work—"let's plant a little something so that when there's a harvest you can build a house, even if it's out of cardboard." Me? I lived with mine for six months. Then an opportunity [to leave] arose. Before [young couples] didn't leave. They would stay for two or three years. The in-laws wanted them to stay until the in-laws died. I don't want my nuera to live with me because it's going to bother me that someone else is in my house, and I didn't like living with my suegra, so I don't think someone else is going to want to live with me. When I lived in my suegra's house there was no door to the room. Everyone came in and out. We'd go live out in the fields for six months. At any rate, it has to be done. "You're here," the husband says, "and my mother isn't going to help you. I'm not going to do your job." [But] it's one thing to help her and another thing to do her job. Some say that if it's the only son he'll never separate from his parents. How can I leave my father alone? Etc. Sometimes the couple fights using very offensive language. The suegra says to her son, "your wife is this way and that way," and the husband hits the nuera (his wife).

There was a couple here. Now they live apart. The girl, the nuera, wasn't free to go out—even to grind corn. The suegra would tell her son that if the nuera were allowed to go out she wouldn't keep up the house. Pigs and goats got into the house when she was wandering around. Since she wasn't supposed to go out, her husband hit her. [A couple] might ask for a house to care for. There's always one. And if not, they make a shack out of wood and cardboard, whatever, next to the in-laws' house.

Judit also told me that a nuera cannot live with her own parents, even if she has children. I witnessed this with Yanaris, who left her husband when he hit her and returned to Rodrigo and Sirina's home with her infant son, who was still nursing and whose paternal family was disinterested. However, Yanaris's return did not mean that Rodrigo and Sirina took responsibility for her, since once a young woman marries her parents' obligations to her are severed. Without a husband, she will have to provide for herself and her children. She will also have no land, which is inherited—with few exceptions—through men.[15] Therefore, at least when children are young, parents might take a daughter in, but soon she will leave San Nicolás to look for work, principally to build a house to be able to return. Yanaris thus stayed with Rodrigo and Sirina for a few months while nursing. She still wanted to socialize with girlfriends, and Sirina had to remind her that she had chosen to flee, had a child, and could no longer go out. When her son was weaned Yanaris left him with Sirina and Rodrigo and went to work in Cabo San Lucas, where she met another man, with whom she had a daughter. She brought the daughter back also for Sirina to look after and returned to Cabo. Both children called Sirina "mommy," while Sirina and Rodrigo joked that they were getting gray hair. Now that the children are school-aged, Yanaris has taken them to Cabo.

Rosa also would not take in Amalia after Alfredo decided to go to el norte and leave her behind, because, like Oscar, he did not want his wife to work in el norte and therefore to be "on the streets." Amalia should have lived with Alfredo's parents, as Chela stayed with her in-laws when Oscar left for el norte, and as Elena stayed with hers while her husband worked in the United States. But because Alfredo's Indian parents split their time between San Nicolás and their Mixtec home in Tecoanapa, Amalia did not want to live with them. Rosa, however, could not take responsibility for her. "If she wanders the streets," Rosa said, shaking her head, "it will cause a scandal." With no other options, Alberto took Amalia to el norte.

Yanaris's choice to stay in Mexico meant that at least she could occasionally return to see her children while they lived with her parents. But many single young women, including mothers, go to el norte. Raising children there without enough extended family or when everyone is working often proves impossible. Children of single mothers might be sent back to live in San Nicolás, as was Alicia's young U.S.-born son, whom I brought back to her family. Single women otherwise certainly have more freedom in el norte—"Even señoritas can build their own houses," Rodrigo once half-joked; "they don't need husbands anymore." But when a woman has a partner migration can mean more extreme confinement in San Nicolás when a husband is gone or in el norte if the woman goes with him, in both cases because of the supposed seduction of the streets. Married women who work might hurt men's "pride," Don Domingo pointed out. "Modernity," then, does not erase traditional values, which in fact might become more extreme if they are threatened (see also Abu-Lughod 1986:72–77). Thus, although Amalia went to el norte with Alfredo he would not allow her to work.[16] She spent her time at home looking after her brother Ismael's eldest child, eating, and sleeping. "We don't fight, but Alfredo's jealous," she told me. "The wife of one of his cousin's went to work and left him for another man." When Amalia had her first child her confinement made cultural sense. Chela, whom Oscar brought to el norte after years of separation, also never worked, and she stays home with her first child. Celia, who is middle-aged, immediately started working in el norte, as she had done in San Nicolás. Often she and her sons are the only ones supporting the family since her husband cannot find steady employment, her eldest son's wife stays home and runs the household, and her oldest daughter moved out, married, and now has a child of her own. Even though Celia must work, her husband once hit her because he thought she was having an affair, pinpointing the motel where he believed she met her lover during the workday.

In el norte the idea that women belong to the house while men belong to the streets therefore does not substantially change. But tensions can mount because people's ability to uphold those standards changes. If a woman works, domestic violence might ensue as she is out in public and therefore "on the streets." If she does not work, she might be locked up, unable to run errands, visit relatives, see her female friends, or simply recline on a hammock and greet passersby as she would in San Nicolás, where she would also be "inside" but not isolated or lonely because of the permeable boundary between public and private, children running around, family close by, work with other women, and the companionship of even elderly women who congregate on stoops to sit and talk, much as in the old days when everyone would bring their sleeping mats (petates) outside to catch a breeze and listen to stories.

Gender Complementarity

As is true in many societies around the world, men not only cannot cook, clean, or sew; they also are not expected to. The ideal in San Nicolás is for a man and a woman to have a complementary union wherein the woman oversees the domestic sphere while the man oversees the public one. This becomes most obvious when a man is alone, which is uncommon but not unheard of. For instance, Don Jesús's wife Doña Greta left him because of his drinking. She moved to Acapulco, leaving her husband and their two youngest children, both daughters, who lived for years with their father and grandparents.

One day Sirina was sewing up a tear in his shirt because one of his daughters refused to fix the shirt or to prepare him food because he was drunk. Sirina, however, took a firm stand. "Even if he's drunk," she said, "she has no right to disobey. He's drunk because he's alone. He doesn't have a woman." From Sirina's point of view, then, Don Jesús's drinking was rooted in his solitude, but as a man he was helpless when it came to day-to-day household chores, which his daughters were expected to carry out in his wife's absence. Soon one of his sons arrived from el norte for a visit. When that son left, his other son died in el norte, and Doña Greta returned for good.

Men like Don Jesús, whose wife left him, need a daughter or other female relative to see to their needs. Sirina stepped in because she was a neighbor and believed Don Jesús's daughter's behavior to be unacceptable. Sometimes elderly men also find themselves alone through no fault of their own, as did Don Domingo when Doña Ana died (Lewis 2009) and their two gifted children were long gone. Don Domingo was unable to care for himself, chiefly because men do not cook. After some negotiation, a niece took him in, even with her own offspring to care for.

Single women also depend on male relatives or ritual kin for help. But they are more resourceful. When Paula's husband left her for several months her brother offered to take her in, but because he lived in Tecoanapa, her young children did not want to go. She therefore cleaned for Doña Lupe to care for her family until her husband returned. Doña Lupe, a widow, depended on her grandsons, but when the last went to el norte she would sometimes go to the fields to fix a corral herself, hire peons to do the work for her, or depend on her only son-in-law in San Nicolás. When Delia's husband died she took a lover, but when he left she managed on her own with the help of her children and extended family.

Gender complementarity extends to the sexes of one's children. Because I only had a boy, people would ask me when I was going to have another child. Sometimes they would say that I needed a second one in case my son died, but more often they would say that I needed a girl: "You need a girl, a partner for Lukas." They would then explain that a daughter looks after aging parents while a son brings a nuera into the home. Thus if I had a girl I would never be alone, and being alone is one of the worst things to befall a San Nicoladense. However, while having many children is a blessing, one also needs to have them in the correct order, again because of gender roles. Having older sons and younger daughters, as Nilda does, is burdensome until daughters are old enough to help around the house. As Rosa pointed out, "Nilda bakes bread six days a week and then she has to wash clothes for eight people."

Queridas and the Danger of the Streets

That men are "of the streets" can be a statement of fact — "Men don't ask permission from their wives to go out," Manuel said. Or it can be a lament when a man leaves a woman high and dry, as happened to Gisela when Pedro was jailed in el norte, or to Angela when her husband went on a drinking binge and could not support the family, or to Petronila when Rubén went off with another woman. Being *of* the street makes men more vulnerable to committing or becoming a victim of violence, a part of the cultural complex of masculinity women try to avoid. Margarita thus told me that as a young woman she feared the streets. Following this early clue that women view the outside with trepidation, I soon realized that the streets lacked protection from extreme violence and that women felt safer at home, whether with parents, in-laws, or husbands.

In the past women had to go to streams and wells to fetch water, which made them vulnerable to sexual assault. Such assaults help in part to explain *queridato*, a term that refers to the extramarital system of having a lover, almost uniformly a mistress or *querida* (the unmarried lover of a married man). San Nicoladenses refer to the offspring of *queridatos* as "illegitimate" or as "bastards." Teresa, for instance, is a *querida* because when she was fifteen in the mid-1970s she was abducted (*agarro por fuerza* or *rapto*) from the streets by Felipe, who raped her. Because Teresa was a virgin and did not want to marry Felipe, the mayor fined him and he had to pay her family. Felipe was subsequently bewitched, Teresa said, and no one knows where he is. They banished him with witchcraft. "Now," Teresa added, "if a girl is taken by force the family isn't going to enter into an agreement. They'd kill him and go to the authorities. A fifteen- or sixteen-year-old señorita is a minor. In the past they'd take them by force at a very young age—twelve, thirteen, or fourteen."

As I discussed in chapter 4, forced abductions were never limited to the Costa Chica, or even to Mexico. But such abductions form part of San Nicoladenses' collective memory, and they help shape their gendered worldview, which is rooted in their colonial history. Abduction "was a Spanish custom," I mentioned Don Domingo telling me. "What could the black and Indian women do?" Occasionally abduction attempts are still made. Quite recently a young woman was dragged from a dance by solteros planning to take her to the bush. As they carried her kicking and screaming up the street, they passed her grandfather's house. He came out in his underwear and rescued her. Everyone talked about it for days and told me as soon as I arrived. I once grew concerned when a female student was not home by nightfall. "If she'd been abducted," Rosa told me, confirming that my fears were justified, "you'd know in an instant because everyone would run to tell you."

Indeed, under the cover of darkness, the convention that men are of the streets and women are of the home is strongest. After dances, for instance, my companions, always women, would wait by the door to make sure I was inside before they left, and the last one home would always have a child with her so as not to be alone. Except for packs of youngsters playing outside or rare evening visits by neighbors and friends, San Nicolás is generally silent by 9:30 P.M.—unless a dance is being held, in which case music audible throughout the village often continues until three or four in the morning or until the electricity fails, whichever comes first.

Because Teresa became a victim of the streets she never married. Instead she became Inocencio's querida because his mother refused a nuera who was not a virgin. Although Teresa and Inocencio never lived together, he fathered all of her children while living with his wife, Josefina, a few blocks away. As Teresa's children grew, Inocencio contributed to their upkeep as he supported his children with Josefina. But now that their youngest is thirteen, Teresa and Inocencio have separated, while their children, many in Winston-Salem, remain connected to their half siblings, also in Winston-Salem. It is not unusual for half siblings to have very strong relationships, as they almost always have the same father and last name. They refer to each other as brother and sister.

In a different category from queridas are prostitutes, who come to San Nicolás from the outside with a freedom not accorded local women, as they "walk the streets" and spend time alone with men in cantinas.[17] Because they are not *from* San Nicolás they are not held to the same standards as local women. Queridas, by contrast, are generally from San Nicolás, and they therefore try to conform to the rules for married women. Thus Teresa, a querida, and Sirina, a wife, both have five children, about the norm for women born in the late 1950s or early 1960s. Neither drinks, except during rituals, smokes, or wears pants or shorts. Neither leaves the house except to run errands, go to church, visit other women, or attend a dance to drink and dance with other women. In Sirina's case, this is because Rodrigo does not like to dance and therefore does not go. But all women who go to dances unaccompanied by husbands maintain propriety by dancing only with other women. In the past Teresa needed Inocencio's permission to go out, and Sirina still needs Rodrigo's. Rodrigo also has a number of illegitimate children with several different women. Thus both Inocencio and Rodrigo have wives, queridas, and illegitimate children.

Men's freedoms extend to choosing whether to financially support those children outside of wedlock. They often do, however, especially when still seeing the child's mother. After Delia's husband died, for instance, she became Octaviano's querida and had three children with him. Octaviano already had several children with his wife. While he and Delia were together, he took care of their children. But when they separated, he stopped, even though the children were still relatively young. From Delia's perspective, men with money "have a lot of women" (see also Díaz 2003:100).[18] She believes that women should take advantage of such men, even though men do not always hold up their end of the bargain: "Single women are assholes. Men fall in love with us—men look for women—whether the women are stuck-up or ugly. They go from house to house and could have seven or eight women without giving any of them money. Women ask these men to give something to their children, even knowing that he's got responsibilities in his own house. The man might pay for [an illegitimate son's] wedding—but everything depends on whether he wants to. Some men don't treat either their legitimate or their illegitimate children well. Even some men with a lot of money don't give anything to their bastard children."

While many men have queridas and children with those queridas, San Nicoladenses believe such men will only leave their wives if queridas bewitch them. Thus when Rubén ran off to Ometepec and left Petronila, everyone said that he was with a *bruja* (a witch). When the "spell" wore off, Rubén returned to Petronila. Rodrigo told me that queridas feel insecure and try to get men to leave their wives "because they don't want to share with another woman." But, he added, men never leave their wives for their queridas. I pointed out that some men, such as Rubén, had, and he explained this was only because he had been bewitched. "One has to be careful," he said, "because the other woman will do witchcraft to get the man to leave his wife and live with her instead."

Women with men who are not their husbands give their husbands something magical, Sirina said, so that the husband does not know what his wife is doing. Indeed, a married woman can take a lover *only* if she has bewitched her husband. Sirina also once confided that some women adulterate food with menstrual blood to bend a man's will, which was also the case during the colonial period (Lewis 2003:223nn35,37). Doña Socorro agreed that married women bewitch their husbands. "They say some women have two or three men, and even have children with them," she said. "They 'cure' them so that they don't know. If his family says 'listen, son, your wife . . .' [the husband] gets angry and says that they don't like her. The husband doesn't do anything because he's bewitched."

Men are therefore more susceptible to love magic, whether they are being ensorcelled by a querida or a wife. Moreover, when men do not honor their marriages it is "not their fault" because they have been ensorcelled, while a woman who leaves her husband, or a querida who ensorcells someone else's husband, is transgressing the ideal of matrimony.

Queridato: An Accepted Institution?

Aguirre Beltrán described queridato as "accepted by the community" (1985:161). "The wife accepts that the husband has a lover" (1985:163). María Cristina Díaz agrees that both queridato and marriage are "accepted and recognized by [the Afromestizo] community" (1995:23). She also argues that a querida and a wife are essentially the same, labeling them "cospouses" (2003:107). Yet it is one thing for a practice to be recognized and another for it to be accepted. Certainly queridato occurs and is not legally or morally condemned collectively, except by evangelicals. But I never met a wife in San Nicolás who did not mind if her husband had a lover, for the wife feels humiliated, and the husband who supports a querida and their children is taking resources from his legitimate children and his legal wife.

As women began to speak freely to me about queridato, it became clear that as much as wives protested, husbands never felt threatened by their wrath and thus never feared that their wives might leave them. But I also never saw a man permanently leave his wife. Thus marriage remains at the heart of San Nicoladenses' social world, despite queridato and despite unhappy moments in marriages, which are often entwined with queridato.

Carmen's decision to marry Donato was made "out of spite" because Donato's mother would not allow him to marry Liliana, who was no longer a virgin. Liliana would laugh at Carmen because Liliana knew that Donato nevertheless loved her, and Carmen retaliated by marrying Donato. Donato continued to consort with Liliana, now his querida, with whom he has four children. When Liliana went to el norte, Donato turned to another woman until he also went to el norte, where he joined Liliana. After months passed without a call from him, his mother casually said, "Everyone knows he's abandoned his family in San Nicolás for one he has there." As the proverb goes, she continued, "se acaban los chiles, se acaban los jitomates, pero nunca se acaba la cosecha de mujeres" (chilis and tomatoes might run out, but the harvest of women never does). Men do not try to hide their queridas. Thus, most of the community will be aware of who she is. When Donato sent fom el norte a television set to the querida he left in San Nicolás, and a sewing machine to Carmen, people joked that he wanted his wife to work and his querida to relax. Eventually Donato and Liliana were forced to split up in el norte when Teo, Donato's nephew, was playing with a gun one New Year's Eve and accidently killed his best friend, a nephew of Liliana's.[19] The intra-family tension destroyed their relationship. Carmen then left for el norte with her and Donato's youngest daughter, and Donato moved in with them.

Rodrigo was with a querida the night he married Sirina, so Sirina went to bed while the band played on. Years later, when I met them, Rodrigo had another querida. "An Indian," Sirina told me. The Indian, Marina, had a son with Rodrigo, the same age as one of Sirina's. Eventually Marina went to northern Mexico for work and then to el norte, leaving the child behind with Rodrigo's parents. Unhappy there, he moved in with Sirina and Rodrigo, against Marina's wishes but as Rodrigo desired. Sirina raised him with her own children and grandchildren, and he always called her "auntie." There are no orphans or abandoned children in San Nicolás, where it is not uncommon for a woman to raise her husband's illegitimate child. Doña Leticia did the same when her husband's querida died, because, as she told me, "it's not the fault of the children." Such a child is referred to as an *internado* (stepchild or boarder) and, as far as I could tell, not treated any differently than a woman's own children. Indeed, Sirina was always pointing out that her internado was smarter than her own kids, whom she often referred to as *burros* (thick-headed).

All this perhaps demonstrates San Nicoladenses' affection for children. But wives who take in their husband's illegitimate offspring might have additional motives, such as competing with the querida. For instance, Marina once called from Tijuana, tearfully pleading that her son not live with Sirina. Yet Rodrigo would not send the boy to live with Marina, nor send him back to his own parents' house, and Sirina was happy to have him.

Queridas and wives might live in the same community and a wife might be friends with a woman who is a querida, just not her own husband's, but wives nevertheless express bitterness. "He's a womanizer," Carmen said of Donato. "He's always looking for women. It makes me angry. The children don't have clothes, food—even if it's twenty pesos it's worth it—but he spends it on women." Husbands with another woman are leading a "double life," Doña Leticia said. "They are hypocrites, *machistas*." As we discussed young men who bring cars and trucks back to Mexico with U.S. plates even though they are often stopped and have to pay off the police, Doña Leticia joked, "They're just showing off; they want the latest model, which they can't get here. The cars are symbols of their success in the United States just like having a new querida is a symbol of a man's success in San Nicolás." Because Doña Leticia's husband was always gone, men would tease her by asking if she was married and express their desire to, like her husband, have two or three wives and many children. "They're jealous," she said, without a hint of incredulity. "Life is difficult here." At the time, her husband, whom I had never met or even glimpsed, lived mostly with another woman. But after a farming accident almost killed him, Doña Leticia nursed him back to health, going back and forth to Mexico City for the three months he was hospitalized there. Isabel did the same for her husband Tomás when he almost died, even though she ran into his querida in his hospital room. Similarly, when Rodrigo became ill, Sirina nursed him devotedly, a situation I discuss at length in chapter 7.

Sirina could not leave Rodrigo, she said, because his family would come after her. And if Rodrigo tried to "kill" her, her family would go after him. A woman cannot report a physically abusive husband to the authorities because that could also start an interfamily feud. "If a man beats his wife," Sirina said, "the mayor can't do anything about it. 'It's his wife,' the mayor will say. He'd be afraid that if he punished the abuser the guy would come after him later." Some men are loyal but "many have other women. People separate," Sirina continued, but "unlike a man, a woman can only go off with someone else if she's separated." Because Sirina wanted and needed to stay with Rodrigo she put up with humiliation: "If you see your man with another woman, it makes you angry; it makes me angry. Women's hearts do break, do ache. It's humiliating when a man goes after a woman who's not his wife. One asks oneself 'aren't I worth as much as she is'? But men don't care. There's so much cancer around here because there's so much pain." She added that women who take other women's husbands do not care what they are doing to other women either. She once asserted that a kind of karmic cycle existed as everyone complicit gets their due. Rodrigo's parents had allowed Marina into their house. As a result, Rodrigo's sister's husband turned out to be a drunkard. "That's his parents' punishment," Sirina said. She also told me that a man who had just died "left his wife for another woman and [dying] was his payback. His wife is still living and he's dead."

Almost every woman I knew had to deal with a husband's infidelity, and I believe I only scratched the surface of a pervasive practice. But as Sirina told me, "a woman from the coast is taught to love only one man." Doña Leticia said more or less the same thing: she had married her husband and she had to stay with him. "You only marry once," Sirina insisted, and indeed San Nicoladenses only marry once. Women also put up with infidelities, Sirina explained, because "children need their father's shadow."

Aguirre Beltrán depicted marriage and other unions as static, as I noted in chapter 4. Yet as I have shown, unions go through cycles (see also Díaz 2003:99), shifting according to unforeseen circumstances or choice. Many if not most couples seem to go through some permutation of this cycle over the years. Sometimes, however, marriages do end, especially if a husband is in el norte. Margarita told me of a woman whose husband had been gone for years. He would return periodically but clearly had a querida in el norte. "Some men can go for years like that, going back and forth," she told me. "Some just stop coming back. The women, in the meantime, have the kids and are lucky if they receive anything from their husbands." But while separations are sometimes permanent and while divorce might be legal in Mexico, divorce never happens in San Nicolás. In fact, if a man who has left his wife dies, his body will still be reunited with hers in burial, as happened with Francisco, allegedly murdered by a querida in el norte but whose wake was held in San Nicolás, with his wife presiding.

The Logic of Queridato

Women do not express personal anger toward any *particular* querida. But I made no attempt to befriend, for instance, Teresa's and Delia's lovers' wives, largely because I was friends with Teresa and Delia and did not believe that I would be received warmly. But the general lack of rancor toward queridas—for instance, Sirina and Teresa are close friends, and Sirina is related to both Delia and Teresa—indicates that many women recognize that queridas are in the position they are in because they were raped or rejected, because men abuse or leave them, or because men die and leave behind children who need to be fed and clothed.

But while neither queridas nor men who have a number of women are outside the bounds of community norms, no one seems to feel positive about it either. Queridas are shamed because of their lost virginity. Unmarried, they do not have as high a status as wives, and they are expected to work to support themselves and their children. Moreover, wives are legally entitled to their husband's assets when he dies. Thus wives enjoy a security that queridas do not have. But wives are also humiliated that husbands have queridas. In addition, queridas can be demanding and make men feel guilty if they do not or cannot adequately support their illegitimate children or if they are neglecting or humiliating their legitimate ones. Meanwhile, community expectations pressure men to take as many lovers as possible, as those who teased Doña Leticia suggested.

As I thought through a cultural logic that did not resort to rooting queridato in a kind of pseudo- (and veiled "African") polygyny, as Díaz suggests (2003:100), or reducing it to women's fertility (Díaz 2003:99), or seeing it as a lower-status form of coupling, it occurred to me that men maintain their autonomy and therefore assert their gender by having a number of women. In other words, queridato is about gendered *meanings* rather than functions. This is not because being a womanizer underscores men's sexual prowess. Rather, access to several women provides a man with a choice of "homes," locations to sleep, women with whom to have intercourse, and places to be fed, enabling him to avoid dependency on any one woman—not just or even most importantly for sex and procreation, but for his very identity as a "free" man. The wealthier a man is perhaps the more lovers he has, but this simply means that wealth enhances his gender identity as men compete with other men. "Winning" is not determined by how many queridas a man has, as conventional wisdom might have it, but by how much *freedom* he has. Such freedom might extend to a man's old age, as having many children augments a man's lineage. But he also has to have treated enough of those children properly to enhance his security.

Because gender is complementary, queridato further encloses women, whether they are wives or queridas. Queridas cannot make too many demands for fear that their lovers will leave them; they also have to obey certain rules of comportment. Wives generally do not leave husbands because being a wife confers status and security. But wives cannot comfortably live with the situation either. Thus, within this cultural complex a woman's condition is at the extreme of what it means to be inside, to the extent that she even has to bottle up feelings, while the circumstances of men with lovers are at the extreme of what it means to be male and outside. It might be said that rather than the fierceness of maroons it is their freedom that characterizes maleness in San Nicolás. Such freedom, in turn, upholds the highest ideals of what it means to be a San Nicoladense in general. As Rosa once emphatically stated with reference to the modest dress worn by many Muslim women, local women would never dress like that because "we are free." Freedom perhaps also explains why women acquiesce to gender roles and raise their children to replay those roles (also Guttmann 1996:103).

Gender and Space: Being Home

Home constitutes the sentimental and social center of people's lives. It is the source of a man's pride insofar as men are supposed to be the providers, and their day-to-day well-being depends in great part on their housebound wives. Yet with modernity have come expenses that often require a woman to work. Don Domingo explained: "In the past," a husband was "proud that his wife wouldn't have to leave [the house], that she didn't conduct business, that she was just at home. Now women have to work to support the children. Now [school] uniforms. Before [just] clean clothes. Everyday ones. Now [school] donations. They didn't let a woman work. Now she doesn't let them [stop her]. Now the woman is more independent because she makes a little money. She's more headstrong. It damages men's pride. Women still ask permission, but it's a formality. It's lovely if both have paid work, but the man no longer feels that he has obligations that include him. Sometimes he goes out drinking and returns bothering her—he hits her. But he can't do that any more because they'll jail him. Now there's no legal right to hit women. This makes men afraid that the woman is going to do well and his pride won't let her. [But] with women working people do get ahead. We have more." Although hitting still occurs without consequences, Don Domingo's comments help to explain contemporary gender dynamics. Because a man's pride will be wounded if his wife is "on the streets," wives in San Nicolás ask permission of their husbands to work, even if it is just a "formality."

All public labor is done by men, who come through town with mattresses, bottled water, hammocks, and the sling-back woven chairs known as Guerrero chairs. Men are the police and the cab drivers, and men work in the fields. But given that men often do not work or that it takes two adults to support a household, women also start small businesses. These extend into the public sphere, but they are always run from home or revolve around domestic items. Because even single women (queridas, widows, women whose husbands have left them) try to make a living from home, it is clear that women internalize the broader gender values that associate maleness with the streets and femaleness with home.

Rosa built a clay bread oven in her yard and sells plastic containers,

A clay bread oven in
a woman's backyard

clothes, and knickknacks from her finished breezeway.[20] Doña Estefanía,
a widow, also has a bread oven in her yard. She employs several women,
including her daughters and daughter-in-law. Doña Lupe, also a widow,
butchers cows at home weekly, has a small pharmacy, also at home, and owns
a cab, which she hires a man to drive. She also sells tacos from home. Margarita and I joke that she should send Margarita remittances, a reversal that
has in fact happened elsewhere in Mexico in the wake of the U.S. recession
(Lacey 2009). Judit runs an ice pop business in the center of San Nicolás.
She and Manuel have a house some distance away. Thus Judit spends most
of the day making ice pops, and the family eats in the central plaza. Judit
also used to run the CONASUPO (the Compañía Nacional de Subsistencias
Populares, or National Company of Popular Subsistence) next door, which
sells food and household items, and is thus also "women's work."

Women make tamales, flan, and cheese at home, and send their young daughters out to sell the food door to door.[21] Young girls also sell bread in the afternoon, often with large plastic containers perched on rolled-up washcloths or towels placed on their heads. "In the old days," Doña Lupe told me, "women had to go to the river or a well for water and carry a lot of it back. Heads came in handy, and they continue to carry things that way."[22] Women also sew clothes from home for their families and for other people. At one point a number of women started a sewing cooperative. Because no one had adequate business training and the promised outside support did not materialize, the cooperative failed. But Margarita, who was a member of the cooperative and also sews in el norte, plans to start a private sewing business from home when she returns to San Nicolás. Women also sell from home clothing bought wholesale.

Apart from home-based businesses, women have few money-making opportunities. In 2009 Doña Lupe became the civil registrar, one of the few public positions for women, but also one that deals with family matters such as births, deaths, and marriages. Several women, including Petronila, Petronila's mother, Doña Hermilinda, and Doña Leticia, own home-based grocery stores of varying sizes where they sell basic foodstuffs, household goods, candy, limited fresh produce, machetes, cowhide sandals, candles, and the like. Doña Leticia's store is the largest, and it contains the only public phone.[23] Other women sell from home sodas, candy, and a few vegetables or other items to get by. Still others slaughter chickens for sale.

For several years Doña Patricia ran the only local restaurant, which she was able to open with remittances from a son. The restaurant had what might be construed as an Indian name: El Nopalito, or the "Little Nopal." Doña Patricia employed several women to cook and wait tables. But when she passed away, the restaurant closed. Women do own billiard halls and cantinas. Although these are lucrative, they are not appropriate businesses for "proper" women as cantineras tend to smoke and drink and spend their days around men who are not their husbands. The few tortillerías in town are run by men because they require heavy machinery. Tortillas are otherwise still homemade by women, some of whom keep small corn-grinding machines and charge others to use them.

Professional opportunities are few, in part because girls' education has not been a high priority, though San Nicolás finally offers a *bachillerato*, the equivalent of the last two years of high school. Pina, the only one of Doña Lupe's children still living in town, is a nurse and the only local woman

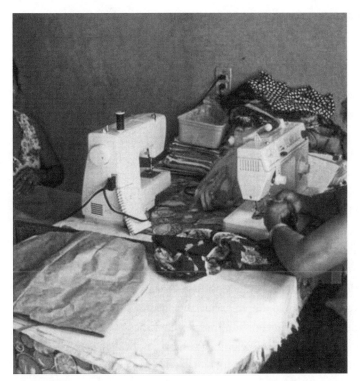

A women's sewing cooperative

A woman sells fresh chicken from home

I know who has attained such a high level of education, although many mothers now have such aspirations for their girl children. But paid work done by women still tends to be associated with the home, including cleaning other women's houses. Such work is interiorized because it does not require a woman—even one not living with a man—to be on the streets to make money.

Gender and Space: Being Outside

"Women are in the home," Rosa offhandedly said one day, "while men are in the fields." Angela also insisted that "men are *for* the street," meaning that the street holds a kind of allure that men cannot resist. Indeed, the only inside space other than their own homes in which men feel completely comfortable are cantinas, where they can keep their sombreros on. Apart from agricultural work, driving one of the dozen or so taxis, or being a policeman, few job opportunities exist on the coast for the men of San Nicolás. Although some young men join the army, the only local federal or state positions, aside from the civil registrar, are for schoolteachers, most of whom are outsiders. Any skilled work, including the mayoralty, requires literacy. Since most older San Nicoladenses are not literate, their opportunities are limited. Thus, although the mayoralty rotates every year, Rodrigo could never take the position because he cannot read. He could, however, become a policeman, a position he held for a while.

Almost all outside work is men's work. I only saw one female cab driver, and no woman has ever been the mayor or a policeman in San Nicolás, although such positions are technically open to them. The work of maintaining the community's infrastructure also falls to men. Much of this work takes place in the town hall or in the ejidal hall. Women are welcome at meetings (*asambleas*) in either place, but since these are public and usually deal with male things such as drainage and agriculture, few of them attend.

When women do attend they sit toward the back of the hall unless the issue directly involves them. Thus when Yolanda wanted her house plot measured because she believed a schoolteacher was infringing on her land, she went to the ejidal hall and spoke up. When Eva was asked to run the CONASUPO because Judit was going to el norte, both Eva and Judit attended a town-hall meeting that included discussion of accounting procedures. But in general the only meetings for which many women turn out have to do with the distribution of food packages (*despensas*) meant to assure a politi-

Men at an ejidal hall meeting

cal party's win in the next election.[24] The only meeting where women and men ever turned out in droves—to which they literally ran—dealt with witchcraft, a meeting and theme I discuss in the following chapter.

In general what happens at a town hall meeting is precisely the opposite of what happens in the Catholic Church, also located in the central plaza but gendered as female, as the Spanish priest intimated. Few men attend church, and they stand in the back. Men have to remove their sombreros in church, as they do at home. Church is thus *like* home, but it is not home because men are surrounded by adult women, they cannot talk, and no man is in charge. Instead, either the priest—sartorially and behaviorally feminized himself, since he wears a long robe, is celibate, and surrounds himself with women (Garber 1992:210–19)—or the rezanderas are. Men will take on the responsibility (*cargo*) of a church fiesta, some belong to religious brotherhoods, and a few are quite actively Catholic, but everything associated with fiestas and caring for a saint takes place outside the church. Only if men have to be in church for a wedding, baptism, or fiesta will they go. And only in desperation—for instance when they need to pray for their health to a saint—will men do what are considered feminine things. Otherwise, as people say, "men can't pray; they don't know the words." "Church is about women's things," Yolanda remarked. "It shames men to be in church. Here they just marry and that's it, until it's time for a baptism and then only because the priest asks the father and mother to go." Then she added that it should not be that way since "the woman and the man are a couple—it was Joseph and the virgin—the two of them."

Manuel said that men did not have time to go to Mass because they were out in the fields or otherwise working. Doña Lupe added that it is women who make promises to the saints. This was clear in Collantes, where we accompanied Jesusa and her family to the shrine of San Gerardo to pray for the health of her son, who had just had his appendix removed. The gathering consisted of women and two boys: Jesusa's son and mine. Carrying flowers, we walked up the main road in the dusk to the shrine, where we waited for the rezandera who arrived with her prayer book and rosary to lead us in giving thanks to the saint.

The several evangelical Protestant groups in San Nicolás do not have many adherents, in part, perhaps, because San Nicolás is not a terribly poor community and evangelicalism in Mexico tends to correlate with poverty. But these groups are more gender balanced insofar as Protestant men do attend services. This is likely because the issues addressed, such as drinking and infidelity, are men's issues. In addition, within Protestant churches the spiritual relationship is between an individual and God, so men have to attend services if they want that relationship. In contrast, a woman represents her family in the Catholic Church. Women are therefore responsible for the day-to-day religious requirements that keep their families and, by extension, their community blessed and healthy.

Right outside the church, in the central plaza in front of the ejidal hall, a tall, leafy tree casts shade over a large boulder. Only men sit under this tree, known as the *palo de chisme* or the "gossip tree." Indeed, even when people are waiting for taxis to Cuaji next to the tree, no woman would ever sit under it. When I came from Mass one day and mentioned that I found only women in church, Ernesto and Susana laughed and told me that while women are at church, men sit under the tree gossiping.

Gender segregation also holds true at wakes. Apart from close kin, only women enter the room where the deceased is laid out surrounded by candles and flowers. They otherwise sit under ramadas made by men, where they pray led by rezanderas. As during weddings, the ramada is essentially an extension of the interior space of the home, and men never join women under it. Instead men arrange themselves in a semicircle outside the ramada and behind the women.

Men under the gossip tree

Wakes are probably the occasions during which men get the drunkest, and they do so collectively. Alcohol is considered a stimulant that helps men stay up all night and thus fulfill the duty to see the wake through to the end and to carry the coffin. While women, too, have a bit of alcohol on these occasions, where cigarettes and sweetened coffee are also served, they are not expected to stay up all night. Instead, they come and go in shifts because of children.

One afternoon I was at Doña Olivia's with her eldest daughter, Yolanda, her daughter-in-law, Doña Socorro, and several other female relatives in the main sitting room, as children ran about. Both Doña Olivia's and Yolanda's husbands passed through and said hello, but they did not stay to chat. I began to ask about gender, which surprised the women because they had never given it much thought. One of Doña Olivia's grandchildren came in, a boy of about ten. He listened for a minute and then immediately interjected as he plopped down beside me: "Women are locked up and men go around outside." A young girl of about eight then ran by without a top and the boy, remarkably astute, commented that she was (un)dressed "like a man."

Doña Socorro's son had just arrived from el norte, and Yolanda had just arrived from Cuernavaca. But Yolanda was inside with her mother, sister, and other women, while Doña Socorro complained that her son had immediately gone out to carouse with his friends. Thus the son, who had come farther and been gone longer, immediately went for the streets, while the daughter, who comes more often and lives closer by, stayed at her mother's side. "We don't see eye to eye," Yolanda said of men and women. "Men think differently. We stay away from each other. There's more trust between women and between men. Women are also a bit scared because men drink and women don't want to go near them. I never thought about it. It all seems normal to me." I assured her that it was.

Trans-Space

San Nicolás is home to a number of people who do not conform to traditional sex roles, despite the town's relatively strong gender differentiation. But the most important aspect of a person's gender is comportment, rather than anatomy. Thus no matter a person's biology or sexual orientation, he or she will conform to the gender rules that best accord with identity. If there is a "third gender" in San Nicolás, insofar as some people are neither male nor female (Herdt 1996; Nanda 1999, 2000:47–48), *volteos* and *lesbianas*, male and female "inverts," respectively, would fit that category, since both have sex with men and women. But only one person ever mentioned a lesbiana to me, and the only volteo I knew always dressed and acted publicly like a man. Thus it would be erroneous to attribute anything but a binary gender system to San Nicolás. Even if some individuals are bisexual, everyone maintains the gendered norms for "being from here." Those who in the United States would be termed lesbians (*marimachos*, or "butch women") thus act *like* heterosexual men; while homosexual men (*putos* or *maricones*) act *like* heterosexual women. Although they often exaggerate their behavior, "no one bothers them," as both Sirina and Leonel told me and as I observed myself. Indeed, San Nicoladenses are extremely tolerant, in part because of their religious faith, in part because gender nonconformists are usually family members, and perhaps in part because of indigenous cultural influences that tolerate gender diversity.

Because of the high degree of tolerance, homosexual men come from other parts of Mexico to live in both San Nicolás and Cuaji.[25] "They work here like women, like servants," said Leonel, using the feminine form for servant (*criada*). "People don't accept them in the cities, but here, yes, whatever God wants; they're put on earth by God." Like women, homosexual men are admired for their skill in food preparation. "In general, maricones are good cooks," said Sirina. "That's why everyone wants them as servants." One homosexual, Luis, told me that he had "arrived lost." He had a friend in San Nicolás and decided to stay; he had not seen his family for forty years. In 1992 he ran a small restaurant. By the late 1990s, he was working for Doña Leticia as a family cook.

Homosexual men have feminine pet names such as La Rubia (the Blonde), La Parota (the Parota Tree), and La Usurpadora (the Usurper). Along with cooking, they prepare young women for weddings and other special occasions that require dressing up. They do makeup, hair, and clothing "because they specialize in it," said Yolanda. When Juana's son married, the family videotaped La Rubia readying the novia at her baptismal godmother's house. As we watched the tape, Juana said that La Rubia did this for everyone.

Leonel and Sirina disagreed on whether homosexual men who worked in someone's home were free to come and go. Leonel, who at the time was struggling with his own fidelity to his young wife, insisted that "the ones that work in a house, they don't let them leave, so that they don't get to know other ones. They can live here quietly, but they can't have a personal life. A village is more delicate, cleaner with respect to sexuality—one doesn't get involved with just anyone. Some of them work in the cantinas, but they just wait on people. They can have sexual relations with clients, but they have to pay the client; a [female] prostitute gets paid by the cantina owner." But Sirina insisted that "at night, they're free. The one that works for Leticia— he's building his house. Right now he's renting. Other ones live in their own houses, but they're free to leave at night. They can visit each other, have sex together, whatever."

My observations are closer to Sirina's assessment. First, Luis lived alone, even though he worked for Doña Leticia. Indeed, unless a homosexual man has his own family in San Nicolás, he is unlikely to live with a family. Second, young homosexual men are not tightly controlled. They freely congregate in the central plaza at night and have sex in empty houses. Although this is not typical for a young woman, a homosexual male teen's virginity is not at stake, and he will not be marrying a young man, reproducing, or otherwise forming a family.

Because gender distinctions are so acute from infancy on, most people identify homosexuals born and raised in San Nicolás, which is the majority, quite easily. By the age of seven or so one can tell if a boy will be homosexual because he will polish his nails and hold himself a certain way, and one can tell if a girl will be because she will enjoy running around topless (as Doña Olivia's grandson was quick to point out) and playing with boys. One time a girl of about ten ran through Doña Lupe's house wearing shorts but no shirt. I was startled in view of her age. Doña Lupe remarked that she was a *marimachito* (a little marimacho) since from the time she was small she had been telling her mother that she was really a boy. "She also likes to ride way up high on her papi's camioneta," Doña Lupe added. Thus, trucks—men's prized possessions that extend their freedom to come and go and that are associated with the streets and the fields, are thus also associated with homosexual girls.

One afternoon I was talking to Don Nicomedes when he told me that his only child still at home was a daughter, Adriana. But he quickly corrected himself and said it was a son, as everyone stood around and giggled. Sirina told me that people reckoned when Adriana was young that she was a mari-macho because she liked to play with boys. And from an early age people would tell her so, and she would listen. "So now she thinks she's a marima-cho," Sirina said.

Adriana went to Rosa's house that New Year's Eve. I watched her arrive with a group of young men. They all stayed on the street instead of entering the breezeway. At the same time, Carlos, a homosexual from Cuaji and a schoolteacher in San Nicolás, arrived with a number of Rosa's female nieces and cousins. Carlos and the young women entered the breezeway. Thus the space around Rosa's house was gendered with the feminine interiorized and the masculine exteriorized. This does not mean that men never sit in breeze-ways or that women do not stop by and lean in for a chat, but the way people placed themselves in this particular instance raised my awareness of gen-dered space.

Gendered space is also evident at dances, where homosexual men social-ize, tease, and dance with each other and with women. Occasionally one man will dance with another. Thus, for instance, at one dance La Parota—whom I had taken for a woman until Sirina pointed out his bra stuffed with cotton—danced in an exaggerated erotic way with a shirtless man (making them appear as a heterosexual couple), and no one took offense. I danced with several homosexual men, including La Parota. This was appropriate, as I was unaccompanied and could only dance with women. As women dance together but men do not, La Parota also danced with La Usurpa-dora. Roberto, who was there with his wife—indeed, the party was for their eldest son's graduation from primary school—also danced with La Parota, but they *appeared* to be heterosexual. Both shimmied as they danced and everyone laughed, including Roberto's wife.

At one dance two homosexual women, including Adriana, wore the baggy pants and long, oversized T-shirts of cholos. "The 'macho' in *marima-cho* means that they fight," Leonel had informed me, and indeed cholos are known for fighting at dances. Once I spotted Adriana driving a truck, again dressed like a man in long pants and a long-sleeved, button-down shirt, surrounded by a number of young men. Juana did not think Adriana was a "true marimacho," however, because in her view this would be an inter-sexed person. "I think if a man grabbed her," Juana said, "she would act like a woman. . . . A marimacho is someone who has two 'parts'—male parts and female parts. Adriana's a woman and not a marimacho. See, a marimacho can have relations with women because she has a man's parts, but Adriana can't. She's a woman." The idea of sexual activity without a penis was thus unthinkable, and Adriana, who did not have a penis, was therefore not a true marimacho. Here, then, a person's gender was related to biological sex. Juana had known Adriana since infancy and therefore knew that she did not have a penis, the exteriority that would make her a man. Rather, her interi-ority, her vagina, meant that she was a woman and that she would act like one given the chance. But most people identify a homosexual woman as a woman who *acts* like a man through dress, comportment, and space. Like a barren woman, she can also be referred to as a machomula. Thus she is another kind of woman who does not completely conform to gender ideals. She is *like* a man but she is *not* a man.

San Nicoladenses do not try to conceal their sexual orientation. Indeed, the public nature of their performances suggests quite the opposite. Even homosexual teenage boys will dress in women's clothes, grow their hair long, and paint their nails. Indeed, one of Doña Lupe's grandsons would take her underwear and a pair of pink wedge sandals that I brought her from el norte. Far from feeling threatened, heterosexual men in San Nicolás are very tolerant. They might tease, but there is no violence, and I never heard very offensive words, except from a Mexican evangelical pastor. Indeed, when the teacher Carlos died of HIV everyone was distraught.[26]

Heterosexual men's attitudes can be attributed to several things. First, many homosexual men and women (who are unthreatening anyway because they are known to be biologically female) are their relatives; second, San Nicoladenses believe that God created them. Indeed, San Nicoladenses are also extremely unprejudiced toward people with mental and physical disabilities, who have their own places in the community and within their families. Third, and perhaps most important, men are so secure in their masculinity that they are not offended by men who are, culturally speaking, women. For how could a woman be a threat to a man?

thousand dollars, enough for a cattle herd, a home addition, or to get a couple to el norte.

I learned the system when I donated several thousand dollars for the road repair, money I had written into a grant proposal for a project towns-people chose. The regidores who led me through the donation process insisted that I pay the gravel company directly, oversee the project, collect the receipts, and let many people know about it, because if I simply gave the money to the mayor he would "eat" it. When I sought advice about leaving money with another mayor to plant trees in the plaza, everyone agreed that he was trustworthy because the house he shared with his wife and eight children was one room with a dirt floor. "If he were corrupt he wouldn't live like that," Doña Socorro said. But when I returned months later, there were no trees, and people quickly told me that he had kept the money.

"You don't understand us," Don Domingo said during a town meeting in which only eight men signed up to ready the road. "They don't want to work." The mayor said people were complaining that the road was only going to benefit the man who owned camionetas, who also did not want taxi service in San Nicolás because it would cut into his business, and did not want the government to pave the road from Montecillos to San Nicolás because it would make the trip to and from Cuaji easier for small vehicles. But when the time came to ready the road for gravel, which became the only passable one during Hurricane Paulina, twenty men showed up.

Yet another problem of the modern is drainage. In the late 1990s Andrés Manzano was Cuaji's municipal president, a member of the PRD and someone in whom many people had placed hope. He was ready to implement a number of infrastructural works (*Noticias del Sur Guerrero-Oaxaca* 1997:5) that included restarting a drainage project aborted several years earlier when another mayor had pocketed most of the funds. The new project was supposed to be completed in two months. "We're going to transform San Nicolás," Manzano's deputy announced during a visit that included a walk-through of an area fast becoming a cesspool because of broken pipes. The state government provided the materials and specialists to design a new system; men from San Nicolás were to provide the voluntary labor. A call for volunteers, however, evoked comments from San Nicoladenses such as people are "selfish"; "people here never agree on anything, they're not united"; "they say that 'the people united will never be defeated,' but we're not like that." Don Samuel sighed, "It makes me sad, the way my people are."

Broken drainage pipes

The completed drainage was scheduled to run through less than half the village.[1] Many believed that only those who would benefit directly should have to work, because if others helped in the initial stages, when the time came to expand the system their neighbors would not reciprocate. Those who had their drainage would just say, "I have mine, why should I cooperate?" "People are apathetic," said Estéban, the builder trying to organize the work brigade. During the same period San Nicoladenses would not pay their water bills, at the risk of having the water completely turned off, because they thought others who did not pay were taking advantage.

Several months later the drainage project had ground to a halt, but not because people would not cooperate. Instead, the architect had miscalculated the width of the pipes, which kept bursting under the pressure. What had previously been a stream of waste water had become a mucky green and brown pond, where diseases and mosquitoes bred and where a child could easily drown. So local people tried, though the project failed, and once again San Nicoladenses shook their heads. As Don Domingo vented frustration over the drainage, he noted that San Nicolás used to be much cleaner because people relieved themselves in the open air, where pigs would consume human waste. But bush and therefore outdoor privacy have become scarce.

Modernity also brought democratization in the form of multiple political parties, which sometimes leads to feuds. Now fingers are marked with indelible ink to limit voting fraud. During the first part of 1997, the PRD was locally in power in Cuaji and in San Nicolás. Attendance at town meetings was deeply affected. Jaime, the mayor at the time, and Doña Lupe, a member of the PRI, told me that PRIistas were boycotting because of the PRD's mayoral and municipal president wins, the latter carrying a three-year term. Doña Lupe started bypassing Cuaji to take groups of women to Ometepec to see the PRI deputy about political issues. In return she occasionally received building materials and the like, but after a few years she stopped because "it was running around for nothing—they never do anything for me." The next mayor, the one who lived in a one-room house with dirt floors, was a PRIista and thought to be incorruptible. But Sirina, a member of the PRD, insisted that he and his brother would try to impose their will on everyone else. When the PRD won Mexico City later in 1997, even though the PRI won San Nicolás, PRDistas commented that "we might have lost the feet but we won the head."

Not long ago, everyone belonged to the PRI. There were no divisions; no election-day tensions; no community friction. Now when the government periodically distributes food packages, people protest that they accord with a person's political affiliation. Thus when the PRI handed them out, Rosa received one but Sirina did not. Sirina complained that this was because the person in charge of distributing them was a PRIista, as was Rosa, while Sirina belonged to the PRD. "There's going to be blood," Sirina angrily said. "We're divided," Ernesto sighed. "Before, when we were hungry, the government would send helicopters with handouts; everyone would line up and they'd be for everyone."

PRIistas especially maintained their political affiliations out of paternalism, both literally and figuratively: their fathers were PRIistas or the president of the Republic was.[2] They expected that, like their fathers, the president would "feed" them if they maintained their loyalty. If Julia and Augustín were PRIistas, Rosa said, Doña Marta would not be trying to close off the entrance to their house by building a fence around the bordering home of one of her sons who was in el norte. Doña Marta told me that she thought Augustín was going to kill her because of the fence, which she never built in the interests of keeping the peace. Political party affiliations can even disrupt family unity. Thus, in one, the wife was a PRIista because her father was, but her husband and his family were PRDistas. Ultimately, no one in the family voted so as not to insult each other. Morenos believe that resident Indians are much more united than they are, despite variations in Indians' political affiliations. "Some of [the Indians] are PRI and some of them are PRD," Don Samuel told me, "but they don't let that affect them. We, the 'rightful' members of this village, cannot work together."

Land, now privatized, continues to cause tensions even among morenos. Thus, for instance, Hugo's mother showed me papers confirming that her former partner, to whom she was not married (both were widowed), had left land to her when he died. His children, however, were threatening her, as they believed the land rightfully belonged to them. Moreover, resident Indians still sometimes express fear that they will be chased out of San Nicolás now that there is more restricted access to land. Angela pointed out that when the Indians first arrived "the land didn't have a boss" and "no one got angry." This again led her to comment about "differences," meant once again to deflect worries about being displaced: "Blacks are different in the way they live," she said. "Also, the way they work, the way they talk . . . we say things the right way: 'dile a tu mujer que venga' [tell your wife to come here], while they say 'dile tu muje,'" she laughed. "Here the men don't go to church. Back where I come from, they do." Thus, much anxiety boils just below the surface, and sometimes it explodes into hostility over money, land, politics, residential rights, water, and many other issues.

The only social sphere seemingly without tension is religion. The number of evangelicals has not yet reached a critical mass—indeed, there are only small pockets—and party affiliation does not map directly onto religious affiliation. The general consensus, even among evangelicals, is that Catholicism and the community's customs are equivalent, and such customs make and remake community. Apart from saint worship, which evangelicals believe to be idolatrous even though they are residents of a town named after a saint, customs include drinking and dancing, which are often banned in evangelical congregations. "Everyone wants to drink and dance," Doña Lupe told me, "so they don't come to the evangelical temple." Manuel said that 90 percent of the people "will go on as they always have." Indeed that has proven to be the case throughout the years because, as Sirina put it, to join an evangelical congregation she would have to change her whole way of being. "Life here revolves around dancing and drinking. To become an evangelical, well, that would be hard. If we were evangelicals," she laughed, "we wouldn't be going to dances."

That Everything Be Clean

The two most significant stages in the life cycle of San Nicoladenses are marriage and death.[3] Both involve days-long rituals with much drinking and, in the case of weddings, dancing. Men also drink with other men in cantinas. Some evangelicals teach that drinking and dancing invite sexual licentiousness, although most San Nicoladenses disagree. I once asked whether drinking made people "hot," a question that drew guffaws from Sirina and Rodrigo, who said no, though they did mention a man who, while drunk, grabbed his wife and chased all of his children out of the house. Alcoholism is nevertheless a problem, especially for men, who normally drink more than women do. Some men attend the occasional AA meeting in San Nicolás. Don Domingo, whose conversations with me frequently become Bible lessons, stops drinking for periods of time, but he can also go on binges. Once I had just arrived and was immediately tapped to drag him out of a cantina, where he had passed out. People thought that if he knew I was there, he would sober up out of respect.[4]

Dancing *can* be sexual, which is why married women dance only with their husbands, with homosexual men, or with other women. But unmarried young people still dance without touching, although older people think that their dancing has become increasingly sexualized, especially when they dance to techno and hip hop, imported from North Carolina. Adults do not like it (they would like it even less if they understood the words) and often leave when the music is not cumbia and therefore "bad." But dancing is central to both Catholic and secular community festivals; it is part of a child's wake because "it celebrates life," and it is considered a form of personal expression. As Héctor, an Indian, noted, "It lets one express oneself. If you feel like it, well, you get up and dance."[5] Thus the freedom to dance when one wants to is important to how San Nicoladenses — including resident Indians — self-identify.

Cooperation and Obligation

Weddings of children with ostensibly evangelical parents might take place in San Nicolás's Catholic Church.[6] Moreover, and perhaps most centrally, the obligations that pass from family to family to sponsor festivals, mostly for saints, are required to maintain community. Thus evangelicals participate fully in some community rituals and partly in others. They will attend a wake for a short time to pay their respects, but they will not participate in what they consider pagan customs. With respect to a wake, the most important of these customs is the soul-shadow calming that takes place during eight days following a person's death. During those days, people pray outside the house of the deceased, where no one sleeps until a cross is carried to the cemetery in a ceremony known as *levantar la cruz*.[7] Once a cross is left at the gravesite, the deceased and his or her soul shadow are reunited, and the body can rest in peace. "Everything is then clean," Manuel explained. This idea that everything be "clean" encapsulates San Nicoladenses' ultimate aspirations for their private lives and for the community.

Festivals are cleansing rites that remake community, and morenos and Indians now participate equally. Once someone has freely committed to sponsorship he or she cannot retreat. Thus, when Javier tried to avoid his obligations because of financial burdens and approached the mayor to plead his case, the mayor told him publicly and in no uncertain terms that if he did not live up to his commitments others would want to duck theirs. The result would be "no more traditions and no more pueblo." Indeed, if someone refuses to fulfill their obligations he or she can be fined, including by the municipal president if the holiday is a national one.

The whole community will be in an uproar if a sponsor deviates from the script, as Judit and Manuel attempted when they planned to hold a dance for the festival of Santiago (Saint James) in the afternoon rather than in the evening. When Manuel was threatened with jail and the couple feared no one would come anyway, they gave in under the pressure that came even from the friends and kin who grumbled about the impending change as they toiled over the decorations. "People were just all over me," said an exasperated Judit.

If sponsors appear to resent a saint's festival expenses—which include food, drink, decorations, music, and elaborate costumes—either that person or their father will be punished by the saint himself. Not only does one have a community obligation to serve a saint, one must also do it wholeheartedly or risk the saint's wrath. Indeed, Santiago's sword is removed from his hand when the festivities start to symbolically forestall any violence. Like Santiago himself, those who participate in the festival's most elaborate rituals, the *empleados* or functionaries, are on horseback. Since functionaries are always paired by gender, they include young women who, for a day anyway, become cowgirls. The horses gallop in the searing heat back and forth between villages, where their riders receive food and drink thus creating not just solidarity but a network of community ties. Although the horses are rested, sometimes they overheat and bleed to death. That only some horses succumb leads people to interpret a horse's death as punishment for its owner's secret lack of devotion to Santiago.

The families of Santiago's outgoing functionaries are obliged to present foodstuffs and other items to the families of incoming ones. Each functionary also sponsors a community dance in the weeks leading up to the main fiesta day and must entertain everyone with fireworks. Together outgoing functionaries provide a final dance for incoming ones, with whom they compete through drinking bouts. A feeling of relief generally prevails after such a financially draining festival. "Salvé," one person said to me after he was done. "I managed."

Although festival expenses are more than many people can bear, it is widely acknowledged that traditions make community, as families and even other villages participate. Because festivals are *for* everyone, not to participate means essentially to not "be from here." Indeed, festivals are so central to village life that people often go to el norte specifically to fulfill their obligations. Juana, for instance, went for a year in anticipation of her son's participation in the Santiago festival. The Indian Héctor also went when his daughter Gisela played a leading role in the same festival. If a festival functionary is in el norte, he or she also might send money for someone else to fulfill his or her obligations.

Like festivals, weddings are community events. While weddings in the United States set themselves apart by their "difference" and "uniqueness," weddings in San Nicolás are fairly generic. They last three days and otherwise follow more general Mexican patterns.[8] Because expenses are so great for the novio's family, large numbers of godparents are invited to pay for everything from the flowers to the rings to the wedding dress to the cake to the music for the evening dance, to which everyone is invited. The dance is generally held outside the novio's family home or at one of the village's basketball courts. The relatively new dance hall is too far from the center of town for people to want to use it, except for exceptional events such as a visiting circus or the entertainment provided during the Meeting for Black Villages.

One of the greatest wedding expenditures, and the area of greatest competition, is the music. Families of lesser means hire local disc jockeys. Wealthier ones hire a band, typically from outside San Nicolás. The most affluent, how-

Tiered wedding
cake on display

ever, hire two bands, one to play at each end of the space. Competition also takes place over the wedding cake: the more tiers and decorations the better. The cake is displayed throughout the evening but not eaten until the following day, when the newlyweds distribute pieces to those who have contributed to the celebration either as godparents or by helping to prepare food. Women might also receive plastic food containers with the date and names of the bride and groom. Other mementos (*recuerdos*), including china figurines, small fabric flowers, and the like, are distributed to guests throughout the event.

Like the music, the cake symbolizes the "wealth" of the novio's family, which is calculated not so much by money as it is by how many godparents of what caliber the family has been able to attract. Some godparents come from as far as Mexico City. Similarly, the number of attendees speaks to a family's popularity and the quality of the celebration. If attendance is sparse, the atmosphere is "sad." Thus wedding success, like festival success, is measured by how many community members are drawn together, which depends on a family's social ties and effort. In this way, individual families make community.

Festival and wedding obligations expand as the years pass and as San Nicolás's population grows both at home and abroad. Rather than restricting access to events traditionally for everyone, however, San Nicoladenses find ways to continue to fulfill their commitments. In the context of a wedding, for instance, the groom's parents need see only to feeding larger numbers of invitees, as even the entertainment for a quickly expanding village with louder and louder music coming from bigger and bigger bands can be sponsored by godparents. Some godparents will be in San Nicolás or in other parts of Mexico, and some will be in el norte but will have sent money, just as people do for festivals.

Along with creating reciprocal obligations, weddings and festivals involve much beef (a luxury but expected food), cooperative cooking (and drinking), and cooperative building to prepare for the perdón and for the evening's festivities. The Santiago festival expresses much of this mutual dependence because while all weddings and festivals involve the whole community, this one culminates in pork and chicken tamales for everyone—another burden undertaken by that year's functionaries with the help of female relatives, neighbors, and ritual kin, who together make the thousands of tamales, the distribution of which marks the end of the festival. Such distribution takes place in front of the town hall, the political and national center of village life as well as the scene of much friction over the consequences of noncooperation. The town hall thus provides an ironic commentary on ideals and stands as a symbol of the embedded contradictions resolved there.

Cooperation is also integral to daily life in Mexico and in el norte. Neighbors and relatives help each other; visitors try not to arrive empty-handed, and hosts always offer a cool drink. Women send token bowls of food to each other's families. Attendees at wakes and memorials make whatever donations they can to the deceased's family to help offset expenses; in el norte they donate for a family to send a coffin home. This climate of cooperation of course contrasts sharply with what San Nicoladenses *say* about their own disunity, about people not working together and bickering among themselves, just as bickering between Indians and morenos belies concordance. In light of this contradiction one might ask whether ritual occasions are reversals or exaggerations of community values. In response I suggest that those values involve competing forces that ultimately work to maintain village life, expanding and contracting to account for historical change, as San Nicoladenses consciously—albeit sometimes under pressure—follow conventions. Those conventions can strain those who must feed and fete more and more people, who feud over access to money, water, drainage, and land, those who try to maintain family ties across geopolitical borders, and who vote for competing political parties. But conventions are also what make *community* possible despite its tensions and strains.

Moreover, traditions themselves necessarily embrace stress and are often lived up to under duress. People do not necessarily want to spend money on public events, nor do family members necessarily jump at the chance to help each other out. For instance, Doña Lupe, who is constantly short of cash for various small business projects, complains that a sister, who is comparatively wealthy, will lend her money, but only at 10 percent interest. This is less than the sister's going rate of 20 percent, but Doña Lupe does not find it very familial. She describes herself as a giving person, who does not hesitate to part with money if she has it and someone else needs it. Indeed, San Nicoladenses do gift money, which can, after all, also come from the ground and is therefore something akin to a gift of fruit. "I'm a chain," Doña Lupe once said, meaning that she depends on others and others on her. Her sister, on the other hand, would "let me fall from a tree like a *guayaba* [a guava] [with a thud]." Doña Lupe also sold a commercial space to Judit and Manuel for two thousand pesos, "even though it was worth twenty thousand." "I gave it to them as a gift," she said. Gifting and being part of a reciprocal chain are therefore "native" values that might compete with more individualistic or egocentric tendencies. However, because of San Nicolás's history as a ranching community, home to both independent, wage-earning cowboys and to cooperative peasants, I would hesitate to pose too much of a contradiction between the individual and the collective, or between a monetary economy and gifting, as in many ways these oppositions overlap and are traceable to the colonial period.

Anger, Intimacy, and the Preservation of Symmetry

Tensions among San Nicoladenses can arise around different axes as certain decisions—such as whether to save money or to spend it—can compete and create discord within the community or between individuals.

While the community takes steps to alleviate such discord, at least by setting generally recognized behavioral standards around the yearly festival
cycle and mechanisms for alleviating disputes, and while group pressure
makes people adhere to these standards, things more intimately related to
family life are not subject to community policing and therefore lack the out-
lets that help resolve public tensions. While private tensions can erupt in a
flash and cause one man to shoot another, they can also simmer for years,
until they cause ailments, which also involve a cleansing for which "soul
calming" is a metaphor.

Although many ailments afflict San Nicoladenses, I devote the rest of
this chapter to *coraje*, which is best translated as "anger," "wrath," "spleen,"
or "bile." In this sense it shares some of the characteristics attributed to the
archaic use of these terms in English. Coraje is closely related to *muina*,
"an annoyance" or "nerves." Like coastal Mixtecs not far from San Nicolás
(Flanet 1977:104), San Nicoladenses often describe coraje and muina as the
same thing, or muina as a side effect of coraje. Thus San Nicoladenses say "I
have coraje" or something "gives me muina."

Coraje affects adults, children, and pet birds. Its physical manifestation
is phlegm (*flema*). Unlike public tensions, it is incurable in adults. People
nevertheless try to alleviate the phlegm to bring their live bodies to rest, and
in so doing to heal personal rifts. Given the sorts of ongoing conflicts I described earlier and in the previous chapter, coraje can constantly threaten
a person's health. Like other ailments,[9] it invites a deeper understanding of
the sociocultural rules of place-making, as it involves the maintenance of
personal boundaries and what happens when they are crossed. It also im-
pedes the freedom of movement so central to people's identities. Importantly, coraje also speaks to Indian supernaturalism: morenos try to avoid
angering especially outside Indians so as not to be ensorcelled, but outside
Indians also soothe through cleansing rituals the strife of moreno life.[10]

I noticed that San Nicoladenses often spit. Initially I thought this was
due to smoking, which it is, but not because San Nicoladenses smoke regularly. Some of the elderly, including women, smoke tobacco leaves, and
some people smoke filtered cigarettes, though only cantineras, who are all
women, appear to. But smoking is usually a purgative that helps to expel
phlegm; hence the spitting. "Homemade cigarettes are better than manufactured ones," Delia said. "If you have coraje, you make a cigarette out
of tobacco leaves," said Margarita as she made a rolling motion with her

hands. "[Manufactured] cigarettes make the phlegm thicker and affect the lungs while [homemade cigarettes] don't. They get the phlegm out without making it thicker," Delia explained.

Phlegm begins in the stomach. "Your stomach hurts when you have coraje," Sirina told me. "Because [phlegm] is cold," she added, referring to the necessary balance between hot and cold that applies to foods and anything else that passes through the body. A stomach ache also prevails among coastal Mixtecs, where "anorexia, pain at the kidney level, or stomach pain is due to muina, to coraje" (Flanet 1977:104). Although Flanet does not explain phlegm in detail, in San Nicolás it moves from the stomach to the throat, which simplifies its expulsion. But left unchecked, it continues to travel through the body, causing the greatest danger to the heart, where it *se pega*, or "gums up the works," and can cause a heart attack.

Phlegm and coraje are "like this," Margarita told me one day while crossing two fingers in front of her face. "You have to avoid coraje in order not to produce phlegm," she continued. "Phlegm builds up—that's why people get sick from coraje," said Sirina. Thus the resultant phlegm, rather than the coraje itself, causes physiological distress. Although coraje is not amenable to absolute cures, morenos seek out especially Indian healers for the condition: a diagnosis of coraje requires effort to expel the phlegm that materially signifies it, and Indians are most adept at purging. But expelling phlegm does not cure coraje. It only keeps it at bay. The best medicine is to avoid it entirely.

But because San Nicolás is relatively small, and disputes can be quite serious, coraje is difficult to avoid. Many kinds of interpersonal tensions cause it, and it accumulates bit by bit from sour or broken social relationships and emotional trauma. Delia used the term to describe her feelings when her half-brother was shot and killed over an agrarian dispute during a festival. Sirina used it to describe how she felt when her father was murdered, also over an agrarian dispute, and when Yanaris would disobey household orders. Such disobedience occasionally ended in a beating. "She's obstinate. Sometimes I hit her so hard with twine or whatever is around that her skin turns purple." Rodrigo asked me if I had coraje after a neighbor accused me of stealing mangoes from her tree, and Sirina told me that my son had it when he was crying. Beatriz used the term to describe her response to her husband's irresponsibility and infidelity. "He's with another woman now," she once told me. "And it gives me coraje." Eugenia also linked coraje, her husband's infidelities, and responsibilities toward children. "Here women suffer," she said. "Sometimes it gives me coraje."

Rosa explained that "people are always trying very hard not to get into arguments, but it's difficult to avoid. That's what's wrong with us." "How does one avoid coraje? Some people can't," Margarita said. According to Cosme, an individual suffering from coraje can "calm it" but never completely pull it out (*arrancarlo*). "Those who have it, including women who argue with other women, try to ignore unpleasant things, so that they don't get even more coraje." Cosme's comments, along with Sirina's observations that "one tries not to have enemies" and that men "have more coraje," helped me to understand why a tipsy Manuel passed by our house one evening to announce that he got along with everyone, before he continued up the road.

Coraje is a form of "embodiment" (Collier et al. 2000; Low 1994). It involves the physical body and is mediated through culturally specific metaphors, in this case phlegm, which is heavy, cold, causes throbbing, wends its way through the body, and is constantly expelled in an effort to rebalance the body. How San Nicoladenses describe coraje resembles *nervios* (nerves) among Costa Ricans, Guatemalans, or Puerto Ricans in New York (Low 1994), *chawaj* among the Highland Maya of Chiapas (Collier et al. 2000), coraje and muina among Zapotecs in the Valley of Oaxaca (O'Nell 1986), coraje among the Yucatec Maya (Woodrick 1995), or *bilis* (bile), used interchangeably with the term *coraje* among Mazahuas in the state of Mexico (DeWalt 1977). Thus, as Setha Low points out, commonalities exist among different groups (1994:157). Phlegm is said to be cold, and along with these other ailments, coraje is likely rooted in the Western European system of humoral balance, often expressed as "hot" and "cold" (DeWalt 1977:6; but see Ortíz de Montellano 1987 for possible syncretic Aztec/Spanish origins).

While comparison can indicate the breadth of general illness categories, "the illness embodiment is metaphorically framed in symbolic terms that are specific to the cultural and social context" (Low 1994:157). Thus, to understand San Nicoladenses, coraje and the disputes that provoke it must be located in meanings and experiences grounded in their specific histories and systems of social relations. These specificities, unlike many of the aforementioned illnesses, which are interpreted as related to socioeconomic struggles, involve spats with neighbors, arguments over land, the raising of children, and men's infidelities. Moreover, both women and men in San

Nicolás suffer from coraje, albeit for different reasons and with different results. In other places similar nervous disorders seem to afflict mostly women, a conclusion that I suspect partially replicates Western understandings of female "hysteria," rather than being a carefully considered analysis of how various kinds of disorders can look one way in a woman and another way in a man, especially in societies with strong gender differentiation. In San Nicolás, while all adults can catch coraje, it is more dangerous for men, whose freedom means that they are more likely to die or to be imprisoned. As Doña Ana said, "people who fight, they have coraje."

Coraje, Children, and Birds

Aguirre Beltrán wrote only one paragraph about coraje. He presented it as particularly affecting children, whom it could kill: "One cause of illness is an intense emotion or passion introduced into a child's body by an adult. Ticha passed in front of Chelo's house. He was full of anger (*ira*). When he saw that Chelo was carrying a child in his arms he said, 'Jesus, Chelo, keep this child inside so that I don't bump into her because she will then get coraje.' Coraje is, in effect, the name of a medical classification with respect to infants, which makes them ill and kills them. . . . Every *cuileña* mother knows the danger of this illness and tries to prevent it with religious relics hung around the neck or the wrist" (1985:193).

Today children—especially infants—are still susceptible to "catching" coraje from adults. But if Aguirre Beltrán's account is correct, coraje is no longer as lethal as it was. Only Patricia told me that one of her children had died from coraje; everyone else claimed that children survived. Birds, however, the only animals San Nicoladenses coddle like children, can also catch coraje, and they do invariably die. "If you're fighting with someone—for example, with your husband—you harm the bird," said Sirina. Parrots and macaws are talkers and said to gossip together. They are taught to speak "like a child, you just repeat words," said Sirina. Birds are caught in the bush, but they are also "of the house. We raise them," Patricia explained. They live among people, perch on their shoulders, peck at their ears, are talked to, given affection, and specially fed. Birds, Maximino told me, are the only animals given names. While dogs and cats also live around houses, they remain outside, are fed scraps, do not talk, and are not indulged or anthropomorphized. "Birds are more delicate than dogs, their lives are more fragile,"

Sirina said. "Dogs are tougher." Dogs go to the fields with their masters, and cats are only kept to kill mice and other small pests. Cats are particularly mischievous since they do not obey and steal food.[11]

Birds are the free creatures that fly out of San Nicolás, the saint's, hand. Thus the affection San Nicoladenses have for them is moderated by the knowledge that enclosing a bird, like enclosing a child, is morally wrong. Indeed, like children, birds that live around adults are defenseless and susceptible to illnesses caught through the air. As Andi explained, pet birds catch muina from people, though *loros* (large parrots) are hardier than *periquitos* (parakeets) because they are larger. When Patricia pointed out that "[birds] are taught to speak," she added that "they're delicate; they're very light, and they get ill from coraje." Now most of the birds are gone, she added, because the bush is gone. Birds thus in some respects represent a past way of life. As Papa Nico lets go of a dove, so people have had to let go of the land's bounty.

Just as in Aguirre Beltrán's day, infants are still protected by their parents, given that any adult—especially an unknown one—can pass coraje on. Because Petronila runs a shop she would always protect her infants from clients. When one had a fever for three days running, she called a doctor, who recommended cough syrup. I was in the store when Petronila mentioned to another customer that the baby might have a bit of coraje. "Yes," the woman said, "there are so many people coming in and out of here—maybe one hurt her." Petronila responded that the syrup did in fact make the baby vomit a lot of phlegm, which was also in her excrement. One of Sirina's infant nieces also caught coraje when Sirina and Rodrigo went by to see her. Sirina and Rodrigo had just argued, and the baby caught their coraje "from the air." Like Petronila's child, the niece was cured with a liquid—in this case sesame oil. When Rosa's daughter Nidia, a toddler at the time, "had a lot of coraje, muina, phlegm," Sirina instructed Rosa to give Nidia oil with a bit of salt.

Remedies involving vomiting and tobacco water hold for older children. The backs of their throats are tickled with feathers to "free" the phlegm, something Petronila said she was not going to do to an infant. One day I saw Sirina put her finger down her youngest son's throat. At first I thought she was trying to brush his teeth, but she told me he was in a foul mood (indeed that morning I had heard him screaming) and that she was trying to make him expel phlegm to cure his coraje. He bit her finger, so she used a feather to tickle his throat until he vomited. Afterward she gave him a bit of tobacco water and he fell asleep. The same day, after my own son had been crying for hours, Sirina suggested that he might have coraje too. Of course I attributed it to fatigue, but then what is the difference between being tired and being angry, especially for a child? After all, Sirina's son slept after his treatment, just as my son needed to do.

Bearing the Great Corajes

In adults, coraje is often connected to events long passed. For instance, when the elderly Doña Cata was explaining her coraje, she included the long-ago murder of her husband in an agrarian dispute. His murder precipitated that of her eighteen-year-old son as he sat in the plaza in San Nicolás drinking a soda, because those who had killed her husband feared the son would seek revenge. Then her fourteen-year-old daughter, who was not even menstruating yet, was raped while working for a storekeeper in Cuaji. One of four men who had taken her away was later fined by the authorities in Omepetec, even though, as Doña Cata explained, "[The boy's family] had money and I had 'dirty teeth.'" In other words, while Doña Cata was poor, she nevertheless won the suit. "These are the great corajes," she said, "the greatest ones—when they kill a family member, when they take a young daughter by force." She connected her coraje to her own powerlessness. Not only did she have "dirty teeth," a reference to her poverty, but "I'm a woman," she said. "I couldn't do anything. People can't do anything," she continued. "They just try to bear [aguantar] it."

Delia died in 2007 relatively young. She had suffered many tragedies before my arrival in 1997. One day Margarita and I were talking about coraje as she walked by. "She has a lot of coraje, that one," Margarita said. As Delia and I became friends, we began to talk about phlegm. One day, as she responded to my questions, she immediately, as it appeared to me then, switched the subject to the story of the (half-)brother who had been shot to death. Yet of course a connection existed between phlegm and her brother's death, as well as between phlegm and her mother's death three months later: Delia and her mother were both full of coraje because of Delia's half-brother's death, as well as that of another brother eleven years earlier.

Delia told me her story in fits and starts, sometimes looping back to a point she had just made. Declaring that she indeed had a lot of coraje, she immediately associated it with phlegm:

I spit. One gets rid of coraje from the inside, and I have to purge myself to get rid of it. I use olive oil, a spoonful, it's like honey. That's how I cure myself. I didn't have this before. But they killed my [half-]brother. If it were God's will it wouldn't hurt so much, but they killed him, and it wasn't God's will, so it caused coraje. One gets angry. Coraje makes phlegm. This is where I feel it [she pointed to her throat]. I smoke tobacco and look, the phlegm comes out. Now it's coming out on its own because I haven't eaten anything. If someone has a lot of phlegm they can't eat chili. If you eat chili when you're taking oils you get blotches all over. You can't drink very strong alcohol either. The oil gives me diarrhea and the phlegm comes out from below. But I have to purge myself. I also vomit to get rid of it. Coraje is air—like now—an adult passes in front of a child—it's air—and the child can catch it from other people. Oil with salt gets rid of it [in a child]. If someone spits a lot it can also be because they have parasites.[12] But that's saliva, not phlegm. Phlegm is thick. With parasites you have to go to a doctor for medicines.[13] Phlegm is thick, green, it comes from coraje. This is why it's bad for me to have a cold soda or an ice pop.[14] It's like curds, beef fat. [There's] phlegm in the heart. It's bad. It doesn't allow the heart to function. [The heart] wants oxygen. If a child gets coraje they take it out and the child is fine. It's easy to get rid of it in a child. But in an adult?

Delia pulled tobacco leaves out of the refrigerator. "I smoke. It gets rid of the phlegm." As she smoked she expelled a great deal of phlegm. "You fall asleep [with tobacco]," she continued. "It makes you drunk. I smoke. I get into the hammock and sleep. There are various ways of getting rid of the phlegm, you see. When my [half-]brother died it gave me a lot of coraje. Children get it from the air, but adults, no. I got it because they did something to me. Children are clean. Adults aren't. They've all got coraje." Delia's reference to cleanliness and frequent references to God give her account something of a sacred nature: in this sense, coraje can be read as a punishment for sin, and purgatives cleanse the soul as much as the body. Because young children cannot be sinners, they cannot die from coraje.

Delia's story did not end there. "My mother was very nervous," she continued. "She had coraje, muina. She had a lot of coraje when they killed my brother [eleven years earlier]. She had it in the esophagus. It was stuck to it, then in the liver, and so on. They were going to operate on her. We took her to the hospital but they couldn't operate. She was quick-tempered and irritable, but not malicious. She died from this phlegm that blocked up her esophagus. Food couldn't get through. This phlegm came from her heart, from the death of her son. She didn't have it before. We tried to cure her with herbs, but it didn't work. Not even an Indian can cure this thing."

Gender, Race, and Coraje

Sirina said that because she and Rodrigo fight a lot, both have coraje. "He has *pure* coraje," she said, while describing her own in a more nuanced way. Like Doña Cata she spoke of "bearing it." A woman, Sirina said, remembers it all the time; it gives her muina and makes her emotional. "I carry coraje in my breast," she continued. "Yes, I have coraje. I have it at one moment but not at another. Just for a minute and then I forget it. I remember it a bit, but not too much. A lot of people become anxious and don't eat.[15] They just drink. Yes, I have coraje, but when it passes I eat. I also cry when I have coraje." "Men," she continued, "go around thinking about their coraje all the time."

Delia's remark that "not even an Indian" can cure coraje identifies Indians as powerful healers, even if they cannot completely dislodge this ailment. By the same token, Indians are feared because coraje directed at one can be returned in the form of witchcraft. This became apparent one day when Sirina was at the health clinic and Rodrigo's Indian lover Marina walked in. Wives and queridas try to avoid each other, but in this case it was impossible, and Sirina lost control.

> I had something to say to her. I told her that this was the moment that I was going to call her on it. I felt coraje. She stood there in the door. I felt like my blood was boiling. "What are you laughing at you motherfucker?" She didn't get angry. I was the angry one. She sat down and then stood up. She pushed me and I went backward and fell into a chair. I reached out like this—she has straight hair; straight like an Indian's. I grabbed her hair with so much force. I felt muina, and I pulled her hair really hard; she flew about and fell on the floor, banging her head twice. "You want a husband . . ." [Sirina started to say to her]. But there were a lot of women there. "Get off of her," they said. "You're going to hurt her really badly." The doctor intervened. A few women grabbed me from behind and others grabbed her. She thought she was biting me, but she was

biting the doctor. The other women said to me, "Get a hold of yourself; don't give yourself so much coraje, you'll hurt yourself." She pulled my shirt away from my shoulder. I drew blood from her, but she didn't leave a mark on me. I came home. On the way I said to myself, "What have I done? I lacked respect for the doctor." I sat until the muina passed. Then I went to a friend's house and later went back to apologize to the doctor.

Sirina then told me that *even though Marina was an Indian*, "I'm not afraid." "Sometimes Indians are evil," she continued. "One doesn't know—some of them do witchcraft and others don't. If she wants to hurt me she can send someone to my house to look for some clothing or a dirty rag and bring it to her—she can then take it to wherever they do witchcraft. She could cause an accident or an illness so that I couldn't walk. If you're sick you can't even make love. There's a lot of evil going around right now."

Rodrigo spent that night away from home, with Sirina convinced that he was with Marina. When he returned the next day he berated Sirina for fighting in public, commented that people could see her underwear, and told her that she was reducing herself to a prostitute, for his reputation was at stake if he could not control his wife (Díaz 2003:108). Sirina made tortillas for his dinner as she listened to him shouting at her. "You can imagine my silence," she later told me. "I thought he was going to hit me."

Soon after this, Rosa and I were at Sirina's and Rodrigo's house after they had argued. "Rodrigo is full of coraje," said Rosa. Apparently Rodrigo had accused Sirina of bewitching him with powders she had purchased from an Indian Indian woman from the mountains, the mother of a woman who lived in San Nicolás. He believed that Sirina had mixed the powders with water and then sent the concoction to Marina's home, meaning to kill both Rodrigo and Marina. But only Rodrigo had consumed the water, after which he vomited and developed a tremendous headache. Hence his coraje over what he thought Sirina might have done.

In the middle of the argument about who had done what to whom, Rosa tried to calm Rodrigo. She denied that the woman had passed by her own house on her way to collect the six hundred pesos Sirina allegedly owed for the powders, and pointed out to Rodrigo that whoever had told him to suspect Sirina "is no friend of yours. If he was your friend he would tell your family, not you directly, because what he told you is giving you coraje. Everyone knows that coraje kills, and people say things just to kill them with coraje." Thus gossip can kill. Friends and birth family are supposed to protect loved ones rather than give them reason to be angry, while an alleged friend can be an enemy in disguise.

Rodrigo then redirected his coraje toward the Indian Indian woman, whom he threatened to kill if he caught her. "It's all her fault," he said. "It started with her." According to him, she had been seen at midday at the church taking two candles. These were later found in the graveyard next to a dead chicken, suggesting that she had conducted a sacrifice. A place of extreme ambivalence, the graveyard is a space where family members—including those who have migrated—rest peacefully together in death, as I discuss in the final chapter, but it is also a place where spirits wander and witches practice their craft in secret.

As if things were not complicated enough, the graveyard again came into play when, a few days later, the mayor, Jaime, called a town meeting about a "little old man." The meeting was held in the ejidal hall, which holds more people than the town hall, where San Nicolás's jail cell is located. As I arrived with Sirina, I saw Cuaji's uniformed police posted in a pickup truck in the plaza with their rifles visible. This indicated that whatever was afoot transcended the ability of San Nicolás's police force, of which Rodrigo was then commander, to handle. I was rather amazed to see the hall full of men and *especially* of women. Indeed, Jaime had gone out personally to gather people, and the church bells were rung for good measure. People literally ran to the meeting.

Inside a slight, gray-haired man in a multicolored blanket, huaraches, and the white trousers and shirt of a Mixtec, sat on a corner bench. His name was Romelio, he had spent the night in jail, and I later spoke with him. The matter at hand was twofold. First, someone had been digging skulls out of San Nicolás's tombs for several months. Second, Roberto had seen Romelio scratching the ground at midnight in front of his mother María's house. The questions were whether Romelio had taken the skulls from the graveyard tombs and sprinkled powders made from them in front of María's house in an attempt to bewitch her, or whether, as he claimed, he was simply scratching the ground for buried money. The tombs, called *bóvedas*, are "hidden things," Cosme told me. Indeed, any place with a lot of money, such as a bank, is also called a bóveda. Thus the ground on which San Nicoladenses walk, in which they bury their dead, in which their ancestors hid money, and in which crops grow, is in itself a source of wealth. But that source is hidden and always seems elusive, except, perhaps, to the cleverest Indian "owners" of Mexico.

As the meeting got under way, Sirina called out: "We want to know who's responsible!" And then Rodrigo spoke: "Yesterday we discovered fifteen tombs disturbed. This began when the old man arrived. His profession is to cure people. He cures people and looks for buried money. Roberto saw him digging around in front of his mother's house at midnight. He says he was looking for a mine with Juana, Juana's son, and another woman. He'd been digging around for about five days. But Juana denies that she was there, and we want to know what he was doing in front of the house."

Romelio stood up, walked over to Jaime, and wagged his finger while refuting the accusation of witchcraft. But Roberto insisted that it was so. "What were you doing over there at midnight?" Jaime asked Romelio. "Listen, Sir," Romelio replied, "everything is a coincidence." Suddenly a man brought out the hooked pole allegedly used to yank the skulls from the tombs. Romelio had not himself been caught with the pole. Yet the pole was found in the graveyard, where Romelio had been spotted during his stay. Thus he was the logical suspect.

Jaime once again tried to make Romelio admit that he had sprinkled powders in the doorway of María's house, which Romelio continued to deny. Jaime then asked the crowd what further proof it wanted. Carmen loudly proclaimed as the din drowned out people's words that Romelio was from Collantes, where he had also performed supernatural acts, as Romelio shook his head in denial. "What'll we do with him?" Jaime asked. Various ideas chaotically tumbled out: "He should return to where he came from"; "Let's run him out of here"; "Who were these women [his accomplices]"?; "Send him to Cuaji; they'll know what to do with him."

At this point Romelio, who seemed angry to me but who, I was later told, had been drinking to quell his fear, was led out as San Nicoladenses continued to talk. "People are angry that graves were opened"; "Some women have his powders" ("They grate the bones to make powders," Sirina explained to me in an aside). "Some people here are accomplices . . . these people who were scratching at the ground." A man read out the names of the families to whom the skulls belonged, while Jaime attempted to bring calm: "People not from here [i.e., "outsider" Indians such as Romelio] must behave with dignity . . . but if an honest person comes to work here and then does something fucked up, well . . . I want to send the police [to the graveyard at night]." Sirina shouted, "I don't agree," because she did not want Rodrigo spending his nights at the graveyard.

Jaime then asked who Romelio's accomplices might have been, since Juana was denying that she was one. "The old man didn't go around by himself," Jaime pointed out. Someone yelled, "it's the [female] schoolteachers: he gives them powders for their rooms."[16] A man pointed to a woman: "She offered me a powder. I said I didn't need it." Jaime insisted that Juana make herself known to the crowd, as people yelled that she go to the front of the room.

María then started shouting at Juana while the deaf-mute Yuyu gesticulated wildly for everyone to calm down. Romelio was brought back in and the mayor asked him if he had had anything to do with Juana, pointing out that Romelio and Juana were contradicting each other since Romelio insisted that he was digging for a mine while Juana insisted that Romelio was doing "an evil thing," but that she had nothing to do with him.

Romelio denied any evil and was again removed. "He's dangerous," people commented as he was escorted out. María then shouted that she had seen Juana in the company of Romelio for at least five days prior to the scraping at her doorway, which everyone understood as an attempt to ruin her successful cantina business. "Someone threw powders in the doorway of the house; bones and earth from the graveyard. I think they wanted to bewitch me," she twice repeated. Although María had not seen Juana with Romelio the night Roberto sighted him in front of the house, and in the dark Roberto could not identify Juana either, María believed Juana to be Romelio's accomplice because the two were friends and because Juana also owned a cantina, which meant that she would have liked to see María's go out of business. "They threw the earth from the graveyard [in front of my door] and made a huge cross out of it," said María. "*Even if she [Juana] were my sister*, I would want her punished."

Jaime implored the crowd, "Look, this guy is old. Let's do this: the police can take him to Cuaji." One man responded, "Let him die"; another, "Let's punish him here"; another, "Let him sleep in Cuaji's prison." People were so angry that, as Rodrigo later told me, if they could have, they would have taken Romelio out to the bush and killed him. When I asked why, Rodrigo simply replied, "Because he's a witch" and because he disturbed the graves.

Jaime handed Romelio over to the Cuaji police. Before they left I stopped to speak to him through the cell bars. He told me he was Mixtec and from

Putla in the Mixteca Alta. His wife was in New York. He was related by marriage to a moreno family of San Nicoladenses. In fact, he had been summoned by a relative to cure the man's son-in-law of *espanto*, a term that literally means "fear" or "fright" and which in Mexico refers widely to a condition that brings on chills after someone has been unwittingly exposed to a spirit. The son-in-law confirmed to me Romelio's story and that Romelio had cured him. Romelio stayed on after the cure, looking for other work as a healer. ("Curo," he told me; "I cure.")

It is difficult to say whether someone who was not an Indian Indian would have been so quickly found guilty. But despite María's insistence that she would want Juana jailed even if they were sisters, Romelio's alleged morena accomplices were not jailed, even though some people claimed the women had roped Romelio into doing their dirty business and accused him only to extricate themselves. Thus one could conclude that Romelio's Indianness contributed to San Nicoaldenses' verdict.

I was still not certain why Romelio had allegedly taken the skulls or why people were so agitated, though I understood the grief and anger. My greatest "aha" moment came when Rodrigo told me that Romelio had taken only the skulls of men killed by bullets, not women's skulls, "because women do not die that way." The crania of men killed by bullets are stronger, he said, because of the coraje in their heads at the moment of death. They can be shot anywhere in their body, but coraje concentrates in the skulls which, once pulverized, are potent. It was never clear to me whether this meant that coraje was a material thing, like phlegm. But this is the only time I heard coraje referred to as a substance rather than as an emotion, and even then it was only a substance insofar as crania in a sense "contain" it at the moment of death. I note in this respect that even Romelio allegedly used pulverized skulls. No one said, for instance, that he tried to extract coraje from them. If Romelio did what he was accused of, he would have revived what was otherwise inert and resting peacefully in the graveyard, the coraje brought on by arguments San Nicoladenses try to avoid.

Men were additionally alarmed because women had allegedly exchanged sexual favors for Romelio's curative powers. Romelio therefore presented a threat to moreno men's control over women. That he had breached the boundaries of what was deemed acceptable behavior in San Nicolás was thus both raced and gendered. That he had kin in San Nicolás did not matter at all. As with Rodrigo's accusation that the mother of a San Nicoladense had given Sirina powders with which to bewitch him shows, kinship is not a defense, which María also made clear when she noted that even if Juana were her sister she would want her punished. Perhaps because of the danger, or perhaps because Indian Indians are most feared, I never became aware of a resident San Nicoladense, Indian or moreno, successfully accused of witchcraft. Indeed, Romelio's alleged accomplices were the only San Nicoladenses I know who were even suspected. Healers exist in the community; but witches do not want to practice their craft there.

I had never before and have never since seen so many women attend a town meeting. But the Romelio incident involved women directly. I felt palpable fear from Romelio and from San Nicoladenses: Romelio feared the wrath of the community's men, and the community feared Romelio's suspected witchcraft, especially the pulverized traces of their own relatives' coraje. Indeed, Romelio's ordeal compelled me to ask pointed questions, thus expanding my understanding of coraje, people's personal ordeals, and their efforts to deal with life's tensions.

The Aftermath

The fallout from Romelio's "trial" continued for months. First, Jaime fell gravely ill, ending up in a Mexico City hospital where he nearly died. Although doctors diagnosed pancreatic failure brought on by drinking, many people believed Romelio had bewitched him because Jaime had ordered Romelio's arrest, thereby giving Romelio coraje. Then Rodrigo fell ill. As he was the police commander, this meant that the two men most involved in the resolution of Romelio's case had been struck down. While Jaime battled for his life in the hospital, Rodrigo complained of stomach pains and that phlegm—which he was constantly trying to expel—had settled in his throat. For months he searched for a cure fearing that it would kill him.

Because the origins of certain ailments and their cure are often hit-or-miss propositions that bring much uncertainty, different theories arise in individual cases, depending on a person's history. San Nicoladenses have three ways of attempting to diagnose and treat particular ailments: biomedicine, saint worship, and magic. The first involves white doctors. Ometepec has two hospitals; San Nicolás has a clinic (sparsely staffed) along with one or two private doctors. But doctors, especially local ones, have few tools with which to diagnose biomedical illnesses beyond common ailments such as high blood pressure and diabetes, both of which are on the rise because of dietary changes and increasingly sedentary living.[17] Their prescriptions for other ailments frequently prove ineffective. San Nicolás also does not have a first-class pharmacy, and many people cannot afford the ride to Cuaji or medications that doctors might prescirbe. Thus, for instance, when Angela took Denalis to the doctor in Cuaji, I paid for the taxi and the baby's treatment.[18]

Unlike doctors, healers recognize themselves as part of a curing *system*, because they do acknowledge some ailments as the purview of biomedicine. As Doña Lupe said, medical doctors cannot tell if a nagual caused an illness, for instance, but a healer can tell if an illness can be cured by a medical doctor. Healers charge more than doctors: "Really expensive," Doña Lupe said, "2,500 to 3,000 pesos" (see also Aguirre Beltrán 1985:194). Morenos will borrow money to see an Indian healer, as Sirina and Rodrigo did, using Sirina's gold jewelry as collateral for their loans. Rodrigo admitted that "some *brujos* tell you the truth and others do not." Nevertheless, like the constant search for a cure, the constant search for the right healer can preoccupy San Nicoladenses.

Rodrigo first saw a white doctor, who gave him Prozac and told him his problems were "all in his head" (see also DeWalt 1977). The quest for a cure then led Rodrigo, accompanied by Sirina, to the Christ King's shrine in Maldonado, where he left flowers and said a prayer. But after consulting doctors and pleading the intervention of a saint, neither of which cured him, Rodrigo came to believe that his ailment, which had all the hallmarks of coraje, resulted from bewitching: either by Marina, now gone; by the Indian Indian woman he thought had given powders to Sirina; or by Romelio, yet another Indian Indian. "Indians are evil," Doña Marta once told me. "My cousin," she continued, "put some Indian peons to work and didn't want to pay one of them. The same day, he was killed by lightning.[19] One has to speak nicely to them. My nephew says 'cousin' to Indians [to placate them] because they're evil." Her reference to this form of address suggests that respect and pseudo-kinship ties might protect someone from an Indian's wrath.

Because Rodrigo was genuinely scared of dying and because his suspicions focused on Indians, whose witchcraft is particularly lethal, he consulted several Indian healers. Although Delia had said that "not even an Indian" can cure coraje, when Cosme discussed coraje, he said that one had to consult "a different kind of healer," by which he meant an Indian. As I observed, people who believe they have coraje, especially if the source is an Indian, do consult Indian healers if they can afford it, if only to keep the phlegm at bay. Therefore, as during the colonial period, Indian power is double-sided: it can harm through what Miguel Angel Guttiérrez refers to as its "destructive side" (1993:24), or it can heal (Lewis 2003). Morenos are implicated in both because, unlike whites, they believe in it. Moreover, while any Indian can potentially be a source of harm, Indian Indians control the most potent supernatural powers. It is no coincidence, then, that although Romelio spoke Spanish, as most Indian Indian healers do to cater to their clientele (indeed Sebastián once said that few people go to the least assimilated Indian Indians because they cannot understand what they are saying), he also wore indigenous dress and came from the mountains. In some ways morenos therefore follow colonialist ideologies and practices, imputing supernaturalism to geographically, culturally, and socioeconomically distant Others (see also Derby 1994; Lewis 2003; Taussig 1987). Yet this distancing is muted by morenos' ready acknowledgment that they are themselves deeply caught up in Indian supernaturalism. Indians thus possess skills "foreign" to non-Indians, but morenos are also *like* Indians because, in contrast to whites, they trust that Indians can both harm and cure them.

Rodrigo first visited an Indian woman north of Ometepec, who palpitated his body and gave him a purgative to induce vomiting and fainting. Sirina was there to catch him as he fell. But when he continued to suffer, he turned to an Indian man in Cuaji who told him that he would be fine, that he had a hair lodged in his throat from witchcraft a woman had inflicted through his food or drink.[20] Although Rodrigo paid 3,500 pesos for the man's services, he insisted that he had not been cured and continued to take the white doctor's Prozac. Cost, therefore, does not act as a placebo. Rodrigo continued to hack up phlegm. "I have coraje," he insisted. "It sticks."

One day he rested in a hammock while Sirina went to work baking bread in her mother's clay oven and Modesto erected chicken-wire fences around their yard to protect young trees from wandering donkeys. I sat with Rodrigo for a while as he told me about his gastritis and acid, which he also believed to be exacerbated by a fish bone lodged in his throat. The white doctor's medicine was curing the phlegm, he said, but the throbbing he felt came from coraje. "The heart palpitates," he said, referring to coraje's latter stages. Cosme wandered over and joined our conversation. "Mexicans are very violent," he said. "We're full of coraje. Gringos, well, they reach an agreement. We don't. If we get into a fucked-up situation we're like animals." Both then again described the symptoms of coraje, along with other

Juan curing a morena in Tlacamama

least in the wider society any kind of supernaturalism is considered highly heterodox.

Juan knew without being told that Rodrigo had seen a doctor, that he had been ill for months, and that he and Sirina had been fighting. He told Rodrigo that two people were bewitching him, which was why he was not improving. Rodrigo asked Juan to cast his affliction back toward those bewitching him, but Juan responded that God would punish him if he did, as he only cured. He did ask if Rodrigo wanted to know his tormentors' names, but Rodrigo declined while speculating about one man with whom he had a minor land dispute, because he did not want to add to his coraje.

I went along for Rodrigo's second visit, during which Juan cleansed Rodrigo and Sirina and informed one of their nieces that he could not cure her because her ailment (likely vitiligo) was the purview of biomedicine. After this session, Rodrigo looked much healthier as his pallor disappeared. When we returned to San Nicolás he explained that he believed in Juan because during his first visit he had seen a man who could barely walk— the man's brother had had to carry him and his fingers were scrunched up like claws. But during Rodrigo's second visit, which was the disabled man's third, the man's hands were straight and he was walking with a cane.

Juan had told Rodrigo that there was something evil in his home and that he would have to come to San Nicolás to perform a midnight cleansing (*limpia*) of the dwelling. One day Juan sent a message that he was coming to "cure the house," and he invited me to observe. He arrived from Tlacamama late that night, accompanied by his wife and son-in-law. Sirina fed them before Juan set up a small washtub in front of the vanity in the bedroom where the four youngest children were sleeping. The washtub held water and a figure of San Antonio, whom Juan mentioned in the chants that were otherwise in Mixtec, with the exception of the first line: "The Father, Son, and Holy Ghost." Propped up on either side of the washtub were bunches of sweet basil, which morenos and Indians use for curing rather than for eating. Lit candles flanked the basil, and beside them were three bottles of liquid, one the strong alcohol *aguardiente* (firewater). Juan sat on a wooden crate facing the washtub and chanted for about ten minutes to the saint figure immersed in the water. He then sprayed Rodrigo with aguardiente from his mouth, and sucked Rodrigo's neck, from which he extracted a bit of paper and three stubby worms, all of which he placed in the water, into which he also spat the aguardiente.

When Juan then rubbed Rodrigo with the saint figure and the basil, Rodrigo keeled over, his eyes rolling up into his head, and passed out. Juan continued to cleanse the rest of the family—the children now wide awake—with the herbs. Sirina developed a sudden headache, and I became nauseous and ran home to vomit, the only time I have done so in San Nicolás, despite the many illnesses I have had there. When I returned Juan was cleansing both rooms with the herbs. He then switched off the lights and beamed a flashlight up to the ceramic-tiled ceiling and into the various corners, settling on one over Modesto's bed. We went to fetch a ladder so that he could reach in from the outside. He poked around, found a gap, and asked for a knife. Soon he found a human figure made of packed earth.

Back inside, Juan dropped the figure in the water, rubbed an egg over the now conscious Rodrigo, cracked the egg, and spilled its contents, polluted with Rodrigo's affliction, into the water. Eggs were also rubbed over Sirina and the children, and dropped whole into the water. Juan reserved Rodrigo's eggshell and brought in a live turkey, rubbed it over everyone and, as he held it over the water, cut off its head, sacrificing the also polluted blood that drained very neatly into the washtub, which also held the herbs. Juan placed the turkey head in the eggshell, and immersed both in the water.

Once Juan completed the cleansing, he instructed Modesto to bury the contents of the washtub at the edge of the yard. We sat outside talking quietly for a while as the children fell asleep on the ground. Sirina and Rodrigo made plans for a visit to Juan for Rodrigo's final cleansing. "It doesn't make sense to have yourself fully cleansed before the house is cleansed," Sirina explained to me, "because you then just return home with the thing still there and you get sick again."

During Juan's same trip to San Nicolás he also cleansed the mayor Jaime's house. Although Jaime's family did not believe in witchcraft or that Romelio had bewitched him, his wife was prepared to try anything to save him, especially as Juan had told her that Jaime had indeed been bewitched. Jaime came home several months after Juan's visit, and while he is still frail, he is alive.

Because home is the center of family life, and family lives and houses make up the community, Juan's curing of both Rodrigo's and Jaime's homes was akin to curing a social illness, thus bringing peace to families. Through families the community is symbolically cured. Indians, then, not unlike priests—who also bless houses but do not "cure" them—make the place most central to moreno life a clean one.

Resident Indians and Witchcraft

Resident Indians linguistically and sartorially resemble morenos: they speak Spanish and do not wear traditional dress. Moreover, their supernaturalism is muted. Although Rodrigo suspected that Marina had bewitched him, and Sirina asserted that she was not afraid of her, Doña Marta explicitly excluded San Nicolás's Indians from her characterization of Indians as evil. Most revealingly, even Angela pointed out the virtues of assimilation as she discussed at length the dangers of witchcraft in her natal Mixtec community.

Her story began with her sister, whose mother-in-law disliked her. The mother-in-law made a doll from a piece of her sister's skirt, which she buried in the earth under her sister's bed. Her sister stopped eating—she felt something in her throat, a needle—and quickly died, along with her one-month-old child. Angela's brother was a Catholic lay preacher. One day he encountered a catechist who could not read, while the brother could. Jealousy ensued and Angela insisted that "it gave the brujo [the other catechist] coraje." The brujo pulled on her brother's hand when they parted with a handshake. "So those brujos are evil," she said in the middle of telling me the story. "If someone has coraje because of me . . ." she drifted off thinking about how she might find herself bewitched, and then returned to her tale. Her brother walked away after the handshake, Angela continued. Married and with a baby daughter, he and his wife still lived with Angela's father and wanted to build their own house. "In my land," she said, "houses are still crude, made of adobe, mud, and hay." Her brother went to gather branches for the house, and as he pulled one down, a large animal fell from the tree. He felt back pain and went home to tell his wife, but he did not tell her about the animal. His condition so worsened that he hired two peons to finish the house, which he only saw once as he rapidly deteriorated and died.

Angela's paternal grandmother was also killed by a witch. A feisty woman who liked to farm and grew abundant crops, she made other people jealous, giving them coraje. One dawn she was passing over a small hill when a "cold, cold, cold" wind hit her. This was caused by a witch, Angela said. Her grandmother lasted for a year while her father searched for healers. He spent a lot of money until one finally said, "Your mama is going to die. If you don't believe me, go to this other settlement. There you'll find a woman who is the voice of Juan Diego."[22] Angela went with another *abuelita* (grandmother) to see the voice of Juan Diego.[23] The woman came to her paternal grandmother's house, and the family went to visit a statue of the Virgin of Guadalupe. "Tell us the truth," said Angela's father, "because the brujo said [my mother] was going to die." The voice of Juan Diego told them not to sell more animals or to waste more money, because yes, she was going to die. Within an hour, she added, they would find a creature in her throat.

When Angela's grandmother died a dog entered the house.[24] The family then found in her throat a thin snake that seemed to be made of blood, which they pulled out and burned. "My father is still alive because he doesn't fight," said Angela. "There are really evil people [in my land]," she said, "brujos. There are a lot of brujos there. I'm afraid to go there." She felt much safer in San Nicolás, she declared, because she had less to fear from Indian witches.

"Some blacks believe in witchcraft," she said, but "we [Indians] all believe in it." She was convinced that Romelio had bewitched both Jaime and Rodrigo and told me that when Rodrigo had caught Romelio, he had told Romelio that he was going to "have you buried alive." "Romelio—he was an Indian," she said, "and they say that Indians are more likely to be witches."

Balance

I began this chapter by sketching sources of community tension that can lead to bitterness but which can also be resolved so that everything is "clean." Coraje invites a more intimate understanding of especially inter-personal tensions such as infidelities and murders, while adding another dimension to the fraught yet conciliatory relationship between morenos and Indians. As black Indians, morenos share cultural habits with Indians, and they are caught up in Indian witchcraft and healing in ways that whites are not. Indeed, an ailment like coraje—which one does not want to give to an Indian and which only an Indian can alleviate—is not even evident to white doctors.

Indian Indians are especially entangled in coraje because not only does the alleviation of this stubborn ailment require "foreign" intervention but someone can also be ensorcelled, especially by an Indian full of coraje, which requires a countervailing force for a cure. As Romelio and Juan dem-onstrate, then, Indian Indians can either imbalance the body or heal that imbalance. Thus morenos often placate Indian Indians, whom they do not wish to anger, by calling them "cousin." But they also approach Indian Indi-ans to cure the symptoms of coraje that so interferes with their lives. Curing is essentially cleansing, and just as a house is cleansed of a wandering soul after a death, bodies are cleansed to bring balance to interpersonal relation-ships and to the homes people make for their families, as Juan's rituals—which illustrate the close relationship between home and family—demon-strated. Such rebalancing stabilizes individuals again, and as it does it heals their relationships.

For family balance all members have to be healed, which healing is a metaphor for the state of interpersonal relationships. Healing, in turn, can be extended to the whole community, as demonstrated in a reverse way by Romelio's alleged desecration of the graveyard. In other words, while most coraje results from interpersonal tensions, the community can have a kind of collective bout of coraje, which Jaime tried to temper by having Romelio taken away. Because the skulls Romelio allegedly took belonged to men, and because they were filled with coraje as the men had died violently, one can argue that within the gendered ideologies that enclose women and give men their freedom, including to express themselves, men are so free that their very beings are in danger. Notwithstanding Sirina's outburst, which is rare among women, Rodrigo was ill for months and Delia's brother was murdered, as were Doña Catalina's husband and son, Doña Marta's cousin, who was also Delia's brother, Sirina's father, Doña Lupe's husband, and a host of other men I have named and not named here. Most of these killings stemmed from agrarian disputes, which makes land central to (male) moreno life, while women's coraje focuses on the maintenance of the home, the female center of moreno life. Being "closed in" protects even as it oppresses women, while being "of the streets" and public makes men vulnerable even as it underscores their freedom. In curing coraje—though perhaps temporarily—Indians put moreno families back together again by recementing the outside and the inside, the male and the female, the streets and the home. Indians thus remake the core of a community otherwise seemingly fraught with discord and tension.

The trappings of modernity, such as literacy, multiple political parties, transportation routes, and even drainage, have all been lightning rods for tensions. Before there was drainage the village was cleaner; before the PRD arrived everyone was united; before there was literacy people had to share knowledge; before there were decent roads there was little competition over transportation. My focus in this chapter has been to connect these wider tensions with more intimate, familial ones. While Indian healers are never called in to cure community-wide conflicts (a function that partially falls to festivals, in which Indians often figure prominently), that Indian healers alleviate conflicts within families is significant to the maintenance of the broader community itself, since families make up that community. Only with peaceful families can the community function.

People perceive migration as the greatest threat to family unity. The final chapter focuses on what seems, like spit, to be a mundane issue: cinderblock houses. But cinder block is a prism for most of the issues discussed in this book: folklorization and history, black-Indian identities, modernity, upward mobility, reconciliation, and finally death, the outcome of coraje in adults and the way in which San Nicolás's extended families finally reconnect to place.

CHAPTER EIGHT

Transnationalism, Place, and the Mundane

Me voy, me voy, me voy	I'm leaving, I'm leaving, I'm leaving
Para los tres Monterreyes	For the three Monterreyes
Me voy, me voy, me voy,	I'm leaving, I'm leaving, I'm leaving
Para más nunca volver	And will return no more
Me voy, me voy, me voy	I'm leaving, I'm leaving, I'm leaving
Yo ya me voy como pájaro perdido	I'm leaving like a lost bird that has
que se encuentra malherido	been badly wounded
Yo ya me voy para más nunca volver	I'm leaving and will return no more
Adiós compañeros míos	Goodbye my companions
Adiós amigos queridos	Goodbye dear friends
Donde yo quise triunfar de por	Where I wanted to succeed, in
diós yo se los pido	God's name, I ask of you
Que no me vayan olvidar	That you not forget me

— TRADITIONAL MEXICAN SONG

Shall I Stay or Shall I Go?

Doña Cata sang this traditional song to me in 2002 as her "good-bye." She was getting too old to dance, sing, and travel, she said. Before she died in 2007 she told me that she had taught a lot of young people to dance, but they had all gone to el norte. Like other Costa Chicans, San Nicoladenses have a migration history more recent than most Mexicans, including those from elsewhere in Guerrero,

Doña Cata

who long ago founded well-established U.S. communities, for example in Chicago (Vaughn 2005:130–31). San Nicoladenses established themselves in Winston-Salem in the mid-1990s, after a decade of migrating to Santa Ana, California, where some families remain. A trickle of Costa Chicans that included San Nicoladenses turned into a stream as the southern United States offered work, cheaper housing relative to wages, and fewer Latinos with whom to compete (see also Quiroz 2004). This internal migration is part of a wider Latino pull toward the global U.S. South (Murphy et al. 2001; Peacock 2007:23–24). In North Carolina the Latino population quadrupled between 1990 and 2004,[1] while Forsyth County, of which Winston-Salem is the seat, saw an 841 percent increase between 1990 and 2000 (*Chronicle of Higher Education* 2002). San Nicoladenses often complained even before the recession of 2009–10 that Winston-Salem was so crowded with other Latinos, including fellow San Nicoladenses, that work proved difficult to find. A few, such as Margarita and Maximino, moved to Chester County, Virgina, which is close enough to Winston-Salem to visit family while offering less labor competition.

As I write, some San Nicoladenses have returned home, principally to wait out the U.S. recession. Yet despite return migrants, the Winston-Salem community probably still numbers close to one thousand. Most hold jobs in the service industry, in construction, and in light manufacturing, including in the remnants of the textile industry that was once a mainstay of North Carolina's economy. Although much construction has halted, it pays relatively well and has been the backbone of San Nicoladenses' survival. Such work corresponds, in fact, to Morenos' status on the Costa Chica itself, where they are sandwiched between rich whites and Indian peons. But expenses are high in the United States, in great part because of remittances sent home. Thus most San Nicoladenses live in substandard and crowded conditions, often in areas scarred by drugs and street violence. Their bosses are typically white, while neighbors and coworkers are mostly African American or Latino (the latter often relatives or friends from San Nicolás).

San Nicoladenses still cross the border at Tijuana, even though their destination is North Carolina. Judit, who has made the journey several times, has family in California and in North Carolina. While North Carolina is her usual destination, she would never consider the Texas border because "Texas is scary. The people, well, they'll turn you in in a second . . . they're Mexicans, but they're residents and think they're better." When a group of San Nicoladenses once did try to cross at Matamoros, "the coyote didn't know what he was doing," Rosa said. The group was robbed on the Mexican side, and most moved on to Tijuana. But a couple returned to San Nicolás, where it emerged that the assailants had forced everyone, including the women, to remove their clothes.

Normally San Nicoladenses leave town at dawn in mixed groups of mostly men and a few women. Men try to protect women from robberies and rapes, while women try to mediate conflicts among their male companions and between them and potential assailants. A hired camioneta takes them from San Nicolás to Acapulco. From there they fly to Tijuana. Doña Leticia organizes these trips, including hotel reservations at the border. For many it is the first time they have left the region. Indeed, sometimes young people have never even been to Pinotepa Nacional. The conventions of travel are often unknown, as they were to Modesto, who, his parents gleefully said, clenched his backpack at the Acapulco airport when security asked to search it. Today the cost to cross the border is several thousand dollars, even though coyotes include family members from San Nicolás. Hence people sell land and cattle or take up collections from friends and family, loans repaid once a migrant begins working.

For those in their teens and early twenties migration has become a rite of passage. Migrants include single young women, which is uncommon in Mexico, remarked Esther, Judit's eldest daughter and one of the few San Nicoladenses married to a northern Mexican. "All young people want to go to el norte," Felipa said, as she was awaiting her parents' permission. "All of them, all of them," she added emphatically. When I asked why, she replied: "They're bored here, and they don't want to work in the fields." It is now generally expected that young couples will leave for el norte immediately after they marry; indeed, often they come from el norte to marry, with no plans to stay. A godmother played a joke on one such couple through public wedding gifts of a gourd, a sombrero, a machete, a tortilla press, a bucket, and other accoutrements of a traditional rural household.

Although Judit was going to North Carolina, in addition to finding Texas scary, she wanted a relative to collect her U.S.-born son Marti in Mexico and drive them both across. Thus she and Marti crossed at Tijuana, with Judit stuffed behind the back seat of the car. She had argued with Manuel about going again for "a better life for my children." Manuel, who could not accompany Judit because he had been jailed in North Carolina, tried to dissuade her, especially from taking the son to whom he was so close. "You have enough to eat here," he argued. Indeed, in general San Nicoladenses do have enough to eat. Although NAFTA has contributed to the destruction of Mexico's agricultural sector, San Nicoladenses do own fertile land, and they are not fleeing political conflict or overwhelming drug violence. Yet most are caught up in the culture and economy of upward mobility, which means leaving field labor behind. Because salaries and hence mobility are attainable in el norte, they go in droves.

San Nicoladenses are thus part of the transnational flows characteristic of past decades, and their lives cannot be contained within national borders (see also Levitt and Glick Schiller 2004:1003). Yet they articulate their rationale for leaving San Nicolás with reference to the village, by linking migration to their desire to build cinder-block houses for their anticipated return. Their stated reason for leaving is therefore to "build my house" in

San Nicolás rather than, for instance, "to feed my family" or to settle permanently in the United States. "Building my house" is not a euphemism. Personal remittances do buy food, clothing, appliances, furniture, and electronics, and attend to other wants and needs,[2] which, Kimberly Grimes notes, means that migrants "[maintain] and [renew] their social relationships and their connections with their home communities" (1998:133). But in San Nicolás most money from el norte goes to accumulate building materials bit by bit and to eventually construct a home.[3] Because those in el norte are powerfully tied to San Nicolás, the village space is a prominent symbol of enduring connections between migrants and nonmigrants, members of the same family and the same community. Like Papa Nico, who returns only once a year although he still loves his people and watches over them, San Nicoladenses plant themselves in el norte while simultaneously sustaining a place in their Mexican community. Houses are the most concrete of the goods remittances buy, and because of the importance of domestic spaces, houses speak most directly to place.

Scholars stress that in great part because of proximity, many Latin Americans live "simultaneously in two countries" (Glick Schiller and Fouron 2001:3),[4] or multilocally through "transnational migrant circuits" (Rouse 1991) and "social fields" (Levitt and Glick Schiller 2004:1008–9). Yet most San Nicoladenses in the United States are undocumented, and migration theory often fails to address the distinct situations of the undocumented and the documented.[5] For the former, simultaneity might not be as characteristic of their lives, for it is almost impossible to fully "live" in the United States, even though they spend their time there. Lack of documentation conspires against cultural fluidity or bifocality, a description that assumes an equal sense of belonging in two places at once.[6] Most San Nicoladenses older than fifteen do not speak English unless they were schooled in el norte, and they cannot communicate with landlords, employers, the electric company, and so on. They are stymied by state and federal laws that make mobility and community involvement within the United States difficult.[7] Furthermore, they do not participate easily in border-crossing processes because the return journey costs too much and proves arduous. This makes it all the more remarkable that I have never known of a San Nicoladense to die in the crossing and that so many people return for festivals, to find partners, and the like. Indeed, because most San Nicoladenses in the United States are "stuck," their orientation is generally toward San Nicolás and Mexico, which permit them fuller social participation than does el norte. Rather than being "radically pulled . . . apart from place" (Inda and Rosaldo 2002:11) many San Nicoladenses therefore appear constantly pulled toward San Nicolás. Without downplaying the fissures and dislocations that characterize migration, and without losing sight of the structural conditions that compel it, it behooves us to ask how undocumented migrants maintain place. By attending to San Nicoladenses' Mexican presence I therefore highlight the meaningful sentiments and obligations that orient them to their village and make them always (affectively) there.[8] This orientation motivates at least the middle-aged with hopes for a future return, even though many of their children and now grandchildren were born or raised in el norte and have no plans to go back for good.

During one of my visits to San Nicolás the taxi driver from Cuaji was a young evangelical who informed me not only that the world was about to end but that Gisela was three months pregnant and marrying Pedro the following day. After their daughter Denalis was born, Gisela followed Pedro, who had already left, to el norte. Amalia and Alberto went several years later, and then Chela joined Oscar, Gisela's brother. Chela finally became pregnant in el norte while Gisela had her second child there (one of Pedro's cousins had brought the now seven-year-old Denalis years earlier).

Amalia and Alberto have a toddler daughter and a newborn son. Today, Amalia, Alberto, their children, Amalia's brothers, their partners and children, and two of Alberto's cousins and their partners and children share a house they bought in Winston-Salem. Pedro, Gisela, Chela, Oscar, and their children all live together in Winston-Salem, too. This immigrant generation, now in its mid-twenties with children of its own, thus often forms lateral households (though young married couples still often live with in-laws in el norte). It also continues to reflect the black Indianness central to the history of San Nicolás and to moreno identities while maintaining, like older generations, what Nina Glick Schiller and Georges Eugene Fouron refer to as "long-distance nationalism" (2001).[9] In this respect, most young people would return periodically, as their nonmigrant parents beg them to do, if they were not undocumented. They are all friends on Facebook, and when someone posts a picture, everyone is tagged. One young woman, who has stayed in Mexico and works in Cuaji (where there is now Internet service), posts images of events in San Nicolás for her family and friends in el norte. The comments on these photos are compelling and often heartbreak-

Chela pregnant
in el norte
with her niece,
Denalis

A young Indian-moreno family in its Winston-Salem house

ing, coming as they do from young adults often separated from extended family and a way of life fondly remembered. But home grows ever more distant as it is impossible for people of all ages to regularly attend the rituals that characterize community life. Those who have left close family behind wonder when they will next see them, and telephone calls and videos of missed events make for lifelines. Indeed, my visits to San Nicoladenses in the United States often include watching lengthy videos of events such as weddings and festivals, taped in San Nicolás, during which the commentary is endless as viewers giggle and point out who is doing what and with whom (see also Quiroz 2004:20). Satellite television now carries a program about coastal customs, and people watch it avidly. I recently promised Margarita, who has been in the United States at least ten years longer than she had planned to be, that the next time she visits me I will show her San Nicolás using Google Earth.

Houses are perhaps the most compelling indication that middle-aged and even younger San Nicoladenses in the United States do not allow migration to disrupt ties to home. Indeed, because people cannot go back and forth, even younger ones symbolize place through home construction and land purchases in San Nicolás: Amalia and Alberto bought a house and land there, and Ismael bought land. Oscar, a bricklayer, built his home there before he brought Chela to el norte, first sending remittances for the building materials that would replace the adobe home in which his parents and Chela lived. Each time I visited, more materials had accumulated until, in 2005, I arrived to find a brick home in place of the adobe. This will eventually belong to Oscar and Chela.

Some young people do return for good—as did Luis after he obtained a high school diploma in el norte and came back to teach English in San Nicolás; as did Eva's daughter when Eva suddenly found herself pregnant and needed help around the house; and as did Marti when, at the age of ten, he missed his parents too much to stay in Santa Ana with his aunt to study and become truly bilingual. But Antonia, who left San Nicolás when she was five and is recently engaged at eighteen, told me that she had no memory of it. Amalia misses her mother but Alberto has no plans for their return. Ismael does not want his children to "grow up in the dirt" as he did. And even though he has bought a house plot in San Nicolás, which suggests what Steven Vertovec calls a kind of "cognitive tension" between "home" and the "foreign" (2004:975), he is reluctant to send his children, all U.S. citizens, even for a visit, though he periodically checks with me to see if I can take the oldest. Modesto has been gone for twelve years and, while he has a room in Sirina's and Rodrigo's house, he has no plans to return. Neither do Gisela and Pedro or Chela and Oscar. All of Margarita's and Maximino's children are in el norte, two now with families of their own. None of this means that migrants will never return. It simply means that what began as a journey of only a few years to "build my house" becomes a sojourn that might stretch until old age, when offspring can support elderly parents who want to return to San Nicolás.

Migration is not for everyone. Not only do the oldest and youngest typically stay home, the *wealthiest* do too. For instance, none of Don Daniel's and Doña Candelaria's children has ever left. All were schooled in Acapulco and live in Cuaji or San Nicolás. Jeffrey Cohen points out that members of "relatively comfortable" households in rural Oaxaca might choose to not migrate (2004:125). Yet in focusing on economic need, he fails to address what wealth "buys": status by allowing some men to have many lovers; elaborate weddings for some families; and the maintenance of a position in and ties to a community, in this case San Nicolás, without "having to" migrate. Indeed, nonmigrant families enhance their status as "true" San Nicoladenses.

Home Is Where the Heart Is

Migrant San Nicoladenses' presence and sentiments are evident in the place they departed, which is central to the logic compelling such departure and confirms their ongoing attachment. Most pointedly, cinder-block houses speak to the violence of a modernity that ruptures family ties. But they also speak to the enduring importance of place, kin, and belonging, and to the paradoxes of being labeled black in Mexico, where blackness is historically tantamount to ongoing displacement. Despite hardships, during the past ten years Margarita and Maximino have built a five-room house in San Nicolás, with an enormous breezeway that runs its length. The breezeway is enclosed with wrought-iron grating, although there is still no front door. As with Amada's and José's house, where I first lived, I have contributed to the construction of Margarita and Maximino's house rather than pay rent. Since I am the only nonfamily member Margarita allows to stay, the house otherwise stands empty, since no relatives need it. In fact, many unfinished houses built with remittances stand empty.

Unfinished and empty cinder-block home with breezeway

San Nicolás is full of cinder-block houses in various stages of construction because the task of building one there while maintaining family in el
norte and at home is a stretch. Returns get pushed back and houses are
built "bit by bit." Indeed, a recent study found that 56 percent of homes in
San Nicolás still lacked a room dedicated to sleeping; 15 percent of families
had only two rooms; and 11 percent had only one (Barragán Mendoza, del
Carmen, and Cañedo Villarreal 2004:221). Thus people's aspirations do not
precisely match the results.

In 2001 during a visit to the Museum of Afromestizo Cultures in Cuaji, I
purchased a Valentine's Day card from its small collection of gifts. The cover
of the card is a cut-out heart; the interior a blurred color photograph of a
redondo. A few barefoot people are outside, on a bench or under a ramada.
The caption describes the redondo as from San Nicolás. Directly above the
photo is a verse, written colloquially but translated as: "My mother told me
not to go to San Nicolás; I am going to San Nicolás even if I die tomorrow."

The words might be a general warning to avoid San Nicolás or a more
specific caution to the subject that his or her problems will only worsen. The
verse and the cut-out heart also suggest, however, that those cautioned are
so strongly drawn to San Nicolás that not even death will stand in the way.

Because the verse on the card was specific to San Nicolás, its content and

MI MADRE ME LO DECIA
QUE A SAN NICOLAS NO FUERA
A SAN NICOLAS ME VOY
A UNQUE MAÑANO ME MUERA

REDONDO SAN NICOLAS, MPIO, DE CUAJINICUILAPA, GRO.
MEXICO

Front of museum notecard   Inside of museum notecard

its placement above the redondo suggest connections to place. One might read those connections in this context as a mummified rootedness in the past. When I read Margarita the verse over the phone, she said that it reminded her of the ballads of her youth: "From a time when people didn't know how to read and were ignorant." The community was rife with violence but, Margarita added, agrarian disputes were endemic throughout rural Mexico then.[10]

Even today, however, as the souvenir implies, many outsiders and Costa Chicans continue to attribute violence on the coastal belt to a local ethos bound to what is construed as the fierce character of "black" people. Thus the card's emblem and verse aim to appeal to those who find the coastal belt compellingly exotic in this way. By the same token, and as the card indicates, blackness is also associated with the primitive (see also Lewis 2004). Within this discourse moreno identities, and the centrality of "modernity" and migration to community life, are ignored. Redondos therefore have a central place in the cultural calculus of the present as culture workers "rescue" local traditions to draw out the exotic. As they do, however, local people not only leave; they replace the earth of the past with the cinder-block of the modern.[11] Because cinder blocks belong to the modern, however, they never become part of the culture work that rests on the difference of the past.

Like spit, cinder blocks might not seem to inspire culturally thick ethnographic description. U.S. Americans, for instance, associate cinder block with bland suburban utopias dotted with strip malls. Cinder block is also denigrated by elites in parts of the world where the maintenance of the quaint or exotic feeds tourist economies (e.g., Perlez 2004). Contemporary houses are invisible in accounts of coastal belt culture. But the sheer ordinariness and ubiquity of cinder blocks beg for an ethnography of the mundane. Like spit, these homes are texts for reading deeper meanings: they signify the routine and extraordinary experiences of people's day-to-day lives, in this case the entwined processes of migration and global restructuring that simultaneously foster new displacements *and* reconnections.

San Nicoladenses tend to look at the past ambivalently, with a mixture of nostalgia and shame. They also see themselves as Mexicans with a future, although elderly people especially lament what is gone. "Building my house" in San Nicolás therefore means to replace structures made of "dirt" with sturdy cinder blocks that withstand earthquakes and hurricanes and are more aesthetically pleasing than adobe or wattle and daub. Cinder blocks, also called *material*, are expensive. But their pull is so strong that cross-border migration has burrowed deeply into village life.[12] In a literal and a figurative sense cinder blocks "cement" people to the community, even though they might never return alive. Cinder blocks change property boundaries and social relations, but they also carry emotive meanings, which are most pointedly replicated in San Nicolás's cemetery, where people are buried next to family, in tombs resembling houses. Romelio's alleged desecration of San Nicoladenses' tombs, and Juan's cleansing of Sirina's and Rodrigo's house, both therefore encapsulate the importance of home.

Houses in San Nicolás indicate how emigrants recall a place that many have not seen for years and that their children may never have seen or may have forgotten. They represent aspirations for upward mobility, the rural and oft-disdained past, and ongoing attachments to a community where family members remain and where most will return to be buried. Migration causes displacement and conflict, but in the end, as is the case with drainage, roads, festivals, or any other community project, the village of San Nicolás is at the center of people's hearts. Houses thus highlight the ironies of the migrant experience, as people replace the ephemeral adobe and wattle and daub and reinforce their ties to a place that changes day by day, in large part due to the accelerating transformations that migration engenders in the community's physical and social landscape. Houses also highlight the disconnection between outsiders' interest in people's "African" heritage and San Nicoladenses' lack of interest in that heritage, in part because of their understandings of cinder blocks and global restructuring, and in part because they are Mexicans for whom the past is not only *not* African but gone.

The Past in the Present

Redondos and other dwellings made of earth, such as adobe structures, are not "real" houses for San Nicoladenses. But redondos do draw attention to San Nicolás's past, for until about thirty-five years ago they were common in the village, and many people remember living in them. Redondos similar to the one depicted on the museum card were typical on the Costa Chica in the 1940s, as Aguirre Beltrán documented. Some displayed crosses at their apex, as they typically did before the revolution that curtailed the authority of the Catholic Church. As I have shown, Aguirre Beltrán emphasized the isolation of the region's blacks, as well as their differences from both national (mestizo) and indigenous populations. His claim that redondos were "Bantu" was adopted by contemporary researchers, such as Robert Farriss Thompson, as I discussed in chapter 4. But as I also showed, there is ample evidence for the Indian origins of redondos, as in Frederick Starr's images from the Mixtec highlands. San Nicoladenses do associate them with Indians. Don Margarito said, "Indians also lived in redondos—I saw them when I went to Ometepec, to Igualapa. The little Indians had their little round houses. They would gather in them—everyone was there . . . now redondos are gone. There aren't any even among Indians." Don Angel, a moreno from Collantes, said that Indians in Jamiltepec also lived in round houses. "There are still some in Chayuco, on the way to Jamiltepec," he added. "Morenos copied it." "Generations of Indians made houses like [redondos]," Maximino said. "They can still be found in the hills and mountains . . . who knows where."

The issue of who had redondos first is of more than casual interest, for it speaks to the crux of contemporary multiculturalism and ethnic identity politics. Are blacks and Indians separate peoples on the Costa Chica?

Does each group have its own history? Did morenos copy redondos from Indians? Or did Africans bring the form, which Indians borrowed? Neither is the problem of origins a question of academic musing or a pointless exercise in outsider essentialism. For as I have shown, Aguirre Beltrán's rather than Tibón's, assessment was carried forward, and the idea that redondos and other cultural forms are vestiges of Africa and have their origins in black culture guides much outsider interest in—and interactions with—coastal belt communities, including San Nicolás, constituting part of the knowledge base we have of those communities.

Like other local traditions, such as artesa music, which some also code as African, redondos are folklorized in ways that spatially and temporally decontextualize them. They are turned into portable pictures and replicas and made available for national and even international consumption. In this vein, I recall how during my first visit to San Nicolás in 1992 Ernesto brought me directly to a redondo on the assumption that I was from la cultura and wanted to see "culture." As noted, this redondo turned out to be a replica built in the 1980s that stood on the outskirts of the village on borrowed land, next to a carved wooden trough used as a dancing platform for performances of artesa music. Ironically, the same redondo now appears on the museum notecard. The image is therefore twice removed from the authenticity it seeks to convey.

Periodically new cultural initiatives arise: culture workers ask for a new redondo, restart plans for a casa de cultura, or tape a watered-down version of artesa music. Redondos otherwise still surface in contexts controlled by outsiders who emphasize the past as the repository and fount of racial difference and value. Despite the shaky ground on which African arguments inspired by Herskovits stand, redondos have become prominent emblems of the past and of supposedly authentic black Mexican spaces. They are not only found inside the museum's gift shop. Its ethnoscape initially included several concrete replicas scattered outside the main building and used for traveling exhibits and meetings.

As noted, an image of a redondo also graced the painted backdrop for San Nicolás's First Traditional Fair and the badges made for participants in the First Meeting of Black Communities in 1997, where attendees seized on redondos as evidence of African influence in the region. At no time, however, does the recreation of redondos—either as model dwellings or as images—come from San Nicoladenses themselves.

San Nicolás's crumbling redondo

The museum ethnoscape

Nostalgia and Shame

San Nicoladenses are cautious about those who profess to act on their behalf in part because culture workers and political activists impose identities without addressing the community's experiences or concerns, which include migration, access to basic infrastructure, and the availability of material goods and the magic of money—the salaries—that late modernity holds out as a promise. The interests of culture workers also focus on only a few local residents, particularly the musicians, who are now mostly deceased or disabled, but who until recently performed principally for outside audiences. Residents see themselves giving away cultural capital and their labor without receiving anything in return. Cosme put the issue rather bluntly one day as we chatted in San Nicolás: "The redondo doesn't interest people here," he said. "That's why they don't take care of it. Someone needs to pay them. Who's going to pay someone to work in the casa de cultura?" Maximino told me much the same thing. "Miguel Angel paid them to make [the redondo]. They don't want to do it anymore. They don't want to cut the wood. They want to be paid."

I believe that San Nicolás's crumbling redondo does not so much indicate people's indifference as it does their realization that they have received nothing for all of the "culture" they have handed to whites. Indifference also indicates the need for local history to be meaningful and public—hence the interest in the documents I brought from the Mexican National Archives. But people have mixed feelings about redondos, which signify their own backwardness because the houses themselves are deemed primitive, as well as nostalgia for the past by the elderly. With the exception of Ernesto, who is familiar with the rhetoric of culture workers, when local people discuss redondos it is not to link them to an ethnicized African history but to a Mexican time at once more bountiful and less comfortable than the present. Thus redondos act as a kind of prism refracting setbacks and aspirations, nostalgias and dreams. For some San Nicoladenses, especially for the elderly, my questions about redondos brought wistfulness and ambivalence, feelings that focused on the "rustic" but also generous environment long ago, before deforestation brought insecticides, before the mango groves fell silent and the wildlife disappeared. Don Margarito recalled the past as "pure sticks . . . no streets, just redondos, just trails; the village full of bush." Doña Lupe described how redondos would be bunched together during her childhood. People would make a bonfire and everyone would bring their sleeping mats outside to smoke tobacco. "Men and women would come out to chat," she continued in a long chain of associations, with her voice—as I remember it—working through a long sigh.

Sirina's grandparents lived in a redondo when she was growing up. "[Redondos] were made of palm fronds with earthen walls," she explained. "People would put more grasses on the roof and then mark off the surrounding area with their feet. The beds were inside and people made a raised platform out of sticks to keep their clothes off the ground. Cows lived among people," Sirina laughed. "They would be milked on the patio in front of the house, and come and go alone." Like Sirina, Manuel linked redondos to "the time of his grandfather." Back then, he added, in a raced assessment of progress, the village was "really, really black and there was nothing here."

Because people link redondos to a past that was simpler, more deprived, more countrified, and "darker" than the present, they can also be negative about them. "Redondos were for poor people," Don Domingo told me. "Rich people—those who had cattle—built square houses." Doña Cata expressed it this way: "Before, there weren't any good houses—just redondos. . . . Now there are only good houses." Don Domingo did not understand why there was even any interest in redondos: "La cultura is concerned with dated things," he said, "but we are in the modern world."

If one walks through San Nicolás today one sees neat rows of "good" houses: square and rectangular cinder-block dwellings (and a few red brick ones) in various stages of construction, on house plots laid out side by side to conform to the electrical grid installed in the 1970s. One also notices a smattering of unreinforced adobe houses with tin or clay tile roofs, and even more rustic wattle-and-daub ones, which are mostly abandoned. Like ancestral redondos, adobe and wattle-and-daub structures are made principally of earth mixed with plant materials.[13] Adobe is sometimes sided with plaster, and all earthen houses are now rectangular or square, shapes that Don Domingo associated with "rich people." Many earthen houses are transformed into storage or kitchen extensions as their owners move into new cinder-block ones. But those who have had to abandon el norte without finishing "my house" will live in adobe or in unfinished cinder-block. Indeed, Judit, Manuel, and their four children lived for years in a cinder-

Wattle-and-daub house in San Nicolás

block house without a wall to encircle it, a breezeway or window guards or doors. Someone always had to be home to keep the house and its contents safe from intruders.

Adobe is also still common in the mountains and elsewhere on the coastal belt. In Collantes, for instance, many people were just beginning to build cinder-block homes when Hurricane Paulina struck in September 1997. As the village flooded with water and mud from a nearby river, adobe houses fell to pieces while even piles of cinder block washed away. Adobes have pitted walls and dirt floors. Like redondos, they are associated with backwardness, poverty, and low status. Sirina told me that it "shames" people to live in a house made of "dirt." "If you build a house out of earth," she said, "people will say you're poor and can't make it." Once she derisively described such houses as "muck." Doña Lupe asked me whether Sirina's house, which is red brick and added onto piecemeal with remittances sent by Modesto, had a dirt floor, as she attempted to gauge how much wealth the family had accumulated. For her part, Sirina pointed out that Angela, who lived in an adobe house with exposed walls before Oscar built a brick one, "should have had 'her house' a long time ago, but Héctor drinks." In Sirina's mind, then, Angela did not yet have a real house because she still lived in one made of earth and because her family was not working as a unit.

On the whole, San Nicolás's Indians, such as Angela and Héctor, have fewer resources—including land—than morenos do. But for the most part, and as intermarriage between morenos and Indians accelerates, migration and cinder-block homes have taken hold in the Indian neighborhood as well. Until Oscar built the brick house, Angela was therefore even more self-conscious about her adobe dwelling. She feared that not just morenos but also her own kin and neighbors pitied her. Her house might not be a "nice" one, she once told me, but I was always welcome to eat there. And then she segued into a discussion of the redondos still inhabited by upland Indians. As Angela anticipated her new house, she told me that Oscar was "an excellent bricklayer. He's going to make us a house in a [city] style. Everyone will like it; he'll then get a lot of work in San Nicolás and he'll never have to go back to el norte again." While Oscar did build an unusually styled brick house anchored with rounded turrets, he also returned to el norte when he finished, thus distressing both his mother and his wife Chela, whom he again left behind for a time as he amassed the funds she would need to cross the border herself.

When remittances are plentiful, construction in San Nicolás provides opportunities for builders, electricians, and even plumbers as people want the indoor flush toilets and faucets they become accustomed to in el norte, or the ability to pipe in water from outdoor cisterns. But as Doña Lupe once observed, during the winter months in el norte there is no work in San Nicolás for builders. Though wages in el norte far exceed those in San Nicolás or even in Mexico City, economic downturns or too much competition in el norte means migrant San Nicoladenses send less or no money home, halting construction in San Nicolás.

Stable Attachments and Tense Mobilities

In the past, plant materials and earth for redondos were freely available from the surrounding bush, even when San Nicoladenses were tenants and workers on Carlos Miller's hacienda (Manzano 1991:30). But today, as Don Samuel put it rather succinctly, "lots of dollars, lots of houses." People migrate for those dollars because in San Nicolás "there's no way to make money to build a house for your children," Rosa told me. "If there weren't opportunities in Carolina, there wouldn't be any houses."

San Nicoladenses' relative success in el norte challenges racist local and national discourses that represent "blacks" as lazy, violent, disinterested in bettering themselves, and as really "not Mexican" at all. Such success also in-

The house Oscar built

The house it replaced

dicates not only that San Nicoladenses migrate like other rural Mexicans but also that their goal is to reinscribe themselves as Mexicans in generic Mexican houses far removed from the ethnicized redondos of the past. With that past perceived as rooted in poverty, dirt, and rurality, in short, in the outdoors and in "wildness" associated with being dark, morenos link progress and upward mobility to their mestizoization. This identity retains an emphasis on Indianness and mixture but it is closer than moreno to the romantic Mexican ideal of a glorified Indianized past and a whiter future. The term *mestizo*, however, is not simply or even primarily race-based for San Nicoladenses. Rather, as Doña Lupe once indicated by associating shoes, the urban, and mestizoization, *mestizo* indexes a move from rurality and poverty, tangentially associated with darkness, to urbanity and wealth, tangentially associated with lightness and belonging to the modern Mexican mostly seen on television (Lewis 2004:493). Because mestizoness posits whitening as a path to the future, San Nicoladenses recreate themselves as urban through migration to urban places, and through what such migration adds to life in San Nicolás. In other words, San Nicoladenses aspire to be urban: Highway 200, as I was often told, was not supposed to run through Cuaji; it was supposed to run through San Nicolás.

Morenos still link dark skin to spending too much time in the sun. For instance, in the collective taxi from Acapulco to Cuaji in March 2009, a man next to me, whom I did not know, covered his arm with a towel because it was near a window, and remarked that he was trying to avoid too much sun. The women in the taxi on the way to San Nicolás then chatted as they always do about how white I am when I arrive and how morena I am when I leave, again because of the sun. And as Don Domingo told me long ago, men want their wives inside and out of the sun because it reflects a man's ability to care for his family. Instead of seeing this as a "racist dichotomization" (Grimes 1998:125), one can understand it as part of the process by which people urbanize and therefore in their minds improve self and community. They do so, to put it bluntly, by "getting out of the sun," building cinder-block houses, and leading more metropolitan lives.

The twin processes of dollarization and mestizoization engage both geographical and economic mobility. As rural San Nicoladenses move to urban areas in el norte, they also develop new aesthetic and ideological tastes, and like other Mexican immigrants, they turn into "eager shoppers" (see also Grimes 1998:66) with the means to acquire things unavailable in

San Nicolás. Consumption, including of abundant and inexpensive food, is of course also fueled by mass media in Mexico, where material goods are racialized in ways that associate them with whiteness and status (Grimes 1998:125; Lewis 2004). Only by going to el norte, however, can San Nicoladenses achieve monetary power to buy things. A favorite pastime of San Nicoladenses in the United States is, in fact, to attend yard sales (see also Grimes 1998:66) where they snap up goods unavailable in San Nicolás or out of economic reach in U.S. commercial establishments. Like U.S. Americans, the more experienced wake early and drive a very hard bargain, as I have had ample occasion to note. Moreover, perceptions of material deficits in San Nicolás keep some from returning home, even if they have money. As Alicia once told me, "If I went back to San Nicolás, well, I would have money, but there would be nothing to buy!"

El norte is not just a place where things—including money—can be acquired. It is also seen as cleaner, more orderly, and more comfortable than Mexico. The highways are smooth and wide, I was told admiringly by Ernesto, who has twice been to California. When Marti was young he insisted on wearing shoes in San Nicolás and repeatedly told Judit that he wanted to go back to North Carolina because "the floors are cleaner there." Sirina showed me with deference Reina's and Roberto's house in San Nicolás. They are documented and have been transmigrating for many years. Sirina raved about the well-built, painted home: its cleanliness, breeziness, tiled kitchen with appliances, smooth floors, and multiple bedrooms. In short, except that the toilet and shower were in a small building outside of the house with a rubber cistern on the roof for running water, there was no confusion between indoors and outdoors. Don Samuel once told me that as people returned from el norte there was more pressure to clean up the public areas of San Nicolás, "because they see how clean it is there." A woman I met in Maldonado, who had come from California for the Santiago festival, discussed life with her children in el norte. She did not have to work and she used face creams and makeup to stay youthful. "I don't look dirty," she said. "I like it clean."

As noted throughout this book, migration and village life are temporally and spatially entwined. Busloads of new emigrants leave after a festival, or if people can they return home for festivals, funerals, and weddings, and leave after them. San Nicoladenses in the United States send remittances for their obligations, even if they cannot be there themselves. Thus Sirina's niece, chosen as one of the functionaries for the Santiago festival, sent money to sponsor the dance she was obliged to give, and someone else filled her role as host. I sent money when Sirina asked me to be godmother to one of her sons as I could not be there in person. As festivals link community members, the long-distance participation of migrants means that they do not shirk their duties, even if they cannot physically attend.

In el norte San Nicoladenses express their attachment to their community in ways that speak to the tastes and smells, the heat and orientation of home. In the dead of winter, people go barefoot indoors, dressed in tank tops, skirts, and shorts in overheated houses and apartments. Like other Mexicans, they watch Mexican channels on television. More subtle are the sudden waves of longing, such as the one Antonio had as we were driving around Winston-Salem in my car and he suddenly rubbed his belly in an exaggerated way, threw his head back, closed his eyes and moaned about the iguana he would like to eat.[14] Margarita prepares in her U.S. kitchen the same tamales, barbequed beef, and cheese she would make in San Nicolás, some of which she sells to U.S. San Nicoladenses to supplement the family income. I haul from Mexico large suitcases and boxes of dried meat, shrimp and herbs, sweet bread, homemade cheese, and Mexican pharmaceuticals for San Nicoladenses in the United States. The foods and medicines are not simply about people's preferences. They fall somewhere between "ways of being" and "ways of belonging" (Levitt and Glick Schiller 2004:1010) as people unconsciously identify through their bodies as Mexicans and as San Nicoladenses.[15] A sense of connectedness remains deeply and unconsciously ingrained in San Nicoladenses' very gestures, which I realized one day as Margarita and I conversed in Winston-Salem about where a particular family lived in San Nicolás. Although by then Margarita had been in el norte for years, she spontaneously and naturally waved her arm as she said "up by the lagoon" to point me in the right direction, as if we were orienting ourselves in San Nicolás itself.

Houses, Reputation, and Class

Manufactured houses have become "symbols of progress," as the Mexican journalist and political commentator Juan Sánchez Andraka writes with reference to northern Guerrero. In contrast, "huts and mud brick have become symbols of social and economic failure." Sánchez views such "progress" as the by-product of a paternalistic state that effects "criminal reconstructions of Catholic churches, covering [even] colonial jewels with cement" (1987:26). "The attitude of politicians toward social problems is paternalistic. Cement in small peasant communities has turned into a symbol of progress. To construct a house out of cement, a town hall with cement, has been a common goal. Disdain for regional materials has become an illness. Even in villages such as Zitlala, where the stone called *tepochacautel* [tepoxaktetl], a traditional construction material is abundant, they opt for cement, losing the great advantages of tepochacautel" (1987:25).

Paternalism and state intervention in local communities began with official school construction through the CAPFCE (Comité Administrador del Program Federal de Construcción de Escuelas, or Federal Government Program for School Construction), which first introduced cement into rural Mexican communities in the 1960s and 1970s. Instead of building local schools with local resources, "schools were made of prefabricated materials and their construction implied specialized knowledge of how to utilize those materials" (Sánchez 1987:26). But while cement might work for schools, which can be almost completely open to breezes, it turns houses—which all have concrete slab roofs—into nearly uninhabitable ovens, especially in the tropical heat and humidity of the coastal belt. Although Guerrero's governor in the mid-1980s encouraged home construction with local materials, such as adobe, people would ask, "are we going backwards?" (Sánchez 1987:35). And so cement is the material of choice to move one's family forward.

San Nicoladenses find cinder blocks more visually pleasing and infinitely more stable than earth. Amalia once told me, as we swung in a hammock in the backyard of the rundown, two-bedroom house in Winston-Salem that she shared at the time with Alberto and his male cousins, that "houses made of earth are from the past. Who would want a house made of dirt?" she asked disparagingly. At the time Alfredo worked for a cement manufacturer to save for what Amalia described as a square or rectangular house in San Nicolás with straight walls and floors, the kind of house they recently bought there, even though they have no plans to return.

In San Nicolás, Sirina pointed out that while cinder-block houses "might be hot, they survive earthquakes. [They] don't collapse or get damaged." In addition, she explained, redondos would "fall to pieces because of the wind and the water." During the rainy season clothes had to be kept off the ground, and during the dry season redondos easily went up in flames from candles. In one account, Papa Nico's disappearance from the village of San Nicolás is linked to a storm that lasted fifteen days and destroyed many redondos, including his own. Neither San Nicolás nor Cuaji would have burned to the ground during the revolution if it were not for building construction. Despite older people's nostalgia for a more bountiful and less monetized era, the materials out of which redondos were made thus symbolize the ephemeral, as well as the poverty and insecurity of the past.

For San Nicoladenses, the government-built primary school is in fact the turning point in their own collective memory of houses and migration. Sirina, for instance, remembers exactly when "good" houses entered people's consciousness: after a cyclone in the mid-1970s, when the state founded San Nicolás's first official primary school.[16] "From the beginning," she explained, "schools were made out of cinder block." Local people watched as the building progressed, learning the techniques and modeling their desire for more secure houses on the school. But they did not have the economic wherewithal to build such houses. Some went to Acapulco for work. "Little by little, people started going to Mexico City," Sirina said. "Now they go to el norte." The larger-scale processes wrought by migration to el norte are thus continuations of changes already under way before such migration became the norm, thereby "broadening, deepening or intensifying conjoining processes of transformation that are already ongoing" (Vertovec 2004:972; see also Quiroz 2004).

Indeed, out-migration from San Nicolás actually began in the 1960s when highway 200 was completed and Indians started arriving. Husbands typically worked the land and cared for livestock at home, while wives found positions as domestics in Mexico City, sending remittances back, including for house plots and adobe bricks. Single women went to support themselves, as did Iris, who worked in Mexico City for many years for a woman who taught her to read. As "bettering oneself" became a more generalized goal, agricultural supports diminished, and NAFTA undercut livelihoods, wage labor became more attractive than farming. Mexico City, with its low wages and vast numbers of un- or underemployed no longer appeals, although the service industry in some tourist destinations, such as Cabo San Lucas, where Yanaris remains, does.

It might also be women's responsibilities for the maintenance of home and inside spaces, coupled with a desire to leave their in-laws' house (Pauli 2008), that prompted Sirina to say that "from the beginning women have been the ones to pay for the houses." "Hermelinda's daughter was the first

Unfinished second stories

to go" to el norte. She sent money to build the cinder-block house with glass windows in which Hermelinda now lives. Sirina continued, "People would pass by Hermelinda's house and say, 'look at her nice house.'" Variations on the kind of home Hermelinda's daughter built are now the norm, and San Nicoladenses freely talk about the economic class dimension of cinder block. "Before," Sirina explained, "the people were poorer; with the opportunities that exist in Carolina now, people can go make money to live well, more or less." Rosa told me that Hermelinda and Rafael were once so poor that Hermelinda mixed milk with water and lived on a hillside out in the bush, while Rafael lived in a tiny stick house. Both families' children went to el norte. Now "Rafael has a two-story house and Hermelinda has a store, two trucks, and a lot of cattle."

Remittances first purchase house plots, which are typically fenced off to keep other people's wandering pigs—and other people—from encroaching and to avoid conflicts with neighbors over fruit trees, waste water, and such. As a house is built, window openings and breezeways are protected with wrought-iron gratings. If the owner can afford it, perimeter walls are erected to protect the whole property and to make it more private, as is typical throughout Mexico. Walls might be topped with broken glass or barbed wire for additional security. Painting the exterior is the final part of the process, and so most houses are still plain. Most are also one story, but they have flat rather than pitched roofs to accommodate a second floor that un-reinforced adobe could never support. While second stories are becoming more common, many are unfinished, and out of the roofs of most houses protrudes the rebar that *anticipates* a future second floor and thus continued and literal upward mobility.

A generation ago, house plots, like agricultural land, were not private property. Twenty men could lift a redondo and move it to another locale, Julio told me. Hence, if a person did not like where he or she was living, the situation was easily remedied and conflicts with neighbors and family members averted. Extended family could also always take in a member in trouble. "I had a cousin," recounted Don Margarito. "She got married and lived in a house on the edge of town. They killed her husband, so she moved closer in. They brought her house from there. About twenty people tied it up, someone stuck their head inside [to lift it], and they brought it here." Sirina added another dimension: "People could move much more easily back then, because there was a lot more space and now there's none. You could move and build another house." "Before there weren't any house plots," Don Margarito added as he linked the spatial organization of the vil-lage to familial solidarity. "[People just took whichever] but they stayed near their families."

New notions of ownership, population growth, and the sheer immobility of cinder block have not only rapidly urbanized the rural; they have also added to social tension because feuds can no longer be resolved by one party moving a dwelling to another location. "Now," Julio said, "if you want to change locations you have to sell." Conflicts between neighbors are more common. Sirina built a massive brick wall with Modesto's remittances to block her home off from that of the sister-in-law she despises; people with trees overhanging someone else's property still have sole rights to the fruit; during the rainy season the runoff from the palm frond shack Doña Delfina's family used to relieve themselves would drain into Greta's outdoor kitchen, but because the shack was on Doña Delfina's property she did not have to move it, and Greta could not move; Doña Lupe did not think she should have to leave room for cars and pedestrians as she contemplated enclosing José and Amada's house; Yolanda insisted that her neighbor had started to fence off a piece on her house plot while she was gone without leaving her an entrance, and so on. Conflicts over property such as these sometimes re-sult in full-blown hostilities resolved only through official intervention.

While new sources of wealth from migration have allowed people to improve their standard of living in ways meaningful to them, such wealth also
escalates tensions between households. Some link such tensions to emerging class differences. Yolanda, for instance, pointed out that "in the past we
were all humbler and poorer. Now those who go to el norte send money, and
we're growing more distant from one another because of jealousy. Nowa-
days someone with a lot of money is proud. Before people helped each
other; neighbors loved each other. My mother, if she killed a pig she would
take a piece to each of her siblings; it would be shared among the family."
Sirina pointed out a woman who had been in el norte for ten years and
sometimes walked around draped in gold necklaces and bracelets to dem-
onstrate her wealth. "That's how people make their reputation," Sirina said.
"Hermelinda and Soccoro go around saying they'd like to be poor to see
what it's like," Rosa said. "But they've both been poor. I wonder why they
say this. To let everyone know how rich they are?" She then expressed her
frustration because San Nicoladenses mostly have the same habits: "Here
someone with money does less [than a poor person] and doesn't even speak
to those with nothing — to poor people. But they live the same way, without
shoes, wearing dirty clothes, without doing anything, the men drinking."
She mentioned the wealthiest man in town. "He goes around barefoot, without a shirt. He doesn't eat good food. Grilled beef. Same as me." Petronila
thought that for some, having money was more important than being with
family. "I'm more of a conformist," she said, as she told me that she did not
mind if Rubén went to el norte, for which he has a resident visa, but that she
wanted to stay close to her extended family and her children.[17]

Reconfiguring Kinship

The processes that have reconfigured the physical space of the village also
index changes in kinship, including the potential destruction of the very
unity of the families for whom cinder-block houses are built. The fact that,
as Rodrigo told me, even señoritas have the wherewithal to purchase their
own homes is one indication of this. So is the fact that San Nicolás has become "a nursery and nursing home" for the children and parents of migrants (Rouse 1991:252). As Vertovec points out, the lives of nonmigrants
are also transformed by migration (2004:976).[18] Doña Lupe, one such nonmigrant, feels abandoned as four of her five children, and all of her grandchildren, are in el norte. She has no one to help her with the demands of

the land and cattle she inherited from her husband. She links her abandonment, the demands her children place on her to take care of their children, and her own isolation to the widespread obsession with houses. "Before," she told me, "no one bothered about their house. Now it's all anyone thinks about—building additions, this and that . . . they go to el norte and forget about us." She oversees several house plots and even home construction for her absent relatives. Doña Estefanía refused to take over the care of her daughter's months-old child when the daughter wanted to go to el norte to join her husband. "My kids take off and leave me with all their kids," she said. When one of her sons and his wife went to el norte, they left her with their five children, the youngest of whom was only a year old. Sirina mentioned a woman who had a baby and immediately gifted it, so that she could emigrate, something that many single women, of course, are forced to do. Since grandparents—including Sirina and Rodrigo, Doña Soccorro and Don Guillermo, and even Doña Estefania, even though she complained—almost always take in grandchildren, what San Nicoladenses say again contradicts what they actually do.

The reconfiguration of living spaces also reflects changes in family structure. In the past redondos, which often sat in the same places people build their houses today, were not self-contained living units, as Starr's image in chapter 4 shows. Not only did different redondos serve different functions—as Sirina told me, "there would be one redondo for sleeping and one for cooking"—but the kitchen redondo would be shared by the women in an extended family. Moreover, there used to be one big bed for everyone. "This is how we did it," said Don Margarito: "We'd encircle the redondo with branches, put hay on top, and make the walls out of earth. The door would be clay." He then pointed out a tree where his redondos once stood. One was whitened with lime, he told me, but it was completely round; the kitchen was enclosed just with branches, nothing more, as many kitchens still are.

Doña Cata pointed out to me where her mother's redondos were. She lived with her mother most of her life as her first husband left her and, unusually, she obtained a divorce and moved back in with her mother until she remarried a year later. When her second husband was killed, she took her children to live with her mother once again. And until she died in her nineties, she still lived on the same plot of land where her mother's redondos once stood.

The communal living of the past is linked to unified families. As Don

Outdoor kitchen made of branches (with iguana)

Margarito said, "Families were united. Everything is changing now." "Before," Rosa lamented, "family members were your neighbors. But that's not the case any longer." Yet Marcos saw things differently. In the past, he told me, everyone lived close to their family and still does. "If you need something, you go to your family. Who's going to go running to the other side of the village looking for their family?"

My own observations, in part based on a mapping of house locations, indicate that family members do still tend to live close to each other. Teresa's sister's house is connected to Teresa's, and they share a yard; their mother lives with them. As Teresa never lived with Inocenio, and her sister separated from her husband, these women form a family compound. Díaz notes that in contrast to a wife, a querida's ties "are closer to her birth family and her children" (2003:107). Yet it is also the case that because many older men have passed away, or because daughters-in-law and mothers-in-law do not get along and remittances enable a faster separation (see also Pauli 2008), or because women are responsible for homes more generally, or because husbands have left for el norte, women often live near their own kin, thus easing their enclosure with proximity to family. Sirina, for instance, is a wife who does not get along with her mother-in-law and whose father passed away long ago. Rodrigo's father often visits, but Sirina and Rodrigo are adjacent to Sirina's brother, whose house is across the road from their mother's and down the road from a sister's. Doña Lupe, a widow, lives next to her sister and her sister's family, her parents (until they died, when her youngest brother arrived from Acapulco to claim their house), her cousins and her cousins' children in a large family compound with a shared yard. Eva lives with her husband and children next to a male cousin and his family. Until she died, Doña Olivia lived in a large compound with a son and his family; her sister lived next door, a brother lived on the other side, a daughter owns a plot of land across the road, and a son lived up the road. Angela and Héctor, whose parents are deceased or in the Ayutla region, share a house with Oscar and Chela, though not all of them are always present. Those of their relatives also in San Nicolás live in the same neighborhood. While patrilocal residence might therefore be the norm, once a couple leaves the husband's parents' home, matrifocal residence is one option, as it is elsewhere in Mexico (Guttmann 1996:157–58, 281n20). Whatever circumstances and choice bring, it is always preferable to live near extended family, which, in fact, might be difficult to avoid in San Nicolás since almost everyone is related. That such arrangements are deliberate choices, however, is easier to see in Winston-Salem, where extended family opt to live in the same apartment complex or in the same house.

However, it is also true that open compounds that once held redondos and extended families have given way to individual plots for individual houses and smaller, nuclear households. Separation from nonfamily members and within the family itself is more of a priority. Although relatives still tend to live close to each other, people still routinely visit friends and family, and front doors are always open if someone is inside, shared compounds with a single outdoor kitchen are much less common than they once were. People prefer houses with more than one room so that they can be both inside and separated; and no one brings mats outside to chat or to sleep anymore, in part because everyone is entertained inside by televisions and cooled by fans as they recline on hammocks strung indoors or on the store-bought mattresses that have replaced petates.

Separation

People now have a heightened sense of privacy. I recounted Judit's story of living with her in-laws; Sirina humorously explained the difficulties of making love while living with children or in-laws in a one-room house. "Very slowly," she said with a chuckle. Back then the beds were just wooden frames with a *mecate* (crisscrossed rope topped with a petate). "They squeaked and moved a bit because they were very light, and you had to be very quiet." Then she made a noise like a squeaky bed. "If someone farted," she guffawed with a laugh I would recognize anywhere, "everyone smelled it!" "Also," she added, "you'd make sure that all the kids were asleep, and then suddenly a head would pop up!" She told me about a couple who would check that their children were asleep and then make love on the floor so as not to make any noise. But, she said, "you know, back then everyone was innocent." When I asked her what had changed, she said: "Television — now the kids see and know everything," and she went on to describe an indecency from a soap opera she had watched the night before. Someone on TV said, "'I want it until a fire is lit under me; doesn't it make you itch?' We don't discuss things like that."

Margarita's and Maximino's house in San Nicolás has two bedrooms and many walls and partitions, a feature they admire in my house in Virginia, even though I think my house is like a rabbit warren. As anyone who watches home-improvement shows in the United States knows, such partitions are out of favor in the public parts of houses, as "great rooms" and combined kitchen-dining areas replace them. But San Nicoladenses want separation and the privacy it brings. In the ideal house, for instance the one Roberta and Reina built, the kitchen is inside with appliances, cabinets, and tiled countertops, separate from the living room, a communal and public space for everyone, even though a cutaway counter might join the two. Bedrooms are to the sides of the main living area, and closed off with doors. Thus while the floors of Maximino's and Margarita's house have not yet been smoothed, while the bathroom holds only a toilet bowl, and while there is no indoor sink in the kitchen, Doña Lupe has purchased wooden doors for their house to delineate two bedrooms. Each time I stay there I take pictures so that Margarita can gauge its progress.

A married couple of course wants a room for "their bed, their wardrobe, their mirror," as Amalia told me. But while the "ideal" U.S. home favors private spaces for each child too, in San Nicolás children are expected to, and prefer to, sleep in the same room. Thus Amalia once envisioned her house in San Nicolás with a large master bedroom, a living room, an indoor kitchen and bath, and two bedrooms for her children—one for the boys and one for the girls. This is in keeping with San Nicoladenses' emphasis on gender segregation and the close relationships among brothers, sisters, and cousins, for children find the idea of sleeping alone completely alien. Amalia's molding of a new form to traditional mores is a fine example of what Jonathan Inda and Renato Rosaldo refer to as the "customization of alien cultural forms," as people absorb outside impositions through the filter of their own deep cultural practices (2002:16). Indeed, when we initially put our son in the only room with a door, the other children were incredulous. "Doesn't he get scared?" they would ask.

Trouble

As some San Nicoladenses grieve the social changes that index widening gaps between the rich and the poor, as well as the loosening of family ties, they also speak of rising crime that largely affects and is committed by unsupervised young people whose parents are in el norte or who are themselves in el norte but on occasion return. Sirina explained that when people first started migrating they were responsible and keen to work. These days, she continued as we talked in 2002, young people do not want to work. Instead, they want a "hidden" business that will make them rich in a short time. As unemployment grew in the United States, Margarita told me in 2008, more and more people there turned to the "business" of dealing drugs. One San Nicoladense was caught with three kilos of cocaine in March of that year, and is currently serving twenty years in North Carolina.

In San Nicolás, Luis laments it all:

People here aren't poor. They're lazy. They have cattle; they have food—elsewhere people don't have anything to eat, not even tortillas. Here they don't understand. A lot of people don't consult their parents. "Let's do this." Now young people want to live a different kind of life. They don't want to go to the fields. They want to take off, to leave. Before there weren't any cars, but now if you have a car you can take your own road. They forget family; they forget everything. For them el norte is a place of liberation. Now you make your cinder-block house and it's more civilized than the provinces. Arriving in a city, some go to work to make their house; others have no idea what they're doing and get into trouble.

Much local crime in San Nicolás is attributed to *marijuaneros* who have been in el norte. "Things weren't like this before," said Rosa. "They brought that [marijuana] from el norte. Before it was really, really quiet—we could sleep outside." Doña Ana struggled with Don Domingo for years to scrape together money from crop sales for a one-room cinder-block home with a dirt floor and an insubstantial wooden door. Like Rosa, she pointed out a few years before she passed away that "before, you could sleep [outside] under a shelter or in a house of sticks." "But now you can't" because of the crime. Indeed, while her house was more solid than one made of earth, it was not quite solid enough. She used to leave the little jewelry she owned with a niece, for fear of someone breaking in.

Older nonmigrant San Nicoladenses speak of a breakdown in traditional forms of respect and reciprocity. Don Gregorio, for instance, described the past as a time when "people were trustworthy, honorable, and didn't steal from others." It was a "golden era," he repeated, with "great quantities of fruit." Youth were more respectful. They knelt before their godparents for a blessing, and they "greeted older folks with 'uncle,' bowed, and tipped their hats. Everything was lovely." Thus, in the past people esteemed one another, crime and class differences did not exist, and the earth was more giving.

Migration has therefore shifted from a promising avenue for security and a shortcut to the modern to a move fraught with dangers that come not just from crossing borders without documents but also from social processes that threaten to undermine the very concept of community. Cinder-block homes might be anchored to the ground, but now the people they are meant to house are scattered all over, as respect and reciprocity give way to a less communal set of values.

Carolina Chica and the Persistence of Family and Place

Yet in the final analysis, houses are deeply paradoxical. On the one hand, they reflect the social displacements that accompany migration, which in a kind of vicious circle make such homes necessary to ensure safety and security, not just because of the weather but also because of the problems that migration itself engenders, in part through the acquisition of immobile property. Thus the houses that protect against the outside world can exist only because of the processes that simultaneously erode what people perceive to be traditional social rules and bonds, as rich people stop talking to poor people, young folks steal and deal drugs, extended families are torn apart, and children stop respecting their parents.

On the other hand, one can perceive in the very presence and immobility of cinder-block homes an ongoing and profound attachment to place and to kin, one that challenges the idea that global restructuring simply dislocates or that displacements have turned morenos into "people without a country," a phrase that becomes even more ironic in the new transnational context. The transatlantic and internal Mexican slave trade, colonialism, land disputes, war, and migration have conspired to fragment the families of San Nicolás. Yet cinder-block homes now cement in/to Mexico the continuing aspirations and desires of people who have moved quite far afield. Those aspirations and desires are coded by class and race, as some people literally own more of the village than others. That such aspirations and desires are also coded by absence, however—a striking number of cinder-block homes stand empty—additionally attests to the central importance of families and their futures.

Achieving that desired future in fact requires an ongoing reliance on family. Migrants preparing for departure depend on kin in el norte, who often send money to pay their passage, find jobs for them, provide a place to sleep, and help them negotiate the complexities of life in a place where the lingua franca is English. Emigrants, on the other hand, have to trust nonmigrant family members to receive remittances, purchase building materials and oversee the construction of the houses to which emigrants aspire to return to live permanently among family before being buried in the local cemetery. That people who are not physically present regularly send money to family to construct sturdy houses in which they cannot yet live, and to which they might in reality never be able to return, suggests that even San Nicolás's most displaced migrants retain abiding ties to—and an abiding confidence in—their home community. Perhaps most tellingly, whatever else happens, almost every San Nicoladense is buried in the local cemetery: the one that Romelio allegedly desecrated with his hooked pole to access the coraje that itself symbolizes the tensions of place, tensions often only laid to rest with death itself. And even if migrants die before they make it home, their final resting place will be San Nicolás.

One year I mentioned that something seemed amiss. People responded that there had been a lot of deaths in el norte. Several coffins had arrived: a car accident victim; two young men dead of long-term ailments; a young woman felled by an infection following a gunshot wound inflicted by her novio; and a young man shot by another one from Huehuetán. A man and his nine-year-old niece had also been killed in a drug dispute in Winston-Salem, a tragedy reported in a North Carolina newspaper.[19] During this period a woman from a nearby town called me in San Nicolás from North Carolina to ask me to intercede with U.S. authorities, who could not find a physiological reason for her niece's death. "It was her nagual," she told me. "You need to explain this so they release the body."

The enormous expense of sending a loved one's body back for burial in San Nicolás is covered collectively—like weddings, funerals, and migration itself—through donations and loans from people in el norte and in San Nicolás. Moreover, the burial plots that migrants young and old sooner or later occupy reflect the house aspirations they left in the first place to fulfill, which made Romelio's desecration of those plots that much more egregious, and Juan's curing of Sirina's and Rodrigo's house that much more significant. The preferred form of interment is in elaborate concrete tombs that stylistically resemble houses. Indeed, as Doña Lupe explained, building a tomb is like building a house, right down to buying the cement and paying a mason. "The person with money has luxuries in life and luxuries in death," she said, while the poor, "those who do not have money, just bury their dead in the soil." Many cement tombs have detailed superstructures, some of them are tiled, and most of them are individually enclosed with fencing and sturdy gates, much like house plots themselves.

Families sweep the dirt surrounding the tombs, just like they sweep the dirt in their yards. Most tombs have crosses and resemble small churches. Yet churches themselves are in many ways modeled on houses, as Sánchez's comments suggest, and redondos had small crosses at their apex too. Women cultivate plants in the spaces that enclose and protect the tombs where the dead reside, and many of the plaques adorning those tombs speak of family and of the deceased, who will "dwell" in the hearts of the living forever.

Cristina seems aware of the ways in which the modernity that is perceived to have destroyed family ties also manages to reaffirm them in the cemetery's tombs. "They have roofs," she said of these residences for the

A "street" of tombs in the cemetery

dead, "and the entire family is buried there. People grab their burial plot and enclose it, just like now they grab a house plot to live." She then spoke of the past and the transience of the earth. "Before, when people died, they weren't entombed; they'd just be buried in the ground," she said. "Family members weren't buried together. Now everyone is united as a family. If the gravesite isn't enclosed and there isn't a tomb," she added, "people will take a bit of the land and even dig it up again." She knows this because her second child died of a fever long ago as an infant. He is no longer where she and her husband buried him—indeed, they cannot find his remains because they had no money to entomb him, and his bones have been scattered over the earth.

As Cristina's comments about her baby suggested, the new burial forms, which cost more money, actually bring families closer together, even if it is in death. Indeed, it is only in the cemetery that people imagine themselves safe from the insecurities of the outside world. I was at first surprised to learn that migrants send money for tombs as well as for homes. But Chela explained to me that the former were in fact more important. "Everything comes from Carolina," she said. "What they say here is 'I'm going to build my house,' but one also says that it's not one's house, that it's simply on loan. One's real house is in the graveyard, because [as people say] 'I'm going to be there forever. No one can take me out of there. In my [everyday] house, well, [I'll be there] no more than a short time.'"

In the cemetery families are thus reunited in fixed dwelling places, replicas of the homes and the violence of modernity that have torn them apart in the first place. It is poignant, of course, that people leave to find work to purchase their own tombs, as well as those of kin they might never see again, in a homeland to which they might not return alive. San Nicoladenses, however, joke about the situation and, in their inimitable fashion, give it an ironic twist, as I discovered one day after I had visited the town's graveyard to look at the tombs and the layout. Afterward, I went by Rosa's home to chat. When I told her I had gone to the cemetery, I expected her to admonish me for going alone, not because it was dangerous in the daytime but because despite changing social norms, people still see being alone as unusual and uncomfortable, especially for a woman and especially in a cemetery far from town. Instead of scolding me, however, Rosa laughed uproariously. "Ahhh," she guffawed, "[you went to] Carolina Chica [Little Carolina]!" I must have looked terribly perplexed because she quickly added — still laughing — "you know, [the graveyard] — it's 'the other side' [*el otro lado*], but you don't need a passport or a coyote to get there."

Although many community conflicts can be traced to migration, people still go, even in the worst economic downturn, and families still encourage their eldest children, especially because rural workers do not earn wages or qualify for Mexican social security. Rosa's three oldest children are now in el norte, along with most of her grandchildren, whom she has never seen. Her children regularly send money to secure Rosa's own cinder-block home in San Nicolás and to pay for the telephone she uses to call them. Rosa once asked me where Africa was and whether there was work there. She would like to go to el norte herself to see her children and grandchildren, but she has no documents and is afraid of attempting the difficult journey on foot. It took her sister fifteen days, she told me, and it once took Juana twenty-eight. When Ismael left in 1997, Rosa did not want to go to Cuaji to see him off. She was too upset. "It hurts my heart," she said at the time. Perhaps I can conclude by imagining a new notecard, like the one from the museum. This one would still bear a heart signifying a profound attachment to place, to family, and to community, but it would evoke the dangers and promises of migration. Its verse might comprise a mother's warning to her child not to go to el norte and of that child's reply that he or she is going anyway, and will defy death to get there. Such a card might be embellished not with a picture of a redondo in a nostalgic rendition of an imagined and folklorized African past, but instead with an ambiguous Mexican cinder-block structure that could be either a house or a tomb.

Conclusion   WHAT'S IN A NAME?

San Nicoladenses's identities rest on a complex calculus of race, history, and custom. That calculus is situational, which makes it fluid and conciliatory rather than bounded and antagonistic. But really two issues are at play: San Nicoladenses as objects and San Nicoladenses as subjects. Culture workers and some scholars essentialize and objectify morenos, imposing racial identities based on mythologies of purity and difference. Using top-down models, they create distinctions between "blacks" and "Indians," thereby ethnicizing and insisting that "in search of a legitimate place in the nation, each group must guard its gains and insist on all credit due" (Williams 1989:435). This potentially undermines rural solidarity by fostering a national "multicultural" legitimacy that rests on competition and that will never rectify the structural inequalities Mexican small farmers suffer.

Despite San Nicoladenses' rejection of the terms *Afromexican*, *Afromestizo*, and *black*, outsiders—many from the United States or informed by U.S. paradigms—continue to use them without engaging the unique experiences of peoples from the coastal belt. The emphasis on an Afro or black identity component follows the rule of hypodescent, a social invention characteristic of U.S. racial classifications (Hoffmann 2006b; Wade 2006a). Thus, U.S. influences recolonize costeños and deprive them of a voice. As Arturo Motta once responded to a student whose parents came from the Costa Chica but who had been raised in the United States: "I'm not one of those who buy into saying that coastal peoples are 'AFRO' something because this is a historically inconsistent label and one recently imposed. . . . There is too much of an *autochthonous* history on the Costa Chica to look for it in something as abstract and hollow as Afro-something" (Motta personal communication 2009; emphasis added). In these pages I have tried to detail such a history for a single village to challenge the objectification through hollow abstractions that occurs when "Afro" is substituted for the complexities of transnational, national, regional, and local processes, as well as for particular worldviews.

Under the guise of culture work, ethnicization has failed precisely because while hyphenated identities might join and strengthen in one context, they can separate and subordinate, or be completely irrelevant, in another. In this respect, local subjectivities challenge the model on which, as Brackette Williams indicates, the scaffold of legitimacy is erected. San Nicolás is not an Afromexican place. It is a Mexican place couched in terms of morenoness, an appellation that destabilizes the black-Indian divide while simultaneously recognizing blackness and Indianness. San Nicoladenses' identities thus challenge state models of multiculturalism and stymie the imposition of such models by state agents. Father Glyn continues the struggle to organize, but he acknowledges that Black Mexico has failed "to force people to take their lives seriously" (Jemmott Nelson 2008). In the meantime, Jean-Philibert Mobwa Mobwa N'djoli continues to work for Mexico's Consejo Nacional para Prevenir la Discriminación (National Council to Prevent Discrimination, www.conapred.org.mx), campaigning to change the wording of the antidiscrimination clause of the Mexican Constitution (Article 4) to specifically reference Mexicans of African descent (personal communication 2008, 2011).

While all efforts for recognition are laudable, discrimination in Mexico targets darker-skinned and rural people in general. It is a historical product best viewed in the context of a colonial society that "put difference to work," as I have explained elsewhere (Lewis 2003), and of a national society in which scientific racism from Europe allowed Mexican "whites" to "modernize" (Velásquez and Motta 2008). Such modernization included a distancing from the rural and from manual—including field—labor that "darkened." Indeed, the role of labor in the construction of race in Latin America tends to be overlooked: San Nicoladenses do not identify someone as rural because they are dark but rather as dark because they are rural (Lewis 2004:484; Pineda 2006).

San Nicoladenses might not make blackness meaningful in terms of a diasporic consciousness of Africa (also Amaral 2005:2). But blackness nevertheless forms part of an amalgamated identity that squares with the Mexican national one. The mestizo emerged as the cosmic race in response to European racism. The moreno is a parallel, likewise mixed, construct that uses Indianness as a touchstone for Mexicanness. Moreover, it *also* emerged in part because of white racism. Thus it both duplicates and challenges national hegemony. San Nicoladenses are tied to their Indian kin and, paradoxically, to a free nation that disparages blackness as not Mexican. Yet whiteness is arguably not Mexican either. And because it is not, and because they are rural people, San Nicoladenses do not incorporate whiteness into their Mexican identities, even though some of their ancestors were white. This occurs largely because socioeconomic class formation and the geography of race separate morenos from whites while affirming moreno affinities with Indians, to whom the nation "belongs" and to whom San Nicoladenses are indebted for a village that is a metonym for that nation.

Like any identity, one informed by Indianness can be "constructed" (Clifford 1988; Jackson 1995), as the independence festival La América demonstrates. But really a *kind* of iconic Indianness lends itself to such construction, for it is certainly the case that contemporary Indian, as well as Indian Indian, identities are meaningful locally and extralocally to San Nicoladenses. Indeed, they are an *ongoing* fact of morenoness. In this respect as in others, San Nicolas's customs, people, gender ideologies, nationalism, attachment to place, and migration experiences are all deeply Mexican, and San Nicoladenses most assuredly see themselves as Mexicans above all.

Yet they are still a distinctive people within the regional and larger national histories of Mexico. In part their distinctiveness is linked not to Mexican slavery but to the freedom that Mexico offered. Maroonage is a trope for freedom, but such freedom is also attributed to Indians writ large (and writ small) and to the white landowner Carlos Miller from the United States. In short, such freedom—often couched in the language of independence and masculinity—defines San Nicolás. Both the black part and the Indian part of morenoness are therefore locally understood in ways confounding to outsiders. This becomes most evident when cultural and geographical borders are crossed.

Race across Borders

Scholars and activists have begun to address the conflictive and conciliatory aspects of Latino (including African descent) and African American relations (Dzidzienyo 2003; Dzidzienyo and Oboler 2005; Hernández 2003). For both Indian and moreno San Nicoladenses, "how African Americans are" leads to negative stereotypes similar to those noted by Kimberly Grimes and Sarah Mahler in their ethnographies of migrants from Oaxaca to New Jersey and from El Salvador to Long Island (Grimes 1998:85; Mahler 1995:228–32; see also Dolnick 2009; Dunn and Stepick 1992:54; Prince 2006:317; Stepick 1992:62). Bobby Vaughn observes that "Afro-Mexicans" "subscribe, at least in part" to prevailing stereotypes that categorize African Americans as "violent, drug-addicted, and generally undesirable" (2005:132).

Despite these conclusions, the processes by which Latin American identities transform (or not) in the United States have been neglected. But these processes are central to understanding relations between Latinos and African Americans, including Latinos of African descent: identities forged in Latin American contexts do not disappear when people migrate to el norte, and blackness, however construed, does not guarantee mutual understanding or respect. Thus the relationships San Nicoladenses living in the United States have with others there are a product of their U.S. experiences as well as of the Costa Chican logic through which they represent their own identities in Mexico. They do not identify with African Americans in great part because they see them as a different people. Nor do African Americans see themselves related to people they call "Mexicans." Indeed, as Father Glyn noted, the two groups are "indifferent to each other" (Jemmott Nelson 2008; Vaughn and Vinson 2007:231–34).

The Dominican Republic provides a broadly comparative case for San Nicoladenses' attitudes and experiences because of its history and because of its migrant population. Dominican racial identities were forged "in the context of separation from Haiti and with pressure from U.S. officials to 'make' the newly independent Dominican Republic a non-black Caribbean nation" (Torres-Saillant 1998:127–29; see also Candelario 2007:13–16). Dominicans therefore commemorate fighting off "black" Haiti in the mid-nineteenth century, some twenty years after first gaining independence from "white" Spain. While in contrast to the Costa Chica there are strong African elements in Dominican speech patterns, foods, oral traditions, and religious expression, many of them Haitian in origin, the identification of Dominicans as "black" has nevertheless been limited since colonial times to "people still living in slavery or engaged in subversive action [maroonage] against the colonial system" (Torres-Saillant 1998:134). Thus, much as on the Costa Chica, even early in Dominican history *black* was a deracialized term. Moreover, again as on the Costa Chica cattle ranching has always constituted a major part of the Dominican economy. Although such ranching rested in part on slave labor, as indeed it did on the coastal belt, it "relied on a far less labor intensive and much more autonomous mode of production than the sugar plantations" (Candelario 2007:4–5). Such autonomy on the coastal belt fostered moreno ties to white bosses.

By the end of the nineteenth century, the Dominican concept of race aligned with most of Latin America's, including with Mexico's, as national ideologies promoted the notion of a single race blended from what were conceived of as different ones, and with Indianness again a touchstone for mixed yet "untainted" identities. Within this context, and again similar to Mexican recognition of the Aztecs, Dominicans recognize the indigenous Taino, who inhabited the island at the time of the Spanish conquest. The Eurocentric and antiblack Trujillo regime especially promoted this association, which afforded the Dominican nation a path to an identity independent of blackness and whiteness. Even though the Taino had mostly died out after the conquest of Hispaniola, "Indio" came to be the "prototypical" Dominican middle (Candelario 2007:17–21; see also Derby 2009:24). It continues to be displayed on Dominican national identity cards, while Dominican negrophobia historically and today targets real or suspected Haitians (Danticat 1999; Derby 1994; Gregory 2006:166–208; Torres-Saillant 1998: 140).

Yet Indianness is variously valued in different parts of Latin America. For instance, the Nicaraguan state all but erased indigeneity from national identity (Gould 1993; Pineda 2006:83). In Puerto Cabezas on Nicaragua's Mosquito Coast, Indian rurality is denigrated, while residents, regardless of racial identification, celebrate their prerevolutionary (1979) cosmopolitanism (Pineda 2006:ch. 4). For San Nicoladenses "the rural" is also negative. Urbanity denotes a higher status even among morenos, while intensities of Indianness and blackness correspond to perceptions of distance and "backwardness." One might thus conclude that, like Dominicans, San Nicola-denses do not identify with blackness per se, while, like Mosquito Coast Nicaraguans, they maintain a certain disdain for the rural, widely associated with Indians. Yet as in the Dominican Republic but unlike in Nicaragua, Indianness also has positive connotations for San Nicoladenses.

Silvio Torres-Saillant recounts a conversation with an African Ameri-can colleague in the United States, who asked him whether he considered himself more black or Hispanic, a question Torres-Saillant found himself unable to answer. For him, Dominicans brought up in the United States, with its "bipolar" racial categories, are more likely to identify as black. He considers this to be empowering in the Dominican diaspora and in the Dominican Republic itself, but he also regards it ambivalently, as it denies the complexities of Dominican racial history (1998:142–43). Ginetta Cande-lario (2007) finesses Torres-Saillant's observations by comparing two trans-national contexts: Washington, D.C., where Dominicans are more likely to identify as black, and New York City, where they are less likely to. A class dimension provides one way to understand these differences: in the first context middle-class African Americans are more visible to Dominicans than they are in the second. An ethnoracial dimension provides another way to understand the differences: in the U.S. capital Haitians are less of a presence than they are in New York, and Dominicans are therefore more accepting of blackness. The Dominican case shows that for Latin Ameri-cans *context*—from the national imaginary to the concreteness of work and everyday life—is central to understanding how racial identities are regu-lated.

The phenotypes of San Nicoladenses and of other coastal belt peoples range considerably. Andrés Manzano realized after his trip to Detroit, they do not neatly fit the "bipolar" race and ethnic categories in the United States that create cognitive correspondences between hair, skin color, and "race" (see also NPR 2007).[1] This means that U.S. Americans do not automatically classify San Nicoladenses as black, and they, in turn, do not classify them-selves that way. No U.S. racial context exists for them. To Latinos, "Hispanic" is not a race, and racial categories do not appear on Mexican census forms. Indeed, Latinos in general, of whatever phenotype or national origin, tend to choose "white" or "some other race" on those forms in the United States (Fears 2002; Navarro 2003).

San Nicoladenses in the United States refer to all native Spanish-speakers with whom they come into contact—such as the Peruvian woman who worked with Margarita and her sister printing logos on T-shirts, the Puerto Rican janitor at Antonia's middle school, or the policemen who help them out—as Hispanics (*hispanos*). Depending on the context, San Nicoladenses also self-identify as Hispanics or, more specifically, as Mexicans. They therefore orient themselves in terms of language and geography, in keeping with the ways in which race is expressed in Latin America and based on the availability of "Hispanic," a category that means they are neither white nor black (Candelario 2007:12). San Nicoladenses typically use *gabacho* or *güero* for whites,[2] terms they do not hesitate to use in front of me but that in general refer to someone else, as *gabacho* can be derogatory while *güero* refers to a blond, blue-eyed, freckled person. *Gabacho*, *gringo*, *blanco*, and *americano* are all conflated, thus linking whiteness to the U.S. nation.

Just as there are derogatory terms for Indians (*macuano*, for example) and for whites, such terms also exist for African Americans: San Nicoladenses employ *mollo* (see chapter 5) interchangeably with *black*. But while they are not self-conscious about how to refer to whites and Hispanics, they are self-conscious about how to refer to African Americans, perhaps because every term with which they are familiar—including *black*—is to them impolite. Thus an uncertain Margarita told me that she once asked an African American woman whether she preferred to be called *negra* or molla. Margarita and Adela both told me that "a mollo would rather be called a mollo than a negro," but Margarita also wanted to know whether blacks knew that *mollo* was as insulting as *black* is for a moreno or *macuano* is for an Indian.

Because of circular migration and African Americans visiting the Costa Chica, San Nicoladenses in Mexico and in the United States view African Americans in similar ways. In both places they refer to them as blacks or as mollos, and they equate their dark skin with backwardness. African Americans are therefore *like* very dark (more rural) coastal belt peoples, from whom San Nicoladenses distance themselves both geographically and temporally. But even if skin color is perceived as similar, differences are still not overcome. As Manuel once said, "even San Nicoladenses who look very black" did not get along with blacks in el norte. Indeed, although citizen, documented, and undocumented Latinos are victims of hate crimes and discrimination by U.S. whites (e.g., Associated Press 2006; Sandoval and Tambini 2004), the undocumented are under increasing pressure as states and localities take immigration measures into their own hands (Aiezenman and Dwyer 2005), and Latinos do not always find sympathy from other Latinos (Navarro 2006), most San Nicoladenses direct their antipathies toward African Americans. In this respect, as in others, they are not unlike Latinos in general. But to understand this attitude as it relates to San Nicoladenses, it is necessary to simultaneously address the Mexican and U.S. contexts, *as well as* the ways in which different concepts "translate."

Civility

The subtext to Manuel's claim that even "very black" San Nicoladenses did not get along with blacks in el norte was that no matter how alike morenos and African Americans might appear, their differences outweighed any superficial similarities. This became apparent when he began to layer behavioral characteristics onto his explanation: blacks were "too loud," he said, while San Nicoladenses liked whites because they were "more peaceful." Moreover, San Nicoladenses did not understand blacks' English, and blacks "do a lot of drugs and don't want to work." Judit, who is usually very measured, once told me that "blacks [in the United States] are nasty [*feo*]." When I asked her what she meant, she replied that "they sell drugs; they stand around—and the police don't pay any attention. They're also lazy. The reason employers prefer us," she continued, "is that we're good workers. Where I worked we had to put together a certain number of boxes. The blacks, well, they didn't care whether they did it right or not; they'd get up and go to the bathroom every five minutes and smoke." Margarita laughed that in her workplace the white bosses had fired all the mollos because they would just "talk all the time." Perceptions of improper sexuality and disease, especially women's, also influence San Nicoladenses' ideas about African Americans, as they do about all U.S. women. Stereotypes of both African American men and women, however, can be much more crude. Overall San Nicoladenses characterize African Americans as noisy loafers with loose morals who like to party and who speak "wrong." These characterizations resemble local Indian and white assessments of Costa Chican "blacks."

Like Dominicans in New York, San Nicoladenses in urban North Carolina and Virginia do not have contact with middle-class African Americans, and they filter the African American experience through their own as undocumented immigrants.[3] Most contact occurs on the street, in the workplace, and in the generally poor neighborhoods where both groups live and travel. Margarita thus once asked me if only blacks lived in Richmond, Virgina, because her experiences of this segregated city meant that she never saw whites there. Many San Nicoladenses are not literate, have not experienced *institutionalized* discrimination as people of African descent,[4] and, though they are not middle class, they are relatively well-off small farmers. Perhaps for these reasons discrimination is not at the forefront of their identities and battles (see also Andrews 2004:200–201). And they find it difficult to understand why discrimination against African Americans continues to be an issue. This became clear one day as I was driving Margarita, Maximino, and Antonia to the family's small apartment. We passed Antonia's middle school, an inner-city public school that is about 15 percent Latino and 50 percent African American, where anti-Latino racism can be a problem.[5] As we drove, Margarita asked about Martin Luther King Jr., as the school was located on a boulevard named for the slain civil rights leader. When I told them who King was, Margarita and Maximino wanted to know about the "rights" (*derechos*) to which I was referring. As I explained slavery, segregation, discrimination, and voting, Margarita burst out: "That was so long ago; it's all passed now; blacks are just lazy—did you see that guy in our apartment complex? The young guy downstairs when we left? He's young and he doesn't even look for work. He asks for money." Maximino chimed in laughing, "A black asking Hispanics for money—immigrants!" Adela told me that U.S. blacks dress in an exaggerated way, with gold chains and brand-name clothing. "They don't have any furniture," she said incredulously. "But they've got nice gold chains. They go shopping with their paychecks, and the next day they're asking for a dollar."

If African Americans are not directly asking for money then they are trying to steal: Amanda and José insisted that mollos had gone around to the rear of their rented house, helping themselves to CDs, a barbeque, and whatever else was left outside. Amalia characterized blacks as thieves: "They steal our car radios." Héctor pointedly told me that a group of African Americans had asked him for a cigarette before one of them shot him in the arm in 2004. As he fell, they stole his money: $6. "They're lazy; they don't work; they go around robbing people," he said, adding that the police who caught the shooter were Puerto Rican and Salvadoran, and thus Hispanics like him. When Margarita and Maximino wanted to move, the property list from the landlord included addresses in "mollo neighborhoods." Maximino shook his head: "They're always firing guns, making a racket," even though his brother had just been deported to Mexico after the police caught him drunk with a pistol on the street. Indeed, the standards that hold for African Americans often do not hold for fellow Mexicans or Latinos.

To some extent San Nicoladenses certainly adopt attitudes from whites and other Latinos, or at least their own prejudices are confirmed. For instance, Margarita and Maximino once attended the wedding of a white woman with whom Margarita worked. They were the only Latinos there, and the mother of the bride told her that Hispanics were welcome while blacks were not. But Paul McClain and his colleagues conclude that Latinos bring antiblack racism with them from their home countries (2006). Such racism—and more general color discrimination—brought from Mexico and other parts of Latin America, was also the subject of a National Public Radio segment in 2007. Even though the explanation given for Latino antiblack racism is often that Latin Americans "learn" racism from whites in the United States (e.g., Harrison 2006:386; Mahler 1995:231), we thus might also look to the complicated face of racism in Latin America, itself a product of Spanish colonialism, as a source.

More specifically, the issue of "cultivation," as I have discussed it throughout these pages, means that San Nicoladenses, themselves upwardly mobile, denigrate the "rural" because its people are "off" the progressive track. Even though the U.S. context is urban, San Nicoladenses see themselves as tenaciously adapting to the rigors of daily life to get ahead. They do not see African Americans as upwardly mobile, even though they are also able-bodied citizens, with advantages unavailable to undocumented immigrants. Their perceived failures render them darker to San Nicoladenses, who "whiten" through intermarriage with Indians and class mobility. San Nicoladenses try to buy into the immigrant dream, in el norte as in San Nicolás, to start a small business, admiring above all immigrant communities such as the Chinese and South Asians.

Reduplication, Language, and Race: *Negro*, Negro, Moreno, and Moreno Moreno

Barriers might come down if language were not such an issue, but in this respect as well San Nicoladenses distance themselves from African Americans, using home categories to make sense of their U.S. experiences. Language asserts itself, for example, when San Nicoladenses claim that African American English is hard to understand. They say this even though only the youngest among them understand even when I speak English. San Nicoladenses rarely, if ever, encounter African Americans who speak Spanish. As Amalia once told me with a shrug, the neighbors to one side of her new house were mollos, to whom she did not speak because "we don't understand each other."

The finer points of linguistic issues might be overlooked in debates about immigrant and nonimmigrant minority group relations. The Spanish word *negro*, to which I now turn, offers clues to tensions not just between San Nicoladenses and African Americans but arguably between many Latinos and African Americans. *How* to identify African Americans, which San Nicoladenses spend quite some time mulling, involves both pronunciation and the linguistic reduplication with which morenos in San Nicolás identify Indian Indians at home.

During my earliest fieldwork in North Carolina San Nicoladenses used the terms *black* and *mollo* to refer to African Americans. Recently, however, they began to employ *moreno*. This does not mean that they identify *with* African Americans. Instead, they also shift *their own* identities via the autochthonous reduplicative logic they use for Indians. My first hint of this came when Margarita told me that San Nicoladenses had begun to use *moreno* for African Americans because African Americans found *negro* disparaging. Initially this confused me because I did not understand why African Americans would find *black* disparaging, even though it is not universally preferred. But I let the matter rest. Sometime later, Ismael and Alberto, both San Nicoladenses but the first moreno and the second Indian, also used the term *moreno* for African Americans. When I asked why, Ismael responded that he was moreno but that in the United States *moreno* is a polite term for *negro*. "We can't use *negro* because blacks feel offended," he said, echoing Margarita's comment in a totally different conversation. He then asked me what the English term was for someone of mixed black and white parentage. When I responded that there was no term, that the person would be black (according to the rule of hypodescent), he was confused. Thus two cultural systems collided, just as they had for Andrés Manzano. There was no logical explanation.

But as I contemplated the issue of *negro* I realized that the word might sound like Negro to non-Spanish-speaking African Americans, who would perceive it as antiquated and insulting. I asked more questions, and Maximino elaborated that negros were "moreno moreno," that is, more moreno than morenos, just as some Indians are more Indian than Indians.

To call African Americans *moreno moreno*, he continued, meant that they were "pure morenos" (*morenos limpios*), whereas San Nicoladenses were just plain morenos or black Indians. As he explained he rubbed his arm to emphasize his lighter skin in reference to his Indian heritage. Since I had never heard morenoness described as pure, I could only conclude that in the *United States* it had become a euphemism for *black*, which Amalia confirmed when she told me that in el norte blacks were morenos while in San Nicolás she was. As San Nicoladenses continue to differentiate themselves from African Americans they "whiten" not only their moreno selves: recently Amalia told me with a chuckle that Alberto now refers to himself as white and to her as Indian. Thus it seems that, depending on the context, even for young San Nicoladenses negros are black, mollo, or moreno moreno; morenos are morenos or become Indians; and Indians are Indian or become white.

Nomenclatures change to maintain distancing. But distancing also occurs among African Americans in Winston-Salem, typically based on stereotypes of "wetbacks." Veronica, an African American administrator who had gained some familiarity with Mexican culture by traveling in Mexico, told me that "in the beginning," in the mid-1990s, African Americans had begun to notice an influx of Latinos, especially at the local Walmart. They would identify them all as "Mexicans." She was surprised when I mentioned that many of these Mexicans were of African descent because her own perceptions of a person of African descent did not include Spanish speakers, nor did it include the wide range of San Nicoladenses' and other coastal belt people's phenotypes. Veronica spoke some Spanish and was sympathetic to the plight of one set of Mexican neighbors, whom she found friendly, hardworking, and poor, and who she knew were escaping the poverty of their home country. But she also identified language as an issue. So did "Big Mama," an elderly African American woman who spends her days sitting on the balcony of an apartment complex where many San Nicoladenses live, making sure that the African American children do not hassle the Latino ones. "They do it," she told me, "because they notice that the Hispanics don't speak English." She speaks no Spanish herself but her heart tells her to protect the children, and this she does.

As Veronica and I spoke about more general African American attitudes, I better understood local dynamics as she focused on changing demographics in Winston-Salem's neighborhoods. "Most blacks," she said, "used to live in the Waughtown area. But when Latinos started moving in, blacks started moving out."

"Blacks [now] call it 'little Mexico,'" Veronica continued. "They started moving to other areas. They tend to look down on Hispanics. They say, 'Oh, look at them, packed in their cars, twelve of them living in their houses, they all have satellite, they take the screen door off of the house or they park their car on the front lawn instead of in the driveway; they don't put money in the bank and carry it around with them instead.'"

Calvin, Veronica's African American husband and a former police officer, was more direct: "There were some robberies," he said, "situations where people would try to take advantage [because] Latinos carry money around with them." Veronica had heard people say that "their money is so wet when they give it to you . . . maybe blacks felt like Waughtown . . . I don't know how to say it—it's almost like when blacks start moving into a white suburb and whites start putting up 'for sale' signs and moving out." She also noted that "a lot of black females go to nursing school . . . and assist live-at-homes and things like that. They see speaking English as an advantage but also as a *status* [emphasis added]—they say there is no comparison between them and Latino women because they speak English. There's even that within the African American community. If you speak better, if you've been to college and have a degree, you're a cut above everybody else. . . . But I don't think [these women] would be as hostile toward whites as they are toward Latinos, because of the 'slave mentality' in which whites in general are seen to be a cut above."

Clearly, then, the structural conditions and racial and language ideologies that influence the attitudes and perceptions of San Nicoladenses are not exclusive to them. Other Latinos share them, and elements of exclusion and superiority influence African American attitudes, as Veronica's openness illustrates. In the United States, Latinos and African Americans are forced to compete for a place in a socioeconomic hierarchy organized around race, skin color, class, and language, a hierarchy broadly construed as "American" with both English and whiteness at its apex. Since most San Nicoladenses' English is nonexistent, they compete by trading on qualities such as a work ethic, peacefulness, honesty, and the lighter skin that joins them to their homeplace, signals their cultivation, and draws them closer to whiteness. Although my sample of African Americans is not generalizable, at least some, according to Veronica, propose that their own command of

An apartment complex in Winston-Salem where many San Nicoladenses live

Waughtown: A house owned by San Nicoladenses

English and conformity to "white" norms, such as not parking a car on the lawn or carrying "wet" money around, makes them better than Latinos. Indeed, perhaps Veronica's final astute observation, which echoes Brackette Williams, best describes the situation: "You step on the ones below you and you're still trying to reach the ones above you."

Place Naming and (Dis)placements

San Nicoladenses incorporate into their day-to-day lives, including across geopolitical borders, their familiarity with a place, in this case the village of San Nicolás. This encompasses food, language, race, custom, and a history grounded on the southern Pacific Coast of Mexico. I began with an analysis of that history, followed by how identities are spoken about and performed in Mexico. I then addressed the U.S. anthropologist Melville Herskovits and his influence on the Mexican researcher Gonzalo Aguirre Beltrán, whose own influence is apparent, in turn, among recent culture workers. The latter have attempted — generally without success — to forge what are in fact new identities for San Nicoladenses, as outlined in chapter 5. Moving to the interior of San Nicolás I examined what it means to be from there, and the tensions and contradictions of daily life. My final chapter links that daily life to migration, as I show how San Nicoladenses use remittances to cement claims to a place in their natal village, through houses sometimes cleansed by Indian healers. Despite culture workers' attempts to fix them in time, San Nicoladenses thus continue to live their processual rather than static lives. With only a first generation born or raised in the United States, San Nicoladenses' racial categories have shifted, but they are still rooted on the Costa Chica, where worldviews feature both distancing from blackness and reduplication of the Other.

Of course there is no "analysis" of San Nicoladenses in their "natural" setting. As Catherine Allen astutely notes, "any stopping place is arbitrary" (1988:11), both for the ethnographer and for the people with whom she or he works. I thus leave to others the future or a reinterpretation of the present and close by noting that from the moment San Nicoladenses' lives were recorded for outside consumption, the recording process itself has been influenced by foreign intellectual paradigms, which I have tried to set aside as best I can. Such paradigms have partially changed the way San Nicoladenses understand the world, as many of them have told me. But the Mexican village of San Nicolás keeps most San Nicoladenses together in North Carolina because they are highly endogamous, most are undocumented, and family is crucial to success. This helps them to maintain strong identities in the United States *as* San Nicoladenses. In this respect, their ways of being challenge the conclusions of recent scholarship that dislocates people whose lives are characterized by a postmodern and postcolonial "loss of territorial roots," and by escalating hybridity as borders and boundaries blur (Feld and Basso 1996; Gupta and Ferguson 1997:37; see also Appadurai 1996:204, 1997).[6] Such processes entail a myriad of spatial and temporal movements that blend centers and peripheries, the local and the nonlocal. Indeed, contemporary anthropology tends to focus on boundaries, movement, deterritorialization, destabilization, and the lack of fixity among place, space, and culture, perhaps as a hypercorrection to what classic ethnography falsely presented as the isomorphism between a community of so-called natives and its boundedness in space and time (Appadurai 1992:34–36; Gupta and Ferguson 1997:34–36). Yet such theorists overlook the fact that hybridity *is* identity for many of the world's peoples, and that it translates to categories other than personhood. These categories might appear stable only in light of a fixed Western gaze that makes it difficult to understand how a migratory saint maintains a community's faith as that community itself migrates to maintain its saint. And those who are allegedly mobile might instead see themselves and the world as fixed, in part because the categories they use to understand that world are themselves fluid and always have been.

This is not to minimize the destructive effects of globalization and the countless numbers of world refugees, nor to forget other massive historical displacements such as the Atlantic slave trade, the colonial concentration of Indian communities, or the fact that San Nicolás and surrounding towns were burned to the ground during the Mexican Revolution. It is to say, however, as Jonathan Amith so eloquently does, that "locations . . . may be considered nodal points uniquely characterized by their embeddedness in wide-ranging webs of social, cultural, political and economic relations. As loci of relations, places are neither static, internally seamless and undifferentiated, nor necessarily bounded" (2005:163). Places are therefore where social relations are maintained and transformed. San Nicolás has been created and recreated by people who have been many times dispersed, whose lives are simultaneously local, regional, national, and, now, international, and whose racial categories reflect the flux of their historical and ongoing experiences. It has thus always been unbounded, and its identities are nodal points for which locations are metonyms.

By attending to historical events such as the slave trade, colonialism, land claims, and migrations, I have therefore tried to embed the displacements of both moreno and Indian San Nicoladenses in the ongoing construction of place. Such displacements are produced and maintained through what Nancy Munn calls the "spatial fields" of "acting subjects" (1996:453)—here the saint, maroons, and migrants—who move through time and space but who never stop making place. The tensions captured by these subjects, and the complicated territorial and identity claims those tensions reflect, are continuously resolved (and continuously recreated) in the material and emotional embodiments of day-to-day life, to which are bound understandings of time, space and place, race, the Other, the past, and movement expressed through narratives, festivals, feuds, emotion, and memory (Casey 1996:36–37).[7] Far from suggesting terminal "loss," ships, maroons, independence, saints, and migration—indeed the everyday lives of San Nicoladenses—suggest that loss itself authenticates what is claimed. In effect, this post-postmodern world of ongoing displacements that build on each other and recall the past, is a world in which, as the late William Roseberry once reminded me, villages, as places that people make real and give meaning to, can and do still exist. Moreover, while stories of displacements, which engage both Indianness and blackness and which are told and enacted by Indians and morenos, do rupture that isomorphism between natives, space, and time, they also indicate that local people find ways to bind themselves as various kinds of natives to the specific places meaningful to them—to the village of San Nicolás and, in the broader narrative, to Mexico itself.[8]

That Indians and morenos alike see themselves as natives with hybrid and hierarchical but essential connections to local and national places might challenge anthropological concerns with essentializing and essentialized identities. Yet it also compels an anthropological understanding that acknowledges the power of identities to strengthen people's political, material, and emotional connections to their locales (also Diskin 1991; Hale 1997:577–78, 1994:18–21). Here those connections accommodate both Indians and morenos, who present themselves as natives in culturally specific ways. Indians are the primordial natives of Mexico, the indigenous ones, the bearers of freedom but also "outsiders" in San Nicolás. Morenos are native-born San Nicoladenses, but ultimately lay claim to their village—and to Mexico itself—through Indians, because blackness makes them outsiders. Moreno or black Indian identities therefore combine the "diaspora cosmopolitanisms" of blacks, which draw on historical contexts of displacement, with indigenous claims to continuity, which rest on "natural" connections to places (Clifford 1994:308).

Notes

Introduction

1. Local names are pseudonyms; I use real names only for public figures.
2. I use the honorifics Don and Doña for people above the age of about fifty-five. For the middle generation I dispense with honorifics because although San Nicoladenses are quite formal, they generally do too. I try to dissuade all but children from referring to me as Doña Laura.
3. This is not to say that land distribution was perfect; it failed miserably in Chiapas, and much land distributed during agrarian reform cannot sustain communities. Nor is it to deny that land disputes are central to coastal history. Indeed, chapter 1 is devoted to such disputes. But many coastal belt communities received some of the best land in Mexico.
4. Today between one-quarter and one-third of Guerrerenses live in el norte (S!Paz International Service for Peace 2009). Despite the U.S. recession, at least in 2008–9 most Mexican immigrants were not returning home (Passell and Cohn 2009). Indeed, even with new and draconian state laws, such as Arizona's SB1070, escalating drug-related violence, increasingly in southern Mexico but especially in Mexico's northern states, continues to send Mexicans across the border.
5. Since the implementation in 1994 of the North American Free Trade Agreement (NAFTA), Mexico's agricultural sector has contracted, and foreign investment has not poured in while agricultural imports have, thus all but destroying local markets. Today, three small farmers must work to achieve the same income that one would have brought in prior to NAFTA, but the agricultural terms of the agreement have not been renegotiated (Carlsen 2008; De Ita 2008).
6. For me foundational theoretical discussions of Latin American and Caribbean

transnationalism include Rouse 1991 and Glick Schiller and Fouron 2001. With respect to my emphasis on meanings and on nonmigrants as well as on migrants, I draw on Vertovec 2004.

Chapter 1: The Lay of the Land

1. After Chiapas, Guerrero has the highest number (29 percent) of monolingual indigenous language speakers (Estrada Castañón 1994:8). Not long ago about half of the Costa Chica's Amuzgo population was monolingual (Valdez 1998:28).

2. The municipal president of San Marcos, at the northwestern edge of the Costa Chica, petitioned Lázaro Cárdenas in January 1940 for funds to initiate the construction of the highway "projected from Acapulco to Puerto Angel" (AGN Dirección General de Gobernación 2.000 [9–48]). Built in fits and starts throughout the 1940s and 1950s, it was completed through southern Mexico in 1964. In 1940 the municipality of Cuaji had 4,819 residents. In 1950 it had 5,124, with San Nicolás accounting for 1,021 and Cuaji for 1,458. Between 1950 and 1960 the municipal population grew by 102 percent; by 1963 it had climbed to 13,500 residents. My own calculations based on the engineer Alejandro Waldimir Paucic's numbers indicate that Cuaji experienced the fastest growth of any municipality in Guerrero during this period. Other Costa Chican municipalities, such as San Marcos, in fact lost population because of instability and proximity to Acapulco (AGEG-AHE, AP 86, 99, 120).

3. Mayors handle civil offenses, interpersonal disputes, and community infrastructure. The *comisariado ejidal*, or ejidal commission, deals with agricultural issues, including disputes over land boundaries and farm animals that are injured or die. It has a president as well as various functionaries. Local community policing also exists. Some crimes, such as rapes and murders, are state offenses, while others, such as drug trafficking and guerrilla activities, are federal ones. San Nicolás has a jail cell for rabble-rousers, but serious crimes are dealt with in Ometepec and then in Chilpancingo. Cuaji does not have courts, though occasionally a judicial agent arrives to investigate crimes.

4. The researchers insisted on using *Afromestizo*, while the reporter used *moreno* or *Afrodescendent*.

5. Ejido refers to lands granted as community property during the agrarian reform period under Article 27 of the Mexican Constitution.

6. Inheritance is bilateral, but men generally inherit land as women are supposed to co-own their husbands' land. In general, women only inherit land when husbands die. They also look after land for migrant husbands and sons.

7. One crop can be planted in the highlands in June at the beginning of the rainy season, and two in the lowlands: one in early September toward the end of the rainy season and, if the owner has access to irrigation, one during the dry season.

8. Tourism is Guerrero's most important industry, though it is uneven, especially as

the beach resort city of Acapulco is now one of Mexico's deadliest cities. Most of the state's assets have historically bolstered Acapulco and Ixtapa, a more exclusive beach resort, as well as the colonial silver mining town of Taxco. Guerrero's tourist industry once brought in 40 percent of Mexico's tourist dollars (Estrada 1994:19). But while most state resources maintain tourist infrastructure, agrarian communities have been "virtually abandoned to their fate" (Estrada 1994:16–17). Even into the 2000s some community land—especially near Acapulco—was appropriated to expand resort hotels. Guerrero's other main industry is forestry. Dominated by multinationals, forest exploitation has caused environmental devastation (Estrada 1994:18).

9. In 1999 the Boise Cascade Corporation contacted the University of Boise, where William Wines was a professor of business ethics. The University of Boise then contacted Denver University, which published the *Denver Journal of International Law and Policy*. The journal subsequently printed a retraction of the article and pulled it from online databases. Wines and others sued and reached a settlement with Denver University (William Wines, personal communication; Patterson 2000).

10. Estrada traces the Guerreran economic model to the 1930s and 1940s while others trace it to the Porfiriato. But Estrada points out that agrarian reform and tourism, both of which have had an enormous impact on Guerrero's economy, are twentieth-century phenomena (1994:15–16n34).

11. The EZLN took its name from the Zapatistas of the Mexican Revolution. It appeared in Chiapas on 1 January 1994, the day NAFTA went into effect.

12. Subcomandante Marcos was one of the most prominent EZLN leaders.

13. Igualapa roughly corresponded to the northern part of the Costa Chica, while Xicayan was a province in what is today southwestern Oaxaca.

14. Pinotepa del Rey is today Pinotepa Nacional. Although it is now a Mixtec-dominant region, *Pinotepa* means "toward the crumbling hill" in Nahuatl.

15. Like *mulatto*, *pardo* referred to mixed black Indians (Love 1971).

16. Norberto Valdez and María de los Angeles Manzano both date this transfer to the post-independence period (Manzano 1991:22; Valdez 1998:64), but the original documentation indicates that it took place in the 1770s, before independence.

17. According to Paucic, San Nicolás became a *pueblo* (town), as opposed to a *cuadrilla* (settlement), in 1883, while Cuaji became a pueblo in 1870 (AGEG-AHE, AP 607).

18. I use *hacendado* for large landowner because San Nicoladenses use the term.

19. San Nicolás was named at least by 1761, around the time Don Juan de Vargas was litigating. Its patron saint was feted in Cuaji by 1782 and possibly earlier (AGN Criminal 457.2–3).

20. In the 1850s Alvarez was one of the architects of the Plan de Ayutla, which called for replacing the then-dictator Santa Ana with an elected government. Alvarez briefly became head of state, with Benito Juárez serving as his minister of justice.

When Alvarez stepped down, Juárez, a Zapotec Indian, returned to his native Oaxaca, reemerging several years later as the chief justice of the Supreme Court, and then declaring himself president of Mexico.

21. For examples, see the collection of Mexican Colonization Papers, July 23, 1887– September 17, 1889, held by the Latin American Library at Tulane University.

22. The Guerrero Trading Company controlled the 190,000 hectares of the San Marcos Hacienda at the northwestern edge of the coast, purchased from the federal government in 1903 (Jacobs 1982:61–62; Valdez 1998:56). Guerrero also hosted the Guerrero Land and Timber Company, the Pacific Wood Company, the Mexican Nollano Company, the Yextla Company, and the holdings of George M. Hurty, also a U.S. citizen (Estrada 1994:38). The Mexican López, Galeana, Solis, Izazaga, Cabrera, and Campos families also owned large tracts of land (Jacobs 1982:62).

23. Aguirre Beltrán uses the pseudonym Juan A. Smith for Miller because the Miller family was still powerful when he conducted his fieldwork in Cuaji. The outlines of the story are similar, but Aguirre Beltrán does not address the Miller legacy as his research was done in the late 1940s.

24. Quoting U.S. National Archives, Records of the Department of State Relating to Internal Affairs of Mexico, 1910–1029, Microfilm #274, RDS 812.00/2178.

25. The author Manzano is a member of this family, as is Andrés Manzano Añorve, her brother and Cuaji's municipal president in the late 1990s. Francisco Madero helped to unseat Díaz. But Madero came from a prominent landholding family and, from exile, appointed a Conservative interim president seen to have betrayed Zapatista ideals. Madero then became president, but he was deposed by one of his generals, Victoriano Huerta, who participated in Madero's assassination in 1913.

26. During this period, Zapata was rebelling in Guerrero against Madero. As the Zapatistas prepared attacks in northern Guerrero, their forces were defeated by Enrique Añorve, who had been redirected by Madero from the Costa Chica. Añorve died in January 1913, without gaining support or payment from Madero for defeating the Zapatistas.

27. Carranza was assassinated in 1920, one year after Zapata.

28. Carnival is no longer celebrated in San Nicolás because whites suppressed it in the 1950s. It is still celebrated by Mixtecs in the sierra north of Pinotepa Nacional, and even in the heavily evangelical Pinotepa de Don Luis, a community of about eight thousand people. When I attended in 1997 there were no morenos, although The Dance of the Devils ("Los Diablos") said by Don Zeferino to be "a moreno dance only from Collantes," was supposed to be performed. Later I was told by Elena, also from Collantes, that the dancers had not been invited.

29. An Añorve, Alfredo, is listed as head of a White Guard that killed twelve peasants "just for asking for a [land] application" (AGN Dirección General de Gobernación 2.012.8[9]20278:22).

30. For documentation on Pastrana, his activities against the Millers, and his com-

plaints to the authorities, see the collection in AGN Dirección General de Gobernación 2.012.8(9)26474. The song Don Domingo refers to is a ballad (*corrido*). See McDowell 2000:95.

31. The ninety-one-year-old Don Margarito feared the history would be forgotten. I brought copies of the Pastrana and other documents from the AGN to San Nicolás, where a schoolteacher was establishing a local archive because a "white municipal president in Cuaji had burned all the papers." See also Añorve 1999.

32. Gifting children is fairly common and usually occurs when a couple is infertile, as Don Domingo and Doña Ana were, or when an older person is otherwise childless. Thus Doña Bertha was gifted a grandchild when all of her children left home. Margarita was gifted as a toddler to her childless great-uncle, who brought her up until she was twelve, when her father took her back against her will into a home where she knew none of her siblings.

33. Eventually five colonies were formed in Cuaji's municipality: Miguel Alemán, Cuije, San José, Tierra Colorada, and El Tamale, all carved from Miller's property.

34. Don Domingo indicated that San Nicolás owns 8,000 hectares, while the ejido documentation indicates 9,840. I am guessing that El Pitahayo, which has almost 2,000 hectares, did not figure in Don Domingo's equation, as he frequently mentioned El Tamale.

35. The Education, Health, and Food Program (Programa de Educación, Salud y Alimentación, PROGRESA), now called Opportunities (Oportunidades), gives direct cash benefits to poor households to keep children in school and to make regular visits to health clinics. Fully implemented in 1998, it targets rural communities like San Nicolás. It has improved school attendance and health, especially for girls and women.

36. Pesticide vendors are required by law to post the dangers and proper usage, but many men working with them do not take precautions.

Chapter 2: Identity in Discourse

1. The 235 kilometers from Huatulco to Cuaji "was a distance not easy to traverse on foot, especially as [it] was indirect and filled with brambles and bush.... To reach Cuaji one would have to circle around a great deal, crossing rivers with rough flows that, in the colonial era, were recognized as impassable in the rainy season. Moreover, such transit implies previous knowledge of where Cuaji was . . . the topography meant at least four months without communication [because of the rainy season] . . . it is not very believable that it was conducive to expedited transit toward Cuaji" (Motta 2006:141). Even today, Motta observes, elderly Oaxacans note that because of distance it is much better to marry locally; one would not even look for a partner elsewhere (2006:141).

2. Bolivians of African descent concentrated in the Yungas region of Bolivia (department of La Paz) learned to plant coca from Aymara Indians, whose dress they also wear (Urioste 1985).

3. Africa, Cuba, and Chile all circulate as part of the local imaginary, but most knowledge of these places and their connection to San Nicolás comes from what people have heard outsiders say. Africa, of course, was the principal source of slaves, but most San Nicoladenses have no geographical knowledge of the continent, nor do they know much about the slave trade itself. References to Cuba are less transparent, although Mexico's Gulf Coast is home to many Cuban immigrants who brought Afro-Cuban cultural forms—especially music—with them. Chile is the alleged source of the *chilena*, a regional Guerreran dance said to have been introduced through the port of Acapulco by Chilean sailors in the early nineteenth century (Lewis 2000 and chapter 5).

4. At least one contemporary Indian account concurs that Indians fled the coastal belt during the conquest, placing the ancestral origins of the contemporary Sierra Madre del Sur Amuzgos of Xochistlahuaca in San Nicolás, which is of course located in an area now recognized as "black" (Valdez 1998:31–33). Although it is likely that Amuzgos once populated the region, Norberto Valdez cites a seventy-two-year-old Amuzgo's claims that there is still a remnant Amuzgo community in San Nicolás, the only such community outside the Amuzgo zone (1998:32). But there is only one Amuzgo family in San Nicolás, and it only recently arrived.

5. Data I collected in 1997–98 from about one-third of the village's families indicate that the average Indian holding is three-quarters the size of the average moreno holding (7.46 versus 9.17 hectares, or 5.07 versus 7.77 eliminating the top holders, who would be one family with 45 hectares in the Indian group and two families with 150 hectares each in the moreno group).

6. According to Jonathan Amith, *cuculuste* is derived from the Nahuatl *xokolochitl*; *cuita* from the Nahuatl *kwitlatl*; and *chochoyote* from the Nahuatl *xokoyotl*, all of which have the same meanings as the moreno terms (personal communication).

7. Bobby Vaughn cites Veronique Flanet's work around Jamiltepec to support his claim (2004:83n13), and Flanet does note hostility between black and indigenous people. But she fails to reconcile such hostility with her own observation that "most mixing appears to be black-indigenous" (1977:227n6).

8. Even the careful etymology by Chege Githiora (1994) of his own first name and the last name of a coastal resident (Chegue) is problematic because *chagüe*, a term common throughout the coastal belt for lowland or irrigated corn plots, is also a place name in Mexico, Nicaragua, Peru, and other parts of Latin America. It is also a common surname stretching from Scotland to Quebec to the northeastern United States (originally with an accent on the final *e* and without the umlaut over the *u*.)

9. *Macuana* is the feminine form of *macuano*, a derogatory term for an Indian. The etymology of *macuano* is unclear, but in Huehuetán *macuana* means "penis" (Aparicio, Díaz, and García n.d.:16) and might be a Nahuatl derivative (Jonathan Amith, personal communication). *Macuache* is also a Mexican Spanish term (likely derived from Nahuatl) for a non-literate Indian (see also note 11).

10. I thank Amy Paugh for the correct linguistic term for this doubling. The first *Indian* has an intensifying function, such that Indian Indians are "very" Indian.

11. Throughout Latin America the term *guanaco* means "dumb" or "rustic"; it is also a species of llama (Rollin 1998); Guanano is also an indigenous language in parts of Colombia, Brazil, Peru, and Ecuador. Otherwise, the word's origins appear unknown.

12. Of course now Indians born in San Nicolás have lost Mixtec altogether, speak the same Spanish as morenos, and have more social mobility than both their parents and Indian Indians.

13. I address this issue, which indeed is a gender issue, in chapter 6.

14. I thank Judy Boruchoff for calling my attention to this distinction.

Chapter 3: Identity in Performance

1. Rafael Rebollar's film *De Florida a Coahuila* (*From Florida to Coahuila*), of 2002, documents the history of Black Seminoles who fled to northern Mexico in 1850.

2. Such peoples and their "culture" are also used to enhance national cosmopolitanisms (e.g., Moore 1997; Wade 2006b).

3. Zitlala might have been a pre-Columbian observatory. Some San Nicoladenses say that San Nicolás the saint was guided at night by a star.

4. This is similar to Loring Danforth's (1989) analysis of genealogical, spatial, and temporal connections between rural ethnic Greek Kostilides, Saint Constantine, and the group's patriarch, Kosti, which is also the name of the Thracian village from which Kostilides were exiled in the first half of the twentieth century.

5. Even today San Nicolás does not have a resident priest. Instead, priests reside in Cuaji and come to San Nicolás twice a week for Mass, weddings, and occasionally for other ritual events such as funerals (though I have never seen a priest at a funeral).

6. Of course some of this help came from Indian groups hostile to Nahuas, but from the perspective of San Nicoladenses the lines are clearly drawn.

Chapter 4: Africa in Mexico

1. Daniel Althoff (1994) notes that despite identification with "old" or "African" Spanish, the word *Cuijla* and other local speech patterns are consistent with popular or rural speech elsewhere in Mexico and Latin America (253–54). Everyone refers to Cuajinicuilapa as Cuaji and has done so since the time of Althoff's work. He does not know how Cuijla came to be Cuaji, or how Cuijla derived from Cuajinicuilapa. He speculates that Cuijla died out because Cuaji is easier to pronounce and Spanish has few instances of a final *h* syllable. Today in San Nicolás "old" Spanish is still occasionally heard in such verbal forms as *vide* instead of *vi*, meaning "I saw." Althoff notes that *voseo*, or the use of the Spanish informal pronoun *vos* (you), still used in parts of Latin America but uncommon in Mexico, was no longer found in Cuaji in the early 1990s. In San Nicolás one occasionally

hears *vos*. However, in most of Mexico (and usually in San Nicolás) *tú* is more common than *vos*.

2. Hugo Nutini (1965) describes bride theft in an indigenous Tlaxcalan community, and Brian Stross (1974) in an indigenous Chiapan community. Barbara Ayers notes that "the forcible abduction of a woman for the purpose of marriage" (1974:238) is present in Eurasia, Africa, the circum-Mediterranean, the Pacific, and North and South America; R. H. Barnes (1999) describes "marriage by capture" as a former practice in Eastern Indonesia.

3. Aguirre Beltrán elaborated this typology, but I discuss marriage and having a lover at length in chapter 6.

4. I have been unable to find this film.

5. Miriam Jiménez, personal communication, 2007.

6. Bobby Vaughn, "Mexico's Black Heritage: The Costa Chica of Guerrero and Oaxaca," Mexconnect, http://www.mexconnect.com (accessed 2 December 2007).

7. Baron Pineda notes that U.S. scholars of the Mosquito Coast, for instance Charles Hale, also link Africanity and violence (2006:51–53).

8. Flanet focuses on Indian and mestizo perceptions of blacks rather than on blacks' self-perceptions. She concludes that violence is a consequence of unresolved land disputes and not specific to any particular group (see also Hernández 1996; McDowell 2000).

9. Jean Jackson uses this term to characterize missionaries, government personnel, and whites who helped bring an ethnic group consciousness to indigenous inhabitants of the Vaupés region of southeastern Colombia (1991:133).

10. Bobby Vaughn, "Mexico's Black Heritage: The Costa Chica of Guerrero and Oaxaca," http://www.mexconnect.com (accessed 2 December 2007).

Chapter 5: Culture Work

1. Carlos Ruíz believes that the drum derives from the boxes used to transport soap on the coast. He considers it part of the original Chilean sailors' repertoire (2001:56–57).

2. Moisés Ochoa (1987) covers the debate over whether this dance was originally introduced to South America by African slaves.

3. The costumes, picked out by one of the musicians, are traditional Veracruzan jarocha outfits, although moreno men used to wear the same homemade white trousers fastened with a tie at the waist as Indians, while substituting store-bought shirts for Indians' handmade ones (a substitution indicating morenos' higher socioeconomic status).

4. Traditionally, unmarried young women and young men dance to minuets with purple bougainvillea in their hands at any unmarried person's wake. Minuets are considered joyful, as is the dance that accompanies them. The goal is to "overthrow the burden" of grief by imitating a happy occasion, in this case a wedding

that a deceased young person will never experience. During the wake and funeral I attended, a tape of minuet music played, and at the soul raising young men and women danced with bougainvillea, gracefully bowing, swaying, and turning before an offering of crepe paper flowers and portraits that included the Virgin of Guadalupe and the only snapshot of the little girl her parents had. I was initially surprised to hear minuets. But all kinds of dance music were introduced from Europe into colonial Mexico during the last century of colonial rule (Koegel 1999). The first dance at weddings in San Nicolás, as elsewhere in Mexico, is always a waltz.

5. This was startlingly inaccurate since slavery was abolished in Mexico in 1824, so no one's grandparent could have been a slave.

6. On this issue, see Penelope Harvey's discussion of contemporary multicultural-ism and the "integrity" of the modern nation-state (1996).

7. Doña Lupe has been trying unsuccessfully to acquire a visa for years with a passport and a son who is a U.S. citizen. She has traveled to Chile, has the funds, and only wants to visit. Don Gregorio has no documented relatives in el norte, has never left the coast except to go to Mexico City, and does not have the money for a visa.

8. Corridos are rooted in Spanish ballad traditions. The Mexican tradition is primarily a mestizo one, and the "Mexican corrido is essentially true to its [Spanish] roots" (McDowell 2000:25–26). Unusually, half the corridos on the coastal belt are in minor keys, a "distinctive feature" (McDowell 2000:29) perhaps due to the influence of chilenas (John McDowell, personal communication, June 2009).

9. There are no church funerals per se in San Nicolás. Instead, after the wake—which is two nights for an adult and one for a child, because a child's body decomposes more quickly—the coffin is carried to the church courtyard, where the pallbearers bow down and touch the coffin to the cross. From there it is taken directly to the cemetery.

10. The origins of *mollo* are unclear, but it might be a Puerto Rican term from the urban United States or derive from the Nahuatl *mollote* for "little black bug" (Jonathan Amith, personal communication).

11. Adela Amaral notes that when the Meeting of Black Villages was held in Corralero, Oaxaca, in 2005, Corralero's morenos, like those of San Nicolás in 2002, also attended only the evening entertainment (2005:13).

12. Under considerable community pressure, he eventually bought instruments for the casa de cultura, as well as bricks to rebuild the structure, though it was never rebuilt. The instruments sat gathering dust as the musicians aged. At one point they tried to sell them, but they never recouped most of the money.

Chapter 6: Being from Here

1. After 1997 I would occasionally bring my son and female students, but I otherwise go alone.
2. A "relic" is a small piece of cloth with a saint's message that protects the wearer.
3. Seven is the age of reason and when first communion takes place.
4. Children born in el norte are often sent to family in San Nicolás so that parents can work. Those who bring them are going to San Nicolás anyway, or are women who charge for their services.
5. Kindergarten begins at age three and lasts for two years.
6. Property extends to fruit trees that overhang a neighbor's yard or house. Hence the neighbor accused us of stealing her fruit.
7. The terms *novio* and *novia* are used for boyfriend and girlfriend, fiancé and fiancée, and groom and bride because the couple is expected to marry.
8. Only baptismal godparents must be a couple because their roles are central to weddings, procreation, and the recreation of gender pairings.
9. Girls often did not finish primary school because their mothers needed them at home. This began to change in the late 1990s when the government began subsidizing families to keep children in school through the program Progresa, which became Oportunidades in 2002. In the early 2000s the Open School also became available for those who never completed primary school.
10. The Catholic Church will not marry anyone under seventeen. Mexican law requires parental consent for those under eighteen, but a boy must be at least sixteen and a girl at least fourteen. Thus with parental permission a fourteen-year-old girl can have a civil marriage and later a Catholic one. Parents who want their daughters in school will do their best to discourage early fleeing.
11. In el norte young couples sometimes live on their own before marriage, as Felipa did with her husband, because his parents were not there. On the other hand, Filadelfo and his wife Dorotea live with Filadelfo's parents because they are there.
12. Aquiles was gifted by his Indian peon parents as a toddler. His adoptive father did not have sons of his own and the Indians could not afford to raise Aquiles, who was brought up in San Nicolás and married a morena.
13. Traditionally a husband would amass enough money to buy his own houseplot and build an adobe house for his family by working with his father in the fields. But as everyone now wants cinder-block houses (see chapter 8), people head to el norte to make more money.
14. A severely mentally or physically disabled woman, such as Rita, will live with her parents her whole life. When the parents die, as Rita's have, she will stay in her parents' home with her youngest brother, who inherits the house.
15. A woman can buy land but since she does not normally work land, this resource makes sense only if she has sons old enough to care for cattle or crops.
16. The fact that Alberto decided that Amalia not finish school, accompany him to

el norte, and not work outside the home there indicates that traditional gender roles are still highly rigid, even for young people.

17. Prostitution is legal in Mexico, where the government issues identity cards and checks monthly for HIV.

18. Although the perception might be that wealthier men are more likely to have queridas, this may not be true since wives often complain that men spend scarce money on their queridas and cannot support their legitimate children.

19. Guns are ubiquitous in San Nicolás as I discovered one New Year's Eve when, at the stroke of midnight, just about every man pulled one out and shot it into the air. But the fact that I did not realize how many guns people had until that point indicates that they are not often used. Indeed, homicides in San Nicolás are much lower than they are in surrounding Mixtec communities (Gutiérrez Avila 1997a:106–7).

20. This is sweet bread. It is made in the afternoon and consumed in the late evening or the following morning. It is the main sweet thing—besides fruit—that San Nicoladenses eat. While I love their cooking, they generally dislike mine because no matter what I make it is deemed "too sweet" (not spicy enough).

21. Young girls are not in any danger on the streets, as older girls would be, and boys do not do this kind of work, which deals with food items and orders from mothers.

22. Women from Bali to Guatemala to Ghana carry things on their heads.

23. When I first arrived in San Nicolás, phone service consisted of public phones in Doña Leticia's store, for which some people had party-line extensions. When someone without an extension received a call, a notice would go out over the loudspeaker. Since no one could pronounce my last name, I became "Laura, la mamá de Lukas" (Laura, Lukas's mom). Telmex, the Mexican national phone company, eventually ran lines through town and people began to acquire private phone numbers. The public phone (known as the caseta) is still in business, however, to serve those without a phone.

24. When World Vision (wv), the only NGO operating in San Nicolás, announces it is giving out toys, school supplies, or food, or will be taking children's photos, women and children line up. It favors registered children's mothers for despensas that include food and discounted medicines. But it announces that anyone can register children while limiting registration. Thus in 1998, 450 children in San Nicolás were registered at registration's close, and some people were unable to register their children. Like other outsiders, wv can cause community tensions. For instance, it formed a health committee with Mayra as president and gave her medicines to sell at a discount even though she did not have the credentials to diagnose illnesses, treat injuries, or give injections. "So," Sirina said, "she'll just sell World Vision's medicine as if it were hers and charge whatever she likes." The majority of San Nicoladenses are Catholic while wv is evangelical, but the oranization's religious orientation does not bother San Nicoladenses. It began one

meeting by seeking volunteers to preach door to door "what the Bible says" and to give Bible classes. Sirina remarked, "No one believes this is going to work for them. They go to the meetings because they want a despensa. If World Vision had announced that the meeting was about preaching no one would have come. You saw how people left as soon as they began to talk about preaching. Well," she continued, "if I have to be an evangelical to get a despensa that's what I'll do. Then I'll stop."

25. Unless quoting someone directly I use the term *homosexual* for both men and women because *marimacho*, *puto*, and *maricón* might seem pejorative and *gay* might become anachronistic.

26. By the early 2000s there had only been one case of HIV in San Nicolás. Carlos was the second, but since he was from Cuaji everyone, including the clinic doctor, counted him as a Cuaji case. Because there are so few cases and I never heard any evidence to the contrary, my impression is that heterosexual men in San Nicolás do not have sexual relations with other men (who, unlike female prostitutes, would not be regularly tested by the government), regardless of the general perception that Latin American men do so without being considered "homosexual."

Chapter 7: A Family Divided?

1. A recent study indicates that only 11.5 percent of homes in San Nicolás have drainage, and only 29.8 percent have indoor bathrooms (Barragán and Cañedo 2004:223). Most people bathe in outdoor enclosures using cistern water for bucket baths. Those in el norte still use buckets. Indeed, every bathtub there holds them. Toilets in San Nicolás are still mostly latrines, even if there is a toilet bowl.

2. In 1997 Ernesto Zedillo was president and adherents of the PRI had in one form or another held political power since 1939. This did not change until the election in 2000 of Vicente Fox, a member of the conservative National Action Party (PAN).

3. Birth is little acknowledged, perhaps because until quite recently many babies died (and some still do) from dehydration and fevers. A celebration might take place if, as was the case with Sirina, a daughter—who now has four younger brothers as well as an older one and who became Sirina's household helpmate— is born. But little is done for the mother, who simply rests for forty days until the baptism, when an infant's most important godparents are appointed.

4. I am not evangelical. I do drink moderately and dance, as people know, so this request to "rescue" Don Domingo had nothing to do with religious affiliation or custom. It was based on our long friendship.

5. Héctor is an Indian born and raised in the Ayutla region. Since I had heard the same thing about dancing during the First Meeting of Black Villages, I can only conclude that dancing as an expression of individual willfulness and freedom is a more generalized regional phenomenon.

6. As with World Vision, people are often unconcerned with the significance of religious affiliation. At a wedding I attended at a Virginia evangelical church, there was no drinking or dancing, a limited number of people, and the reception remained brief. While not all members of a family will necessarily belong to the same church, I was a godmother for another wedding for the same family at the Catholic Church in San Nicolás. That wedding included drinking and dancing, and it lasted for days.

7. Veronique Flanet notes that soul calming in Jamiltepec is both indigenous and "mestizo," "the body dies but the sombra lives on after death" (1977:104). The sombra is "the soul (*alma*) of the dead person that has not found rest in the beyond, and because of this is tormented" (Flanet 1977:105). In Jamiltepec the ceremony to calm it is called raising the shadow (*levantar la sombra*) and also involves a cross taken to the tomb (Flanet 1977:104–9).

8. If a wedding takes place in el norte, customs might mix. Thus, when Amada's eldest daughter married in June 2008 at a Catholic Church, even though Amada attends a Moravian Protestant one, about forty godparents were listed on the invitation, some grouped together to sponsor more expensive items, such as the band. But the husband's family, also from the Costa Chica, observed the U.S. convention of a church ceremony followed by a three-hour dinner and dance in the evening, and they included a reply card with the invitation.

9. Although I do not have the space to describe other ailments here, the most prominent is probably *vergüenza*, or shame, which causes parts of the body to swell (see also Aguirre Beltrán 1985:193) and which, like coraje, is carried in the air. Twins are particularly adept at both causing and curing swelling: one causes it, the other cures it. *Espanto* is mentioned in the text. Diabetes is on the rise, but people do not control their diets because of it, nor have I ever seen anyone test their blood sugar or take an insulin shot, although clinicians do advise about diets. San Nicoladenses call it "sugar," and many believe that it comes from *susto*, a fright, which can be healed traditionally. Arthur Rubel notes that susto transcends race, class, the rural-urban divide, and geopolitical boundaries among Latin Americans. He also argues that susto and espanto refer to the same condition (1964:270), yet San Nicoladenses distinguish the two. Sirina gave me an example of susto: "You're riding along in a truck and are stopped by a bunch of young men with guns, who make everyone get out. That is a susto." Unlike espanto, which is caused by an unseen force, susto is caused by a seen one. *Mal aire* (bad or evil air) is like coraje insofar as it is airborne and caused by adults but hurts children. Like Indians, San Nicoladenses also believe in naguals, as do other morenos. Once I saw the recent burial mound of a two-year-old girl in the moreno town of Collantes. When I asked the young woman accompanying me how the toddler had died, she replied "diarrhea and vomiting." When I asked if a doctor had seen the child she responded affirmatively, but added that it was her nagual and that the doctor could not cure her. (For an account of *nahuales*

in Jamiltepec, see Flanet 1977:74.) Some of these ailments are treated the way coraje is.

10. My interest in Indian supernaturalism and non-Indians was first sparked by my historical work (Lewis 2003). While piecing together its contemporary manifestations gratified my historical conclusions, it also made me wary of reading too much into my observations. Yet ongoing conversations with morenos and Indians put those fears to rest.

11. During the Santiago festival a cat is hanged by its legs from a wooden cross beam outside of the church, as the incoming and outgoing male functionaries gallop on horseback underneath, grabbing for a monetary prize a medallion draped around the cat's neck. By the time the medallion is secured, the cat is dead. No one was able to tell me the significance of the cat, which, according to Don Samuel, is apparently only hanged in San Nicolás. Historically, cats might represent Islam. In San Nicolás they might also represent men in the sense that they do not obey, and overcoming masculinity is one of the themes of the festival, during which roosters are also killed.

12. Sirina elaborated: "They also say that people spit a lot because they have parasites. Some people spit because their stomach hurts. They get watery mouths, but it's saliva, not phlegm. The majority of people here spit. I don't know. It's the custom. There aren't remedies as there are elsewhere. Here it's the custom that if one smells something bad or if someone farts, or you smell a dead thing, you have to spit. This means that it disgusts you."

13. Intestinal parasites are endemic, especially among children, who are routinely treated by the clinic doctor. Such parasites and their causes were documented in 1951 by a doctor visiting Cuaji. The reasons he gave are still causes today: poorly cooked or handled foods; nonpotable water that people do not boil; bare feet; and living in proximity to animals (Fuentes 1951:33).

14. Like phlegm, sodas and ice pops are "cold" and would exacerbate the imbalance.

15. Just as among the Mixtecs about whom Flanet writes, anorexia can be a side effect of coraje in San Nicoladenses.

16. Most female schoolteachers do not come from the community, are single, and do not live with families. On occasion they complain about intruders in the houses they rent, often together, and this comment might have referred to their attempts to protect themselves (perhaps unnecessarily) through magic.

17. Throughout most of the 1990s vascular ailments were the leading causes of death, while violent deaths came third after old age (Villalobos 1997).

18. Perhaps the most effective biomedicine is for children, whose diarrhea, high fevers, and parasites are relatively easily cured with rehydration therapy, antibiotics, and deworming medications.

19. Gutiérrez notes that certain Indians are highly feared. If someone looks at them in the wrong way or mistreats them, they can seek vengeance by turning into a ray of lightning and killing the person (1993:24).

20. Again this parallels the colonial period, during which women often ensorcelled men through food (Behar 1987; Lewis 2003:110, 153–54).

21. Some people associate swelling with coraje.

22. Juan Diego is the Indian to whom the Virgin of Guadalupe, Mexico's mestiza patron saint is said to have appeared in the early sixteenth century.

23. In the Anglo kinship system this would have been her great-aunt, her grand-mother's sister, with whom her father's mother lived, but in San Nicolás the kin-ship system is probably closest to what anthropologists call "Eskimo," wherein both generational and lateral distinctions are made, but without distinction between matrilineal and patrilineal kin. Descriptive terms exist for a person's closest family members: parents and siblings. Classificatory terms are more com-mon for relatives further removed, such as cousins and grandparents' siblings. Thus a first cousin is sometimes called a *primo hermano* (a sibling cousin) and a great-aunt is a grandmother.

24. During the colonial period Indian witches sometimes took the form of dogs, as I have documented elsewhere (Lewis 2003:103–5).

Chapter 8: Transnationalism, Place, and the Mundane

1. See the census information at http://census.osbm.state.nc. us/lookup (accessed 15 August 2007); Associated Press 2004; Peacock 2007:23–24.

2. Steven Vertovec distinguishes between personal remittances to families and collective ones sent to communities by migrant organizations, particularly by hometown associations (2004:986–87; Goldring 2002). San Nicoladenses' remit-tances are personal. The result is what Vertovec calls "'private affluence and pub-lic squalor,' or new homes reachable only over dirt roads" (2004:986).

3. See Barragán, del Carmen, and Villarreal 2004:233 for remittance statistics. With much labor, farming profits can underwrite the cost of a house. My household survey indicated that people build houses without leaving for el norte at all and without receiving money from there. But most people's perceptions are that houses and el norte are coterminous, and remittances do speed up the process considerably. They also enable larger and more elaborate homes.

4. Examples of studies that do link the different locales Mexicans inhabit include Boruchoff 1999; Cohen 2001, 2004; Fletcher 1999; Grimes 1998; Hellman 2008; Rouse 1991.

5. For an exception see Chavez 1998, who uses an older assimilation model but also portrays the complexity of Mexican families whose members have different legal statuses in el norte.

6. The term *cultural bifocals* is from Inda and Rosaldo 2002:20. Their essay gener-ally fails to distinguish between documented and undocumented immigrants, instead assuming that the position of not fully belonging to any one place is due entirely to the state of living in two places at once. But immigrants' legal statuses must be taken into account in any discussion of transnationalism because such

statuses affect people's sense of, and ability to, belong. Hilary Cunningham makes similar points when she argues that anthropologists need to "stay attuned to . . . issues of exclusion, access, and stratification in a context of global interconnections" (2004:332).

7. U.S. state and federal laws deny many undocumented immigrants drivers' licenses, bank accounts, access to in-state public higher education tuition and federal loans, scholarships, and other services, making it difficult, if not impossible, for even those brought to the United States as babies to receive higher education and find well-paying jobs.

8. In this respect I look to Nina Glick Schiller and Georges Eugene Fouron, who define transmigrants as people who "remain tied to their ancestral land by their actions as well as their thoughts" (2001:3). Although she does not make it explicit, Karen McCarthy Brown does the same in her wonderful ethnography of Haitian voudon (2001).

9. Glick Schiller and Fouron's definition of long-distance nationalism refers to the political and sentimental claims immigrants make on their home country. While they emphasize the political, in this case Haitian social justice (2001:17–35), I emphasize the sentimental.

10. The verse was more likely a chilena. Violence is a common theme in Mexican ballads, not just in ones from the coast. Such themes can even be traced back to Spain (John McDowell, personal communication).

11. Cinder-block homes exist throughout Mexico, as well as in other parts of the "developing" world where globalization, and ideas about modernity and progress, have made it the material of choice for construction in rural areas. Although I have not researched cement companies and cement distribution, this would add a dimension to the analysis. The Mexican government sparked the idea of building with cement in San Nicolás and in other parts of rural Mexico, and the Mexican company Cemex (Cementos de México) is the third-largest cement producer in the world.

12. Jeffrey Cohen notes that in a number of rural Oaxacan towns a high percentage of remittances also go to home construction (2004:112–13). He again focuses wholly on economic benefits as families use new rooms for workshops or dry-goods stores, a phenomenon also seen in San Nicolás.

13. Both kinds of houses are dirt mixed with plant materials, but the building processes differ. Adobe bricks are made of a mud-and-straw mixture; wattle-and-daub homes consist of interlaced posts covered with mud.

14. Iguana is one of the few wild animal foods still available. However, iguana and armadillo, which also used to be hunted, are very scarce and expensive to buy.

15. On food and self-identification in the wider context of consumption, see Friedman 2002:233–36.

16. San Nicolás received a secondary school in 1984 (Jile 1997:321–22).

17. On emergent socioeconomic class differences in Mexican migrant communities, see Cohen 2001; 2004:102–30; and Conway and Cohen 1998.

18. Cohen notes that "with so much migration in the news and with such an emphasis in anthropology on the study of migration, it is easy to forget that many Oaxacans never leave their hometown" (2004:8).

19. I do not cite the article to protect the family's privacy.

Conclusion: What's in a Name?

1. Bobby Vaughn disputes this by arguing that some costeños have adopted the hairstyles and clothing of African Americans, thereby helping them evade immigration services (2005:132). I have seen little evidence for this among San Nicoladenses, who dress differently, style their hair differently, adorn themselves differently, and look physically distinct from African Americans, including with respect to their height and comportment, such as the way they walk and hold themselves. In addition, what some term "African American" culture, such as hip hop and low-slung trousers, is also part of U.S. youth culture. However, different contexts (urban California and urban North Carolina) might produce different forms of self-expression.

2. In peninsular Spanish *gabacho* means "froggy," with specific reference to foreigners, especially to the French. Thus it is similar to the English term *frog*.

3. Kimberly Grimes notes that Putlecans, who are not of African descent, are also "especially ignorant about the discrimination African Americans have suffered" (1998:86).

4. Of course, I have made clear the extent of antiblack racism in Mexico. For recent examples that made headlines, see Thompson 2001 and Habana 2003. See also Lewis 2004:477 and Hernández 2003. One young woman from San Nicolás told me that she was sexually and racially harassed in Mexico City with the comment: "Black woman, big hot black woman, were you born like that [lit. are you like that?] or do you grease yourself up?" (*Morena, morenaza,¿asi eres o te echas grasa?*). Despite all of this, and despite San Nicoladenses' obvious awareness of it, on the coastal belt and within the community itself antiblack racism is not institutionalized and San Nicoladenses have more immediate concerns.

5. See the local North Carolina school directory, http://nc.localschooldirectory .com/schools.php/cPath/12884 (accessed 1 October 2007). For instance, Margarita once told me that the African American girls would not allow Antonia to sit with them at lunch because she was "Hispanic." When Antonia recently changed high schools she complained to me in perfect English that there were "too many blacks" at her new school.

6. Akhil Gupta and James Ferguson seem to want to argue both that "interconnected spaces," mobility, and unfixed identities have always existed and that "post-coloniality" has produced an "erosion of the cultural distinctiveness of

places" and a "generalized sense of homelessness" (1997:35–37). As is clear from my argument, I think past displacements are just as meaningful today as the "post-colonial" border crossings that displace many of the world's peoples. In that sense, I use the concept of the "coloniality of power" (Quijano 2000) in a deeply cultural way.

7. Edward Casey privileges place and lived experience as prior to the "dense historicities and geographies" to which place and experience refer (1996:36–37). Yet ethnographers come to know things in a different order than, and in a different way from, natives. For instance, I heard the ship stories long before I "sensed" the place, and San Nicolás the saint did not enter my consciousness in a significant way until I was familiar with the place. I thus clearly understand place with the boat stories in mind, and I try to understand the saint with a much finer sense of a place that is already constituted (in my mind) by the "dense historicities and geographies" of which Casey speaks.

8. Jeffrey Cohen (2004:2–3) notes that at least in song, ties to home are also significant to the migrant experiences of rural Oaxacan Mixtecs.

Bibliography

Archival Sources

Archivo General de la Nación (AGN), Mexico City
  Bienes de Comunidad volume 6, dossier 30, 1786
  Criminal volume 457, dossiers 2 and 3, 1783
  Dirección General de Gobernación 2.34.66, box 6, 1922
  Dirección General de Gobernación 2.317.4 (9)-58, box 45, 1934
  Dirección General de Gobernación 2.012.8 (9)26474, box 102, 1937
  Dirección General de Gobernación 2.012.8 (9) 20278, box 101, 1938
  Dirección General de Gobernación 2.000 (9–48), box 8, 1940
  Dirección General de Gobernación 2.380 (9) 42, box 13, 1952
  Dirección General de Gobernación 2.380 (9) 59, box 14, 1953
  General de Parte, volume 4, dossier 328, 1591
  Indios volume 102, dossier 1, 1659
  Indios volume 30, dossier 393, 1690
  Indios volume 30, dossier 472, 1691
  Inquisición volume 439, dossier 14, 1656
  Inquisición volume 1223, dossier 13, 1787
  Padrones volume 18, pp. 209–306, 1791
  Propios y Arbitrios volume 10, #239, 1780
  Tierras volume 48, dossier 6, 1583
  Tierras volume 2164, dossier 86, #2, 1609
  Tierras volume 2955, dossier 123, #2, 1611
  Tierras volume 32, dossier 21, 1692

Tierras volume 472, dossier 2, 1726–28
Tierras volume 3668, dossier 3, 1755
Tributos volume 34, dossier 1, pp. 1–33, 1761

Archivo General de Las Indias (AGI), Seville, Spain
Indiferente volume 107, dossier 1, pp. 104f–114v, 1743

Archivo Histórico del Estado de Guerrero, Chilpancingo, Guerrero, Archivo
Histórico del Estado, Archivo Paucic (AGEG-AHE, AP)
Volume 86, Demografía Guerrero
Volume 99, Estadística Demografía
Volume 120, Caminos y Carrateras
Volume 607, Analisis de Comunidades Guerrero

Despatches from United States Consuls in Acapulco, 1823–1906 (DUSCA)

Instituto Nacional de Antropología e Historia, Biblioteca del Museo Nacional
de Antropología, Mexico City, Collection Manuel Martínez Gracida (INAH)
Microfilm number 7.2.38 (38)

Northwestern University Archives, Evanston, Ill., Herskovits Papers (NUA-HP)
1906–1963; series 35/6, box 32/folder 14

Schomburg Center for Research in Black Culture, New York City, Melville and
Frances Herskovits Papers (SCRBC-MFHP)
Personal Papers, box 1, folder 9
Personal Papers, box 54, folder 574
Personal Papers, box 67, folder 685

Tulane University, New Orleans, Latin American Library, Mexico Colonization
Papers, July 23, 1887–September 17, 1889

U.S. National Archives, Atlanta, Records of the Department of State Relating
to Internal Affairs of Mexico, 1910–29
Microfilm #274, RDS 812.00/2178

Secondary Sources

Abu-Lughod, Lila. 1986. *Veiled Sentiments: Honor and Poetry in a Bedouin Society.*
Berkeley: University of California Press.
Afroamerica: Journal of the International Institute of Afromamerican Studies vol. 1,
nos. 1–2; vol. 2, no. 3 (January 1945–January 1946). Mexico City: Fondo de Cultura Económica.
Aguirre Beltrán, Gonzalo. 1945. "Comercio de esclavos en México por 1542." *Afroamerica* 1, no. 1, 25–40.
———. 1946. "Problema, metodo y teoria en los estudios afroamericanos, según
Melville J. Herskovits." *Afroamerica* 2, no. 3, 187–96.

———. 1951. "Casamiento del monte." *Homenaje al Doctor Alfonso Caso*, 41–54. Mexico City: Imprenta Nuevo Mundo.

———. 1963. *Medicina y magia: El proceso de aculturación en la estructura colonial.* Mexico City: Instituto Nacional Indigenista.

———. 1970. "The Integration of the Negro into the National Society of Mexico." *Race and Class in Latin America*, ed. Magnus Mörner, 11–27. New York: Columbia University Press.

———. 1972 [1946]. *La población negra de México.* Mexico City: Fondo de Cultura Económica.

———. 1976. *Francisco Xavier Clavijero: Antología.* Mexico City: Secretaría de Educación Pública.

———. 1985 [1958]. *Cuijla: Esbozo etnográfico de un pueblo negro.* Mexico City: Secretaria de Educación Publica.

———. 1994. *El negro esclavo en Nueva España y otros ensayos.* Mexico City: Fondo de Cultura Económica.

Aizenman, N. C., and Timothy Dwyer. 2005. "In Herndon, Only Feet Away but Worlds Apart: The Minutemen, Foes of Illegal Immigration, Turn Cameras on Their Cause." *Washington Post*, 9 December.

Allen, Catherine. 1988. *The Hold Life Has: Coca and Cultural Identity in an Andean Community.* Washington: Smithsonian Institution Press.

Althoff, Daniel. 1994. "Afro-Mestizo Speech from Costa Chica, Guerrero: From Cuaji to Cuijla." *Language Problems and Language Planning* 18, no. 3, 242–56.

———. 1998. "The Afro-Hispanic Speech of the Municipio of Cuajinicuilapa, Guerrero." PhD dissertation, University of Florida.

Amaral Lugo, Adela. 2005. "Morenos, Negros, and Afromestizos: Debating Race and Identity on Mexico's Costa Chica." Bachelor's thesis, University of California, Los Angeles.

Amith, Jonathan. 2005. "Place Making and Place Breaking: Migration and the Development Cycle of Community in Colonial Mexico." *American Ethnologist* 32, no. 1, 159–79.

Anderson, Mark. 2007. "When Afro Becomes (Like) Indigenous: Garifuna and Afro-Indigenous Politics in Honduras." *Journal of Latin American and Caribbean Anthropology* 12, no. 2, 384–413.

Andrews, George Reid. 2004. *Afro-Latin America, 1800-2000.* New York: Oxford University Press.

Añorve Zapata, Eduardo. 1999. "Crónica municipal e historia en el municipio de Cuajinicuilapa." *El Sur*, 28 June.

Aparicio Prudente, Francisca, María Cristina Díaz Pérez, and Adela García Casarrubias. n.d. *Choco, chirundo y chando: Vocabulario afromestizo.* Chilpancingo: Dirección General de Culturas Populares, Unidad Regional Guerrero.

Appadurai, Arjun. 1992. "Putting Hierarchy in Its Place." *Rereading Cultural Anthropology*, ed. George E. Marcus, 34–47. Durham: Duke University Press.

————. 1996. *Modernity at Large: Cultural Dimensions of Globalization*. Minneapolis: University of Minnesota Press.

————. 1997. "Fieldwork in the Era of Globalization." *Anthropology and Humanism* 22, no. 1, 115–18.

Arce, Francisco O. 1870. *Memoria presentada ante la H. Legislatura del Estado de Guerrero, por el gobernador del mismo*. Ompetec: Estadistica del Distrito de Ometepec.

Así somos. 1994. Organo Quincenal de Información Cultural, Centro de Investigación y Cultura de la Zona de la Montaña, Año 3, 15 de Febrero, Número 58, Guerrero Indígena [broadsheet].

Associated Press. 2004. "North Carolina Preps for Latino Boom." 9 July.

————. 2006. "Houston Jury Convicts White Teen for Racial Attack on Hispanic Teen." 16 November.

Ayers, Barbara. 1974. "Bride Theft and Raiding for Wives in Cross-Cultural Perspective." *Anthropological Quarterly* 47, no. 3, 238–52.

Baker, Lee. 1998. *From Savage to Negro: Anthropology and the Construction of Race, 1896–1954*. Berkeley: University of California Press.

Banks, Taunya Lovell. 2006. "*Mestizaje* and the Mexican Self: *No Hay Sangre Negra*, So There Is No Blackness." *Southern California Interdisciplinary Law Journal* 15, 199–233.

Barnes, R. H. 1999. "Marriage by Capture." *Journal of the Royal Anthropological Institute* 5, no. 1, 57–73.

Barragán Mendoza, María del Carmen, and Roberto Cañedo Villarreal. 2004. "San Nicolás Tolentino: Calidad de vida y migración de un pueblo Afromestizo." *Migrantes indígenas y Afromestizos de Guerrero*, ed. Gabriela Barrosso, 212–43. Acapulco: Editorial Cultural Universitaria.

Bartra, Armando. 1994. "On Subsidies and Self-Management: Lessons from Provisioning Experiments on the Guerrero Coast." *Economic Restructuring and Rural Subsistence in Mexico: Maize and the Crisis of the 1980s*, ed. Cynthia Hewitt de Alcántara, 131–44. Geneva: United Nations Institute for Social Development.

Bashkow, Ira. 2006. *The Meaning of Whitemen: Race and Modernity in the Orokaiva Cultural World*. Chicago: University of Chicago Press.

Bateman, Rebecca B. 1990. "Africans and Indians: A Comparative Study of the Black Carib and the Black Seminole." *Ethnohistory* 37, no. 1, 1–24.

Behar, Ruth. 1987. "Sex and Sin, Witchcraft and the Devil in Late-Colonial Mexico." *American Ethnologist* 14, no. 1, 34–54.

Bennett, Herman Lee. 2003. *Africans in Colonial Mexico: Absolutism, Christianity, and Afro-Creole Consciousness, 1570–1640*. Bloomington: Indiana University Press.

Besserer, Federico. 2004. *Topografías transnacionales: Hacia una geografía de la vida transnacional*. Mexico City: Plaza y Valdes.

Blau, Harold. 1966. "Function and the False Faces: A Classification of Onondaga Masked Rituals and Themes." *Journal of American Folklore* 79, no. 314, 564–80.

Blu, Karen I. 1996. "'Where Do You Stay At?' Homeplace and Community among the Lumbee." *Senses of Place*, ed. Steven Feld and Keith H. Basso, 197–227. Santa Fe: School of American Research Press.

Bonfil Batalla, Guillermo. 1990. *México profundo*. Mexico City: Grijalbo.

Boruchoff, Judith. 1999. "Creating Continuity across Borders: Reconfiguring the Spaces of Community, State and Culture in Guerrero, Mexico and Chicago," PhD dissertation, University of Chicago, Department of Anthropology.

Bourdieu, Pierre, and Loïc Wacquant 1999. "On the Cunning of Imperialist Reason." *Theory, Culture, and Society* 16, no. 1, 41–58.

Bourgois, Philippe. 2003. *In Search of Respect: Selling Crack in El Barrio*. 2nd edn. Cambridge: Cambridge University Press.

Brooks, James. 2002. Introduction to *Confounding the Color Line: The Indian-Black Experience in North America*, ed. James Brooks, 1–18. Lincoln: University of Nebraska Press.

Brown, Karen McCarthy. 2001. *Mama Lola: A Vodou Priestess in Brooklyn*. Rev. and exp. edn. Berkeley: University of California Press.

Candelario, Ginetta. 2007. *Black behind the Ears: Dominican Racial Identity from Museums to Beauty Shops*. Durham: Duke University Press.

Carlsen, Laura. 2008. "NAFTA and Immigration: Toward a Workable and Humane Integration." Unpublished manuscript.

Carroll, Patrick. 1977. "Mandinga: The Evolution of a Mexican Runaway Slave Community, 1735–1827." *Comparative Studies in Society and History* 19, no. 4, 488–505.

Casey, Edward S. 1996. "How to Get from Space to Place in a Fairly Short Stretch of Time: Phenomenological Prolegomena." *Senses of Place*, ed. Steven Feld and Keith H. Basso, 13–52. Santa Fe: School of American Research Press.

Cervantes Delgado, Roberto. 1984. "La Costa Chica. Indios, negros y mestizos." *Estratificación étnica y relaciones interétnicas*, ed. Margarita Nolasco, 37–50. Mexico City: Instituto Nacional de Antropología e Historia.

Chavez, Leo. 1998. *Shadowed Lives: Undocumented Immigrants in American Society*. 2nd edn. Fort Worth: Harcourt Brace.

Chávez Carbajal, María Guadalupe. 1997. Introduction to *El rostro colectivo de la nación mexicana*, ed. Gerardo Sánchez Díaz, 11–14. Morelia, Michoacán: Instituto de Investigaciones Históricas de la Universidad Michoacana de San Nicolás de Hidalgo.

Chronicle of Higher Education. 2002. "Wake Forest University Medical School Adds Spanish-Language Requirement." 25 April.

Clifford, James. 1988. *The Predicament of Culture*. Cambridge: Harvard University Press.

———. 1994. "Diasporas." *Cultural Anthropology* 9, no. 3, 1–24.

Cohen, Jeffrey. 1994. "'Danza de la Pluma': Symbols of Submission and Separation in a Mexican Fiesta." *Anthropological Quarterly* 66, no. 3, 149–58.

———. 2001. "Transnational Migration in Rural Oaxaca, Mexico: Dependency, Development, and the Household." *American Anthropologist* 103, no. 4, 954–67.

———. 2004. *The Culture of Migration in Southern Mexico*. Austin: University of Texas Press.

Collier, George A., Pablo J. Farias Campero, John E. Perez, and Victor P. White. 2000. "Socio-economic Change and Emotional Illness among the Highland Maya of Chiapas, Mexico." *Ethos* 28, no. 1, 20–53.

Conway, Dennis, and Jeffrey H. Cohen. 1998. "Consequences of Return Migration and Remittances for Mexican Transnational Communities." *Economic Geography* 74, 1, 26–44.

Cunningham, Hilary. 2004. "Nations Rebound? Crossing Borders in a Gated Globe." *Identities: Global Studies in Culture and Power* 11, no. 3, 329–50.

Danforth, Loring. 1989. *Firewalking and Religious Healing: The Anastenaria of Greece and the American Firewalking Movement*. Princeton: Princeton University Press.

Daniel, G. Reginald. 2003. "Multiracial Identity in Global Perspective: The United States, Brazil, and South Africa." *New Faces in a Changing America: Multiracial Identity in the Twenty-first Century*, ed. Loretta I. Winters and Herman L. De-Bose. Thousand Oaks, Calif.: Sage.

———. 2006. *Race and Multiraciality in Brazil and the United States: Converging Paths?* University Park: Pennsylvania State University Press.

Daniel, G. Reginald, and Gary L. Haddow. 2010a. "All Mixed Up: A New Racial Commonsense in Global Perspective." *Color Struck: Essays on Race and Ethnicity in Global Perspective*, ed. Julius O. Adekunle and Hettie V. Williams, 311–48. Lanham, Md.: University Press of America.

———. 2010b. "Race, Class, and Power: The Politics of Multiraciality in Brazil." *Color Struck: Essays on Race and Ethnicity in Global Perspective*, ed. Julius O. Adekunle and Hettie V. Williams, 269–310. Lanham, Md.: University Press of America.

Danticat, Edwidge. 1999. *The Farming of Bones*. New York: Penguin.

Davidson, David M. 1979. "Negro Slave Control and Resistance in Colonial Mexico, 1519–1650." *Maroon Societies: Rebel Slave Communities in the Americas*, 2nd edn., ed. Richard Price, 82–103. Baltimore: Johns Hopkins University Press.

Dávila, Arlene M. 1997. *Sponsored Identities: Cultural Politics in Puerto Rico*. Philadelphia: Temple University Press.

Dawson, Alexander Scott. 1997. "México Indígena: Indigenismo and the Paradox of the Nation, 1915–1940." PhD dissertation, State University of New York, Stony Brook.

Dehouve, Daniele. 1994. *Entre el caimán y el jaguar: Los pueblos indios de Guerrero*. Mexico City: Centro de Investigaciones y Estudios Superiores en Antropología Social.

———. 1995. "L'apparition d'une mémoire afro-indienne dans le mexique colonial: Les tribulations d'un saint sur la route d'Acapulco." *Mémoirs en devenir: Amérique Latine, XVI–XX siècles*. 113–35. Bordeaux: Maison des Pays Ibériques.

De Ita, Ana. 2008. "Fourteen Years of NAFTA and the Tortilla Crisis." American Red Cross, http://www.cipamericas.org (accessed 6 September 2009).

De la Cadena, Marisol. 1991. "'Las mujeres son más indias': Etnicidad y género en una comunidad de Cusco." *Revista Andina* 9, no. 1, 7–47.

———. 2000. *Indigenous Mestizos: The Politics of Race and Culture in Cuzco, 1919–1991*. Durham: Duke University Press.

De la Torre, Carlos. 2005. "Afro-Ecuadorian Responses to Racism: Between Citizenship and Corporatism." *Neither Enemies nor Friends: Latinos, Blacks, Afro-Latinos*, ed. Anani Dzidzienyo and Suzanne Oboler, 61–74. New York: Palgrave.

Del Val, José. 1994. Introduction to *Tierra negra: Fotografías de la Costa Chica en Guerrero y Oaxaca, México*, by Maya Goded. Mexico City: Consejo Nacional para la Cultura y las Artes.

Derby, Lauren. 1994. "Haitians, Magic, and Money: *Raza* and Society in the Haitian-Dominican Borderlands, 1900 to 1937." *Comparative Studies in Society and History* 36, no. 3, 488–526.

———. 2009. *The Dictator's Seduction: Politics and the Popular Imagination in the Era of Trujillo*. Durham: Duke University Press.

DeWalt, Kathleen Musante. 1977. "The Illnesses No Longer Understood: Changing Concepts of Health and Curing in a Rural Mexican Community." *Medical Anthropology Newsletter* 8, no. 2, 5–11.

Díaz Pérez, María Cristina. 1993. Introduction to *Jamás fandango al cielo: Narrativa afromestiza*, ed. María Cristina Díaz Pérez, Francisca Aparicio Prudente, and Adela García Casarrubias, 19–26. Mexico City: Dirección General de Culturas Populares.

———. 1995. "Descripción etnográfica de las relaciones de parentesco en tres comunidades afromestizas de la Costa Chica de Guerrero." Bachelor's thesis, Escuela Nacional de Antropología e Historia.

———. 1998. Introduction to *Soy el Negro de la Costa*, exhibit, Cuajinicuilapa, Guerrero.

———. 2003. *Queridato, matrifocalidad y crianza entre los afromestizos de la Costa Chica*. Mexico City: Consejo Nacional para la Cultura y las Artes.

Díaz Pérez, María Cristina, and Juan Carlos Catalán. 1991. "Negros de Guerrero." *Nuestra Palabra* 11, no. 11.

Díaz Pérez, María Cristina, Francisca Aparicio Prudente, and Adela García Casarrubias. 1993. *Jamás fandango al cielo: Narrativa afromestiza*. Mexico City: Dirección General de Culturas Populares.

Diskin, Martin. 1991. "Ethnic Discourse and the Challenge to Anthropology: The Nicaraguan Case." *Nation-States and Indians in Latin America*, ed. Greg Urban and Joel Sherzer, 156–80. Austin: University of Texas Press.

Dolnick, Sam. 2009. "For African Immigrants, Bronx Culture Clash Turns Violent." *New York Times*, 20 October.

Dunn, Marvin, and Alex Stepick III. 1992. "Blacks in Miami." *Miami Now! Immigration, Ethnicity, and Social Change*, ed. Guillermo J. Grenier and Alex Stepick III, 41–56. Gainesville: University Press of Florida.

Dzidzienyo, Anani. 2003. "Coming to Terms with the African Connection in Latino Studies." *Latino Studies* 1, no. 1, 160–67.

Dzidzienyo, Anani, and Suzanne Oboler, eds. 2005. *Neither Enemies nor Friends: Latinos, Blacks, Afro-Latinos*. New York: Palgrave Macmillan.

Estrada Castañón, Alba Teresa. 1994. *Guerrero: Sociedad, economía, política, cultura*. Mexico City: UNAM, Centro de Investigaciones Interdisciplinarias en Humanidades.

Fears, Darryl. 2002. "People of Color Who Never Felt They Were Black: Racial Label Surprises Many Latin Immigrants." *Washington Post*, 26 December.

Feinberg, Benjamin. 2003. *The Devil's Book of Culture: History, Mushrooms, and Caves in Southern Mexico*. Austin: University of Texas Press.

Feld, Steven, and Keith H. Basso. 1996. Introduction to *Senses of Place*, ed. Steven Feld and Keith H. Basso, 3–11. Santa Fe: School of American Research Press.

Flanet, Veronique. 1977. *Viviré si Dios quiere: Un estudio de la violencia en la mixteca de la costa*. Mexico City: Instituto Nacional Indigenista.

Fletcher, Peri L. 1999. *La Casa de Mis Sueños: Dreams of Home in a Mexican Migrant Community*. Boulder, Colo.: Westview.

Fortún, Julia Elena. 1961. *La danza de los diablos*. La Paz: Ministerio de Educación y Bellas Artes, Oficialía Mayor de Cultura Nacional.

Foster, George M. 1944. "Nagualism in Mexico and Guatemala." *Acta Americana*, no. 2, 85–103.

Freyre, Gilberto. 1986. *The Mansions and the Shanties: The Making of Modern Brazil*. Berkeley: University of California Press.

Friedlander, Judith. 1975. *Being Indian in Hueyapan*. New York: St. Martin's.

Friedman, Jonathan. 2002. "Globalization and Localization." *The Anthropology of Globalization: A Reader*, ed. Jonathan Xavier Inda and Renato Rosaldo, 233–46. Malden, Mass.: Blackwell.

Fuentes de Maria J., Roberto. 1951. *Parasitos intestinales en el municipio de Cuajinicuilapa*. Mexico City: UNAM, Facultad Nacional de Medicina.

Garber, Marjorie. 1992. *Vested Interests: Cross-Dressing and Cultural Anxiety*. New York: Routledge.

Gerhard, Peter. 1973. *A Guide to the Historical Geography of New Spain*. Cambridge: Cambridge University Press.

————. 1993. *A Guide to the Historical Geography of New Spain*. 2nd rev. edn. Oklahoma: University of Oklahoma Press.

Githiora, Chege. 1994. "Afromexican Names: A Trail of History and Kinship." *Conexões* 6, no. 2, 4–5.

Glick Schiller, Nina, and Georges Eugene Fouron. 2001. *Georges Woke Up Laughing: Long-Distance Nationalism and the Search for Home*. Durham: Duke University Press.

Gobierno del Estado de Guerrero. 1933. *Periódico Oficial*, 17 January.

Goded, Maya. 1994. *Tierra negra: Fotografías de la Costa Chica en Guerrero y Oaxaca, México*. Mexico City: Consejo Nacional para la Cultura y las Artes.

Godoy, Emilio. 2009. "Mexico: Black Minority Invisible in Bicentennial Celebrations." Global Geopolitics Net Sites/IPS, 2 October, http://globalgeopolitics.net.

Godreau, Isar. 2002a. "Changing Space, Making Race: Distance, Nostalgia, and the Folklorization of Blackness in Puerto Rico." *Identities: Global Studies in Culture and Power* 9, no. 3, 281–304.

————. 2002b. "Peinando diferencias, bregas de pertenencia: El alisado y el llamado 'pelo malo.'" *Caribbean Studies* 30, no. 1, 82–134.

Goldring, Luin. 2002. "The Mexican State and Transmigrant Organizations: Negotiating the Boundaries of Membership and Participation." *Latin American Research Review* 37, no. 3, 55–99.

Goldstein, Donna. 2003. *Laughter Out of Place: Race, Class, Violence, and Sexuality in a Rio Shantytown*. Berkeley: University of California Press.

González, Anita. 2009. "Indigenous Acts: Black and Native Performances in Mexico." *Radical History Review*, no. 103, 131–41.

Gonzalez, Nancie. 1988. *Sojourners of the Caribbean: Ethnogenesis and Ethnohistory of the Garifuna*. Urbana: University of Illinois Press.

Gordon, Edmund T., and Mark Anderson. 1999. "The African Diaspora: Toward an Ethnography of Diasporic Identification." *Journal of American Folklore* 112, no. 445, 282–96.

Gould, Jeffrey. 1993. "Vana Ilusión! The Highlands Indians and the Myth of Nicaragua Mestiza, 1880–1925." *Hispanic American Historical Review* 73, no. 3, 393–429.

Graeber, David. 2001. *Toward an Anthropological Theory of Value: The False Coin of Our Own Dreams*. New York: Palgrave.

Gregory, Steven. 2006. *The Devil behind the Mirror: Globalization and Politics in the Dominican Republic*. Berkeley: University of California Press.

Grimes, Kimberly M. 1998. *Crossing Borders: Changing Social Identities in Southern Mexico*. Tucson: University of Arizona Press.

Grossberger-Morales, Lucia. 1995. "Sangre Boliviana." *Leonardo* 28, no. 4, 246–47.

Gruzinski, Serge. 1990. "Indian Confraternities, Brotherhoods, and Mayordomías in Central New Spain: A List of Questions for the Historian and the Anthropologist." *The Indian Community of Colonial Mexico: Fifteen Essays on Land*

Tenure Corporate Organizations, Land Tenure, and Village Politics, ed. Arij Ouweenel and Simon Miller, 205–23. Amsterdam: CEDLA.

Guardino, Peter. 1996. *Peasants, Politics, and the Formation of Mexico's National State: Guerrero, 1800–1857.* Stanford: Stanford University Press.

Guerrero, José. n.d. *La chilena: Estudio geomusical.* Mexico City: Fondo Nacional para el Desarrollo de la Danza Popular Mexicana.

Gupta, Akhil, and James Ferguson. 1997. "Beyond 'Culture': Space, Identity, and the Politics of Difference." *Culture, Power, Place: Explorations in Critical Anthropology,* ed. Akhil Gupta and James Ferguson, 33–51. Durham: Duke University Press.

Gutiérrez Avila, Miguel Angel. 1987. "Negros e indígenas: Otra historia que contar." *México Indígena* 16, no. 3, 53–56.

———. 1988. *Corrido y violencia entre los afromestizos de la Costa Chica de Guerrero y Oaxaca.* Chilpancingo: Universidad Autónoma de Guerrero.

———. 1993. *La conjura de los negros: Cuentas de la tradición Afromestiza de la Costa Chica de Guerrero y Oaxaca.* Chilpancingo: Universidad Autónoma de Guerrero.

———. 1997a. *Derecho consuetudinario y derecho positivo entre los mixtecos, amuzgos, y afromestizos de la Costa Chica de Guerrero.* Mexico City: Comisión Nacional de Derechos Humanos.

———. 1997b. Letter. *Amate: Arte, Cultura y Sociedad de Guerrero,* no. 6, 47.

Gutiérrez, Maribel. 2004. "Masacre en Aguas Blancas: Misión cumplida." *El Sur,* 28 June.

Guttman, Matthew. 1996. *The Meanings of Macho: Being a Man in Mexico City.* Berkeley: University of California Press.

Habana de los Santos, Misael. 2003. "Finalmente aprobó materia estudiante reprobado 'por ser negro' en la UAG." *La Jornada,* 23 September.

Hale, Charles. 1994. *Resistance and Contradiction: Miskitu Indians and the Nicaraguan State, 1894–1987.* Stanford: Stanford University Press.

———. 1997. "The Cultural Politics of Identity in Latin America." *Annual Review of Anthropology,* no. 26, 567–90.

———. 2006. *Más Que un Indio = More Than an Indian: Racial Ambivalence and Neoliberal Multiculturalism in Guatemala.* Santa Fe: School of American Research Press.

Hamilton, Ruth Simms, and Javier Téllez. 1992. "African-Descent Populations in Mexico: Survival through Resistance and Maroonage." *Conexões* 4, no. 1, 6–8.

Harris, Max. 1997. "The Return of Moctezuma: Oaxaca's 'Danza de la Pluma' and New Mexico's 'Danza de los Matachines.'" *Drama Review* 41, no. 1, 106–34.

Harrison, Faye V. 2006. "Building on a Re-historicized Anthropology of the Afro-Atlantic." *Afro-Atlantic Dialogues: Anthropology in the Diaspora,* ed. Kevin Yelvington, 381–98. Santa Fe: School of American Research Press.

Harvey, Penelope. 1996. *Hybrids of Modernity: Anthropology, the Nation-State, and the Universal Exhibition*. New York: Routledge.

Hellman, Judith Adler. 2008. *The World of Mexican Migrants: The Rock and the Hard Place*. New York: The New Press.

Hendrickson, Carol. 1991. "Images of the Indian in Guatemala: The Role of Indigenous Dress in Indian and Ladino Constructions." *Nation-States and Indians in Latin America*, ed. Greg Urban and Joel Sherzer, 286–306. Austin: University of Texas Press.

Herdt, Gilbert. 1996. "Introduction: Third Sexes and Third Genders." *Third Sex, Third Gender: Beyond Sexual Dimorphism in Culture and History*, ed. Gilbert Herdt, 21–81. New York: Zone.

Hernández, Tanya Katerí. 2003. "'Too Black to Be Latino/a': Blackness and Blacks as Foreigners in Latino Studies." *Latino Studies* 1, no. 1, 152–59.

Hernández Cuevas, Marco Polo. 2003. "Memín Pinguín: Uno de los cómicos mexicanos más populares como instrumento para codificar al negro." *Afro-Hispanic Review*, spring, 52–59.

———. 2004. *African Mexicans and the Discourse on the Modern Nation*. Dallas: University Press of America.

Hernández Moreno, Taurino. 1996. "Una historia de poder regional." *Amate: Arte, Cultura y Sociedad de Guerrero*, no. 5, 20–24.

Herrera Casasús, Maria Luisa. 1994. "Raíces africanas en la población de Tamaulipas." *Presencia africana en México*, ed. Luz María Martínez Montiel, 463–524. Mexico City: Consejo Nacional para la Cultura y las Artes.

Herskovits, Melville J. 1945. "Problem, Method, and Theory in Afroamerican Studies." *Afroamerica* 1, no. 1, 5–24.

———. 1990 [1941]. *The Myth of the Negro Past*. Boston: Beacon.

Hill, Jane. 1991. "In Neca Gobierno de Puebla: Mexicano Penetrations of the Mexican State." *Nation-States and Indians in Latin America*, ed. Greg Urban and Joel Sherzer, 72–94. Austin: University of Texas Press.

Hoffmann, Odile. 2006a. "Negros y afromestizos en México; Viejas y nuevas lecturas de un mundo olvidado." *Revista Mexicana de Sociología* 68, no. 1, 103–35.

———. 2006b. Review of *Afroméxico. El pulso de la población in México: Una historia recordada, olvidada y vuelta a recorda*, by Ben Vinson III and Bobby Vaughn. *Desacatos*, no. 20, January–April, 175–78.

———. 2007. "Las narrativas de la diferencia étnico-racial en la Cosa Chica, México: Una perspectiva geográfica." *Los retos de la diferencia: Los actores de la multiculturalidad entre México y Colombia*, ed. Odile Hoffmann and María Teresa Rodríguez, 363–97. Mexico City: La Casa Chata.

Hoffmann, Odile, and María Teresa Rodríguez. 2007. Introduction to *Los retos de la diferencia: Los actores de la multiculturalidad entre México y Colombia*, ed. Odile Hoffmann and María Teresa Rodríguez, 13–54. Mexico City: La Casa Chata.

Holland, William R. 1961. "El tonalismo y el nagualismo entre los Tzotziles: Estudios de cultura maya." *Estudios de cultura maya* 3, 167–81. Mexico City: Centro de Estudios Mayas, UNAM.

Hooker, Juliet. 2005. "Indigenous Inclusion/Black Exclusion: Race, Ethnicity, and Multicultural Citizenship in Latin America." *Journal of Latin American Studies* 37, no. 2, 285–310.

Inda, Jonathan Xavier, and Renato Rosaldo. 2002. "Introduction: A World in Motion." *The Anthropology of Globalization: A Reader*, ed. Jonathan Xavier Inda and Renato Rosaldo, 1–34. Malden, Mass.: Blackwell.

Jackson, Jean. 1991. "Being and Becoming an Indian in the Vaupés." *Nation-States and Indians in Latin America*, ed. Greg Urban and Joel Sherzer, 131–55. Austin: University of Texas Press.

———. 1995. "Culture: Genuine and Spurious; The Politics of Indianness in the Vaupés, Colombia." *American Ethnologist* 22, no. 1, 3–27.

Jackson, Walter. 1986. "Melville Herskovits and the Search for Afro-American Culture." *Malinowski, Rivers, Benedict, and Others: Essays on Culture and Personality*, ed. George W. Stocking Jr., 95–126. Madison: University of Wisconsin Press.

Jacobs, Ian. 1982. *Ranchero Revolt: The Mexican Revolution in Guerrero*. Austin: University of Texas Press.

Jemott Nelson, Father Glynn. 2008. "The Road to Blackness: A Search for Identity within the Afro-Mexican Community." Paper presented at "The African Presence in Mexico," Texas A&M University, 22 October.

Jile, Pepe. 1997. *Historia de la fundación de las secundarias de Guerrero: 1932-1992*. Mexico City: Anaya.

Julien, Catherine. 2007. "Kandire in Real Time and Space: Sixteenth-Century Expeditions from the Pantanal to the Andes." *Ethnohistory* 54, no. 2, 245–72.

Kaplan, Lucille N. 1956. "Tonal and Nagual in Coastal Oaxaca, Mexico." *Journal of American Folklore* 69, no. 274, 363–68.

Katz, William Loren. 1997. *Black Indians: A Hidden Heritage*. New York: Simon and Schuster.

Katzew, Ilona. 2004. *Casta Painting: Images of Race in Eighteenth-Century Mexico*. New Haven: Yale University Press.

Knight, Alan. 1990. "Racism, Revolution, and Indigenismo: Mexico, 1910–1940." *The Idea of Race in Latin America, 1870-1940*, ed. Richard Graham, 71–113. Austin: University of Texas Press.

Koegel, John. 1999. "New Sources of Music from Spain and Colonial Mexico at the Sutro Library." *Notes*, 2nd ser., 55, no. 3, 583–613.

Lacey, Marc. 2009. "Money Trickles North as Mexicans Help Relatives." *New York Times*, 15 November.

LaFaye, Jacques. 1976. *Quetzalcoatl and Guadalupe: The Formation of Mexican National Consciousness*. Chicago: University of Chicago Press.

———. 1990. "La sociedad de castas en Nueva España." *Artes de México*, no. 8, 25–34.

La Jornada. 2001. "Versión en español del estudio de Marcus y Flannery." 31 July.

La Jornada El Sur. 2001. "Identidad afromexicana en Costa Chica." 20 June.

La Jornada Guerrero. 2007. "Negros de México piden reconocimiento." 25 July.

Lane, Kris. 2002. *Quito 1599: City and Colony in Transition*. Albuquerque: University of New Mexico Press.

Lara, Gloria. 2007. "El recurso de la diferencia étnico-racial en las lógicas de inclusión política: El caso Pinotepa Nacional, Oaxaca." *Los retos de la diferencia: Los actores de la multiculturalidad entre México y Colombia*, ed. Odile Hoffmann and María Teresa Rodríguez, 81–110. Mexico City: La Casa Chata.

Leland, Andrea E., and Kathy L. Berger. 1998. *The Garifuna Journey*. Hohokus, N.J.: New Day Films.

Levitt, Peggy, and Nina Glick Schiller. 2004. "Conceptualizing Simultaneity: A Transnational Social Field Perspective on Society." *International Migration Review*, no. 3, 1002–39.

Lewis, Laura A. 2000. "Blacks, Black Indians, Afromexicans: The Dynamics of Race, Nation, and Identity in a Mexican Moreno Community (Guerrero)." *American Ethnologist* 27, no. 4, 898–926.

———. 2001. "Of Ships and Saints: History, Memory, and Place in the Making of Moreno Mexican Identity." *Cultural Anthropology* 16, no. 1, 62–82.

———. 2003. *Hall of Mirrors: Power, Witchcraft, and Caste in Colonial Mexico*. Durham: Duke University Press.

———. 2004. "Modesty and Modernity: Photography, Race, and Representation on Mexico's Costa Chica (Guerrero)." *Identities: Global Studies in Culture and Power* 11, no. 4, 471–99.

———. 2006. "Home Is Where the Heart Is: North Carolina, Afro-Latino Migration, and Houses on Mexico's Costa Chica." *South Atlantic Quarterly* 105, no. 4, 801–29.

———. 2009. "'Afro' Mexico in Black, White, and Indian: An Anthropologist Reflects on Fieldwork." *Black Mexico: Race and Society from Colonial to Modern Times*, ed. Ben Vinson III and Matthew Restall, 183–208. Albuquerque: University of New Mexico Press.

Lloréns, Hilda, and Rosa E. Carrasquillo. 2008. "Sculpting Blackness: Representations of Black–Puerto Ricans in Public Art." *Visual Anthropology Review* 24, no. 2, 103–16.

Lomnitz-Adler, Claudio. 1993. *Exits from the Labyrinth: Culture and Ideology in the Mexican National Space*. Berkeley: University of California Press.

López Victoria, José Manuel. 1985. *Historia de la revolución en Guerrero*, vol. 1, *1901–1912*. Chilpancingo: Gobierno del Estado, IGC.

Love, Edgar F. 1971. "Marriage Patterns of Persons of African Descent in a Colonial Mexico City Parish." *Hispanic American Historical Review* 51, no. 1, 79–91.

Low, Setha M. 1994. "Embodied Metaphors: Nerves as Lived Experience." *Embodiment and Experience: The Existential Ground of Culture and Self*, ed. Thomas J. Csordas, 139–62. Cambridge: Cambridge University Press.

Mahler, Sarah. 1995. *American Dreaming: Immigrant Life on the Margins*. Princeton: Princeton University Press.

Malkin, Elisabeth. 2008. "San Isidro Tilantongo Journal: Ways of Ancient Mexico Reviving Barren Lands." *New York Times*, 13 May.

Malkki, Liisa. 1992. "National Geographic: The Rooting of Peoples and the Territorialization of National Identity among Scholars and Refugees." *Cultural Anthropology* 7, no. 1, 24–44.

Mallon, Florencia. 1992. "Indian Communities, Political Cultures, and the State in Latin America, 1780–1990." *Journal of Latin American Studies*, no. 24, supplement, 35–53.

Manzano Añorve, Maria de los Angeles. 1991. *Cuajinicuilapa, Guerrero: Historia Oral (1900–1940)*. Mexico City: Artesa.

Marcus, Joyce, and Kent Flannery. 2001. *La civilización zapoteca*. Mexico City: Fondo de Cultura Económica.

Martínez Maranto, Alfredo. 1991. "Coyolillo: Presencia de Nuestra Tercera Raiz." *Nuestra Palabra* 2, no. 11, 7.

Martínez Montiel, Luz María. 1991. "Nuestra Tercera Raíz." *Nuestra Palabra* 2, no. 11, 2.

———, ed. 1994. *Presencia africana en México*. Mexico City: Consejo Nacional para la Cultura y las Artes.

———. 1997. "La Costa Chica y la Tercera Raíz." *Pacífico Sur: ¿Una region cultural?*, ed. Javier V. de León Orozco, 9–13. Mexico City: Consejo Nacional para la Cultura y las Artes.

Martínez Rescalvo, Mario, and Jorge R. Obregón Téllez. 1991. *La montaña de Guerrero: Economia, historia y sociedad*. Mexico City: Instituto Nacional Indigenísta, Universidad Autónoma de Guerrero.

Matory, J. Lorand. 2006. "The 'New World' Surrounds an Ocean: Theorizing the Live Dialogue between African and African American Cultures." *Afro-Atlantic Dialogues: Anthropology in the Diaspora*, ed. Kevin Yelvington, 151–92. Santa Fe: School of American Research Press.

McClain, Paul D., Niambi V. Carter, Victoria M. DeFrancesco Soto, Monique L. Lyle, Jeffrey D. Grynaviski, Shayla C. Nunnally, Thomas J. Scotto, J. Alan Kendrick, Gerald F. Lackey, Kendra Davenport Cotton. 2006. "Racial Distancing in a Southern City: Latino Immigrants' Views of Black Americans." *Journal of Politics* 68, no. 3, 571–85.

McDowell, John H. 2000. *Poetry and Violence: The Ballad Tradition of Mexico's Costa Chica*. Urbana: University of Illinois Press.

———. 2008. "'Soy el Negro de la Costa': Visions of Blackness on Mexico's Costa

Chica." Paper presented at "Blackness in Latin America and the Caribbean," Indiana University, Bloomington, April.

"Mexican Masks: An Exhibition of Mexican Folk Carvings from the Collection of Mr. and Mrs. Donald Cordry of Cuernavaca, Morelos, Mexico." 1974. *American Indian Quarterly* 1, no. 2, 154–74.

Meza Herrera, Malinali. 1993. Presentación. *Jamás fandango al cielo: Narrativa afromestiza*, ed. María Cristina Díaz Pérez, Francisca Aparicio Prudente, and Adela García Casarrubias, 9–11. Mexico City: Dirección General de Culturas Populares.

Miles, Tiya. 2005. *Ties That Bind: The Story of an Afro-Cherokee Family in Slavery and Freedom*. Berkeley: University of California Press.

Miles, Tiya, and Sharon P. Holland, eds. 2006. *Crossing Waters, Crossing Worlds: The African Diaspora in Indian Country*. Durham: Duke University Press.

Mintz, Sidney. 1990. Introduction to *The Myth of the Negro Past*, by Melville J. Herskovits, ix–xxi. Boston: Beacon.

Moedano Navarro, Gabriel. 1980. "Estudio de las tradiciones orales y musicales de los afromestizos de Mexico." *Antropología e Historia*, no. 31, 19–29.

———. 1986. "Notas etnográficas sobre la población negra de la Costa Chica." *Primer coloquio de arqueología y etnohistoria del estado de Guerrero*, 551–60. Mexico City: Instituto Nacional de Antropologia e Historia, Gobierno del Estado de Guerrero.

———. 1997. "Los Afromestizos y su contribución a la identidad cultural del Pacífico Sur: El caso de la tradición oral en la Costa Chica." *Pacífico Sur: ¿Una region cultural?*, ed. Javier V. de León Orozco, 1–7. Mexico City: Consejo Nacional para la Cultura y las Artes.

Moore, Robin D. 1997. *Nationalizing Blackness: Afrocubanismo and Artistic Revolution in Havana, 1920–1940*. Pittsburgh: University of Pittsburgh Press.

Motta Sánchez, J. Arturo. 2006. "Tras la heteroidentificación: El 'movimiento negro' costachiquense y la selección de marbetes étnicos." *Dimensión Antropológica* 13, no. 38, 115–50.

Munn, Nancy. 1996. "Excluded Spaces: The Figure in the Australian Aboriginal Landscape." *Critical Inquiry* 22, no. 3, 446–65.

Muratorio, Blanco. 1993. "Nationalism and Ethnicity: Images of Ecuadorian Indians and the Imagemakers at the Turn of the Century." *Ethnicity and the State*, ed. Judith D. Toland, 21–54. New Brunswick, N.J.: Transaction.

Murphy, Arthur D., Colleen Blanchard, and Jennifer A. Hill, eds. 2001. *Latino Workers in the Contemporary South*. Athens: University of Georgia Press.

Nanda, Serena. 1999. *Neither Man nor Woman: The Hijras of India*. Belmont, Calif.: Wadsworth.

———. 2000. *Gender Diversity: Cross-Cultural Variations*. Prospect Heights, Ill.: Waveland.

Nash, June. 1993. *We Eat the Mines and the Mines Eat Us: Dependency and Exploitation in Bolivian Tin Mines*. Rev. edn. New York: Columbia University Press.

National Public Radio. 2007. "Color Line Divides the Latino Community." 7 August, http://www.npr.org.

Navarro, Mireya. 2003. "Going beyond Black and White, Hispanics in Census Pick 'Other.'" *New York Times*, 9 November.

———. 2006. "For Hispanics, Familiar Faces Might Not Be Friendly Bosses." *New York Times*, 22 October.

Noticias del Sur Guerrero-Oaxaca. 1997. "Paquete de obras y servicios para San Nicolás, Guerrero." 30 December.

Nutini, Hugo. 1965. "Polygyny in a Tlaxcalan Community." *Ethnology* 4, no. 2, 123–47.

———. 1967. "A Synoptic Comparison of Mesoamerican Marriage and Family Structure." *Southwestern Journal of Anthropology* 23, no. 4, 383–404.

Ochoa Campos, Moisés. 1987. *La chilena guerrerense*. Chilpancingo: Instituto Guerrerense de la Cultura.

O'Nell, Carl W. 1986. "Primary and Secondary Effects of Violence Control among the Nonviolent Zapotec." *Anthropological Quarterly* 59, no. 4, 184–204.

Ortíz de Montellano, Bernard. 1987. "Caida de Mollera: Aztec Sources for a Mesoamerican Disease of Alleged Spanish Origin." *Ethnohistory* 34, no. 4, 381–89.

Pagden, Anthony. 1987. "Identity Formation in Spanish America." *Colonial Identity in the Atlantic World, 1500-1800*, ed. Nicholas Canny and Anthony Pagden, 51–93. Princeton: Princeton University Press.

Palmer, Colin. 1976. *Slaves of the White God: Blacks in Mexico, 1519-1650*. Cambridge: Harvard University Press.

Parsons, Elsie Clews. 1936. *Mitla Town of the Souls*. Chicago: University of Chicago Press.

Passel, Jeffrey, and D'Vera Cohn. 2009. "Recession Slows—But Does Not Reverse—Mexican Immigration." Paper presented at Pew Hispanic Center, 22 July, http://pewresearch.org.

Patterson, Wendy. 2000. "Prisoner of Conscience." *Amicus Journal* 22, no. 2, 25.

Patterson, Tiffany Ruby, and Robin D. G. Kelley. 2000. "Unfinished Migrations: Reflections on the African Diaspora and the Making of the Modern World." *African Studies Review* 43, no. 1, 11–45.

Pauli, Julia. 2008. "A House of One's Own: Gender, Migration, and Residence in Rural Mexico." *American Ethnologist* 35, no. 1, 171–87.

Peacock, James L. 2007. *Grounded Globalism: How the U.S. South Embraces the World*. Athens: University of Georgia Press.

Perlez, Jane. 2004. "Where Pagodas Draw Tourists, Concrete Is Unwelcome." *New York Times*, 8 July.

Petre Velásquez, Edwin Ricardo. 2003. "Güiro." *Continuum Encyclopedia of Popu-*

lar *Music of the World: Performance and Production*, ed. John Shepherd, 372–74. New York: Continuum.

Phelan, John Leddy. 1960. "Neo-Aztecism and the Genesis of Mexican Nationalism." *Culture and History: Essays in Honor of Paul Radin*, ed. Stanley Diamond, 760–70. New York: Columbia University Press.

Pineda, Baron. 2006. *Shipwrecked Identities: Navigating Race on the Mosquito Coast*. New Brunswick, N.J.: Rutgers University Press.

Prescod, Paula, and Adrian Fraser. 2008. "A Demolinguistic Profile of St. Vincent and the Grenadines; or, A Successful Attempt at Linguistic Disenfranchisement." *Anthropos*, no. 103, 99–112.

Price, Richard, and Sally Price. 2003. *The Root of Roots; or, How Afro-American Anthropology Got Its Start*. Chicago: Prickly Paradigm Press.

Price, Sally. 2006. "Seaming Connections: Artworlds of the African Diaspora." *Afro-Atlantic Dialogues: Anthropology in the Diaspora*, ed. Kevin Yelvington, 83–114. Santa Fe: School of American Research Press.

Prince, Sabiyha Robin. 2006. "Manhattan Africans: Contradiction, Continuity, and Authenticity in a Colonial Heritage." *Afro-Atlantic Dialogues: Anthropology in the Diaspora*, ed. Kevin Yelvington, 291–326. Santa Fe: School of American Research Press.

Quijano, Aníbal. 2000. "Coloniality of Power, Eurocentrism, and Latin America." *Nepantla: Views from the South* 1, no. 3, 533–80.

Quintana, Claudia. n.d. "De manera póstuma, Gutiérre Tibón recibió la medalla Ignacio Manuel Altamirano." CONACULTA website, http://www.cnca.gob.mx (accessed 20 November 2007).

Quiroz Malca, Haydée. 2004. "La migración de los afromexicanos y algunos de sus efectos culturales locales: Una moneda de dos caras." *Migrantes indígenas y afromestizos de Guerrero*, ed. C. G. Barroso, 244–70. Acapulco: Editorial Cultural Universitaria.

Rahier, Jean Muteba. 1999. Introduction to *Representations of Blackness and the Performance of Identities*, ed. Jean Muteba Rahier, xiii–xxvi. Westport, Conn.: Bergin and Garvey.

———. 2008. "Soccer and the (Tri-)Color of the Ecuadorian Nation: Visual and Ideological (Dis)continuities of Black Otherness from Monocultural *Mestizaje* to Multiculturalism." *Visual Anthropology Review* 24, no. 2, 148–82.

Ravelo Lecuana, Renato. 1990. *La revolución zapatista en Guerrero*. Chilpancingo: Universidad Autónoma de Guerrero.

Rebollar Corona, Rafael. 2002. *De Florida a Coahuila*. Mexico City: Producciones Trabuco.

Robichaux, David L. 1997. "Residence Rules and Ultimogeniture in Tlaxcala and Mesoamerica." *Ethnology* 36, no. 2, 149–71.

Rodríguez, Héctor Manuel. 2008. "Sufren afromestizos en Guerrero de pobreza y exclusión, concluye estudio de la UNAM y Conapred." *El Sur de Acapulco*, 18 July.

Rollin, Nicholas, ed. 1998. *The Concise Oxford Spanish Dictionary*. Oxford: Oxford University Press.

Rouse, Roger. 1991. "Mexican Migration and the Social Space of Transnationalism." *Diaspora* 1, no. 1, 8–23.

Rowe, William, and Vivian Schelling. 1991. *Memory and Modernity: Popular Culture in Latin America*. New York: Verso.

Royce, Anya Peterson. 1993. "Ethnicity and the Role of the Intellectual." *Ethnicity and the State*, ed. Judith D. Toland, 103–22. New Brunswick, N.J.: Transaction.

Rubel, Arthur J. 1964. "The Epidemiology of a Folk Illness: Susto in Hispanic America." *Ethnology* 3, no. 3, 268–83.

Ruiz Rodríguez, Carlos. 2001. "Sones de artesa de San Nicolás Tolentino, Guerrero." Bachelor's thesis, Universidad Nacional Autónoma de México.

———. 2004. *Versos, música y baile de artesa de la Costa Chica: San Nicolás, Guerrero y Ciruelo, Oaxaca*. Mexico City: El Colegio de México, Centro de Estudios Linguísticos y Literarios; Consejo Nacional para la Cultura y las Artes.

Saler, Benson. 1964. "Nagual, Witch, and Sorcerer in a Quiche Village." *Ethnology* 3, no. 3, 305–28.

Sánchez Andraka, Juan. 1983. *Zitlala: Por el mágico mundo indígena guerrerense*. Vol. 1. Chilpancingo: Fondo de Apoyo Editorial del Gobierno del Estado de Guerrero.

———. 1987. *¡Hablemos Claro! ¿Que occurió en Guerrero durante el gobierno de Alejandro Cervantes Delgado? Testimonios*. Mexico City: Costa-Amic.

Sánchez Díaz, Gerardo, ed. 1997. *El rostro colectivo de la nación mexicana*. Morelia: Instituto de Investigaciones Históricas de la Universidad Michoacana de San Nicolás de Hidalgo.

Sandoval, Carlos, and Catherine Tambini. 2004. *Farmingville*. New York: New Video Group.

Saudolet, Elisabeth, Alain de Janvry, and Benjamin Davis. 2001. "Cash Transfer Programs with Income Multipliers: PROCAMPO in Mexico." International Food Policy Research Institute, Food Consumption and Nutrition Division, Discussion Paper No. 99, January.

Sheriff, Robin E. 2001. *Dreaming Equality: Color, Race, and Racism in Urban Brazil*. New Brunswick, N.J.: Rutgers University Press.

Signorini, Italo. 1982. "Patterns of Fright: Multiple Concepts of Susto in a Ladino-Nahua Community of the Sierra de Puebla (Mexico)." *Ethnology* 21, no. 4, 313–23.

S!Paz International Service for Peace. 2009. "The Two Faces of Migration in Guerrero." *Problemáticas*, 7 September, http://www.sipaz.org.

Smedley, Audrey. 2007. *Race in North America: Origin and Evolution of a Worldview*. 3rd edn. Boulder, Colo.: Westview.

Smith, Carol, ed. 1990. *Guatemalan Indians and the State, 1540–1988*. Austin: University of Texas Press.

———. 1995. "Race-Class-Gender Ideology in Guatemala: Modern and Anti-modern Forms." *Comparative Studies in Society and History* 43, no. 7, 723–49.

Stanford, E. Thomas. 1972. "The Mexican Son." *Yearbook of the International Folk Music Council*, no. 4, 66–86.

———. 1998. "La chilena de la Costa Chica de Guerrero y Oaxaca." *Tierra Adentro*, no. 92, 49–53.

Starr, Frederick. 1908. *In Indian Mexico*. Chicago: Forbes.

Stepan, Nancy Leys. 1991. *The Hour of Eugenics: Race, Gender, and Nation in Latin America*. Ithaca: Cornell University Press.

Stepick, Alex, III. 1992. "The Refugees Nobody Wants: Haitians in Miami." *Miami Now! Immigration, Ethnicity, and Social Change*, ed. Guillermo J. Grenier and Alex Stepick III, 57–82. Gainesville: University Press of Florida.

Stross, Brian. 1974. "Tzeltal Marriage by Capture." *Anthropological Quarterly* 47, no. 3, 328–46.

Stutzman, Ronald. 1981. "El Mestizaje: An All-Inclusive Ideology of Exclusion." *Cultural Transformations and Ethnicity in Modern Ecuador*, ed. Norman Whitten, 45–94. Urbana: University of Illinois Press.

Taussig, Michael. 1983. *The Devil and Commodity Fetishism in South America*. Chapel Hill: University of North Carolina Press.

———. 1987. *Shamanism, Colonialism, and the Wild Man: A Study in Terror and Healing*. Chicago: University of Chicago Press.

Tayac, Gabrielle, ed. 2009. *Indivisible: African-Native American Lives in the Americas*. Washington: Smithsonian Institution, National Museum of the American Indian.

Thompson, Ginger. 2001. "Race Strains a Mexican Campaign." *New York Times*, 11 November.

Thompson, Robert Farriss. 1984. *Flash of the Spirit: African and Afro-American Art and Philosophy*. New York: Random House.

Tibón, Gutierre. 1981 [1961]. *Pinotepa Nacional: Mixtecos, negros y triques*. 2nd edn. Mexico City: Posada.

Torres, Arlene, and Norman E. Whitten Jr. 1998. "General Introduction: To Forge the Future in the Fires of the Past; An Interpretive Essay on Racism, Domination, Resistance, and Liberation." *Blackness in Latin America and the Caribbean: Social Dynamics and Cultural Transformations*, ed. Arlene Torres and Norman E. Whitten Jr., 3–33. Bloomington: Indiana University Press.

Torres-Saillant, Silvio. 1998. "Tribulations of Blackness: Stages in Dominican Racial Identity." *Latin American Perspectives* 25, no. 3, 126–46.

Trexler, Richard. 1984. "We Think, They Act: Clerical Readings of Missionary Theatre in Sixteenth-Century New Spain." *Understanding Popular Culture: Europe from the Middle Ages to the Nineteenth Century*, ed. Steven L. Kaplan, 189–227. Berlin: Mouton.

Tylor, Edward. 1889. "On a Method of Investigating the Development of Institutions, Applied to Laws of Marriage and Descent." *Journal of the Royal Anthropological Institute of Great Britain and Ireland* 18, 245–72.

Urban, Greg, and Joel Sherzer. 1991. "Introduction: Indians, Nation-States, and Culture. *Nation-States and Indians in Latin America*, ed. Greg Urban and Joel Sherzer, 1–18. Austin: University of Texas Press.

Urioste, Armando de. 1985. *Razas y costumbre: Los negros de las Yungas*. Washington: Human Studies Film Archives, Smithsonian Institution.

Valdez, Norberto. 1998. *Ethnicity, Class, and the Indigenous Struggle for Land in Guerrero, Mexico*. New York: Garland.

Valencia Valencia, Enrique. 1993. Prologue to *Jamás fandango al cielo: Narrativa afromestiza*, ed. Cristina María Díaz Pérez, Francisca Aparicio Prudente, and Adela García Casarrubias, 13–17. Mexico City: Dirección General de Culturas Populares.

Van Young, Eric. 1994. "Conclusion: The State as Vampire: Hegemonic Projects, Public Ritual, and Popular Culture." *Rituals of Rule, Rituals of Resistance: Public Celebrations and Popular Culture in Mexico*, ed. William H. Beezley, Cheryl English Martin, and William E. French, 343–74. Wilmington, Del.: Scholarly Resources.

Vasconcelos, José. 1924. *La raza cósmica: Misión de la raza iberoamericana*. Paris: Agencia Mundial de Librería.

Vaughn, Bobby. 1998. "Mexico's Black Heritage: The Costa Chica of Guerrero and Oaxaca." Mexconnect, http://www.mexconnect.com (accessed 2 December 2007).

———. 2004. "Los negros, los indígenas y la diáspora: Una perspectiva etnográfica de la Costa Chica." *Afroméxico. El pulso de la población negra en México: Una historia recordada, olvidada y vuelta a recordar*, ed. Ben Vinson III and Bobby Vaughn, trans. Clara García Ayluardo, 75–96. Mexico City: Fondo de Cultura Económica.

———. 2005. "Afro-Mexico: Blacks, Indígenas, Politics, and the Greater Diaspora." *Neither Enemies nor Friends: Latinos, Blacks, Afro-Latinos*, ed. Anani Dzidzienyo and Suzanne Oboler, 117–36. New York: Palgrave.

Vaughn, Bobby, and Ben Vinson III. 2007. "Unfinished Migrations: From the Mexican South to the American South; Impressions of Afro-Mexican Migration to North Carolina." *Beyond Slavery: The Multilayered Legacy of Africans in Latin America and the Caribbean*, ed. Darién J. Davis, 223–45. Lanham, Md.: Rowman and Littlefield.

Velásquez, María Elisa, and Arturo Motta. 2008. "Where Did the Blacks Go? Post-slavery Mexico." Paper presented at "The African Presence in Mexico," Texas A&M University, 23 October.

Vertovec, Steven. 2004. "Migrant Transnationalism and Modes of Transformation." *International Migration Review* 38, no. 3, 970–1001.

Villalobos Morales, Carlos Alberto. 1997. "Servicios estatales de salud, Jurisdicción Sanitaria 06, Costa Chica." Unpublished manuscript.

Vinson, Ben, III. 2000. "The Racial Profile of a Rural Mexican Province in the 'Costa Chica': Igualapa in 1791." *Americas* 57, no. 2, 269–82.

———. 2001. *Bearing Arms for His Majesty: The Free-Colored Militia in Colonial Mexico*. Stanford: Stanford University Press.

———. 2006. "Introduction: African (Black) Diaspora History, Latin American History." *Americas* 63, no. 1, 1–18.

Viramontes, Celia. 2008. "Civic Engagement across Borders: The Promise and Challenge of Mexican Immigrant Hometown Associations in Southern California." *Civic Hopes and Political Realities: Immigrants, Community Organizations, and Political Engagement*, ed. S. Karthick Ramakrishnan and Irene Bloemraad, 351–82. New York: Russell Sage Foundation.

Wade, Peter. 1995. "The Cultural Politics of Blackness in Colombia." *American Ethnologist* 22, no. 2, 341–57.

———. 1997. *Race and Ethnicity in Latin America*. London: Pluto.

———. 2002. "The Colombian Pacific in Perspective." *Journal of Latin American Anthropology* 7, no. 2, 2–33.

———. 2006a. "Afro-Latin Studies: Reflections on the Field." *Latin American and Caribbean Ethnic Studies* 1, no. 1, 105–24.

———. 2006b. "Understanding 'Africa' and 'Blackness' in Colombia: Music and the Politics of Culture." *Afro-Atlantic Dialogues: Anthropology in the Diaspora*, ed. Kevin Yelvington, 351–78. Santa Fe: School of American Research Press.

Weitlaner, Roberto J. 1961. "La ceremonia llamada 'levantar la sombra.'" *Revista mexicana de estudios antropológicos*, no. 17, 67–95.

Whitten, Norman E., Jr., and Rachel Corr. 1999. "Imagery of 'Blackness' in Indigenous Myth, Discourse, and Ritual." *Representations of Blackness and the Performance of Identities*, ed. Jean Muteba Rahier, 213–34. Westport, Conn.: Bergin and Garvey.

Widmer, Rolf. 1990. *Conquista y despertar de las costas de la Mar del Sur (1521–1684)*. Mexico City: Consejo Nacional para la Cultura y las Artes.

Williams, Brackette. 1989. "A Class Act: Anthropology and the Race to Nation across Ethnic Terrain." *Annual Review of Anthropology*, no. 18, 401–44.

Wines, William, and Dan Smith. 1998. "The Critical Need for Law Reform to Regulate the Abusive Practices of Transnational Corporations: The Illustrative Case of Boise Cascade Corporation in Mexico's Costa Grande and Elsewhere." *Denver Journal of International Law and Policy* 26, 453–515.

Woodrick, Anne C. 1995. "A Lifetime of Mourning: Griefwork among Yucatec Maya Women." *Ethos* 23, no. 4, 401–23.

Yelvington, Kevin, ed. 2006a. *Afro-Atlantic Dialogues: Anthropology in the Diaspora*. Santa Fe: School of American Research Press.

———. 2006b. "The Invention of Africa in Latin America and the Caribbean: Political Discourse and Anthropological Praxis, 1920–1940." *Afro-Atlantic Dialogues: Anthropology in the Diaspora*, ed. Kevin Yelvington, 35–82. Santa Fe: School of American Research Press.

Yunez-Naude, Antonio. 2003. "The Dismantling of CONASUPO, a Mexican State Trader in Agriculture." *World Economy* 26, no. 1, 97–122.

Zepeda, Eduardo, Timothy A. Wise, and Kevin P. Gallagher. 2009. "Rethinking Trade Policy for Development: Lessons from Mexico under NAFTA." *Carnegie Endowment for International Peace: Policy Outlook*. December.

Index

Africa: culture workers' use of, 148–50, 155–56, 166–67, 170, 178–79, 184, 187, 189, 277–78, 328n8; Herskovits, Melville, and, 121–22; San Nicoladenses' perceptions of, 4–5, 63–64, 86–87, 93–94, 152–53, 156–57, 164–65, 176, 277, 302, 307, 328n3. *See also* Aguirre Beltrán, Gonzalo; Herskovits, Melville

African Americans: attitudes toward Latinos, 316–19; Latinos in Winston-Salem and, 308, 339n5; San Nicoladenses' attitudes toward, 308, 311–14, 339n5; San Nicoladenses' racial labels for, 315

Afroamerica (journal), 125–26

Afromestizo, 2, 9, 18, 57, 64, 94, 119, 145–51, 156, 158, 165, 173, 175–77, 187, 213, 274, 305, 324n4

Afromexican, 2, 4, 8, 9, 119, 141, 146–51, 156, 165, 175, 181, 184, 187, 305–6

agrarian activists (*agraristas*), 37, 43; Pastrana, Porfirio, the "Father" of San Nicolás's ejido, 44–46, 326n30, 327n31. *See also* Revolution, Mexican

agrarian reform, 8, 42–43, 46–48, 126, 323n3, 324n5; and ethnic organizing, 148

agriculture, 15, 20, 21–22, 48–51, 324n7; holdings, 328n5

Aguirre Beltrán, Gonzalo, 13, 58; and "Africanisms," 127–28; on blacks, 127, 133–34, 137–38; on bride theft, 128–30; and ethos of violence, 127, 129; fieldwork in Cuajinicuilapa, 126–27; influence on contemporary culture workers, 123; influence of Melville Herskovits, 122–33; on marriage, 128–30, 132; at Northwestern University, 124; on race, 136–38; on religion, 130–31; on round houses (*redondos*), 134; training, 123. *See also* bride theft; marriage; religion; round houses

anger (*coraje*), 242–61, 263, 335n9, 336n15, 337n21; adults and, 242, 245, 247–61; children and, 242, 245, 246–47; as embodiment, 244; gender and, 249, 250, 263–64; pet birds and, 242, 245–46; skulls and, 250, 263

antidiscrimination clause, Mexican Constitution, 306

biomedicine and biomedical ailments, 255–56, 257, 259, 263, 334n26, 335n9, 336n13, 336nn17–18

birds: as pets, 190, 242, 245–46; and Saint Nicholas of Tolentino, 190; in the wild, 246. *See also* wildlife, disappearance of

birth, 334n3

black Indians, 2, 4, 6, 56–59, 85–86, 96, 109, 117, 263, 306, 316, 322, 327n2

blacks, 2, 5, 7, 58, 61, 63–64, 74–76, 100, 106, 107, 109, 116, 140, 152–53, 168–69, 306; in coastal discourse, 25–26; colonial period and, 3–4, 27–29, 55–57, 88, 94, 124, 142–43; folklorized, 158, 162, 178, 277–78; independence and, 32–34; national invisibility of, 26–27, 77, 88–89, 94–95, 117, 144–46, 151, 156–57, 273, 275; San Nicoladenses' attitudes toward, 78–80, 87–88, 95, 113, 116–17, 156–57, 162, 177, 189, 311–16; San Nicolás's resident Indians and, 70–71, 93, 104, 176, 235. *See also* Aguirre Beltrán, Gonzalo; Meetings of Black Villages; racism; Third Root, Our; Tibón, Gutierre

bride theft, 75, 135, 148, 180, 247, 330n2; as African, 128–30, 132, 148; as Spanish, 75, 129–30, 210. *See also* Aguirre Beltrán, Gonzalo

Catholicism. *See* religion

cattle, 20–22, 35–37, 39–40, 42, 44, 49–52, 57, 74, 152, 232, 268, 293, 309, 332n15; and colonial period, 4, 27–28, 30; and Saint Nicholas of Tolentino, 100–101; and wealth, 50, 281, 290, 297. *See also* Miller, Charles A. "Carlos"

children, 190–97, 297, 332nn3–5; discipline and, 192–94; and enclosure, 191; as free, 191; gender and, 194, 197, 209; gifting of, 46, 203, 204, 241, 327n32, 332n12; having, as culmination of womanhood, 204; homosexuality and, 227–28, 229; household contributions and, 194–95, 220; as like crops, 193; as like young animals,

191; Saint Nicholas of Tolentino and, 190–92

Ciruelo, 165, 168, 170, 171

class, economic, 69–70, 77, 81, 152, 162, 186, 196, 217, 238–39, 247, 267, 290, 292, 307, 313, 314, 339n17

Clavijero, Francisco Javier, 89

Collantes, 22, 26, 49, 61, 66, 73, 79, 224, 252, 282, 335n9

colonies, agricultural (*colonias*), 46–47, 327n33

community "culture house" (*casa de cultura*), 8, 161, 183, 278, 280, 331n11

conquest plays, 107–9, 112

Corralero, 165, 331n11

Costa Chica: location, 1–2; colonial period, 4, 27–32, 57–58; geography of, 15; Independence period, 32–34; Revolutionary period, 34–42; seasons, 20; socioethnic stratification, 15–16, 57. *See also* Revolution, Mexican

cowboys and cowboy culture, 4, 28–30, 33, 36, 38–39, 42–43, 45, 55–56, 101, 103–4, 107, 190, 241, 309

crime, 25, 297, 324n3, 333n19

Cuajinicuilapa, 16–23, 28, 30, 32–33, 35–37, 40, 42–45, 49, 57–58, 91, 96, 157–58, 165–82, 186, 201, 226, 228, 232, 252–53, 256, 289, 324n2, 325n17, 325n19, 326n23, 326n25, 327n31, 327n1, 329n1, 334n26; 336n13; location of, 17; as maroon settlement, 56, 87, 128, 140; as municipal seat and town, 2; Nahuatl meaning, 66; relationship with San Nicolás, 18–19, 92, 95, 98, 285. *See also* Aguirre Beltrán, Gonzalo

Cuba, 63, 87, 93, 103, 164, 328n3

cultural survivals, 4, 116, 120–39, 140, 143, 144, 146–47. *See also* Aguirre Beltrán, Gonzalo; Herskovits, Melville

dancing and dances, 5, 60, 97, 99–104, 110–13, 121, 136, 159–64, 168, 171–81, 195, 198, 201, 210, 228–29, 235–36, 238, 326n28,

328n3, 330nn2–4, 334n5, 335n6. *See also* festivals and performances; weddings

death, 236; cemetery, 251, 252, 301–2; cemetery as "little Carolina" (*Carolina chica*), 302; cross raising (*levanter la cruz*), 169, 237; funeral processions, 181, 331n9; tombs, 251–52, 276, 300–302; in the United States, 172–73, 300; wakes, 169, 224–25, 237, 330n4, 331n9

demographics, coastal belt: colonial, 3–4, 27–28, 57–58, 107; twentieth century, 3, 16–17, 18, 324n2

destiny (*tono*), 179; in work of Gonzalo Aguirre Beltrán, 130–32

domestic violence. *See* violence

Dominican Republic: race in, 308–9; Dominican identities, 309–10; Dominicans in the United States, 310, 313; negrophobia in, 309; parallels with coastal belt, 309–10; parallels with Mexico, 309

drinking, 208, 209, 218, 235–36, 238, 240, 252, 255, 292, 335n6

education and literacy, 4, 14, 157, 176, 220–22, 231, 264, 313, 328n9, 332n9, 338n16

ejidos and ejidatarios, 20–21, 32, 40, 43, 49, 65, 95, 324n5, 327n34. *See also* agrarian activists

elopement (*huir*), 68, 128, 198–201, 206, 332n10

endogamy. *See* kinship and family

entregamiento, 202, 203

essentialism, 149, 157, 170, 305, 321

festivals and performances: Carnival, 326n28; Dance of the Devils (*danza de los diablos*), 136, 147, 326n28; Independence Day, *La América/Los Apaches*, 85, 91, 106–17; *Los Tejorones* (Mixtec), 107–8; maintenance of community and, 236–38; "masked ones" (*mojigangas*), 103; Pancho and Minga, 101–3; Saint Nicholas of Tolentino, *el toro de petate*,

98, 101–3; Santiago (Saint James), 103–4, 237–38, 240, 286, 336n11

folklorization: artesa music and, 5, 8, 144, 162–63, 164, 169, 176, 178, 181, 183–84; images and, 180; round houses (*redondos*) and, 5, 144, 158, 275–76, 278–80. *See also* music; round houses

food, 4, 15, 17, 22, 26, 51, 52, 53, 70, 178, 184; ailments and, 243; beef (*carne*), 20, 240, 256, 292; cooperative preparation of, 201, 239, 256; corn, 16, 21, 48–49; festivals and, 237–38; gender roles and, 136, 194, 204, 208, 219–20, 227, 333n21; gifting of, 51, 68, 92, 98, 172, 174–75, 190, 222, 234; hunted, 37, 51, 338n14; identity and, 338n15; migrants and, 50, 70, 73, 77, 269, 285, 287, 297; sweet bread, 333n20; tamales, 219, 240; witchcraft and, 212, 257, 337n20

forced abduction. *See* bride theft

freedom: cooperation and, 197; local identity and, 217–18, 307; maroons and, 86, 88, 189, 307; masculinity and, 189, 190–93, 197, 217, 263–64, 307; Mexico and, 86–88, 93–94, 95, 113, 117; migration and, 207

fright (*espanto*), 131, 254, 335n9; Aguirre Beltrán, Gonzalo, and, 131

fright (*susto*), 130, 335n9

gachupines, 107, 109, 112, 113

gang members (*cholos*), 175, 195, 229

gender: anger (*coraje*) and, 249, 250, 263–64; childhood and, 190–96; complementarity of, 208–9; dancing and, 228–29; La América and, 114–16; men and, 189, 201, 211, 217–18, 224, 228, 245, 263–64; migration and, 207–8; moreno/Indian marriages and, 66–68; nonconformists, 226–30; public/private dichotomy and, 14, 68, 203, 209, 210, 222–26, 228; religion and, 223–24; segregation and, 189–90, 222–26, 297; traditional roles and, 332n16; women and,

gender (*continued*)
189, 191, 204, 207–8, 211, 217, 225, 263–64; work and, 218–22

godparents. *See* ritual kin

Guerrero (state): agroforestry in, 22–23, 325n9; compared to Oaxaca, 18; economic growth, 325n10; militarization, 24; municipalities in, 2, 18; poverty in, 23; reputation for violence, 23, 25–26; tourism in, 22–23, 325n8

hair, 62–64, 115; kinky (*cuculuste*), 62, 70, 80, 81, 96–97, 158; straight (*lacio*), 81, 114, 115; very kinky (*chino*), 62, 69, 79, 115; wavy (*crespo*), 81, 114

healing, 242–43, 256–58, 262–63; cleansing (*limpieza*), 259–61, 263, 276

Herskovits, Melville, 13, 119–21, 143; and Africa, 121–22; and *Afroamerica* (journal), 125–26; influence on Gonzalo Aguirre Beltrán, 122–33. *See also* Aguirre Beltrán, Gonzalo

Hispanic, San Nicoladenses' U.S. identity, 311

homosexuals, 226–30, 334n25; children as, 227–28, 229; female, 226, 229; male, 226; outsiders as, 226–27; sexuality and, 227, 229; tolerance for, 226–30; work and, 226–27

houses, 205, 274, 334n1; adobe and wattle-and-daub, 281, 282–83, 288, 338n13; cinder block, 5, 10, 14, 264, 268, 273–77, 281, 282, 283, 285, 288–92, 298, 332n13, 338n11; class and, 290; homeplace and, 11, 272–73, 276, 299; privacy and, 295–97; unfinished, 273–74, 281–82; women's responsibility for, 289–90. *See also* migration; round houses

Huehuetán, 28, 33, 61, 66, 106, 108, 142, 300, 328n9; colonial, land donation, 29–32; free mulattoes in, colonial period, 31–32, 58; Revolution and, 38–39; San Nicolás's land claims and, 36; Third Root and, 147

humoral balance, 243, 244, 248, 336n14

hypodescent, 59, 120, 121, 123, 137, 152, 165, 305, 316. *See also* one drop rule

illegitimacy, children, 211, 212, 214

Independence, Wars of, 32–34; and Indians, 33; and morenos, 33–34

Indians: Amuzgos, 16, 70, 71, 131, 134, 328n4; as "Apaches," 107, 110–13; colonial period, 27–32, 55–57; considered distinct from "blacks," 151, 167, 187–88; as Mexican national icons, 6, 89, 92, 113–14, 116, 307, 322; Mixtecs, 16, 26, 64, 66, 70, 72, 131, 134, 135, 136, 242, 253, 326n28, 333n19, 336n15; as rural, 7, 13, 70–72, 277, 309–10; as rustic, 7, 329n11; San Nicolás's resident, 64–66, 67–68, 71–72, 92–93, 186

indigenism, 89, 95

infrastructure, local, 9, 18, 222, 280; bridges, 22, 197; drainage, 11, 18, 232–33, 334n1; electricity, 82; roads, 18, 22, 34

inheritance, 68, 195, 206, 293, 324n6; ultimogeniture and, 68, 332n14

insecticides, 52, 327n36

kinship and family, 12, 59, 75, 117, 291, 292–93, 297, 307, 337n23; endogamy and, 12, 81–82, 195, 295, 320; importance of, 9, 195, 196, 208, 238, 240, 250–51, 261, 272, 291, 299–302, 320; Saint Nicholas of Tolentino and, 96, 100, 105; spatial organization and, 68–69, 294–95

land. *See* agrarian reform; ejidos and ejidatarios; Revolution, Mexican

landowners, large, 15–16, 27–28, 32, 33, 325n18, 326n22; Ambrosia de Vargas, Doña María (Indian *cacica*), 29–32, 325n16. *See also* Miller, Charles A. "Carlos"

language, 16, 71–72, 75, 78, 81, 87, 235, 311, 329n1; as barrier to communication in the United States, 315, 316–17; English in

the United States, 269, 312; indigenous
monolinguism, 60, 64, 67, 324n1; loss of,
329n12; reduplication, linguistic, 70, 72,
315–16, 329n10
literacy, 222, 231, 313

maroons and maroonage, 56, 64, 86,
127–28, 130, 140, 180, 327n1, 329n1; and
moreno identity, 88, 104, 307; and shipwrecks, 85–86, 87
marriage, age of consent for, 332n10;
Catholic Church and, 200–201, 332n10;
civil, 200; daughters-in-law (*nueras*)
and, 199, 200–201, 203, 204–7; groom
and bride (*novio* and *novia*) and, 198–
99, 200–201, 332n7; importance of,
213–16, 236; Indian-moreno, 60, 66–69,
82; matrifocality and, 295; mothers-in-
law (*suegras*) and, 79, 203–6, 261, 295;
pardon (*perdón*), 68, 198, 199, 201; patrilocality and, 68, 199, 203, 295, 332n11; by
request, 135. *See also* Aguirre Beltrán,
Gonzalo; elopement; weddings
Meetings of Black Villages (*Encuentros de
pueblos negros*), 9, 165–88; and blackness, 166–71, 181, 184, 186–88; Ciruelo
meeting (1997), 165–72; Cuajinicuilapa
meeting (1999), 172–81; San Nicoladenses' disinterest in, 166, 173, 177, 182,
184, 331n11; San Nicolás meeting (2002),
181–87; San Nicolás as visitor destination, 172–75, 177
Memín Pinguín, 186–87
migration, 7–13, 49, 60, 168, 170, 179, 203–
4, 206–7, 268–69, 272, 299, 310, 323n4,
324n6, 337n6; border crossing and, 75,
267–68, 269; cost of, 268; crime and,
195, 297–98; death and, 300; displacement and, 320–21, 339n6; family unity
and, 194, 264, 292, 293–94, 299–300;
gender roles and, 207–8; history of in
San Nicolás, 265–66; household formation in the United States, 270; legal
status and, 269, 270, 337nn5–6, 338n7;

marriage and, 216, 270; nonmigrants
and, 273, 292–93, 302–3, 339n18; North
Carolina census data and, 337n1; obligations at home and, 237; orientation
toward San Nicolás, 269, 276–77, 287,
299, 321, 338n9; property rights and, 291,
299; race and, 75, 305–19; reasons for,
50, 166, 268–69; remittances and, 49,
269, 272, 283, 290, 337nn2–3, 338n12; as
rite of passage, 268, 297–98; technology
and, 270–71; upward mobility and,
286, 292; urbanity and, 285, 291; village
events and, 53, 286; visas and, 331n7;
work and, 267. *See also* African Americans; houses, cinder block; Winston-
Salem, North Carolina
Miller, Charles A. "Carlos," 32, 35–42,
307, 326n23; San Nicoladenses' view of,
36–37; son Germán, 39, 43–45, 46; son
Guillermo, 45, 46. *See also* landowners,
large; Revolution, Mexican
mistress, having a (*queridato*), 132–33, 199,
210, 211–12; men's freedom and, 217;
as Spanish custom, 133; virginity and,
199, 216; wealth and, 333n18; wives and,
211–12, 213–16
"mixture," racial: colonial, 4, 55–58, 113;
contemporary, 6, 48, 58–69, 74–75,
80–81, 85–88, 93, 114–17, 135, 167–69,
285, 307, 315, 328n7; fluidity, 305–6, 316,
319, 320. *See also* black Indians; race
money: fetishization of, 53; gifting, 53, 241;
hidden mines (*minas*), 52–53, 251, 253;
wealth and, 52–53, 87, 94
multiculturalism, 8–9, 148, 150, 158, 178,
184, 277–78, 305–6; official (state), 156,
177–78, 184, 331n6
Museum of Afromestizo Cultures (Museo
de las culturas afromestizas, Vicente
Guerrero), 25, 94, 151, 158, 165, 177–78,
180, 274, 275, 277–79
music: ballads (*corridos*), 137, 149, 160, 174,
179, 326n30, 331n8; *chilenas*, 160–61,
175, 176; *chilenas*, Chilean origins of,

music (*continued*)
160, 328n3, 330n2; *cumbia*, 161; European, 330n4; minuets, 169, 330n4; *sones
de artesa*, 5, 159–64, 170–71, 183, 202–3,
238–39, 330n1. *See also* folklorization

nagual, 57, 179, 256, 300, 335n9; in work of
Gonzalo Aguirre Beltrán, 131
Nahuatl derivatives, 51, 66, 81, 328n6,
328n9
National Company of Popular Subsistence
(CONASUPO), 48, 219, 222
natives (*naturales* and *criollos*), 31, 69, 82,
189; colonial mulattoes as, 83; Indians
as, 70, 83; San Nicoladenses as, 82–83,
112, 321–22
nerves (*muina*), 242–50
Nicaragua: and indigeneity, 309; Mosquito
Coast of, 309; parallels with Mexico's
Southern Pacific Coast, 309–10
Nicholas of Tolentino, Saint (Nicolás de
Tolentino, San): authentic statue of,
29, 90–91, 95; birds and, 100, 190, 246;
childhood of, 99, 101, 190–91; childhood and, 190; Costa Chican history of,
29, 90, 96, 325n19; fertility and, 100, 193;
festival for, 91, 101–3; freedom and, 190;
homeplace and, 322, 329n4; as moreno,
92, 96, 115, 116; stories about, 96–98;
slaves and slavery, parallels to, 104–6.
See also festivals and performances
North American Free Trade Agreement
(NAFTA), 21, 48, 268, 289, 323n5

Ometepec, 16, 17, 29, 30, 32, 35, 36, 38, 45,
58, 62, 70–71, 115, 142, 143, 166, 212, 234,
257, 258, 277, 324n3; Revolution and,
39–41; whites and, 16, 74, 116, 162, 178,
255
one drop rule, 7, 59, 137, 152, 156

pardo militias and militiamen, 29, 33
phlegm (*flema*), 242–43; related to anger

(*coraje*), 242–43, 244, 247–49, 255, 257.
See also anger
Pinotepa Nacional, 16, 17, 26, 28, 37, 61, 62,
107–8, 168, 258, 267, 325n14
politics and political parties: community
friction and, 234–35; Institutional Revolutionary Party (PRI), 24, 234, 334n2;
National Action Party (PAN), 334n2;
Party of the Democratic Revolution
(PRD), 23, 24, 234
Popular Revolutionary Army (EPR), 23,
24, 25
prayer women (*rezanderas*), 68, 76, 223,
224, 258. *See also* religion
Program for Direct Assistance in Agriculture (PROCAMPO), 48–49
prostitutes, 198, 211, 227, 333n17
Protestantism. *See* religion
Punta Maldonado (El Faro), 22, 24, 25,
86, 87

race (*raza*): black, 2, 3, 5–6, 7, 78–81, 315;
blanco, 6, 15, 62, 72; *gabacho*, 75, 311,
339n2; *guanaco*, 71, 329n11; *güero*, 72,
311; Indians, 3, 6, 7, 15, 56, 60–62, 64,
67, 69, 70, 71, 72, 77, 78, 81, 82, 83, 94,
97, 98, 106, 107, 113, 169, 235, 249–50,
256, 261, 307; local meanings, 15, 59–60,
145; *macuano*, 69, 328n9; mestizos, 33,
88, 185, 285, 307; mixture (*mestizaje*),
83, 88–90, 114, 137; *mollo*, 181, 311–16,
331n10; *morado*, 62; morenos, 2, 6–7, 12,
13, 15, 33, 47, 58–59, 60, 63, 70, 73, 76,
77–83, 87, 90, 95, 96, 106, 112–15, 151–52,
163, 165, 189, 285, 307, 315–16; mulattoes,
3, 31–32, 33; *pardo*, 33, 325n15; *prieto*, 48,
62, 79, 81; purity (*limpieza*), 7, 61–63, 72,
82, 316; racial geography in San Nicolás,
67–69; terms used in United States,
311–15. *See also* African Americans;
black Indians; blacks; Indians; "mixture," racial; whites
racism, 26, 47, 70, 71, 76–77, 89, 184, 185,

186–87, 306–7, 339n4; brought from Mexico to the United States, 314

reciprocity, 53, 190, 236–41

religion: Catholicism, 96–98, 167, 200, 223, 235, 236, 261, 277, 332n10, 333n24, 335n6; Catholic prayer women (*rezanderas*), 68, 76, 223–24, 258; Evangelical Protestantism, 11, 73, 101, 196, 213, 224, 229, 235–36, 326n28, 333n24, 335n6; gender and, 223–24

Revolution, Mexican, 34–42; Huehuetán and, 38; Mexican Peasant Federation (CCM), 44, 45; San Nicolás and, 38; White Guard (Guardia Blanca), 44, 326n29; Zapata, Emiliano, 37, 325n26, 325n27; Zapatistas and, 37, 39, 40–42, 326nn25–26. *See also* agrarian activists; landowners, large; Miller, Charles A. "Carlos"

ritual kin: coparent (*comadre* and *compadre*), 3; godparenthood (*compadrazgo*), 190; godparents (*madrina* and *padrino*), 3, 52, 79, 198, 200, 201, 202, 238–39, 240, 268, 287, 298, 332n8, 334n3, 335n6

roots (*raíces*), 14; as metaphor, 144–45; and place, 145, 275

round houses (*redondos*), 5, 8, 141–42, 144, 158, 167, 180, 274, 277–81, 288, 289, 291, 293; as African, 134, 139–41, 277–78; history of, 277, 281, 283; as Indian, 134–35, 141–43, 277, 283; San Nicoladenses' attitudes toward, 280–81. *See also* folklorization

rural/urban contrast, 7–8, 12, 13, 18, 72, 78, 80, 157, 169, 276, 285, 291, 306–7, 309, 310, 311, 314

Santiago Tepextla, 25, 41, 79

shadow/soul (*sombra*): calming, 169, 237, 242, 263, 335n7; in work of Gonzalo Aguirre Beltrán, 130–32

shame (*vergüenza*), 258, 335n9

slaves and slavery, 3–4, 55–58, 74–75, 89,

134, 139, 140, 170, 180, 328n3, 330n2; parallels with Saint Nicholas of Tolentino, 104–6; San Nicoladenses' associations with freedom and, 113–17; San Nicoladenses' ideas about, 85–88, 93–95, 180, 331n5. *See also* maroons and maroonage

social death, 105

spit, 242, 248, 264, 276, 336n12

Third Root, Our (Nuestra Tercera Raíz), 2, 5, 165; Africa and, 144–48; blacks and, 146–53; inception of, 143, 145; objectives of, 143–44, 145–46; San Nicolás and, 156; U.S. influences on, 146. *See also* Africa; blacks

Thompson, Robert Farriss, on round houses, 139–41. *See also* round houses

Tibón, Gutierre, in Collantes, 134–36; on Afromixtecans, 135; on marriage, 135–36

tobacco, 241, 297; cultivation of, 34, 36; as purgative, 242–43, 246–47, 248

town-hall meetings (*asambleas*), 47, 222–23, 251–53

Vasconcelos, José, 89

violence: attributed to Guerrero, 21–22; attributed to morenos, 26, 117, 127, 129, 147–48, 180, 274–75, 330nn7–8, 338n10; domestic, 208, 215, 218; men as victims of, 209–10, 237

virginity: female, 129, 130, 198–99, 232; interiority and, 198; loss of, as public, 199; male, 197–98, 227

Virgin of Guadalupe, 70, 115, 262, 330n4, 337n22

weddings, 238–40; in the United States, 335n6, 335n8

whites, 58, 59, 61–63, 65, 67, 71–73, 80, 81, 162, 171, 175, 178, 182, 185, 186, 187, 285–86, 311, 314, 316, 326n28, 327n31; excluded from local identities, 5, 64, 74–76, 83, 86–117, 162–64, 257, 263; ex-

whites (*continued*)
cluded from the nation, 109, 114, 306–7; local racism of, 26, 76–77, 137, 152, 196; moreno history of loyalty to, 33–34, 36–39, 42, 56; regional history of, 30–48; as rich, and the government, 37, 38, 45, 49, 59, 72, 74, 77, 87, 114, 123, 162; in the United States, 267, 311–14, 315, 316, 318; U.S. racial logics and, 155–57

wildlife, disappearance of, 51–52, 246, 280, 338n14

Winston-Salem, North Carolina, and San Nicoladenses, 3, 10, 11, 50, 63, 227, 266–68, 270–72, 287, 288, 300; residence patterns in, 201, 270, 295, 332n11; Waughtown area as historically African American, 317; Waughtown as "Little Mexico," 317. *See also* African Americans; migration

witchcraft, 212–13, 250, 251, 253, 256; Indians and, 242, 249, 250, 251–52, 256, 261–62, 283, 336n19, 337n24; women and, 212. *See also* food

World Vision (NGO), 333n24, 335n6

Zapata, Emiliano, and Zapatistas. *See* Revolution, Mexican

Zapatista Army for National Liberation (EZLN), 24, 325n11, 325n12

Zitlala, home of authentic statue of Saint Nicholas of Tolentino, 29, 90–92, 96–101, 104–6, 116, 288, 322, 329n3; goat-herding connections to coastal belt, 29, 90

Laura A. Lewis is a professor of anthropology
at James Madison University.

Library of Congress Cataloging-in-Publication Data
Lewis, Laura A.
Chocolate and corn flour : history, race, and place in the
making of "Black" Mexico / Laura A. Lewis.
p. cm.
Includes bibliographical references and index.
ISBN 978-0-8223-5121-4 (cloth : alk. paper)
ISBN 978-0-8223-5132-0 (pbk. : alk. paper)
1. Blacks—Mexico. 2. Blacks—Race identity—Mexico.
3. Mexico—Race relations. I. Title.
F1392.B55L38 2012
305.800972—dc23   2011035989